lonely planet

Discover
Malaysia &
Singapore

Contents

Throughout this book, we use these icons to highlight special recommendations:

The Best...
Lists for everything from bars to wildlife – to make sure you don't miss out

Don't Miss
A must-see – don't go home until you've been there

Local Knowledge Local experts reveal their top picks and secret highlights

Detour
Special places a little off the beaten track

If you like...
Lesser-known alternatives to world-famous attractions

These icons help you quickly identify reviews in the text and on the map:

Sights

Eating

Drinking

Sleeping

ℹ
Information

This edition written and researched by

Simon Richmond,
Cristian Bonetto, Celeste Brash, Joshua Samuel Brown,
Austin Bush, Adam Karlin, Daniel Robinson

Langkawi

p139

The Perhentians &
the East Coast
p167

Penang p107

p83

Taman Negara &
the Hill Stations

Kuala Lumpur p51

Melaka, Johor
& Tioman
p193

p221

Singapore

p263

Malaysian
Borneo

Contents

Contents

On the Road

In Focus

Survival Guide

This is Malaysia & Singapore

Southeast Asia's dynamic duo offer wildlife-rich jungles, beautiful beaches, idyllic islands, culinary sensations, and multiethnic culture in 21st-century metropolises.

Malaysia's primary jungle is among the most ancient ecosystems on earth.

Significant swathes remain intact, protected by national parks and conservation projects. Join a ranger-led nature walk and you'll be alerted to the mind-boggling biodiversity all around: the pitcher plants, lianas and orchids of the humid lowlands, and the conifers and rhododendrons of the high-altitude forests. The icing on this verdant cake is the chance to encounter wildlife in its natural habitat. The most common sightings will be of a host of insects or colourful birdlife, but you could get lucky and spot a foraging tapir, a silvered leaf monkey, or an orang-utan swinging through the jungle canopy. The oceans are just as bountiful – you can snorkel or dive among shoals of tropical fish, paint-box corals, turtles, sharks and dolphins.

Urban explorers won't be disappointed either.

Singapore is a city showstopper that combines a historical legacy of elegant colonial buildings with stunning contemporary architecture and world-class attractions like its zoo, museums and amazing botanical gardens (two of them!). Malaysia's capital Kuala Lumpur (KL) is less organised but perhaps more appealing because of that – a place where Malay *kampung* (village) life stands cheek by jowl with the glitz of the Petronas Towers, and shoppers shuttle from traditional wet markets to air-conditioned mega-malls. The historical cores of Melaka and George Town (Penang) are inscribed on the Unesco World Heritage list for their unique architectural and cultural townscapes, developed over a half a millennium of Southeast Asian cultural and trade exchange. Both should be high on your to-visit list.

The region's potpourri of cultures mirrors the natural environment's diversity.

Each ethnic group has its own language and cultural practices that you can best appreciate through a packed calendar of festivals and a delicious variety of cuisines.

> 66
> The icing on this verdant cake is the chance to encounter wildlife in its natural habitat
> 99

Kek Lok Si Temple (p125), Penang

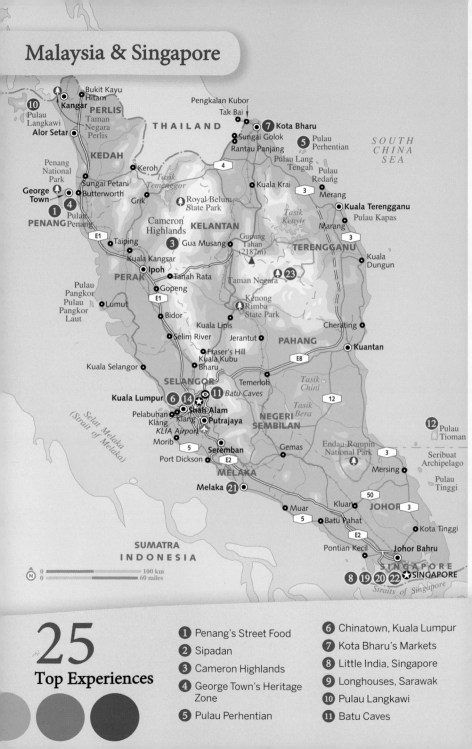

Malaysia & Singapore

25 **Top Experiences**

1. Penang's Street Food
2. Sipadan
3. Cameron Highlands
4. George Town's Heritage Zone
5. Pulau Perhentian
6. Chinatown, Kuala Lumpur
7. Kota Bharu's Markets
8. Little India, Singapore
9. Longhouses, Sarawak
10. Pulau Langkawi
11. Batu Caves

Borneo

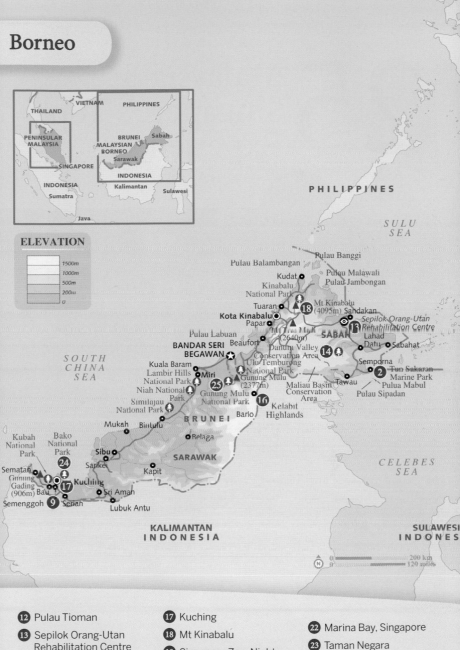

ELEVATION

1500m
1000m
500m
200m
0

12 Pulau Tioman

13 Sepilok Orang-Utan Rehabilitation Centre

14 Petronas Towers, Kuala Lumpur

15 Danum Valley

16 Kelabit Highlands

17 Kuching

18 Mt Kinabalú

19 Singapore Zoo, Night Safari & River Safari

20 Orchard Rd, Singapore

21 Jonker's Walk Night Market, Melaka

22 Marina Bay, Singapore

23 Taman Negara

24 Bako National Park

25 Gunung Mulu National Park

25 Malaysia & Singapore's Top Experiences

Penang's Street Food

In Malaysia the best food is served in the humblest surroundings and involves the least amount of fuss. The country's seemingly countless vendors serve delicious dishes from mobile carts, stalls and shophouses, many employing recipes and techniques handed down through the generations. In addition to informality, ubiquity and quality you're also spoilt for choice – on a single Malaysian street you're likely to encounter Malay, regional Chinese, southern Indian and Western cuisines. Like most locals we reckon the best street food is found on Penang (p129). Indian market stall in George Town's Little India (p132), Penang

DAVID PARKER/ALAMY ©

2

Sipadan

Sometimes it seems as if the world's most vibrant marine life, from the commonplace to the utterly alien fish, mollusks and reptiles, considers the seawall of Sipadan (p293) to be prime real estate. They live here, play here, hunt here and eat here, and you, lucky thing, may dance an underwater ballet with them. For any diver – green amateurs or the seasoned Cousteau-esque veterans – Sipadan is the ultimate underwater adventure. Lined sweetlips

Cameron Highlands

Land Rovers, misty mountains, gumboots, Tudor-themed architecture, scones, strawberries and tea plantations all converge in this distinctly un–Southeast Asian destination. But it's not all about tea time and nostalgia for a bygone era; activities such as self-guided hiking, nature trekking and agricultural tourism make the Cameron Highlands (p98) one of Malaysia's more worthwhile and approachable active destinations. The area also represents a clever escape within a vacation, as the weather in the Cameron Highlands tends to stay mercifully cool year-round. Boh Sungai Palas Tea Estate (p96)

3

The Best...
Beaches

PULAU PERHENTIAN
Sun yourself on these two blissful beach-fringed islands. (p181)

PULAU LANGKAWI
Pantai Cenang is the best all-round beach; head to Tanjung Rhu for perfect sunsets. (p150)

PULAU TIOMAN
Hollywood's stand-in for Bali H'ai is practically castaway perfection (p212)

PULAU KAPAS
An emerald coated in powder-white sand. (p185)

13

The Best...
Diving & Snorkelling

SEMPORNA ARCHIPELAGO
Great diving around Mabul and the legendary deep walls of Sipadan. (p292, p293)

PULAU PERHENTIAN
Wade out to a living coral reef in front of one of the islands. (p184)

PULAU TIOMAN
One of few places where you have a good chance of seeing a pod of dolphins. (p215)

PULAU REDANG
Package tours are the best bet for dives in this marine park. (p183)

4 George Town's Heritage Zone

Once abandoned by locals and seemingly forgotten by tourists, in recent years George Town (p120) has emerged as one of Southeast Asia's hottest destinations. Its 2008 Unesco World Heritage declaration sparked a frenzy of cultural preservation, with the city's charismatic shophouses turned into museums, boutique hotels and chic restaurants. Aggressive drivers aside, it's also one of the best cities in Southeast Asia to explore on foot. And did we mention that it's home to some of Malaysia's best food? Town Hall (p118)

5 Pulau Perhentian

Though eastern Peninsular Malaysia has several islands offering unparalleled underwater activities, Pulau Perhentian (p184) wins flippers-down for snorkelling. The surrounding seas draw a huge variety of marine life, including sharks, tropical fish, turtles and nesting urchins. Living coral beds lie close to shore, so you won't often have to swim far from the shore before finding yourself inside a veritable rainbow cloud of fish.

Chinatown, Kuala Lumpur

Plumes of smoke curl upwards from smouldering coils of incense, flower garlands hang like pearls from the necks of Hindu statues and the call to prayer punctuates the honk of traffic in Kuala Lumpur's (KL) most ethnically diverse and iconic neighbourhood (p67).

Kota Bharu's Markets

Visitors to Malaysian crafts centre Kota Bharu can lose themselves shopping for traditional items like batik, *kain songket* (fabric with gold thread), hand-crafted silverware, hand-carved puppets and locally made kites. Both the Central Market (p180) and the nearby Bazaar Buluh Kubu (p180) are great places to buy spices, brassware and other local goods. For shoppers inclined to roam, the bikeable road from town to PCB beach is dotted with factories and workshops dedicated to the creation of all sorts of crafts.

Little India, Singapore

Riotous Little India (p238) is as close as you'll get to the chaotic Singapore of old. It slaps you across the face with its teeming five-foot ways, incense-scented markets, blaring Bollywood tunes and crayon-hued shophouses. Originally a European enclave, the district bloomed into an Indian hub after a Jewish-Indian businessman started farming buffalo here. For the full Mumbai effect, head in on a crowded Sunday afternoon when it seems all of Singapore's Indian community congregates here.

Sri Veeramakaliamman Temple (p238)

8

The Best...
Museums & Galleries

NATIONAL MUSEUM OF SINGAPORE
Pays homage to the island's history in a beautifully restored colonial building. (p234)

SINGAPORE ART MUSEUM
An excellent showcase of Asian contemporary art. (p235)

ASIAN CIVILISATIONS MUSEUM, SINGAPORE
Packed to the gills with a wide variety of exhibits from across Asia. (p234)

ISLAMIC ARTS MUSEUM, KUALA LUMPUR
Outstanding collection of arts and crafts inspired by Islam. (p68)

PINANG PERANAKAN MANSION
Knock-your-socks-off opulent home turned museum. (p121)

17

Longhouses, Sarawak

There's no better way to get a sense of indigenous tribal culture than to visit a longhouse (p308) – or, better yet, stay over. Essentially a whole village under a single roof, these dwellings can be longer than two sports fields and contain dozens of family units, each of which opens onto a covered common verandah used for economic activities, socialising and celebrations. All longhouses now enjoy at least some modern amenities, but many still have a few head-hunted skulls on display. Iban woman in a traditional longhouse near Kuching

The Best...
Historic Sites

MERDEKA SQUARE
KL's most impressive architectural ensemble is ringed by heritage buildings. (p62)

STADTHUYS
This salmon-pink Melaka landmark is the oldest Dutch building in the East. (p195)

KHOO KONGSI
Outrageously ornate clanhouse in the heart of George Town's heritage zone. (p120)

RAFFLES HOTEL
Grand dame of the region's hotels and the birthplace of the Singapore sling. (p235)

9

 ## Pulau Langkawi

Pulau Langkawi (p150) isn't called the Jewel of Kedah for nothing, and its white-sand beaches, isolated resorts, acclaimed diving and pristine jungles live up to the metaphor. Cheap booze (Langkawi is duty-free) and a decent restaurant and bar scene provide a hint of party vibe, while a glut of kid-friendly activities make it a great destination for families. Best of all, it's not just a holiday island: off-the-beaten-track exploration will reveal that Pulau Langkawi has managed to retain its endearing *kampung* (village) soul.

Batu Caves

It's always a very busy and colourful scene at this sacred Hindu shrine (p79) but, if you can, time your visit for a holy day. The biggest event is Thaipusam, when around one million pilgrims converge on this giant limestone outcrop a few kilometres north of KL. Guarding the 272 steps that lead up to the main Temple Cave is the 43m gilded statue of Lord Murugan, assisted by a platoon of lively macaques who show little fear in launching raids on tourists' belongings.

12

Pulau Tioman

Welcome to Paradise. What's your pleasure? Swimming off any of the dozens of serenely beautiful beaches that run from north to south along Pulau Tioman's western shore? Challenging the serious surf that pounds the island's eastern beaches at Kampung Juara? Perhaps hiking is more your thing. If so, Tioman's myriad trails will challenge your legs, lungs and internal compass. Care to chill out by a waterfall? Swing in a hammock all day with a good book? Or simply do nothing? All of these goals (and others) are infinitely obtainable on Pulau Tioman (p212).

13

Sepilok Orang-Utan Rehabilitation Centre

There's no primate quite like the orang-utan. These great apes are a stirring combination: brawn, grace, raw power and gentle restraint. And behind their sparkling eyes lie deep reserves of what we can only call wisdom and, sometimes, sadness. Such observations occur at the Sepilok Orang-Utan Rehabilitation Centre (p287), the highlight of many a trip to Sabah.

Petronas Towers, Kuala Lumpur

It's impossible to resist the magnetic allure of the Petronas Towers (p65): the 452m-high structure is beautiful to look at, as well as being the embodiment of Malaysia's transformation into a fully developed nation. Designed by César Pelli, this glistening, steel-wrapped structure is the focal point of the Kuala Lumpur City Centre (KLCC), a 40-hectare development that also includes an imaginatively designed tropical park (p64), a fun aquarium (p65), a world-class concert hall (p77) and one of KL's best shopping malls (p79).

14

The Best...
Temples & Mosques

THIAN HOCK KENG TEMPLE
Singapore's most famous Chinese temple, decorated with carved and gilded beams. (p238)

SRI MAHAMARIAMMAN TEMPLE
This venerable Hindu shrine, the oldest in Malaysia, is in KL's Chinatown. (p67)

MASJID JAMEK
Beautiful palm-tree-shaded, onion-domed mosque in KL. (p68)

KEK LOK SI TEMPLE
Penang's 'Temple of Supreme Bliss' is presided over by a 36.5m-high statue of the goddess Kuan Yin. (p125)

The Best...
Shopping

PUBLIKA
KL's most innovative mall is packed with independent stores, galleries and arty events. (p68)

PAVILION KL
All the brands you could wish for in the heart of Malaysia's capital. (p78)

ORCHARD ROAD
Check out www. orchardroad.sg for all the options on Singapore's top retail strip. (p258)

HAJI LANE
Alternative Singapore shopping at cute independent boutiques. (p257)

MAIN BAZAAR
Kuching's promenade of souvenir shops offers plenty of local arts and crafts. (p299)

15

Danum Valley

'Walk quickly,' our guide tells us. 'Fire ants.' Again we wonder: why is this fun? But it is. It is one of the most stirring experiences in Borneo, walking through a forest (p291) that is older than our species. And while this is no open African savannah, and spotting animals can be difficult in the brush, the wildlife we see is all the more amazing for that: iridescent flying lizards, curious frogs, emerald pit vipers and, peering from behind its headlight eyes, an adorable slow loris. Left: Canopy walkway near Borneo Rainforest Lodge; Above: Wallace's flying frog

© ACHIM BERANEK/FISCHER/GETTY IMAGES © LEFT: © PER-ANDERS BLOMQVIST/GETTY IMAGES ©

Kelabit Highlands

16

The air is clean and cool, the rice fields impossibly green, the local cuisine scrumptious and the trekking – from longhouse to longhouse – some of the best in Borneo, but the star attraction is the people, justifiably famous for their ready smiles and easy way with visitors. Getting to Sarawak's remote northeastern corner (p319) is half the fun. You can either bump your bum on logging roads for 12 hours or take an exhilarating flight in a 19-seat Twin Otter turboprop.

Kuching

17

Borneo's most sophisticated and stylish city (p294) brings together an atmospheric old town, an aromatic waterfront, fine cuisine and chic nightspots. But its biggest draw is what's nearby: some of Sarawak's finest natural sites. You can spot semi-wild orangutans or a giant rafflesia flower, look for proboscis monkeys and wild crocs on a sundown cruise in the South China Sea, and then dine on super-fresh seafood or crunchy *midin* fern tips. Chinatown and the State Assembly Building (p297)

Mt Kinabalu

It is the abode of the spirits, the highest mountain in Malaysia, the dominant geographic feature of North Borneo, the bone-shaking hike that has worn out countless challengers. Mt Kinabalu (p280) is all this, and one of the most popular tourism attractions in Borneo. Don't worry: you will still have moments of utter freedom, breathing in the only alpine air in Sabah and, if you're lucky, enjoying a horizon that stretches to the Philippines. Or it will be cloudy. Whatever: the climb is still bloody exhilarating.

18

The Best...
Trekking Locations

KELABIT HIGHLANDS
Trek from longhouse to longhouse in the cool Sarawak uplands. (p319)

CAMERON HIGHLANDS
Another climatically chilled spot to stretch your legs while taking in lush scenery. (p98)

BAKO NATIONAL PARK
A chance to see proboscis monkeys while trekking. (p304)

GUNUNG MULU NATIONAL PARK
Aim high for the Pinnacles, but be prepared for sore knees. (p315)

PENANG NATIONAL PARK
Follow trails to some of Penang's finest and quietest beaches. (p133)

Singapore Zoo, Night Safari & River Safari

19

One of the world's best designed zoos (p245) just keeps getting better and better. No cages here, just roomy open-air enclosures that do a fab job of keeping the animals happy (as far as we can tell) and visitors enthralled, and situated on a lush peninsula that juts out into the waters of the Upper Seletar Reservoir. The latest addition here is the spectacularly ambitious River Safari, showcasing the environments of ten of the world's greatest rivers.

White tigers, Singapore Zoo

LONELY PLANET/GETTY IMAGES ©

The Best...
Local Food

JALAN ALOR
Scrumptious eats and street theatre on KL's most famous food drag. (p73)

MAXWELL ROAD HAWKER CENTRE
Dish up a great selection of hawker favourites, including chicken rice. (p249)

KOTA BHARU'S NIGHT MARKET
Malay dishes rule at this nightly east-coast nosh-up. (p180)

MELAKA
Sample it all from Nonya delights to *satay celup* – like fondue, but better! (p203)

(20) Marina Bay, Singapore

Less than 50 years ago this was where the Strait of Singapore lapped up to the steps of the grand colonial post office. Today the Marina Barrage has created a freshwater reservoir and the post office is now the luxurious Fullerton Hotel (p247), squaring off against the contemporary eye-candy of the Marina Bay Sands and the dazzling Esplanade – Theatres on the Bay (p235). View it all from on high from the Singapore Flyer.

COLJIERE PHOTOGRAPH/GETTY IMAGES ©

Jonker's Walk Night Market

It starts by the river across from the pink Stadthuys building that glows in the street lights (p205). Dr Ho Eng Hui is doing his nightly street show with a crowd in a circle around him; he makes kung fu moves to the theme music of *Hawaii Five O*. Haggle, nibble and maybe stop by the Geographér Cafe (p204) for a cold beer and some streetside people watching.

Orchard Road

Over 20 malls are packed into Singapore's premier retail strip (p258) – this is retail therapy at its decadent best. Should you be in danger of maxing out your finances the mall food courts provide affordable tasty eats, with street vendors offering that unique Singaporean snack, the ice-cream sandwich. When you need a break, make a detour up Emerald Hill for its gorgeous Peranakan architecture and happy-hour bar specials.

Taman Negara

To visit Taman Negara (p94) is to step back in time and experience the land as it was before primeval jungle was replaced with rubber trees and palm oil plantations. Inside this shadowy, nigh-impenetrable jungle, ancient trees with gargantuan buttressed root systems dwarf luminescent fungi, orchids, and flora rare and beautiful. Making their home within are elephants, tigers and leopards, as well as smaller wonders like flying squirrels, lizards, monkeys, deer, tapirs and serpents.

Reticulated python

23

The Best...
Urban Adventures

MENARA KL
Look across to the Petronas Towers and the rest of the city from the observation deck. (p64)

LITTLE INDIA, SINGAPORE
Head here on a Sunday for the full-on Bollywood effect. (p238)

GEORGE TOWN'S HERITAGE ZONE
Explore this living community of traders and craftspeople. (p120)

MELAKA'S CHINATOWN
Hop in a tricked-out trishaw for a no-sweat tour of this heritage zone. (p194, p201)

KUCHING
Sarawak at its most sophisticated. (p294)

Bako National Park

Wild jungle animals – think proboscis monkeys, bearded pigs and families of long-tailed macaques – are easier to spot on the rocky Bako peninsula (p304) than almost anywhere else in Borneo, although the park is just a short trip (by bus or car and then motorboat) from the bustle of Kuching. Over a dozen hiking trails take you to sandstone plateaus, waterfalls, secret bays and secluded beaches, passing through mangrove and heath-forest ecosystems that provide the ideal conditions for pitcher plants and terrestrial orchids. Pig-tailed macaques

The Best...
Gardens

LAKE GARDENS
Location of the lush KL Bird Park and a 70-hectare colonial park featuring native flora. (p69)

GARDENS BY THE BAY
Fabulous 21st-century designed gardens on Singapore's Marina Bay with super-trees and giant climatically controlled zones. (p235)

SINGAPORE BOTANIC GARDENS
A blissful green escape at the end of Singapore's Orchard Rd. (p239)

BOTANICAL GARDENS, PENANG
Dubbed the Monkey Gardens for the many long-tailed macaques that scamper around. (p126)

Gunung Mulu National Park

Sarawak's Gunung Mulu National Park (p315) is a place of spelunking superlatives. It's got the world's second-largest cave passage (the Deer Cave, 2km in length and 174m in height), the world's largest cave chamber (the Sarawak Chamber, 700m long, 400m wide and 70m high) and Asia's longest cave (the Clearwater Cave, over 170km in length). Several of the park's caves are – like their counterparts in Niah National Park – accessible to non-spelunkers: you can walk through them on well-maintained walkways. Clearwater Cave

Malaysia & Singapore's Top Itineraries

Kuala Lumpur to Taman Negara

City & Jungle Adventures

Punctuate a stopover in Malaysia's capital with a road trip to the country's top national park and a visit to Batu Caves, location of a polychromatic Hindu temple and spectacular limestone caverns.

① Kuala Lumpur (p64)

Ease yourself into Malaysian life by spending your first couple of days in Kuala Lumpur (KL). On your to-see and -do list should be the **Petronas Towers** or **KL Tower**, both of which provide bird's-eye views across the city; **Chinatown** for shopping and eating along **Jalan Petaling** and **Central Market**, and the Lake Gardens for the **KL Bird Park** and **Islamic Arts Museum**. Leave time to browse the retail offerings in glitzy malls like **Pavilion KL** and **Suria KLCC** and spend one night digging into the delicious local cuisine offered along **Jalan Alor**.

- -
KUALA LUMPUR ◯ BATU CAVES
🚆 **25 minutes** KTM Komuter train from KL Sentral to Medan Pasar. 🚌 **45 minutes** Medan Pasar to Batu Caves.
- -

② Batu Caves (p79)

One of KL's most popular attractions lies a few kilometres outside the city limits, at a giant limestone outcrop that nature has riddled with cavities. Climb the 272 steps leading to the **Temple Cave** then peel off from the crowds to explore the **Dark Cave** on a guided tour. All this shouldn't take you more than half a day, allowing you to return to KL in the afternoon, to explore or to relax in one of the city's many **spas**.

- -
KUALA LUMPUR ◯ TAMAN NEGARA
🚌 **Three hours** Kuala Lumpur to Kuala Tembeling. 🚣 **Three hours** Kuala Tembeling to Kuala Tahan by riverboat.
- -

③ Taman Negara (p94)

The easiest way to access **Taman Negara**, Malaysia's top national park, from KL is on one of the daily bus and boat services. Basing yourself for the night in **Kuala Tahan**, you can follow day trails to the **Canopy Walkway** or up to the high point of **Bukit Teresik**. The dense jungle makes it difficult to spot big wildlife but a ranger-led walk will clue you into the amazing diversity here. Also consider taking a **boat trip** deeper into the park.

Sultan Abdul Samad Building, Merdeka Sq (p62), Kuala Lumpur

5 DAYS

Singapore to Pulau Ubin Island to Island

Singapore is the perfect Southeast Asian stopover. A fascinating melange of urban pleasures is on offer: world-class museums, galleries, shopping and eating as well as rural escapes to smaller islands.

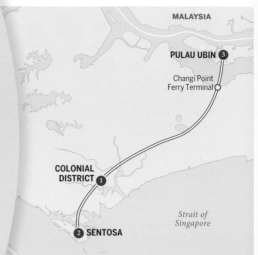

MALAYSIA

PULAU UBIN 3

Changi Point Ferry Terminal

COLONIAL DISTRICT 1

2 SENTOSA

Strait of Singapore

① Singapore (p234)

Get acquainted with Sir Stamford Raffles' grand plan by exploring the **Colonial District**, dropping by the **National Museum** and **Asian Civilisations Museum** for visual history lessons and the **Singapore Art Museum** for artistic stimulation. Later, **Raffles Hotel** beckons for tiffin or a fortifying cocktail. Spend your next day in **Chinatown**, dropping by the **Sri Mariamman Temple**, **Thian Hock Keng Temple** and **Buddha Tooth Relic Temple** as well as digging into hawker delights at **Maxwell Road Hawker Centre**. On day three head to vibrant **Little India** and the nearby Malay area of **Kampong Glam**, location of the gold-domed **Sultan Mosque**. Spend the afternoon at **Singapore Zoo**, then stick around for the **Night Safari.**

ORCHARD MRT STATION ❷ SENTOSA

🚇 **15 minutes** Orchard to HarbourFront MRT station. Either catch the monorail from the VivoCity mall or walk across Sentosa Boardwalk.

② Sentosa (p241)

Essentially one giant theme park, the island of **Sentosa** is brilliant for families and those looking for fun and relaxation. Headline attraction **Universal Studios** is attached to the **Resorts World casino complex** of hotels and restaurants. **Underwater World** provides a window on the region's marine life, and the **beaches** on the south of the island are pretty decent. At least one way, ride the **cable car** to the island from **Mt Faber**. Once at this peak, follow the **Southern Ridges** route to **Kent Ridge Park**, crossing the undulating sculptural **Henderson Waves** bridge along the way.

ORCHARD MRT STATION ❸ PULAU UBIN

🚇 **30 minutes** Orchard to Tanah Merah MRT station. 🚇 **30 minutes** Tanah Merah to Changi Point Ferry Terminal. ⚓ **10 minutes** Changi Point to Pulau Ubin by bumboat.

③ Pulau Ubin (p251)

This island nestling northeast between between Singapore and Malaysia seems worlds apart from the mainland. It's the perfect city getaway for those who love the outdoors, and is best explored by bicycle which can be rented in **Pulau Ubin Village**. Head to the coastal boardwalk around the **Chek Jawa Wetlands**, which includes protected mangrove swamps and a lookout tower with stunning coastal views.

Gardens by the Bay (p235), Singapore
THANK YOU/GETTY IMAGES ©

10 DAYS

Kota Kinabalu to Kuching
Sampling Malaysian Borneo

The East Malaysian states of Sabah and Sarawak contain some of the world's most species-rich equatorial rainforests, prime patches of which are easily accessible from lively, multiethnic cities. Here you'll also find Malaysia's highest mountain.

1 Kota Kinabalu (p274)

Launch your assaults on **Mt Kinabalu,** the Roof of Borneo, from Sabah's capital, **Kota Kinabalu (KK)**. You'll be obliged to spend a day or two here sorting permits, during which you can stoke up on energy by indulging in the flavourful local cuisine and learning a little about the local culture at the **Sabah Museum**. Your reward for the tough overnight hike to Low's Peak, the highest point of the mountain, will be a brilliant sunrise. Thrill seekers should not miss the *via ferrata* rock-climbing route down.

KOTA KINABALU ➲ SEPILOK

🚌 **Six hours** KK to Sepilok ✈ **50 minutes** KK to Sandakan. 🚌 **40 minutes** Sandakan to Sepilok.

2 Sepilok (p286)

Head east from KK to **Sepilok** and its famous **orang-utan sanctuary**, the **Rainforest Discovery Centre** and the **Borneo Sun Bear Conservation Centre**. There are a couple of great places to stay here, too, avoiding the need to overnight in the nearest large town of Sandakan. Return to KK for the next leg of your journey.

KOTA KINABALU ➲ GUNUNG MULU NATIONAL PARK

Backtrack to Kota Kinabalu. ✈ **One hour** to Miri. ✈ **40 minutes** to Mulu.

3 Gunung Mulu National Park (p315)

From the oil-rich boom town **Miri** fly to **Mulu** for spectacular **Gunung Mulu National Park**. Twenty-fours hours here is sufficient to explore several of the park's show caves – including bat-packed **Deer Cave**, the world's largest cave passage open to the public – and join a ranger-led **nightwalk**. The fit can challenge themselves to reach **the Pinnacles**, an incredible stone formation spiking out of the mountainous jungle; set aside at least three days for this trek.

MIRI ➲ KUCHING

✈ **One hour** Miri to Kuching. 🚌 **14 hours** Miri to Kuching.

4 Kuching (p294)

Pass through Miri once more on a quick flight down to **Kuching**. Sarawak's capital is a real charmer and will easily keep you occupied for several days. Meander along the **Waterfront Promenade** and shophouse-lined **Jalan Carpenter**. Also explore the several sections of the **Sarawak Museum** and go shopping for local crafts at the **Main Bazaar**. Break up your time in town with a visit to **Semenggoh Wildlife Rehabilitation Centre**, **Bako National Park**, and the **Annah Rais Longhouse** where you can also spend the night.

Summit of Mt Kinabalu (p280), Sabah
YVES ANDRE/GETTY IMAGES ©

10 DAYS

Kota Bharu to Johor Bahru Beach- & Island-Hopping

Amble down the east coast of Peninsular Malaysia, hopping from the idyllic Perhentian islands to equally gorgeous Pulau Tioman. End up in Johor Bahru just across the Causeway from Singapore.

THAILAND

KOTA BHARU ❶

❷ PULAU PERHENTIAN

Kuala Besut

❸ KUALA TERENGGANU

❹

TASIK KENYIR

SOUTH CHINA SEA

Kuantan

Selat Melaka (Strait of Melaka)

PULAU TIOMAN ❺

Mersing

INDONESIA

JOHOR BAHRU ❻

SINGAPORE

1 Kota Bharu (p178)

Start your trip just across the Thai border in **Kota Bharu**. There's a cluster of museums around the **Padang Merdeka** but this staunchly Malay city's strongest suits are displays of traditional performance arts and crafts at the **Gelanggang Seni** and the tasty, cheap meals at its lively **night market**. Thai-style Buddhist temples surround the city, including **Wat Phothivihan**, one of the largest such complexes in Southeast Asia.

KOTA BHARU 🔾 PULAU PERHENTIAN
🚗 **One hour** Kota Bharu to Kuala Besut by taxi.
🛥 **40 minutes** Kuala Besut to Pulau Perhentian by speedboat.

2 Pulau Perhentian (p181)

Two main islands make up the tropical paradise of the **Perhentians**. **Kecil** ('Small') is popular with the backpacker crowd, while **Besar** ('Large') offers higher standards of accommodation and a quieter, more relaxed ambiance. On both you'll find lush, thick jungles fringed by white-sand beaches. The sparkling blue waters act like a magnet for tropical fish and the divers and snorkellers who come to see them.

KUALA BESUT 🔾 KUALA TERENGGANU
Backtrack to Kuala Besut. 🚌 **Two hours** Kuala Besut to Kuala Terengganu.

3 Kuala Terengganu (p186)

The petro-boom town of Kuala Terengganu has a boardwalk and a pretty **Chinatown**. Other major sights, like the **Kompleks Muzium Negeri Terengganu**, packed with traditional architecture, arts and crafts, and the 'floating mosque' **Masjid Tengku Tengah Zaharah**, are slightly out of town.

KUALA TERENGGANU 🔾 TASIK KENYIR
🚗 **One and a half hours** Kuala Terengganu to the jetty at Pengkalan Gawi by taxi.

4 Tasik Kenyir (p190)

The construction of a dam in 1985 flooded some 2600 sq km of jungle, creating **Tasik Kenyir**, Southeast Asia's largest manufactured lake. Make boat trips from the lake's main access point, Pengkalan Gawi, to waterfalls and caves and journey up the **Sungai Petuang** into beautiful virgin jungle.

KUALA TERENGGANU 🔾 PULAU TIOMAN
Backtrack to Kuala Terengganu. 🚌 **One hour** Kuala Terengganu to Kuantan. 🚌 **Three hours** Kuantan to Mersing. 🛥 **Two to three hours** Mersing to Kampung Genting, Pulau Tioman.

5 Pulau Tioman (p212)

Gorgeous **Pulau Tioman** has steep green peaks and turquoise, coral-rich waters. It's an ideal holiday destination offering an appealing mix of diving, hiking and sunbathing opportunities. **Tekek** is Tioman's commercial hub, and with **Salang** and **ABC** the backpacker hubs; **Juara** on the idyllic east coast has the best surf beaches.

MERSING 🔾 JOHOR BAHRU
Backtrack to Mersing. 🚌 **Two hours** Mersing to Johor Bahru.

6 Johor Bahru (p208)

Singaporeans flock across the 1038m-long causeway to **Johor Bahru** for the city's authentic Malaysian food. The main sight is the **Royal Abu Bakar Museum**, housed in the former main palace of the Johor royal family.

Masjid Tengku Tengah Zaharah (p186), Kuala Terengganu
NAZARUDIN WIJEE/GETTY IMAGES ©

2 WEEKS

Kuala Lumpur to Singapore
Colonial Memories

Ponder the legacy of European colonisation of the Malay Peninsula on this itinerary that covers two Unesco World Heritage zones, the hill station of the Cameron Highlands and the best of Kuala Lumpur and Singapore.

① Kuala Lumpur (p64)

The showpiece of KL's collection of colonial-era buildings is the architectural ensemble surrounding Merdeka Sq including the Moorish domes and 41m clocktower of the **Sultan Abdul Samad Building** and the **National Textiles Museum**. The old **KL Train Station** and **Masjid Jamek** are other Moorish-Mogul inspired constructions and the nearby **Lake Gardens** were originally laid out under colonial rule. To find out more drop by the headquarters of **Badan Warisan Malaysia**, the national heritage protection organisation.

KUALA LUMPUR ⊙ IPOH
🚌 **Four and a half hours** KL to Ipoh.

② Ipoh (p104)

Chock full of colonial architecture and some of the country's best food, **Ipoh** – once one of the wealthiest cities in Southeast Asia – is seeing a revival in its fortunes. Follow the **Ipoh Heritage Trail**, a self-guided walk past architectural gems like the **Train Station**, **Town Hall** and **Court House**.

IPOH ⊙ TANAH RATA
🚌 **Two hours** to Tanah Rata.

③ Cameron Highlands (p98)

Exchange the heat and humidity of lowland Malaysia for the refreshing breezes and cool climate of the **Cameron Highlands**. The hill stations' hub, **Tanah Rata**, is the place to organise visits to lush tea plantations such as the **Boh Sungai Palas Tea Estate**. Take your pick from **14 hiking trails** or relax over afternoon tea and strawberries.

TANAH RATA ⊙ PENANG
🚌 **Five hours** Tanah Rata to George Town, Penang.

④ Penang (p120)

The island of **Penang** is one of Malaysia's most tolerant, cosmopolitan and exciting destinations. Base yourself in the atmospheric World Heritage zone of the capital, **George Town** – stroll the bustling streets, sampling the delicious hawker fare as you go or hop in one of the trishaws and head to the **Eastern & Oriental Hotel** for afternoon tea. Write up **Penang Hill**, **Kek Lok Si Temple**,

⑥ **Melaka** (p194)

Melaka was the seat of a great Malay sultanate for over a century before the Portuguese muscled in, followed by the Dutch and English. Each power left a legacy behind in this historic town, the **Chinatown** area of which is a Unesco World Heritage zone. Take a **trishaw tour** around the sights including the **Stadthuys**, **Porta De Santiago**, **St Paul's Church** and the replica of the **Sultanate Palace**.

MELAKA ⊙ SINGAPORE

🚌 **Four and a half hours** Melaka to Singapore.

⑦ **Singapore** (p234)

Wrap up your travels in **Singapore**, where the grand ambition of Sir Stamford Raffles is so perfectly realised. For crash courses in Straits Chinese culture drop by the **Peranakan Museum**, **Asian Civilisation Museum** and the **Baba House**. Finally, toast the colonial legend at **Raffles Hotel**.

the **Botanical Gardens** and the quiet beaches and trails of **Penang National Park** on your to-do list.

PENANG ⊙ LANGKAWI

✈ **30 minutes** Penang International Airport to Langkawi Airport. 🚢 **Two hours** George Town to Kuah, Pulau Langkawi.

⑤ **Pulau Langkawi** (p150)

Kick back on beautiful **Langkawi**. Top-class resorts are scattered around the main island of Pulau Langkawi, several so lovely you might just decide never to stray from the pool, sun lounger and nearby beach. That would be a shame as there are idyllic smaller islands to visit, diving opportunities and a **cable car** to the summit of **Gunung Machinchang** for incredible views. Pulau Langkawi is big, so hire a car to get around.

LANGKAWI ⊙ MELAKA

✈ **One hour** Langkawi Airport to KLIA. 🚌 **Two hours** KLIA to Melaka.

Month by Month

Hindus, Muslims and Chinese all follow a lunar calendar, so the dates for many religious festivals vary each year. Muslim holidays typically move forward 11 days each year, while Hindu and Chinese festivals change dates but fall roughly within the same months. Dates have been given where they are known, but may be subject to slight change.

January

New Year is a busy travel period. It's monsoon season on Malaysia's east coast and Sarawak.

Thai Pongal

A Hindu harvest festival marking the beginning of the Hindu month of Thai, considered the luckiest month of the year. This Tamil celebration is always held on 14 January.

Thaipusam

Enormous crowds converge at the Batu Caves north of Kuala Lumpur (KL), at Nattukotai Chettiar Temple in Penang and in Singapore for this dramatic Hindu festival involving body piercing. Falls between mid-January and mid-February.

February

Chinese New Year is a big deal throughout the region and a busy travel period, so book transport and hotels well ahead.

Chinese New Year

Dragon dances and pedestrian parades mark the start of the new year. Families hold open house. Celebrated on 31 January 2014, 19 February 2015 and 8 February 2016.

Top Events

- **Thaipusam**, January or February

- **Chinese New Year**, January or February

- **Festival of the Hungry Ghosts**, August

- **Chingay**, February

- **Rainforest World Music Festival**, July

February Chingay parade, Singapore
ANDREW JK TAN/GETTY IMAGES ©

Chingay

Singapore's biggest street parade (www. chingay.org.sg), a flamboyant, multicultural event, falls on the 22nd day after Chinese New Year.

March

The northeast monsoon peters out and the mercury starts rising.

Birthday of the Goddess of Mercy

Kuan Yin (also spelled Guan Yin) is such a popular Chinese deity that she's celebrated three times a year at her temples across the region. The first of these celebrations typically fall in March (or the end of February), while the others are at the end of June or early July, and end of September or early October.

April

The light monsoon season ends on Malaysia's west coast, but you should still always be prepared for rain.

Petronas Malaysian Grand Prix

Formula One's first big outing of year (www.malaysiangp.com) in Southeast Asia is held at the Sepang International Circuit over three days usually at the start of the month. Associated events and parties are held in KL.

May

This quiet month, prior to the busy school holidays, is a good time to visit the region.

Wesak (Vesak) Day

Buddha's birth, enlightenment and death are celebrated with various events, including the release of caged birds to symbolise the setting free of captive souls, and

processions in KL, Singapore and other major cities. Celebrated on 24 May 2013, 13 May 2014 and 1 June 2015.

June

School holidays and one of the hottest months so get ready to sweat it out.

George Town Festival

This arts and performance festival (www. georgetownfestival.com) includes international artists, innovative street performances and new street art.

Gawai Dayak

Held on 1 and 2 June but beginning on evening of 31 May, this Sarawak-wide Dayak festival celebrates the end of the rice harvest season.

Festa de San Pedro

Christian celebration on 29 June in honour of the patron saint of the fishing community; notably celebrated by the Eurasian-Portuguese community of Melaka.

Dragon Boat Festival

Commemorates the Malay legend of the fishermen who paddled out to sea to prevent the drowning of a Chinese saint, beating drums to scare away any fish that might attack him. Celebrated from June to August, with boat races in Penang.

July

Busy travel month for Malaysian Borneo so book ahead for treks, caving, diving, guides and tours.

Rainforest World Music Festival

A three-day musical extravaganza (www. rainforestmusic-borneo.com) held in the Sarawak Cultural Village near Kuching on the second week of July.

🏵 Malaysia's National Day

Join the crowds at midnight on 31 August to celebrate the anniversary of Malaysia's independence in 1957. Events are usually held in Merdeka Square in KL. There are parades and festivities the next morning across the country.

🏵 Night Festival

Art comes out onto the streets of the Bras Basah and Bugis districts of central Singapore in this fun after-dark event that includes late-night openings of the National Museum and Singapore Art Museum. For details see www.nhb.gov.sg.

📆 September

Haze from forest and field clearance fires in Indonesia create urban smog across the region.

🏵 Mooncake Festival

The overthrow of the Mongol warlords in ancient China is celebrated by eating mooncakes and lighting colourful paper lanterns, hence it's also known as the Lantern Festival. Mooncakes are filled with soy bean paste, lotus seeds and sometimes a hard-boiled duck egg-yolk.

🏵 Hari Raya Puasa

The Muslim fasting month of Ramadan culminates in this major festival traditionally celebrated at home with big banquets; the Malaysian prime minister opens his official home in Putrajaya to the public.

☆ Singapore Grand Prix

It's Singapore's turn to host the Formula 1 crowd with a night race (www.singaporegp.sg) on a scenic city centre circuit. Book well in advance for hotel rooms with a view.

🏵 Singapore Food Festival

This month-long celebration of food (www.singaporefoodfestival.com) includes events, cooking classes, food-themed tours and more.

📆 August

Ramandan may fall in this month, so look out for night food markets.

🏵 Singapore National Day

Held on 9 August (though dress rehearsals on the two prior weekends are almost as popular), the Singapore National Day (www.ndp.org.sg) includes military parades, fly-overs and fireworks.

🏵 Festival of the Hungry Ghosts

Chinese communities perform operas, host open-air concerts and lay out food for their ancestors. Celebrated towards the end of the month and early September.

October

The west-coast monsoon season begins, but it's mostly not severe enough to affect travel.

😎 Deepavali

Tiny oil lamps are lit outside Hindu homes to attract the gods Rama and Lakshmi. Indian businesses start the new financial year, with Little Indias ablaze with lights.

😎 Hari Raya Haji

This event, which can also fall in early November, celebrates the end of the pilgrimage to Mecca. Animals are ritually slaughtered, with the meat traditionally given to the poor.

November

😎 Thimithi

At this fire-walking ceremony Hindu devotees prove their faith by walking across glowing coals at temples in Melaka and Singapore.

December

A sense of festivity (and monsoon rains in Singapore and east-coast Malaysia) permeates the air as the year winds down.

😎 Zoukout

Held on Siloso Beach, Sentosa, this annual outdoor dance party (www.zoukout.com) is one of the region's best such events with a 25,000-strong crowd bopping to international DJs.

😎 Christmas

Religiously not such a big deal in mainly Muslim Malaysia but enthusiastically embraced for its commercial aspects in the shopping precincts of Singapore. The dazzling light display that stretches the length of Orchard Rd is well worth seeing.

Far left: August Offerings during the Festival of the Hungry Ghosts
Below: September Singapore Grand Prix
(FAR LEFT) PAUL KENNEDY/ GETTY IMAGES ©; (BELOW) AFP/GETTY IMAGES ©

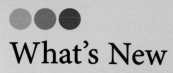

What's New

For this edition of Discover Malaysia & Singapore our authors have hunted down the fresh, the revived and the happening. Here are a few of our favourites. For up-to-the-minute reviews see www.lonelyplanet.com/Malaysia and /Singapore.

1 GEORGE TOWN'S HERITAGE REVIVAL
The Unesco World Heritage area of the city has been revived to create unique hotels, guesthouses, restaurants and galleries amid a living community of trades and crafts-people. (p121)

2 PUBLIKA
This next-generation mall, in the up-market Kuala Lumpur (KL) suburb of Solaris Dutamas, combines shopping with arts, culture and the fostering of local creative industries and nonprofit organisations. (p68)

3 SEKEPING RETREATS
Landscape architect Ng Seksan has crafted a collection of chic rough-luxe guesthouses in KL and Ipoh, including one in Bangsar Baru with access to his private gallery of contemporary Malaysian art. (p72, p104)

4 MARINA BAY & GARDENS BY THE BAY
Singapore's dazzling contemporary architectural centrepiece is home to the iconic Marina Bay Sands integrated resort and the botanic landscape of Gardens by the Bay. (p233, p235)

5 AMBONG AMBONG
This new hotel made up of minimalist decorated rooms surrounded by lush jungle greenery is one of the more sophisticated places to stay on Pulau Langkawi. (p157)

6 TERRAPURI HERITAGE VILLAGE
Equal parts resort and conservation and restoration museum, this luxurious stopover on Peninsular Malaysia's east coast is also graced by fireflies and green turtles. (p190)

7 IPOH
Colonial Ipoh is one of the peninsula's emerging destinations, with a hip urban core and outdoorsy activities in the surrounding areas. (p104)

8 RAINFOREST DISCOVERY CENTRE
Eight canopy towers and walkways have been erected so you can look down from this Sepilok centre onto the rainforest's green rooftop. It's a great spot to while away time between feedings at the nearby orang-utan sanctuary. (p286)

9 RIVER SAFARI
Pandas are just one of the many draws at this new zoological attraction in Singapore, which aims to recreate the aquatic and botanic environments of eight major world rivers. (p245)

10 45 LEKIU & THE STABLE
This pair of Melaka properties is perfect if you want self-catered meals – and you get the whole of each of these sensitively resorted heritage buildings to yourself. 45 Leiku also has a lap pool. (p202)

Get Inspired

Books

o **Singapore: A Biography**
(Mark Ravinder Frost &
Yu-Mei Balasingchow;
2010) A well-written and
handsomely illustrated
history of Singapore.

o **Malaysia at
Random** (2010) Quirky
compendium of facts,
quotes and anecdotes.

o **The Garden of the
Evening Mists** (Tan Twan
Eng; 2012) Intrigue in the
Malaysian highlands.

o **Little Ironies: Short
Stories of Singapore**
(Catherine Lim, 1978) A
collection by the doyenne
of Singaporean fiction.

o **Urban Odysseys** (Janet
Tay & Eric Forbes, eds;
2010) Short stories set in
Kuala Lumpur that capture
the city's multifaceted,
multicultural flavour.

Films

o **Penarik Becha** (*The
Trishaw Man*; 1955) A
classic of Malay cinema
from legendary director
and singer P Ramlee.

o **Talentime** (2009)
Yasmin Ahmad's final
movie, about an inter-
school performing arts
contest.

o **The Blue House**
(2009) Penang's
Cheong Fatt Tze Mansion
hosts this Singaporean
comedy thriller directed
by Glen Goei.

o **881** (2007) Royston
Tan's camp musical
comedy about *getai*
(stage singing).

Music

o **Ghostbird** (Zee
Avi; www.zeeavi.com)
Sophomore album from
the folksy pop diva.

o **Harapan** (Reshmonu;
www.reshmonu.com) The
Malaysian dance master's
latest album.

o **Life Deluxe** (Dick
Lee; www.dicklee.com)
Legendary Singaporean
songsmith's 2010 album.

Websites

o **Tourism Malaysia**
(www.tourismmalaysia.
gov.my) Official national
tourist-information site.

o **Visit Singapore** (www.
visitsingapore.com)
Official tourism board site.

o **Lonely Planet** (www.
lonelyplanet.com)
Information, bookings,
forums and more.

o **The Nut Graph** (www.
thenutgraph.com)
Malaysian politics and
popular culture.

o **The Edge** (www.
theedgemalaysia.com)
Business news and more
general features.

Short on time?

This list will give you in-
stant insight into Malaysia
and Singapore.

Read *Malaysia Bagus!* (Sha-
ron Cheah; 2012) Engaging
travelogue with stories from
all of Malaysia's states and
Singapore.

Watch *Sepet* (2004) A Chinese boy falls for a Malay girl
in Yasmin Ahmad's movie.

Listen *Yuna* (www.yunamusic.
com) First all-English album
by a soulful Malaysian diva.

Log On *Malaysiakini* (www.
malaysiakini.com) Find out
what's really going on in
Malaysia.

Pantai Cenang (p154), Pulau Langkawi
MATTHEW MICAH WRIGHT/GETTY IMAGES ©

Need to Know

Currency
Malaysian ringgit (RM)
Singapore dollar (S$)

Language
Bahasa Malaysia
English
Chinese dialects
Tamil

ATMs
Widespread but check first
whether overseas cards are
accepted

Credit Cards
Accepted by most
businesses

Visas
Mostly not needed for
stays under 60 (Malaysia)
and 90 days (Singapore)

Mobile Phones
Use local SIM cards or set
your phone to roaming

Wi-Fi
Widespread; access is
cheap or free

Internet Access
Internet cafes are common
in tourist centres

Driving
It's easy to hire cars and
motorcycles; drive on the left

Tipping
10% in high-end hotels and
restaurants, plus 6% tax

When to Go

Kota Bharu
GO Mar–Nov

Penang
GO Mar–Nov

Kuala Lumpur
GO Mar–Nov

Singapore
GO Mar–Nov

Kuching
GO Mar–Nov

Tropical climate, rain all year round
Tropical climate, wet and dry seasons

High Season
(Dec–Feb)
○ End-of-year
school holidays and
Chinese New Year
push up prices, so
advance transport
and hotel bookings
are important

○ It's monsoon
season for the east
coast of Peninsular
Malaysia and
western Sarawak

Shoulder
(Jul–Nov)
○ From July to
August vie with
visitors escaping
the heat of the Gulf
States as the region
enjoys what it calls
Arab Season

○ The end of
Ramadan (Hari
Raya) also sees
increased travel
activity in the region

Low Season
(Mar–Jun)
○ Avoid the worst
of the rains and
humidity; plus there
are more chances
to enjoy places
without the crush
of fellow tourists

○ Be flexible with
travel plans

Advance Planning

○ **Two months before** Book tickets for short-run major shows and
events such as Formula One Night Race in Singapore. Reserve table
at hot top-end restaurants.

○ **One month before** Book accommodation, especially if you plan to
stay over a weekend or are travelling during a busy holiday period.

○ **One week before** Confirm your flight. Look for last-minute deals
on accommodation and for the latest events and festivals.

Your Daily Budget

Budget less than RM100/$S150

o Dorm beds: RM12–35/S$16–40

o Hawker centres and food courts for meals

o Use public transport; plan sightseeing around walking tours, free museums and galleries

Midrange RM100–400/ S$150–350

o Double room in midrange hotel: RM100–400/ S$100–250

o Two-course meal in midrange restaurant: RM40-60/S$50

o Take taxis and guided tours of cities and sights

Top End more than RM400/ S$350

o Luxury double room: RM450–1000/S$250–500

o Meal in top restaurant: RM200/S$250

o Take a private tour

o Hire a car

Exchange Rates

Australia	A$1	S$1.27	RM3
Canada	C$1	S$1.23	RM3
Euro zone	€1	S$1.66	RM4
Japan	¥100	S$1.32	RM3
NZ	NZ$1	S$1.03	RM3
UK	UK£1	S$1.94	RM5
US	US$1	S$1.24	RM3

For current exchange rates see www.xe.com.

What to Bring

o **Light wash-and-wear clothes** Pack light and take advantage of cheap laundry services.

o **A warm top and jacket** For over-airconditioned places and for the cool highland regions.

o **Slip-on shoes or sandals** For quick removal when entering mosques and temples.

o **Other handy items** A small torch, waterproof money/passport container, leech socks (if planning jungle hikes), antifog solution for spectacles, earplugs, SPF30+ sunscreen and a travel umbrella.

Arriving in Malaysia & Singapore

o **Kuala Lumpur International Airport** Trains RM35; every 15 minutes from 5am to 1am; 30 minutes to KL Sentral. Taxis from RM75; one hour to central KL.

o **Changi International Airport** MRT train, public and shuttle bus to town, S$1.80 to S$9, 6am to midnight. Taxis S$18 to S$35.

Getting Around

o **Air** Domestic routes from KL, other major Malaysian cities and Singapore are plentiful.

o **Bus** Intercity buses are affordable, comfortable and often frequent; buy tickets at bus stations.

o **Car and taxi** Singapore's metered taxis are affordable, reliable and honest; KL's are less so. It's easy to rent self-drive cars everywhere.

o **Public transport** Singapore's metro and buses are excellent; KL's public transport (metro, monorail, trains and buses) is less reliable.

o **Train** Slow but scenic. Popular for overnight trips from the Thai border to Singapore.

Accommodation

o **Guesthouses and hostels** A common and often characterful option; at their most basic they are simple rooms in a family's home, while others are small hotels and hostels for small budgets.

o **Hotels and resorts** Hip and fashionable in major destinations. In smaller provincial towns Chinese-Malaysian hotels can be dour and impersonal.

Be Forewarned

o **Check travel advisories** Prior to your trip look for advisory warnings to Malaysia on the website of your government's diplomatic mission abroad.

o **Health** Dengue fever is a concern throughout the region; bedbugs are also a common problem.

o **Dress** Cover up when visiting mosques and temples; women shouldn't sunbathe topless, particularly on Peninsular Malaysia beaches.

o **Public holidays** Domestic transport and accommodation can be crowded or booked out during major holidays.

o **Rainy season** Some resorts close; boat services may be limited.

Kuala Lumpur

Hacked out of the jungle in the 19th century, Kuala Lumpur (KL) has evolved into an affluent metropolis remarkable for its cultural diversity. Ethnic Malays, Chinese tin prospectors, Indian migrants and British colonials all helped shaped this city, and each group has left its indelible physical mark and a fascinating assortment of cultural traditions.

KL lacks much of an overall plan and has few obvious sights. Still it's a fascinating place to explore, with historic temples and mosques rubbing shoulders with contemporary towers and shopping malls.

Here you'll also find traders' stalls piled high with pungent durians and counterfeit handbags, monorail cars zipping by lush jungle foliage and neatly clipped public gardens and parks, and locals sipping cappuccinos in wi-fi–enabled cafes or feasting on delicious streetside hawker food.

Kuala Lumpur's skyline

Kuala Lumpur

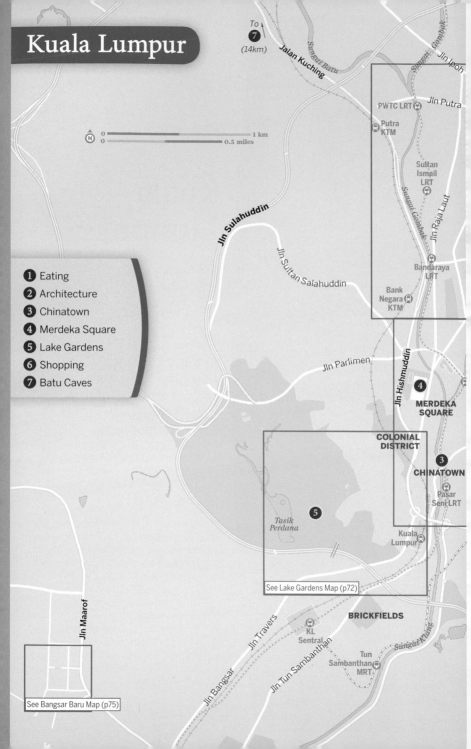

1 Eating
2 Architecture
3 Chinatown
4 Merdeka Square
5 Lake Gardens
6 Shopping
7 Batu Caves

To
7
(14km)

Jalan Kuching

Sungai Batu

Sungai Gombak

Jln Ipoh

PWTC LRT

Putra KTM

Jln Putra

Sultan Ismail LRT

Jln Raja Laut

Sungai Gombak

Bandaraya LRT

Jln Sulahuddin

Jln Sultan Salahuddin

Bank Negara KTM

Jln Parlimen

Jln Hishmuddin

4

MERDEKA SQUARE

COLONIAL DISTRICT

3

CHINATOWN

Pasar Seni LRT

Tasik Perdana

5

Kuala Lumpur

See Lake Gardens Map (p72)

Jln Maarof

BRICKFIELDS

KL Sentral

Jln Travers

Jln Bangsar

Tun Sambanthan MRT

Jln Tun Sambanthan

Sungai Klang

See Bangsar Baru Map (p75)

0 ___ 1 km
0 ___ 0.5 miles

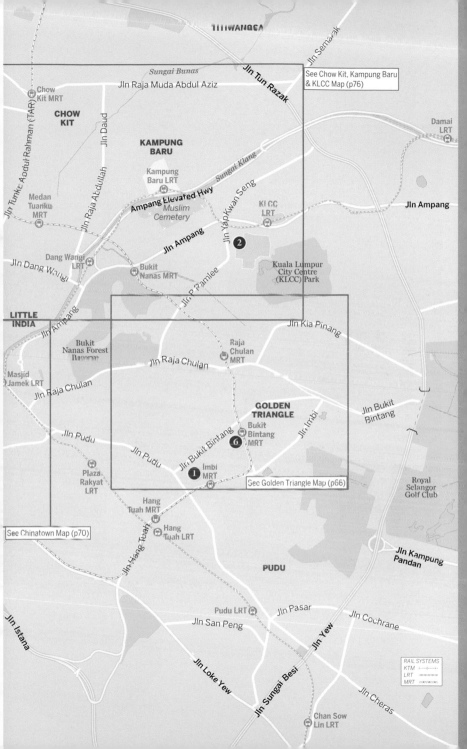

TITIWANGSA

Sungai Bunas

Jln Tun Razak

Jln Raja Muda Abdul Aziz

See Chow Kit, Kampung Baru
& KLCC Map (p76)

Chow
Kit MRT

CHOW
KIT

Damai
LRT

KAMPUNG
BARU

Kampung
Baru LRT

Sungai Klang

Medan
Tuanku
MRT

Muslim
Cemetery

KLCC
LRT

Jln Ampang

Jln Ampang

Dang Wangi
LRT

Jln Dang Wangi

Bukit
Nanas MRT

Kuala Lumpur
City Centre
(KLCC) Park

2

LITTLE
INDIA

Jln Kia Pinang

Bukit
Nanas Forest
Reserve

Raja
Chulan
MRT

Masjid
Jamek LRT

Jln Raja Chulan

Jln Raja Chulan

GOLDEN
TRIANGLE

Jln Bukit
Bintang

Jln Pudu

Bukit
Bintang
MRT

6

Plaza
Rakyat
LRT

Jln Pudu

Imbi
MRT

1

Royal
Selangor
Golf Club

Sec Golden Triangle Map (p66)

Hang
Tuah MRT

Hang
Tuah LRT

See Chinatown Map (p70)

PUDU

Jln Kampung
Pandan

Jln Istana

Pudu LRT

Jln Pasar

Jln Cochrane

Jln San Peng

Jln Yew

Jln Loke Yew

Jln Sungai Besi

Jln Cheras

RAIL SYSTEMS
KTM
LRT
MRT

Chan Sow
Lin LRT

Kuala Lumpur Highlights

① Culinary Kuala Lumpur

KL might not be Malaysia's top culinary destination (that accolade goes to George Town) but it's a close-run race. The city is a nonstop feast where you can dine in incredible elegance or mingle with locals at thousands of street stalls. Top Right: Jalan Alor (p73); Right: A Bukit Bintang night market

Need to Know

TOP TIP For international food, try malls, top hotels and Bangsar Baru **AVOID** Hawker stalls are generally safe, but stick to ones with lots of customers **For further coverage, see p72**

Local Knowledge

Culinary Kuala Lumpur Don't Miss List

BY HONEY AHMAD, FOOD WRITER,
WWW.FRIEDCHILLIES.COM

1 JALAN ALOR

A little pricey but a great way to start sampling street food. The road is long and mind-boggling and deals with mostly Chinese fare; you'll find the fishy broth *asam* laksa, freshly dropped durians and many more. Do not miss **Wong Ah Wah's** (p73) smoky-sticky chicken wings at the end of the road.

2 NIGHT MARKETS

Makeshift markets pop up in different neighbourhoods on different nights. Bangsar Baru's Sunday market is the most civilised, offering fresh produce alongside street fare like *chee cheong fun* (rice noodles). On Saturdays Little India is excellent – the scent of fresh curries and biryani will accompany your fabric and bric-a-brac shopping. The same night hit **Kampung Baru** (p65) for Malay grub: Jln Raja Muda Aziz has everything from street porridge to the rice dish *nasi lemak*.

3 WET MARKETS

A brisk walk from Kampung Baru will take you to **Chow Kit Market** (p65), where chefs shop for last-minute menu items like chicken livers and tropical fruits. Kampung Baru is where Southeast Asian Muslims settle down first, so you can get top-notch *som tam* (green papaya salad) from Pattani ladies and delicious Padang food from Indonesian immigrants. Keen for a visceral experience? Take a gander at **Pudu Market** (Jln Pasar Baru; ⏱6am-2pm); it's long, humid and heady, replete with hanging meats and frog butchers.

4 YUT KEE

Yut Kee (p78), a favourite *kopitiam* (coffee shop), has been open for over 80 years. Here you get a bracing cup of local joe with beans roasted in margarine and toasted Hainanese bread with gritty homemade *kaya* (coconut jam). It also serves British throwbacks like chicken chop, and a pork po' boy called *roti babi*.

Eclectic Architecture

KL's multiculturalism attains a supreme physical expression in the city's eclectic range of architectural styles. Glittering skyscrapers stand cheek by jowl with the grand flourishes of colonial buildings, the sacred ornament of temples and mosques and the simplicity of wooden Malay homes. Below: Petronas Towers (p65); Right: Sultan Abdul Samad Building, Merdeka Sq (p62); Bottom Right: KL's original railway station

Need to Know

TOP TIP KL has some architecturally eye-boggling malls ISLAMIC INFLUENCE Evident in the Petronas Towers and the Menara Maybank For further coverage, see p64

2

Eclectic Architecture Don't Miss List

BY ALEX YONG, EVENTS MANAGER, FZ.COM

1 PETRONAS TOWERS

The world's tallest buildings from 1998 to 2004, these twin towers (p65) were designed by Argentinian architect César Pelli. For stunning illuminated night views head to Sky Bar (p69), or dine at the new **Troika Sky Dining (Level 23A, The Troika)**, which features two glass-encased bridges spanning its three towers.

2 MERDEKA SQUARE

Merdeka Square (p62) was once the focal point of British colonial rule. Situated on one end of the square is the Tudor-styled Selangor Club. St Mary's Cathedral, designed by AC Norman in 1894, sits at another end with the Moorish-style Sultan Abdul Samad Building that once housed the British Secretariat Building built across from it. Here you can learn about the city's history through prints, photos and an architectural scale model at the **KL City Gallery**.

3 ORIGINAL KUALA LUMPUR RAILWAY STATION

This flamboyantly architectural terminus, built in 1910, was designed by Arthur Benison Hubback. Having served in India, he employed Anglo-Asian architecture from the region. After the 2001 opening of Kuala Lumpur Sentral station less than a kilometer south, the original station's importance has diminished. Southwest of the station is the newly restored **Majestic Hotel**.

4 KAMPUNG BARU

This brightly painted Malay enclave (p65) was gazetted by the British in 1900 to maintain the district's culture and lifestyle. The square-kilometre area still maintains several authentic Malay wooden houses on stilts surrounding shabby shophouses and food stalls.

5 PUBLIKA

Aspiring to bring 'art to life and life to art', this arty and edgy mall (p68) has brought together tenants that are a mix of local fashion brands, art galleries, restaurants and cafes that double as performance venues. Sculptures, murals and floor text are scattered around.

Chinatown

The temples and mosques of the city's Hindus, Muslims and Chinese Buddhists are crammed shoulder to shoulder with shops, market stalls and great places to eat in this atmospheric neighbourhood that epitomises multicultural Malaysia. Don't miss eating at the daytime Madras Lane hawker stalls (p75) or savouring the bustle and fun of the night market along Jalan Petaling (p68).

Merdeka Square

Ringed by handsome heritage buildings, **Merdeka Square** (p62, Dataran Merdeka, or Independence Sq) is KL's most impressive architectural ensemble. Once known as the Padang, up until 1987 this vast lawn was the cricket pitch belonging to the neighbouring Royal Selangor Club. The square hosted Malaya's independence from Britain in 1957 and continues to be a place of national celebration. Sultan Abdul Samad Building

Explore the Lake Gardens

5

Covering 92 hectares, the Lake Gardens were created during the colonial era as an urban retreat where the British administrators could escape the hurly burly of downtown (as well as people of other races). The sculpted parks and dense foliage still serve a similar purpose today and are home to several of KL's top sights including the **Islamic Arts Museum** (p68) and **KL Bird Park** (p69). Striated heron, KL Bird Park

6

Malls & Markets

If browsing markets and malls were an Olympic sport, KLites would be gold medalists. And who can blame their enthusiasm with such a tempting range of options on offer in complexes that make shopping fun and comfortable? Take your pick from glitzy mega-malls such as **Pavilion KL** (p78) and **Suria KLCC** (p79) or the night street markets in Chinatown and Little India. Suria KLCC

7

Batu Caves

It's always a very busy and colourful scene at this sacred **Hindu shrine** (p79) but, if you can, time your visit for a holy day – the biggest is Thaipusam. A 43m gilded statue of Lord Murugan guards the 272 steps leading up to the **Temple Cave**, assisted by a platoon of cheeky macaques who show little fear of launching raids on visitors' belongings.

Kuala Lumpur's Best…

Museums & Galleries

○ **Islamic Arts Museum** (p68) Prime examples of artistic expression from across the Islamic world, plus an excellent shop.

○ **National Museum** (p69) A crash course in Malaysian history and culture.

○ **National Visual Arts Gallery** (p74) Dip into the country's historical and contemporary art scene.

○ **National Textiles Museum** (p68) View rare and beautiful fabrics and clothing.

Dining

○ **Kedai Makanan Dan Minuman TKS** (p72) Amazing, spicy Chinese food; one of the best places on buzzing Jln Alor.

○ **Rebung** (p75) The best Malay spread in town, prepared under the gaze of a celebrity chef.

○ **Frangipani** (p74) Contemporary dining in high style; the bar is also very chic and gay friendly.

○ **Sri Nirwana Maju** (p76) Tuck into delicious, cheap Indian food.

Drinking & Clubbing

○ **Palate Palette** (p77) This arty cafe-bar is a respite from the rowdiness of nearby Changkat Bukit Bintang.

○ **Taps Beer Bar** (p77) Sample craft beers from across the globe while listening to live acoustic music.

○ **Zouk Club** (p78) Dance the night away at this vast complex with three separate event spaces.

○ **Luna** (p69) Chink glasses to the glittering backdrop of KL's illuminated skyline.

Mosques & Temples

o **Masjid Negara** (p69) A serene complex on the edge of the Lake Gardens, inspired by Mecca's Grand Mosque.

o **Thean Hou Temple** (p80) Pay your respects to the heavenly mother at this riotously colourful Chinese temple.

o **Sri Mahamariamman Temple** (p67) Hindu temple dedicated to Mariamman, the South Indian mother goddess.

o **Masjid Jamek** (p68) Onion-domed mosque designed by colonial architect AB Hubbock.

Need to Know

VITAL STATISTICS
o **Area code** ☎03

ADVANCE PLANNING
o **One month before** Book accommodation.

o **One week before** Book a Malaysian cooking course.

o **One day before** Check on festivals and events, and tickets for Petronas Towers.

RESOURCES
o **Time Out Kuala Lumpur** (www.timeoutkl. com) What's on in KL.

o **Visit KL** (www.visitkl.gov. my) Official city site.

o **Malaysian Tourism Centre** (MaTiC; www.mtc. gov.my) KL's most useful tourist office.

GETTING AROUND
o **Bus** Most are provided by Rapid KL (www.rapidkl. com.my) or Metrobus. There's an information booth in Chinatown.

o **Monorail** Easiest way of navigating the city centre; runs from KL Sentral to Titiwangsa.

o **KTM Komuter Trains** Suburban rail lines link

with the city hub at KL Sentral.

o **Light Rail Transit** Three poorly integrated lines supplement the trains and monorail.

o **Taxi** Plentiful. Some work on a coupon system; fares are otherwise calculated by meter.

BE FOREWARNED
o **Walking** Highways and flyovers slice up the city, and footpaths are often cracked or nonexistent. However, some sights are so close together that it's often quicker to walk than take public transport or grab a cab (which can easily become snarled in traffic and KL's tortuous one-way system).

o **Dress** Remove your shoes and dress respectfully when visiting mosques.

o **Smoking** Allowed in bars, clubs and most restaurants.

o **Wet markets** Closed on Monday.

o **Taxi** Some taxi drivers will refuse to use their meter, particularly those loitering at major tourist sites and top hotels.

Left: Sri Mahamariamman Temple (p67);
Above: National Museum (p69)

Kuala Lumpur Walking Tour

Gems of colonial KL architecture can be viewed on this walk from Masjid Jamek to Chinatown via Merdeka Square. Start early to beat the heat or go late to enjoy Jalan Petaling Street Market at full throttle.

WALK FACTS

- **Start** Masjid Jamek LRT Station
- **Finish** Jln Petaling Street Market
- **Distance** 1.6km
- **Duration** 1½ hours

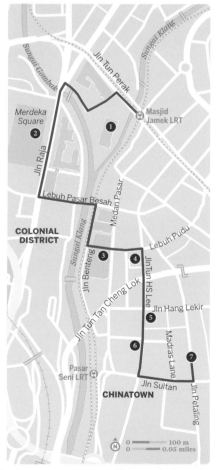

1 Masjid Jamek

From the station head northwest up Jln Tun Perak to pass Masjid Jamek. If you're dressed appropriately, and it's not prayer time, enter to explore this lovely palm-tree-shaded mosque with its Mogul-inspired architecture.

2 Merdeka Square

At the junction with Jln Raja turn left and continue to Merdeka Square where Malaysia's independence (Merdeka) was proclaimed at midnight on 31 August 1957. Once a colonial cricket pitch, the square is speared by a 100m-high freestanding flag-pole claimed to be the world's tallest. The square is surrounded by a handsome architectural ensemble. On the east side is the red-brick Sultan Abdul Samad Building with its distinctive copper-plated cupolas and blend of Victorian, Moorish and Mogul architecture. To the west is the Royal Selangor Club, a mock-Tudor building that was the social centre for high society in KL's tin-boom days of the 1890s. It remains a gathering place for the city's elite. At the square's north end are low memorial arches inscribed with 'Dataran Merdeka' (Merdeka Square). Across the road is another of AC Norman's creations, St Mary's Cathedral, dating from 1894.

3 Central Market

From the National Textiles Museum at the southeast corner of Merdeka Sq recross the Klang River and enter Central Market via Jln Benteng. Housed in a handsome art deco building, Central Market was built in 1888 as KL's wet market. The building was nearly demolished in the 1970s before the Malaysian Heritage Society intervened to save it. The main building now houses a touristy market with some fine handicrafts and souvenirs.

④ Sze Ya Temple

Follow Lebuh Pudu east of Central Market to Jln Tun HS Lee. Turn right and look for the entrance to the Sze Ya Temple, one of the most atmospheric in Chinatown.

⑤ Guandi Temple

Continue south along Jln Tun HS Lee. The shophouses along here are among China-town's oldest; note the unique feature of a five-foot way (footpath) lower than the road level. Just after the junction with Jln Hang Lekir is the bright red, incense-wreathed Guandi Temple. Duck into the alley after this to find Chinatown's pungent wet market.

⑥ Sri Mahamariamman Temple

Back on Jln Tun HS Lee pause to admire the deity encrusted *gopuram* (temple tower) of Sri Mahamariamman Temple and to breathe in the sweet jasmine of the flower sellers outside.

⑦ Jalan Petaling Street Market

Turn left at the junction with Jln Sultan and continue until you hit Jln Petaling. Traders start to fill this central street from mid-morning; by early evening it's jam-packed with market stalls selling wares including fake Gucci handbags, pirate DVDs, *nasi lemak* (coconut rice) and bunches of lychees.

Kuala Lumpur in ...

ONE DAY

For sky-high city views take your pick between the **Petronas Towers** or **Menara KL** where you can have lunch in the revolving restaurant **Atmosphere 360**. Explore Chinatown's temples, street food and **Jalan Petaling Night Market**.

TWO DAYS

Explore the lush Lake Gardens, including the **Islamic Arts Museum** and the **KL Bird Park**, which has a good lunch cafe. Continue on to the **National Museum**. Enjoy the culinary delights of **Jalan Alor** and a nightcap at **Palate Palette**.

THREE DAYS

Amble through the traditional Malay district **Kampung Baru**. Take a taxi to **Thean Hou Temple**. Shop at the nearby mall **Bangsar Village I & II**, and eat at curry heaven **Sri Nirwana Maju**.

FOUR DAYS

Climb 272 steps to view the spectacular **Batu Caves**. Catch the contemporary KL vibe at **Publika**. Check if there's a concert at the **Dewan Filharmonik Petronas** or **No Black Tie**.

Central Market (p78)

Discover Kuala Lumpur

Thean Hou Temple (p80) decorated with lanterns for Chinese New Year

ANDERS BLOMQVIST/GETTY IMAGES ©

History

Kuala Lumpur was founded by Chinese tin prospectors in the late 1850s. Less than 30 years later the boomtown burnt to the ground in a conflict that broke out between local sultans. This allowed British government representative Frank Swettenham to push through a radical new town plan that transferred the central government from Klang to KL. In 1896 the city became the capital of the newly formed Federated Malay States.

After occupation by Japanese forces during WWII (when many Chinese were tortured and killed, and many Indians sent to work on Burma's 'Death Railway'), the British temporarily returned, only to be ousted when Malaysia declared its independence here in 1957.

◉ Sights

Golden Triangle, KLCC & Around

MENARA KL
Observation Tower
(KL Tower; Map p66; ✎2020 5448; www.kltower.com.my; 2 Jln Punchak; observation deck adult/child RM47/27; ⊙observation deck 9am-10pm, last tickets 9.30pm, shuttle bus every 15min 9am-9.30pm) The best view of KL is from atop this telecommunications tower which sits amid the leafy surrounds of **Bukit Nanas Forest Reserve** (Map p66; ⊙7am-6pm). The **observation deck** is in the bulb at the top of tower; its shape is inspired by a Malaysian spinning toy. One floor above is the revolving restaurant Atmosphere 360 (p74); having a meal here is likely the best deal. A free **shuttle bus** runs up to the tower from the gate on Jln Punchak.

FELIX HUG/GETTY IMAGES ©

Don't Miss **Petronas Towers**

Headquarters of the national oil and gas company Petronas, the 88-storey steel clad twin towers, nearly 452m tall and resembling twin silver rockets plucked from an early episode of *Flash Gordon*, epitomise contemporary KL. They are the perfect allegory for the city's meteoric rise from tin miners' shanty town to space-age metropolis.

Get in line before 8am to be sure of securing one of the 960 tickets issued daily (half of which are sold in advance) for a guided 45-minute tour up to the 86th floor, including a 15 minutes to walk across the Skybridge connecting the towers on the 41st floor. The ticket office is in the tower basement at the KLCC.

NEED TO KNOW

Map p76; www.petronastwintowers.com.my; Jln Ampang; adult/child RM80/30; ⏰9am-9pm Tue-Sun

AQUARIA KLCC   Aquarium
(Map p66; ☎2333 1888; www.klaquaria.com; concourse level, KL Convention Centre; adult/child aquarium RM45/35, aquarium & aquazone RM80/52; ⏰11am-8pm) As well as tanks of colourful fish and touch-a starfish–type activities, you can walk through a 90m-long underwater tunnel at this impressive aquariam to view sinister-looking sand tiger sharks and giant gropers.

KAMPUNG BARU   Neighbourhood
Somehow this Malay district has managed to retain its sleepy village atmosphere in the midst of the city: traditional Malay wooden houses stand amid leafy gardens and people go quietly about their daily lives – with the exception of Saturday night when a lively *pasar malam* (night market) takes over the area close to the Kampung Baru Light Rail Transit (LRT) station. A stroll in the area could be combined with a visit to **Chow Kit Market** (Map p76; 469-473 Jln TAR; ⏰6am-8pm) to the west. Even outside of Saturday night, this is a great area to come for tasty home-cooked Malay food at unpretentious roadside cafes and stalls.

Golden Triangle

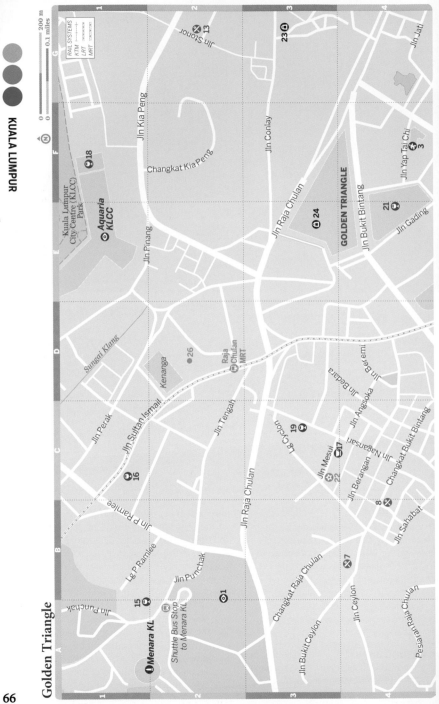

Golden Triangle

RAIL SYSTEMS
KTM
LRT
MRT

200 m
0.1 miles

Kuala Lumpur
City Centre (KLCC)
Park

Aquaria
KLCC

GOLDEN TRIANGLE

Sungai Klang

Kenanga

Raja
Chulan
MRT

Menara KL

Shuttle Bus Stop
to Menara KL

Jln Stonor
Jln Kia Peng
Changkat Kia Peng
Jln Conlay
Jln Raja Chulan
Jln Pinang
Jln Bukit Bintang
Jln Yap Tai Chi
Jln Gading
Jln Jati
Jln Perak
Jln Sultan Ismail
Jln P Ramlee
Lg P Ramlee
Jln Punchak
Jln Punchak
Jln Tengah
Jln Raja Chulan
Lg Cyclon
Jln Mesui
Jln Nagasari
Jln Berangan
Jln Angsoka
Jln Beremi
Jln Bedara
Changkat Bukit Bintang
Jln Sahabat
Changkat Raja Chulan
Jln Bukit Ceylon
Jln Ceylon
Pesiaran Raja Chulan

13
23
18
3
21
24
26
16
19
17
22
8
7
1
15

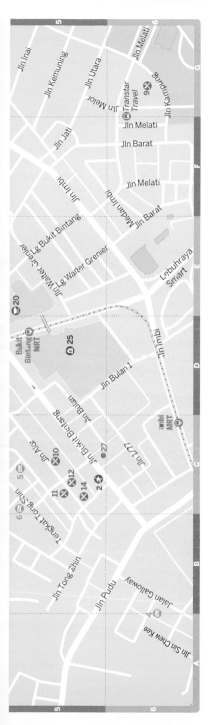

Golden Triangle

Chinatown & Around

**SRI MAHAMARIAMMAN
TEMPLE**   Hindu Temple
(Map p70; 163 Jln Tun HS Lee; ⊙6am-8.30pm)
The oldest Hindu shrine in Malaysia was
founded by migrant workers from the

Detour:
Publika

Publika (www.publika.com.my; 1 Jln Dutamas, Solaris Dutamas), a five minute taxi ride northwest of the Lake Gardens and Bangsar isa mall where contemporary art, culture, shopping and dining combine to create a vibrant, liberal vibe.

Low rents have encouraged new talents to open up shops and creative spaces and business in the mixed-use development. Dazzling murals in the food court, quirky themes for the toilets, a great kids' play space and inspirational quotes carved into the flagging of the public piazza all add to visual interest. There are plenty of great places to eat and drink including the **Bee** (☏ 673 6142; www.thebee.com.my; 36B, level G2, Publika, Solaris Dutamas; mains RM15-20; ⊙9am-midnight Mon-Thu, 9am-1am Fri, 10am-1am Sat, 10am-midnight Sun; 🛜), which stages various events.

Free films are screened each Monday in the piazza, there's an interesting arts and crafts market on the last Sunday of the month, as well as other ocassional events.

Indian state of Tamil Nadu in 1873. Flower-garland vendors crowd the entrance and the temple is crowned by a huge *gopuram* covered in riotously colourful statues of Hindu deities.

SZE YA TEMPLE   Chinese Temple
(Map p70; Jln Tun HS Lee; ⊙7am-5pm) On a narrow alleyway near the Central Market, this atmospheric Taoist temple was constructed in 1864 on the instructions of 'Kapitan China' Yap Ah Loy. You can see a statue of the man just left of the main altar. Its odd position, squished between rows of shophouses, was determined by feng shui. You can enter the temple through the stucco gatehouse on Jln Tun HS Lee or the back gate on the next alley west.

MASJID JAMEK   Mosque
(Friday Mosque; Map p70; off Jln Tun Perak; ⊙8.30am-12.30pm & 2.30-4pm Sat-Thu, 8.30-11am & 2.30-4pm Fri) Chinatown's Muslim population prays at this beautiful onion-domed mosque. Constructed in 1907 at the confluence of the Klang and Gombak rivers, the mosque is an island of serenity, with airy open pavilions shaded by palm trees.

NATIONAL TEXTILES MUSEUM   Museum
(Muzium Tekstil Negara; Map p70; ☏ 2694 3457; www.jmm.gov.my; Jln Sultan Hishamuddin; ⊙9am–6pm daily) Four darkened exhibition spaces help preserve the delicate textiles on display – there are some beautiful pieces and plenty of explanation of how they are made. The sad thing is that many of the time-consuming skills necessary for the production of such textiles are dying out, making these pieces increasingly rare.

JALAN PETALING   Market
(Map p70; ⊙10am-11pm) Chinatown's commercial heart is one of the most colourful and busiest shopping parades in KL, particularly at night when stalls cram the covered street. It offers everything from fresh fruit and cheap clothes and shoes to copies of brand-name watches and handbags, and pirated CDs and DVDs. Be prepared to bargain hard.

Lake Gardens

ISLAMIC ARTS MUSEUM   Museum
(Muzium Kesenian Islam Malaysia; Map p72; ☏ 2274 2020; www.iamm.org.my; Jln Lembah Perdana; adult/child RM12/6, restaurant set lunch RM43, Friday buffet RM28; ⊙10am-6pm, restaurant closed Mon) This outstanding museum is home to one of best collections of Islamic decorative arts in the world. Aside from the quality of the exhibits, which include fabulous textiles, carpets, jewellery and calligraphy-inscribed pottery, the

building itself is a stunner, with beautifully decorated domes and glazed tilework.

KL BIRD PARK
Aviary

(Map p72; ☑ 2272 1010; www.klbirdpark.com; Jln Cenderawasih; adult/child RM48/38; ⊙9am-6pm) This fabulous aviary brings together some 200 species of (mostly) Asian birds flying free beneath an enormous canopy. The park's **Hornbill Restaurant** (Map p72; ☑ 2693 8086; www.klbirdpark.com; 920 Jln Cenderawashi, KL Bird Park, Lake Gardens; mains RM40-60; ⊙9am-8pm; 🔊) is also recommended.

NATIONAL MUSEUM
Museum

(Muzium Negara; Map p72; ☑ 2282 6255; www.muziumnegara.gov.my; Jln Damansara; adult/child RM5/2; ⊙9am-6pm, tours 10am Mon-Thu & Sat in English, Tue & Thu in French, Thu in Japanese) A major renovation has resulted in four main galleries with interesting, well-organised displays. Time your visit to coincide with one of the free tours given by enthusiastic volunteer guides. The easiest way here is by taxi, the hop-on hop-off bus (p71), or via the walkway over the highway south of the Lake Gardens.

 TUN ABDUL RAZAK HERITAGE PARK (LAKE GARDENS PARK)
Park

(Map p72; Jln Tembusu; ⊙daylight hours) This 70 hectare park, laid out during colonial times, is planted with a variety of native plants, trees and shrubs. In the middle is a good children's adventure playground and nearby is the sprawling lake for which the gardens are named.

MASJID NEGARA
Mosque

(National Mosque; Map p72; Jln Lembah Perdana; ⊙9am-noon, 3-4pm & 5.30-6.30pm, closed Fri morning) The main place of worship for KL's Malay Muslim population is this gigantic mosque, inspired by Mecca's Grand Mosque. Its umbrella-like blue-tile roof has 18 points symbolising the 13 states of Malaysia and the five pillars of Islam. Non-Muslims are welcome to visit outside prayer times but dress appropriately and remove your shoes before entering.

♥ If You Like…
Rooftop Bars

Dazzling views of KL's illuminated urban geography are guaranteed from these high-rise watering holes:

1 LUNA
(Map p66; ☑ 2332 7777; Menara PanGlobal, Jln Punchak; ⊙3pm-1am Sun-Thu, to 3am Fri & Sat) Sophisticated bar surrounding a swimming pool. Also up here, inside and facing towards KL Tower, is the smoke-free **Cristallo**, a playboy-esque bar lined with silver velour sofas and draped with strings of glittering crystals.

2 TEEQ BRASSERIE
(Map p66; ☑ 2782 3555; www.teeq.com.my; Level 8, Lot 10, 50 Jln Sultan Ismail; ⊙6.30-10.30pm, bar open to 1am Tue-Sun) This contemporary-styled brasserie has a relaxed alfresco bar from which you can observe the commercial frenzy of Bintang Walk at a calm distance.

3 SKY BAR
(Map p66; ☑ 2332 9888; Level 33, Traders Hotel; ⊙7pm-1am, to 3am Fri & Sat) The perfect spot for sundowner cocktails or late-night flutes of bubbly, with grandstand views of the Petronas Towers.

🏃 Activities

SPA VILLAGE
Spa

(Map p66; ☑ 2782 9090; www.spavillageresort.org; Ritz Carlton, 168 Jln Imbi; ⊙9am-9pm) Indoor and outdoor beauty and massage treatments, a sensory room, and a second outdoor pool with waterfalls. Health club facilities include 24 hour fitness centre, sauna, steam room and whirlpool.

REBORN
Massage, Spa

(Map p66; ☑ 2144 1288; www.reborn.com.my; 18 Jln Bukit Bintang; ⊙11am-3am) One of the more pleasantly designed massage and reflexology joints along Jln Bukit Bintang, offering various spa treatments as well as a fish spa. The latter involves immersing

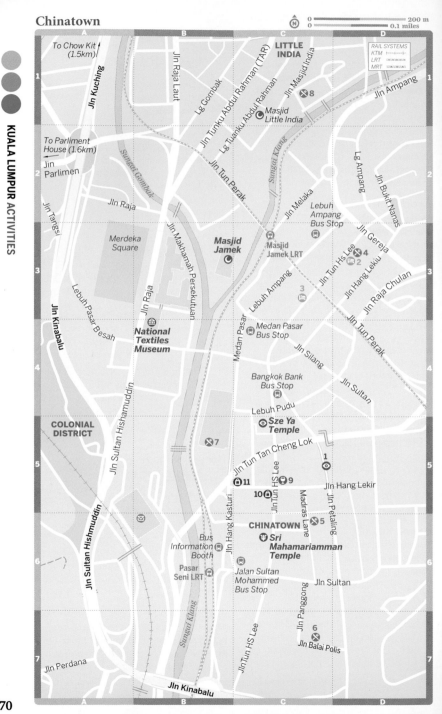

Chinatown

N · 0 — 200 m · 0 — 0.1 miles

RAIL SYSTEMS
KTM
LRT
MRT

To Chow Kit (1.5km)

Jln Kuching

To Parliment House (1.6km)
Jln Parlimen

Jln Tangsi

Jln Raja Laut

Lg Gombak

Jln Tunku Abdul Rahman (TAR)

Lg Tuanku Abdul Rahman

Jln Masjid India

LITTLE INDIA

Masjid Little India

8

Jln Ampang

Jln Tun Perak

Jln Raja

Sungai Gombak

Merdeka Square

Jln Makhamah Persekutuan

Jln Raja

Masjid Jamek

Masjid Jamek LRT

Sungai Klang

Jln Melaka

Lebuh Ampang Bus Stop

Lg Ampang

Jln Bukit Nanas

Jln Gereja

4
2

Jln Tun HS Lee

Jln Hang Lekiu

Jln Raja Chulan

3

Lebuh Ampang

Medan Pasar

Medan Pasar Bus Stop

Jln Silang

Jln Tun Perak

Lebuh Pasar Besah

Jln Kinabalu

National Textiles Museum

Jln Sultan Hishamuddin

COLONIAL DISTRICT

Jln Sultan Hishmuddin

Bangkok Bank Bus Stop

Jln Sultan

Lebuh Pudu

Sze Ya Temple

7

Jln Tun Tan Cheng Lok

Jln Tun HS Lee

1

9

Jln Hang Lekir

11

10

Madras Lane

5

Jln Petaling

CHINATOWN

Sri Mahamariamman Temple

Jln Hang Kasturi

Bus Information Booth

Pasar Seni LRT

Jalan Sultan Mohammed Bus Stop

Jln Sultan

Jln Panggong

Jln Tun HS Lee

6

Jln Balai Polis

Sungai Klang

Jln Perdana

Jln Kinabalu

Chinatown

your feet in a tank and allowing Dr Fish to gently nibble away at the dead skin.

Tours

SIMPLY ENAK   Food Tour

(📞017-287 8929; www.simplyenak.com; tours RM150, minimum of 2 people) 'Food Experience Captain' Pauline Lee will guide you on an informative and tasty voyage of Chinatown and Bangsar. 'Eat a local' home-cooked dinners (RM200) and cooking classes (RM550) can also be arranged.

KL HOP-ON HOP-OFF   Bus Tour

(📞2166 6162; www.myhoponhopoff.com; adult/child 24hr RM38/17, 48hr RM65/29; ⏱8.30am-8.30pm) This double-decker wi-fi-enabled air-con tourist bus makes a circuit of the main tourist sites half-hourly throughout the day. Tickets, which can be bought on the bus, last all day and you can get on and off as often as you like.

Sleeping

Always ask about special deals as practically all midrange and top-end places offer promotions that can substantially slash rack rates; booking online will almost always bring the price down. The only time you should book ahead to be sure of accommodation is public holidays, when room discounts will not apply.

Chinatown & Around

BACKHOME   Backpackers $

(Map p70; 📞2022 0788; www.backhome.com.my; 30 Jln Tun HS Lee; dm/d incl breakfast from RM42/120; ❄@🛜) This chic pit stop for flashpackers offers polished concrete finishes, Zen simple decoration, fab rain showers and a blissful central courtyard sprouting spindly trees. It can be noisy on the street outside, but they've got that covered by offering earplugs for light sleepers. Also check out their fab café **LOKL** (Map p70; http://loklcoffee.com; 30 Jln Tun HS Lee; mains RM14-20; 🛜).

REGGAE MANSION   Backpackers $

(Map p70; 📞03-2072 6877; www.reggaehostels-malaysia.com/mansion/; 49-59 Jln Tun HS Lee; dm/d from RM38/120) Grooving to a superior beat than most backpackers, including its own guesthouses in the heart of Chinatown, this is one cool operation. The decor is white-washed faux colonial with contemporary touches including a flash cafe-bar on the ground floor, rooftop bar and a mini cinema (RM7) where the ticket includes a drink and popcorn.

Golden Triangle, KLCC & Around

VILLA SAMADHI   Hotel $$$

(📞2143 2300; www.villasamadhi.com.my; 8 Jln Madge; r from RM500; ❄@🛜🏊) It's hard to believe you're in the heart of KL while staying at this gorgeous 21-room boutique villa. The black polished concrete, bamboo

Lake Gardens

Lake Gardens

◎ Top Sights

◎ Sights

⊗ Eating

and reclaimed timber rooms with luxurious light fixtures, idyllic central pool, lush foliage, rooftop bar (serving complimentary cocktails) and intimate modern Malay restaurant **Mandi Mandi** combine to conjure an antidote to urban stress.

THE COURTYARD   Hotel **$$**
(Map p66; ☑03-2141 1017; www.courtyard.com.my; 623 (No 51D) Tengkat Tong Shin; d from R192; ❄@🛜) A former backstreet hostel has been transformed into this calm, stylish oasis steps away from both the eats of Jln Alor and the bars of Changkat Bukit Bintang. Contemporary design rooms are very comfy and great value for what they offer.

YY38 HOTEL   Hotel **$$**
(Map p66; ☑2148 8838; www.yy38hotel.com.my; 38 Tengkat Tong Shin; s/d/loft from RM100/120/360; ❄🛜) The bulk of the rooms here are fine, but no-frills. However, the 7th floor offers 17 creatively designed duplexes, each sleeping three, with fun themes ranging from Marylin Monroe to circus and *kampung;* classic Mini features a sawn-in-half Mini Minor as part of the decor!

SEKEPING SIN
CHEW KEE   Apartment **$$$**
(Map p66; www.sekeping.com; 3 Jln Sin Chew Kee; apt RM700; ❄🛜) Architect Ng Seksan's pared-back, quirky style is in full evidence at his latest venture, tucked away on the edge of the Golden Triangle on a street of old houses. Raw and beautiful, the two apartments here sleep up to six and have full kitchens and outdoor relaxation spaces. If this is full consider the sister property **Sekeping Tenggiri** (☑017-207 5977; www.tenggiri.com; 48 Jln Tenggiri; ❄🛜🏊) within walking distances of Bangsar Baru.

HOTEL MAYA   Hotel **$$$**
(Map p76; ☑2711 8866; www.hotelmaya.com.my; 138 Jln Ampang; r/ste incl breakfast from RM700/1000; @🛜🏊) Even though it remains one of KL's most stylish hotels, the Maya is beginning to show some wear and tear in its sleek timber-floored studios and suites. Promotional rates – nearly half the official ones – include breakfast and wi-fi.

Eating

KL is a nonstop feast. You can dine in incredible elegance or mingle with locals at thousands of street stalls – it's all good and it's seldom heavy on the pocket. A short journey out of the city centre, traditional enclave Bangsar Baru is one of KL's top dining destinations.

Golden Triangle, KLCC & Around

KEDAI MAKANAN DAN
MINUMAN TKS   Chinese **$$**
(Map p66; Jln Alor; mains RM15-30; ⊙5pm-4am) Our favourite place to eat on KL's busiest

KYLIE MCLAUGHLIN/GETTY IMAGES ©

Don't Miss Jalan Alor

The great common denominator of KL's food scene, hauling in everyone from sequined society babes to penny-strapped backpackers, are the restaurants and stalls lining Jln Alor. From around 5pm till late every evening the street transforms into a continuous open-air dining space with hundreds of plastic tables and chairs, and rival caterers shouting out to passers-by to drum up business (avoid the pushiest ones!). Most places serve alcohol and you can sample pretty much every Malay Chinese dish imaginable, including grilled fish, satay, *kui-lan* (Chinese greens) in oyster sauce and fried noodles with frogs' legs. Thai food is also popular.

Recommended options include Kedai Makanan Dan Minuman TKS (p72) for amazing Szechuan dishes; the small complex **Restoran Beh Brothers** (Map p66; 21A Jln Alor; meals R10-15; ⊙24hr), one of the few places open from 7am for breakfast, where the **Sisters Noodle** (Map p66) stall does delicious 'drunken' chicken mee (noodles) with rice wine, and there's also a good Hong Kong–style dim sum stall (24 hours); and **Wong Ah Wah** (Map p66; Jln Alor; ⊙4pm-4am), unbeatable for addictive spicy chicken wings, as well as grilled seafood, tofu and satay.

NEED TO KNOW
Map p66; Jln Alor; ⊙5pm-late; 🚇Bukit Bintang

food street is this non-touristy Szechuan joint that has a menu only in Chinese (don't panic, there are pictures and the friendly staff speak English). Prepare for a taste explosion from the chilli-oil fried fish to the gunpowder chicken buried in a pile of mouth-numbing fried chillies.

IMBI MARKET Hawker **$**
(Map p66; Jln Kampung, Pasar Baru Bukit Bintang; meal RM10; ⊙6.30am-12.30pm Tue-Sun) The official name is Pasar Baru Bukit Bintang, but everyone knows it simply as Imbi Market. Breakfast is like a party here with all the friendly and curious locals happily recommending their favourite stalls. We

If You Like...
Contemporary Art

Take the pulse of Malaysia's vibrant art scene at these public and commercial galleries:

1 NATIONAL VISUAL ARTS GALLERY
(Balai Seni Lukis Negara; ☏4026 7000; www.artgallery.org.my; 2 Jln Temerloh; ☺10am-6pm) Fascinating temporary shows of local and regional artists often feature here. The gallery's permanent collection of 4000 pieces includes paintings by Zulkifi Moh'd Dohalan, Wong Hoi Cheong, Ahad Osman and renowned batik artist Chuah Than Teng.

2 MAP
(☏6207 9732; www.facebook.com/mapkl; 1 Jln Dutamas) This ambitious art space is part of the innovative Publika shopping mall; there are several other galleries here, too.

3 WEI-LING GALLERY
(Map p72; www.weiling-gallery.com; 8 Jln Scott; ☺noon-7pm Mon-Fri, 10am-5pm Sat) The top two floors of this old shophouse have been imaginatively turned into a contemporary gallery to showcase local artists.

like **Sisters Crispy Popiah**; and **Teluk Intan Chee Cheung Fun**, where Amy Ong serves a lovely oyster-and-peanut *congee* (rice porridge) and egg puddings. The market will be moving to a new building in the next few years, as the area in which it currently sits is slated for redevelopment.

FRANGIPANI   French $$$
(Map p66; ☏2144 3001; www.frangipani.com.my; 25 Changkat Bukit Bintang; 3-course menu RM170; ☺6.30-10.30pm Tue-Sun) Much feted for its innovative approach to European fusion cooking, Frangipani is leagues ahead of most of the competition. The decor is as slick as the menu, with a stunning dining room surrounding a reflecting pool, and there's an equally stylish bar upstairs.

BIJAN   Malay $$$
(Map p66; ☏2031 3575; www.bijanrestaurant.com; 3 Jln Ceylon; mains RM30-70; ☺6.30-11pm Mon-Sat) Bijan serves skilfully cooked traditional dishes in a sophisticated dining room that spills out into a tropical garden. Must-try dishes include *rendang daging* (dry beef curry with lemongrass), *masak lemak ikan* (Penang-style fish curry with turmeric) and *ikan panggang* (grilled skate with tamarind).

TOP HAT   Nonya, English $$$
(Map p66; ☏2142 8611; www.top-hat-restaurants.com; 3 Jln Stonor; meals RM60-110; ☺noon-10.30pm) This restaurant is set in a spacious bungalow surrounded by peaceful gardens. It serves both traditional English cuisine – think oxtail stew and bread-and-butter pudding – and local dishes, including Nonya laksa (RM28). All meals come with signature 'top hats' (pastry shells filled with sliced veggies) and your choice of local dessert.

ATMOSPHERE
360   Malay, International $$$
(Map p66; ☏2020 2020; www.atmosphere360.com.my; Menara KL, 2 Jln Puncak; buffet lunch/afternoon tea/dinner RM88/58/198; ☺noon-2.30pm & 6.30-11pm) It takes 90 minutes for you to take in the full KL panorama from your seat at this revolving restaurant atop KL Tower. The buffets features a wide range of Malay and international dishes and are consistently good. Book at least a day ahead for a window seat or for dinner, when there's also a live band and more dishes on offer.

SARAVANAA BHAVAN   Indian $$
(Map p70; ☏2287 1228; www.saravanabhavan.com; 52 Jln Maarof, Bangsar; meals RM10-20; ☺8am-11pm; ☏) This global chain of restaurants offers some of the best quality Indian food you'll find in KL. Their banana-leaf and mini-tiffin feasts are supremely tasty and you can also sample southern Indian classics such as *masala dosa*.

Chinatown & Around

MADRAS LANE HAWKERS   Hawker **$**
(Map p70; Madras Lane; noodles RM5; ⊗8am-4pm Tue-Sun) Weave your way through Chinatown's wet market to find this short alley of stalls tucked between Jln Tun HS Lee and Jln Petaling. Standout operators including the one offering 10 types of *yong tau fu* in a fish broth (9.30am to 3.30pm) and, at the far end of the strip, the one serving *asam* and curry laksa.

OLD CHINA CAFÉ   Malay, Nonya **$$**
(Map p70; ☎2072 5915; www.oldchina.com.my; 11 Jln Balai Polis; mains RM40-50; ⊗11.30am-10pm) Housed in the old guild hall of the Selangor & Federal Territory Laundry Association, this long-established, atmospheric cafe serves Nonya dishes from Melaka and Penang, including a fine beef rendang (coconut and lime-leaf curry) with coconut rice and fiery Nonya laksa soup with seafood. Its branch **Precious** (Map p70; ☎2273 7372; www.oldchina.com.my; 1st fl, Central Market; mains RM40-60; ⊗11.30am-10pm) in Central Market serves a similar menu and tends to be less busy.

Bangsar Baru

Bangsar Baru

REBUNG   Malay **$$**
(☎2283 2110; www.rebung.com.my; 4-2 Lorong Maarof; buffet RM50; ⊗11am-11pm; ✳) The flamboyant celebrity chef Ismail runs the show at this excellent Malay restaurant, one of KL's best, respected for its authenticity and consistency. The buffet spread is splendid, with all kinds of dishes that you'd typically only be served in a Malay home, several such as *onde onde*

Chinatown

Chow Kit, Kampung Baru & KLCC

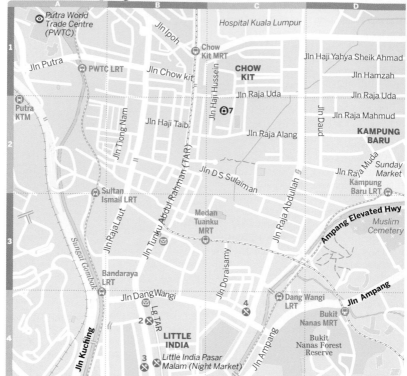

Chow Kit, Kampung Baru & KLCC

(glutinous rice balls filled with jaggery) made freshly. Check the website for cooking-class details.

SRI NIRWANA MAJU Indian $
(☎2287 8445; 43 Jln Telawi 2; meals RM10-20; ⊙7am-2am) There are far flashier Indian restaurants in Bangsar, but who cares

about the decor when you can tuck into food this good and cheap? This place serves it all from roti for breakfast to banana-leaf curries throughout the day.

WONDERMAMA Malay $$
(☎2284 9821; www.facebook.com/ mywondermama; Bangsar Village 1, 1 Jln Telawi 1,

Bangsar Baru; mains RM14-24; ☺9am-10.30pm; 🛜) Traditional meets contemporary at this design-savvy two-level space serving Malay comfort foods and burgers with a creative twist.

🍷 Drinking

PALATE PALETTE
Cafe

(Map p66; www.palatepalette.com; 21 Jln Mesui; ☺noon-midnight Tue-Thu, to 2am Fri & Sat; 🛜) Colourful, creative, quirky and super cool, this cafe-bar is our favourite place to eat, drink, play board games, and mingle with KL's boho crowd. The menu (mains RM10 to RM30) features dishes as diverse as shepherd's pie and teriyaki salmon. Check the website for details of event such as free indie movie nights.

TAPS BEER BAR
Bar

(Map p66; www.tapsbeerbar.my/; One Residency, 1 Jln Nagansari; ☺5pm-1am; 🛜) A very welcome addition to KL's drinking scene, Taps specialises in real ale from around the world with some 80 different microbrews on rotation, 14 of them on tap. Sample three for RM30. It has live accoustic music, too.

VILLAGE BAR
Bar

(Map p66; Starhill Gallery, 181 Jln Bukit Bintang; ☺noon-1am) Columns of glasses and bottles and cascades of dangling lanterns lend an *Alice in Wonderland* quality to this basement bar.

NEO TAMARIND
Bar

(Map p66; www.samadhiretreats.com; 19 Jln Sultan Ismail; ☺11.30am-2.30pm & 6.30-10.30pm) This sophisticated restaurant-bar feels like a slice of Bali smuggled into the heart of KL. Sip cocktails by flickering tealights under leafy trees.

REGGAE BAR
Bar

(Map p70; www.reggaebarkl.com.my; 158 Jln Tun HS Lee; ☺10.30am-3am) Travellers gather in droves at this pumping bar in the thick of Chinatown, which has outdoor seats if you'd like to catch the passing parade. There are beer promos, pool tables and pub grub served till late.

⭐ Entertainment

DEWAN FILHARMONIK PETRONAS
Concert Hall

(Map p76; ☎2051 7007; www.mpo.com.my; Box Office, Tower 2, Petronas Towers; tickets RM10-210; ☺box office 10am-6pm Mon-Sat) Don't miss the chance to attend a concert at this gorgeous concert hall at the base of the Petronas Towers. The polished Malaysian Philharmonic Orchestra plays here (usually Friday and Saturday evenings and Sunday matinees, but also other times) as well as other local and international ensembles.

NO BLACK TIE
Live Music

(Map p66; ☎2142 3737; www.noblacktie.com.my; 17 Jln Mesui; cover RM20-50; ☺5pm-2am

If You Like...
Old-School Dining

Each of these long-time survivors of KL's dining scene oozes retro charm as well as providing lip-smacking meals:

1 COLISEUM CAFÉ
(Map p76; ☎ 2692 6270; 100 Jln TAR; meals RM15-60; ☻10am-10pm) Little has changed here since Somerset Maugham tucked into sizzling steaks and downed a G'n'T in the wood-panelled bar next door. A KL classic, not to be missed; it also serves Chinese food.

2 YUT KEE
(Map p76; ☎ 2698 8108; 35 Jln Dang Wangi; meals RM10-15; ☻7.30am-4.45pm) It can get very busy at this beloved Hainanese *kopitiam* (coffee shop), but the staff remain calm and polite. House specialities include toast with homemade *kaya*, *roti babi* (deep-fried bread filled with shredded pork and onions) or the fried Hokkien mee noodles. Yut Kee's roast rolled pork with apple sauce, available from Friday to Sunday, usually sells out by 2.30pm.

3 CAPITAL CAFÉ
(Map p76; 213 Jln TAR; dishes RM3.50-5; ☻7am-8.30pm Mon-Sat) Since it opened in 1956, this truly Malaysian cafe in Little India has had Chinese, Malays and Indians all working together. Try their excellent mee goreng, *rojak* or satay (only in the evening).

Tue-Sun) NBT, as it's known to its fans, is owned by Malaysian concert pianist Evelyn Hii who has a knack for finding talented singer-songwriters, jazz bands and classical-music ensembles who play here from around 9.30pm.

ZOUK CLUB   Club
(Map p76; www.zoukclub.com; Street 113 Jln Ampang ; ☻Zouk 10pm-late Wed, Fri & Sat, Phuture 9pm-late Wed, Fri & Sat, Velvet Underground 9pm-late Wed-Sat, Wine Bar 6pm-2am Tue, to 3am Wed & Thu, to 4am Fri & Sat) KL's top club offers spaces to suit everyone and a line-up of top local and international DJs.

ACTORS STUDIO@LOT 10   Theatre
(☎2142 2009; www.theactorsstudio.com.my; 50 Jln Sultan Ismail, Lot 10) In addition to staging shows at **KLPac** (☎4047 9000; www.klpac.com; Jln Strachan, Sentul Park; tickets RM20-300), the Actors Studio theatre and comedy group has its base at this splendid, state-of-the-art venue located on the roof of Lot 10. Other theatre and dance companies also get to put on shows here.

Shopping

PAVILION KL   Mall
(Map p66; www.pavilion-kl.com; 168 Jln Bukit Bintang) Pavilion sets the gold standard in KL's shopping scene. Its basement food court is excellent and for a quick trip to Japan head to **Tokyo Street** on the 6th floor.

PETER HOE EVOLUTION   Homewares
(Map p70; 2 Jln Hang Lekir; ☻10am-7pm) Both here and at the much bigger **Peter Hoe Beyond** (Map p70; 2nd fl, Lee Rubber Bldg, 145 Jln Tun HS Lee; ☻10am-7pm) around the corner you can satisfy practically all your gift- and souvenir-buying needs, with selections from the KL-based designer's creative and affordable range of original batik designs on sarongs, shirts and dresses and home furnishings. The Beyond branch has a **cafe** that's worth visiting in its own right.

CENTRAL MARKET   Market
(www.centralmarket.com.my; Jln Hang Kasturi, Pasar Seni; ☻10am-9pm) It's easy to spend an hour or more wandering around this treasure house of souvenirs, batik, kites, clothes and jewellery. Asian artefacts and antiques are also available, but you'll need to bargain hard to get good deals; **Art House Gallery Museum of Ethnic Arts** in the annex has interesting pieces from Borneo and Tibet.

SUNGEI WANG PLAZA   Mall
(Map p66; www.sungeiwang.com; Jln Sultan Ismail) This ragbag of retail fun is confusing to navigate but jam-packed with youth-oriented fashions and accessories. Teens

STUART DEE/GETTY IMAGES ©

Don't Miss Batu Caves

Just north of Kuala Lumpur a towering limestone outcrop is home to these impressive caves, officially 'discovered' around 120 years ago by American naturalist William Hornaday. A short time later a small Hindu shrine was built in the vast open space, later known as Temple Cave.

A flight of 272 steps leads up to Temple Cave. Beyond the towering main cavern, the space opens to an atrium-like cave at the rear. Many visitors are more spellbound by the monkeys that scale the vertical cliff faces than by the shrines which are dwarfed by the scale of the cave. The whole spectacle is enhanced by an enormous golden statue of Muruga, also known as Lord Subramaniam, to whom the caves are dedicated.

For a more traditional caving experience branch off the main stairs to explore the **Dark Cave** (www.darkcavemalaysia.com/site; adult/child RM35/25; ⏰10am-5pm Tue-Fri, 10.30am-5.30pm Sat & Sun, tours every 20min).

Each year in late January or early February up to a million pilgrims visit here during the three days of Thaipusam. Lord Murugan's silver chariot takes pride of place as it makes its way from the Sri Mahamariamman Temple in KL's Chinatown to the caves.

NEED TO KNOW
admission free, car park RM2; ⏰8am-9pm

and youthful fashionistas should hunt out **HK Station** on the 6th floor.

SURIA KLCC Mall
(Map p76; www.suriaklcc.com.my; Jln Ampang)
Even if shopping bores you to tears, you're sure to find something to interest you at this fine shopping complex at the foot of the Petronas Towers. There's also an excellent branch of the bookshop **Kinokuniya** (level 4), scores of restaurants and cafes, two food courts, a cinema, a gallery and a kids' museum.

Detour:
Thean Hou Temple

The multilayered and highly ornate **Thean Hou Temple** (☎2274 7088; www.hainannet.com; Off Jln Syed Putra; ⏲9am-6pm) is one of the most visually impressive in Malaysia. It's dedicated to the heavenly mother, Thean Hou. Her statue takes centre stage in the main hall, with Kuan Yin (the Buddhist goddess of mercy) on her right and Shuiwei Shengniang (the goddess of the waterfront) to her left. Statues of Milefo (the laughing Buddha), Weituo and Guandi further contribute to this Taoist-Buddhist hodgepodge.

There are great views from the temple's upper decks while at its base are tourist restaurants and shops. To reach the temple, 3km south of the centre of town, take either a taxi or the monorail to Tun Sambanthan station, cross Jln Syed Putra using the overpass and walk up the hill.

KOMPLEKS BUDAYA KRAF Handicrafts
(Map p66; ☎2162 7533; www.malaysiancraft.com; Jln Conlay; ⏲9am-8pm Mon-Fri, to 7pm Sat & Sun) A government enterprise, this huge complex mainly caters to coach tours, but it's worth a visit to browse the shops and stalls selling batik, wood carvings, pewter, basketware, glassware and ceramics. The complex also has a small museum and offers batik-making courses.

BANGSAR VILLAGE I & II Mall
(www.bangsarvillage.com; cnr Jln Telawi 1 & Jln Telawi 2) These twin malls – linked by a covered bridge – offer upmarket fashions, including international brands and local Malaysian designers.

🛈 Getting There & Around

Air
KL's main airport is Kuala Lumpur International Airport (p363), 75km south of the city centre at Sepang. AirAsia's flights are handled by the nearby Low Cost Carrier Terminal (LCCT; ☎8777 8888; http://lcct.klia.com.my), which will be replaced during 2013 by the new KLIA2 (http://klia2.org) terminal.

Firefly and Berjaya Air flights go from SkyPark Subang Terminal (Sultan Abdul Aziz Shah Airport; ☎7845 1717; www.subangskypark.com), around 20km west of the city centre.

Bus
KL has several bus stations, the main one being Pudu Sentral (formerly Puduraya), just east of Chinatown. From here services fan out all over Peninsular Malaysia as well as to Singapore and Thailand. The only long-distance destinations that Puduraya doesn't handle are Kuala Lipis and Jerantut (for access to Taman Negara), buses to which leave from Pekeliling bus station (next to Titiwangsa LRT and monorail stations); and Kota Bharu and Kuala Terengganu, buses for which leave from Putra bus station.

Other long-distance bus services are operated by Aeroline (☎6258 8800; www.aeroline.com.my), Nice (p364) and Transtar Travel (☎2141 1771; www.transtar.com.sg).

Car
KL is the best place to hire a car for touring the peninsula. However, navigating the city's complex (and mostly one-way) traffic system is not for the timid.

All the major companies have offices at the airport. City offices include the following companies:

Avis (☎2144 4487; www.avis.com.my; main lobby, Crowne Plaza Mutiara Kuala Lumpur, Jln Sultan Ismail)

Hertz (Map p66; ☎2148 6433; www5.hertz.com; ground fl, Kompleks Antarabangsa, Jln Sultan Ismail)

Orix (Map p66; ☎2142 3009; www.orixauto.com.my; ground fl, Federal Hotel, 35 Jln Bukit Bintang)

KLANG VALLEY RAIL TRANSIT MAP

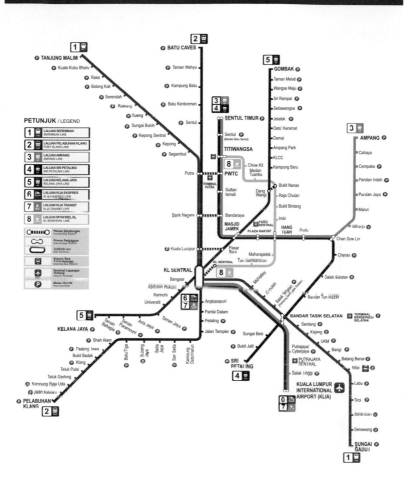

Taxi

Long-distance taxis – often no faster than taking a bus – depart from upstairs at Pudu Sentral bus station. If you're not prepared to wait to get a full complement of four passengers, you will have to charter a whole taxi. Prices should include toll charges.

Train

Kuala Lumpur is the hub of the **KTM (Keretapi Tanah Melayu Berhad;** ☎ 1300-885862; www. ktmb.com.my; ⊙ info office 9am-9pm, ticket office 7am-10pm) national railway system. All long-distance trains depart from KL Sentral, where an information office in the main hall can advise on schedules and check seat availability.

Taman Negara & the Hill Stations

Just three hours from Kuala Lumpur (KL) is Malaysia's premier national park, Taman Negara. Taman Negara (meaning National Park) was first gazetted in 1937 and today is a Noah's Ark of fauna and fauna. Deep in vast tracts of virgin jungle, parts of which are 130 million years old, live elephants, tigers and rhinos. Even on the shortest visit you can have a very close encounter with nature by taking a day hike around the park HQ and swinging high above ground along the Canopy Walkway. You can spot more wildlife at the Royal Belum State Park, an emerging nature destination in the north of the state of Perak.

Take a break from the steamy lowlands higher up the mountain ranges that form the peninsula's backbone. Cool off in the soothing environs of the colonial hill stations of the Cameron Highlands, Fraser's Hill (Bukit Fraser) and Bukit Larut (Maxwell Hill).

Cameron Bharat Tea Plantation (p98)

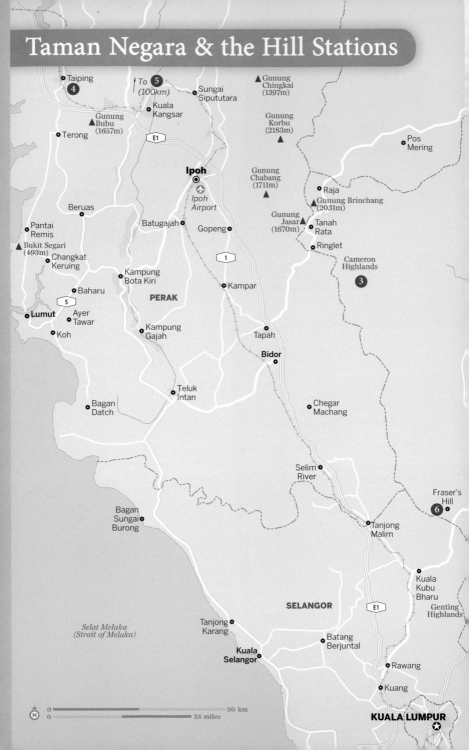

Taman Negara & the Hill Stations

Taiping ④

To ⑤ (100km)

Sungai Siputura

▲ Gunung Chingkai (1397m)

Gunung ▲ Bubu (1657m)

Kuala Kangsar

Terong

Pos Mering

E1

Gunung Korbu (2183m) ▲

Ipoh

Ipoh Airport

Gunung Chabang (1711m) ▲

Raja

Gunung Brinchang (2031m) ▲

Beruas

Batugajah

Gopeng

Gunung Jasar (1670m) ▲

Tanah Rata

Pantai Remis

Ringlet

▲ Bukit Segari (493m)

1

Changkat Keruing

Cameron Highlands ③

Kampung Bota Kiri

Baharu

Kampar

5

PERAK

Ayer Tawar

Lumut

Kampung Gajah

Tapah

Koh

Bidor

Teluk Intan

Chegar Machang

Bagan Datch

Selim River

Fraser's Hill ⑥

Bagan Sungai Burong

Tanjong Malim

Kuala Kubu Bharu

SELANGOR

Genting Highlands

Selat Melaka (Strait of Melaka)

Tanjong Karang

E1

Batang Berjuntal

Kuala Selangor

Rawang

Kuang

N

0 ────── 50 km
0 ────── 25 miles

KUALA LUMPUR ★

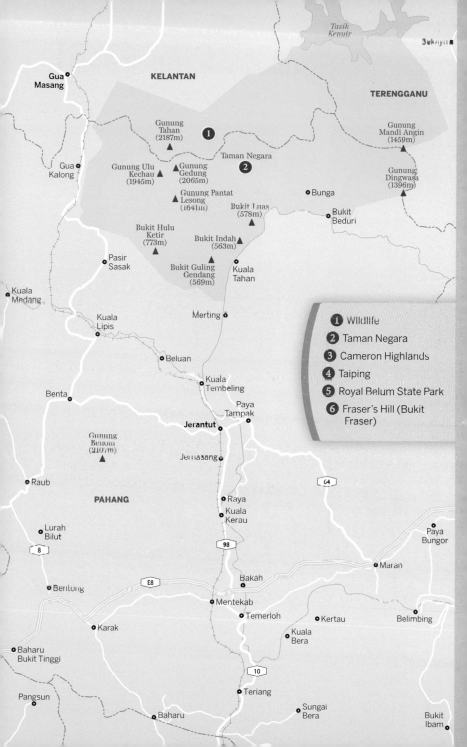

Taman Negara & the Hill Stations Highlights

1

Wildlife

Peninsular Malaysia's lightly populated interior, blanketed with ancient rainforests and mountain ridges, contrasts starkly with its urban coastlines. Swathes of land are protected within national parks, the ideal location for intimate wildlife encounters. Above: Elephant in Kuala Gandah; Top Right: Chestnut-breasted Malkoha, Taman Negara; Right: Macaques, Taman Negara

Need to Know
BEST TIME TO VISIT February to September **TOP TIP** Consider an overnight trek or a boat trip to increase chances of wildlife spotting **For further coverage, see p94**

Wildlife Don't Miss List

BY ANDREW SEBASTIAN,
MALAYSIAN NATURE SOCIETY

1 ELEPHANTS

There was great excitement in 2012 at Taman Negara when a couple of elephants were spotted breakfasting opposite the park's resort. However, such easy sightings of these highly endangered animals are very rare – most herds live deep in the jungle. To be sure of a sighting visit the **Kuala Gandah National Elephant Conservation Centre** (www.myelephants.org), which is en route to Taman Negara near Temerloh. This is the base for the Department of Wildlife and National Parks' Elephant Relocation Team, which helps capture and relocate rogue elephants from across Southeast Asia to other suitable habitats throughout the peninsula.

2 BIRDLIFE

Malaysia's jungles and hill stations are fantastic places for birding tourism – 673 species live on the peninsula alone. All 10 species of hornbill can be spotted in the Belum-Temengor Forest Reserve, which encompasses the Royal Belum State Park. The Malaysian Nature Society also promotes **Genting Highlands**, a hill station resort within easy day-trip range of KL, as a prime birding location.

3 MONKEYS

Peninsular Malaysia isn't the native habitat of the orang-utan or proboscis monkey, the star simians of Borneo, but on a visit to any of the national or state parks chances are high that you'll spot plenty of macaques. A more elegant species is the silver langur (or silvered leaf monkey), which feeds on young leaves and fruits.

4 REPTILES

One species of flying snake inhabits the rainforests of Peninsular Malaysia; they don't literally fly, but glide from trees by extending a flap of loose skin along either side of their bodies. There are also 'flying' lizards and frogs. The reptile you're most likely to see is the monitor lizard.

The Rivers of Taman Negara

Trekking in **Taman Negara** (p94) is a sweaty and leech-ridden business with slim chances of spotting larger fauna close to the park headquarters. If time is short, consider taking a river boat trip deeper into the park. Even on the boat trip to the park from Kuala Tembeling you'll see several local villages, fishers and domestic animals such as water buffalo.

Tea in the Cameron Highlands

No trip to the Cameron Highlands (named after the government surveyor WIlliam Cameron) is complete without a visit to one of the many tea estates whose bushes ripple in organised ranks across the region's gently rounded hills. Tea has been grown on the **Boh Sungei Palas Tea Estate** (p96) since 1929, so they really know how to make a good cuppa!

CARLINA TETERIS/GETTY IMAGES ©

Colonial Architecture

4

The British made their first real colonial incursion on the peninsula in 1874 in Perak. Remnants of their colonial rule stand out across the state in the form of elegant, stately architecture. **Taiping** (p100), the 'town of everlasting peace', is particularly graced with historic buildings including the **Muzium Perak** (p100). Close by is **Kuala Kangsar** (p100), a pleasant royal capital where the British and Malay rulers erected several grand edifices. Royal Museum, Kuala Kangsar

ATLANTIDE PHOTOTRAVEL/CORBIS ©

5

Royal Belum State Park

Advance permission is needed to visit this **park** (p102), part of the Belum-Temengor Forest, but that can easily be arranged with any of the hotels in the area. Because much of the area was flooded after Temengor Dam was completed in 1972, all excursions are conducted by boat. Keep your eyes peeled for the 10 species of hornbill that live here. Rhinoceros hornbill

6

Fraser's Hill (Bukit Fraser)

Named after Louis James Fraser, an adventurous Scotsman who set up a mule train operation in the area in the 1890s, this 'little England' (p103) was developed as a hill station resort in the early 20th century. Come here for relaxing hillside walks, a round of golf and bird spotting; some 265 species are supported here including the Malaysian whistling thrush and the Kinabalu friendly warbler.

Taman Negara & Hill Stations' Best...

Colonial Charm

○ **Taiping** (p100) A pleasing, quiet little place with a nice colonial district and great street food.

○ **Ipoh** (p104) Join in the revival of this colonial boom town that is another fantastic food destination.

○ **Fraser's Hill** (Bukit Fraser, (p103) Surrey in the jungle with its stone clock tower and bungalows surrounded by neatly clipped gardens.

Scenic Journeys

○ **Bukit Larut** (Maxwell Hill, p101) Swing around 72 hairpin bends on the steep ascent to the oldest hill station in Malaysia.

○ **Fraser's Hill** (Bukit Fraser, (p103) On the windy road up from Kuala Kubu Bharu pause at the Gap to take in the view.

○ **Kuala Tembeling to Kuala Tahan** (p94) See wildlife and village life on the boat trip to Taman Negara.

Local Cuisine

○ **Ipoh** (p104) Sample local specialities like curry mee (noodles), *ayam tauge* (boiled chicken served with beansprouts and rice) and dim sum.

○ **Taiping** (p101) Enjoy open-air meals at food courts serving great Malay and Chinese street food.

○ **Cameron Highlands** (p99) Spread locally made strawberry jam on your scone while sipping afternoon tea.

Need to Know

Unusual Accommodation

- **Sekeping Kong Heng** (p104) Easily the quirkiest place to stay in Ipoh, this shabby-chic hotel hides above and around an ancient cafe.

- **Belum Eco Resort** (p102) Be a guest of the Khong family on their own private island.

- **Smokehouse hotels** These traditional English hotels in the Cameron Highlands (p99) and Fraser's Hill (p104) offer pukka rose gardens and a chintzy colonial experience.

- **Bus** For extensive travel between main urban centres, particularly Ipoh.

- **Car** Hiring a car will give you the most flexibility and roads are excellent.

- **Taxis & shared taxis** Faster and more flexible than the bus.

- **Train** Ipoh, Kuala Kangsar, Taiping and Jerantut (for access to Taman Negara) are all on the KTM network.

BE FOREWARNED

- **Park entrance fees** Taman Negara's park entrance fee is rumoured to rise to as much as RM90.

- **Leeches** Wearing boots with gaiters or long socks tucked over your trousers and doused in DEET will make hiking more pleasant.

- **Accommodation** Hill station resorts are at their busiest during school holidays in April, August and December, so book accommodation in advance at these times.

- **Rainy season** The November to February rainy season can affect boat service into and around national and state parks.

- **Clothing** Pack something warm and waterproof for the chilly, damp highlands.

Left: Smokehouse (p99), Cameron Highlands;
Above: Bukit Larut (p101, Maxwell Hill)

Taman Negara & the Hill Stations Itineraries

You can sample Taman Negara in a few days if your trekking plans aren't too ambitious. The hill stations' relaxed ambience and cool climate will tempt you to linger.

4 DAYS

KUALA LUMPUR TO TAMAN NEGARA
Mountains & Jungle

Although this road trip across the Banjaran Titiwangsa mountain range, from hill station to steamy lowland rainforest, is doable by a combination of buses and taxis, you'll save time and have more flexibility if you hire a car in **(1) Kuala Lumpur**. The drive from the capital to Fraser's Hill, via **(2) Kuala Kubu Baru**, also accessible by train, takes under three hours. Stay overnight in **(3) Fraser's Hill**, and spend the rest of the day following one of the walking trails and taking lunch or afternoon tea at Ye Olde Smokehouse.

Continue downhill to the goldmining town of **(4) Raub**, from where you'll follow the signs to **(5) Jerantut**. There are taxis and several daily buses from here to Kampung Kuala Tahan and the headquarters of **(6) Taman Negara**. Spend the next two nights in Taman Negara, enough time to climb up to the canopy walkway, do a short hike and take a river trip.

Catching the boat back to Jerantut on the third afternoon will be faster going as you're not going against the flow of the river. You can hire a car for the return journey to KL.

ROYAL BELUM STATE PARK 6

TAIPING

BUKIT LARUT (MAXWELL HILL) 5

KUALA KANGSAR 4

3

IPOH 1

TANAH RATA 2

TAMAN NEGARA 6

JERANTUT 5

FRASER'S HILL (BUKIT FRASER) 3 4 **RAUB**

2 **KUALA KUBU BHARU**

1 **KUALA LUMPUR**

Selat Melaka (Strait of Melaka)

6 DAYS

IPOH TO THE ROYAL BELUM STATE PARK

On the Colonial Trail

Travel in the footsteps of Victorian colonial adventurers and Chinese prospectors on this journey to far northern reaches of Perak. Your starting point is historic **(1) Ipoh**, a pleasant midsized city that is experiencing a burst of touristic fortunes thanks to interest in its grand colonial architecture, surrounding jungle-clad limestone hills riddled with cave temples and delicious food scene.

On day two wind your way up over 1300m above sea-level to **(2) Tanah Rata**, the main town at the heart of the Cameron Highlands, pulling on a sweater to ward off the soothing chilled climate. Spend a couple of days based here, hiking one or more of over a dozen trails and relaxing over cups of tea made from the leaves growing in the surrounding estates.

Move on to another charming colonial-era town, **(3) Taiping**, which can be used as a base for day trips to **(4) Kuala Kangsar**, the royal Malay seat of the sultans of Perak, and **(5) Bukit Larut (Maxwell Hill)**, Malaysia's oldest hill station.

End your trip with a visit to the magnificent **(6) Royal Belum State Park**; the gateway town is Gerik, about 100km north of Kuala Kangsar.

Discover Taman Negara & the Hill Stations

TAMAN NEGARA

Malaysia's top national park blankets 4343 sq km in shadowy, damp, impenetrable jungle. Inside this buzzing tangle, ancient trees with gargantuan buttressed root systems dwarf luminescent fungi, orchids, two-tone ferns and even the giant rafflesia (the world's largest flower). Hidden within the flora are Asian elephants, tigers, leopards and rhinos, as well as smaller wonders such as flying squirrels, but these animals stay far from the park's trails and sightings are extremely rare. What you might see are snakes, lizards, monkeys, small deer and perhaps tapir.

The park headquarters and the privately run Mutiara Taman Negara Resort (p95) are at small gateway town Kuala Tahan at the edge of Taman Negara National Park; buy your park entry permit (park entrance/camera/fishing RM1/5/10) from the Tourist Information Counter here. Other accommodation options and restaurants are across Sungai Tembeling at Kampung Kuala Tahan. River taxis commute between the two sides of the river (RM1 each way) throughout the day.

Guides

Guides who are licensed by the Wildlife Department have completed coursework in forest flora, fauna and safety. Often the Kuala Tahan tour operators offer cheaper prices than those available at the Tourist Information Counter at Park Headquarters (whose guides are licensed), but we recommend talking with these guides first to find out what training they've had. Licensed guides cost RM180 per day (one guide

Hill mynah, Taman Negara
CHRISTER FREDRIKSSON/GETTY IMAGES ©

NORBERTO VUENICA/GETTY IMAGES ©

can lead up to 12 people), plus there is an additional RM100 fee for each night spent out on the trail.

 ## Activities

Trekking brings folks here and there's a wide variety of possibilities – from an hour's stroll to nine arduous days up and down 2187m-high Gunung Tahan. The trails around the park headquarters are convenient but heavily trafficked. Relatively few visitors venture far beyond the headquarters, and longer walks are much less trammelled.

Anglers will find the park a real paradise. The best fishing months are February, March, July and August. Fishing permits are RM10; you can hire rods in Kuala Tahan for between RM20 and RM30 per day.

CANOPY WALKWAY & AROUND
Trekking
(adult/child RM5/3; ⏱10am-3.30pm Sat-Thu, 9am-noon Fri) This is easily the area's most popular hike. It begins past the park headquarters and leads along Sungai Tembeling to the canopy walkway, 30 minutes away. The walkway is suspended between huge trees and the entire circuit takes around 40 minutes.

From behind the canopy walkway a trail leads to Bukit Teresik (344m), there are fine view across the forest from this vantage point. The trail is steep and slippery in parts, but is easily negotiated and takes about an hour up and back. You can descend back along this trail to the Mutiara Taman Negara Resort or, near the Canopy Walkway, take the branch trail that leads across to Lubok Simpon, a swimming area on Sungai Tahan. From here it is an easy stroll back to park headquarters. The entire loop can easily be done in three hours.

 ## Sleeping

Kampung Kuala Tahan, directly across the river from park headquarters, is where most of Taman Negara's lodging, restaurants and shops are found.

MUTIARA TAMAN NEGARA RESORT
Resort $$
(☎09-266 3500, in KL 03-2145 5585; www. mutiarahotels.com; camp site RM5, dm/

95

LOUISE HEUSINKVELD/GETTY IMAGES ©

Don't Miss Boh Sungei Palas Tea Estate

This breathtakingly beautiful tea plantation is set in an almost otherworldly green patchwork of hills and tea plants. The narrow approach road leads past worker housing and a Hindu temple (tea pickers are predominantly Indian) to the modern visitor centre, where you can witness tea production first-hand. There's also a gift shop selling every version of Boh tea you can imagine and a modern **cafe** (⊙9am-4.30pm Tue-Sun) where you can sip tea while looking out over the lush plantations below.

Free 15-minute tours showing the tea-making process are conducted during opening hours. There's also hour-long **Tea Appreciation Tours** (RM35; ⊙9am, 11am, 1pm & 3pm Tue-Sun), which include a guided walk through tea plantations, a factory tour and tea sampling.

The estate is located in the hills north of Brinchang, off the road to Gunung Brinchang. Public buses running between Tanah Rata and Kampung Raja pass the turn-off to Gunung Brinchang. From there it's 4km along the winding road, after which it's another 15 minutes' walk downhill to the visitors centre. Taxis in Tanah Rata will take you to the estate and back for RM50.

NEED TO KNOW

Map p98; www.boh.com.my; admission free; ⊙9am-4.30pm Tue-Sun

guesthouse/chalets/bungalows incl. breakfast RM60/300/470/1800; ❄) Conveniently located right at park headquarters, there's a huge range of accommodation here from OK guesthouse rooms (all with garden terraces) to colonial-style family and honeymoon suites in wooden chalets and clean, eight-person dorms with air-con.

YELLOW GUESTHOUSE   Guesthouse $
(☏09-266 4243; dm/d RM70/80; ❄@🛜) In better shape than most of the other guesthouses in Kuala Tahan. All rooms have hot showers; the building across from the main house has slightly larger rooms, but both have brightly painted

walls and new mattresses and the owner is super-friendly and helpful.

TAHAN GUESTHOUSE Guesthouse **$**
(☏09-266 7752; dm/d RM10/50) Has excellent four-bed dorms and even better, colourfully painted bright rooms upstairs. The whole place feels like a happy preschool with giant murals of insects and flowers all over the place.

MAT LEON VILLAGE Chalet **$$**
(☏013-998 9517; dm/chalets RM50/120 inc. breakfast) This boasts a supreme forest location with river views, a good restaurant and free boat pick-up from the Kampung Kuala Tahan jetty.

Eating

Floating barge restaurants line the rocky shore of Kampung Kuala Tahan, all selling the same ol' cheap basic noodle and rice meals plus bland Western fare. All are open from morning until late, though most take rest breaks between two and four.

Mama Chop (meals around RM7), at the far northern end of the strip, serves Indian vegetarian banana leaf meals at lunchtime and has very good clay-pot dishes for dinner.

At **Wan's Floating Restaurant** (meals around RM8) you'll find some of the best *kue teow* (flat noodles) in town; a large bowl of *hailam kue teow* (RM12), or noodles with chicken and gravy will hit the spot.

Information

Tourist Information Counter (park entrance/camera/fishing RM1/5/10; ☺8am-10pm Sun-Thu, 8am-noon & 3-10pm Fri) Register here before heading off into the park. The counter, located in the building behind the Mutiara Iaman Negara Resort's reception, also offers park information and guide services.

Getting There & Away

Most people reach Taman Negara by taking a bus (RM26; departs 8am) from Jerantut to the jetty at Kuala Tembeling, then a river boat (one way RM35; departs daily at 9am & 2pm, 9am & 2.30pm Friday) from here to the park. A taxi from Jerantut to Kuala Tahan is RM50.

However, there are also popular private minibus services that go directly to/from several tourist destinations around Malaysia. Han Travel (☏012-674 9208; www.taman-negara.com), NKS (☏03-2072 0336) and Banana Travel & Tours (☏017-902 5952; Information Centre, Kampung Kuala Tahan) run several useful private services, including daily buses to KL (RM35), a bus/boat combination (RM70) and minibuses to Penang (RM120), the Perhentian Islands (RM165 including boat) and the Cameron Highlands (RM95).

Masjid Ubudiah, Kuala Kangsar (p100)
WALTER BIBIKOW/GETTY IMAGES ©

CAMERON HIGHLANDS

♪05

Malaysia's most extensive hill station is an alpinescape of blue peaks, green humps, fuzzy tea plantations, small towns and white waterfalls. Trekking, tea tasting and visiting local agrotourism sites is the done thing here. And best of all, with an altitude of 1300m to 1829m, the temperature rarely drops below 10°C or climbs above 21°C; practically cool enough to make you forget you're in Malaysia.

◎ Sights

CAMERON BHARAT
TEA PLANTATION   Tea Plantation
(Map p98; bharattea.com.my; ⊙8.30am-7pm; admission free) Located at the side of the road around 4km south of Tanah Rata, the views over this plantation are breathtaking. There are no guided tours here, but you can wander around parts of the plantation, and there's a tea house, attractively set overlooking the estate. A taxi here will cost RM10. There's another

Cameron Highlands

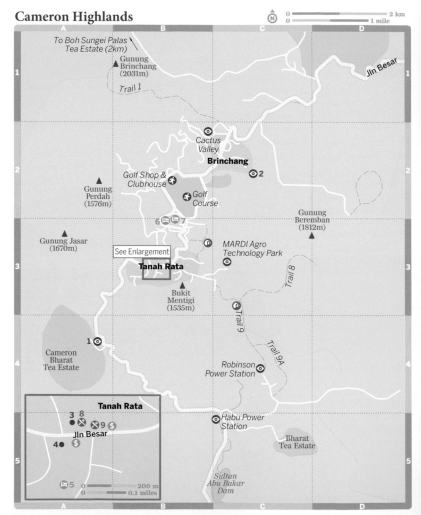

branch (⏰7.30am-6pm), likewise equipped with a cafe, located 12km away on the main road heading northeast Brinchang, although the views aren't as impressive.

SAM POH TEMPLE   Temple
(Map p98) As unexpected sites in the hills go, a temple dedicated to a eunuch and naval officer just about tops the list. This temple, just below Brinchang about 1km off the main road, is a brilliant pastiche of imperial Chinese regalia, statuary dedicated to medieval admiral and eunuch Zheng Ho.

Tours

The distance between sights plus infrequent public transport makes booking a guided tour a popular option in the Cameron Highlands. Most are half-day tours that focus on the tea plantation/strawberry picking/flower farm highlights of the area. Recommended agencies include **CS Travel & Tours** (Map p98; ☏ 491 1200; www.cstravel.com.my; 47 Jln Besar, Tanah Rata; ⏰ 7.30am-7.30pm) and **Eco Cameron** (Map p98; ☏ 491 5388; www.eco-cameron.com; 72-A Psn Camellia 4, Tanah Rata; ⏰ 8am-9.30pm).

Sleeping

Tanah Rata has the greatest spread of hotels in the Cameron Highlands, including quite a few decent budget places.

SMOKEHOUSE   Boutique Hotel **$$$**
(Map p98; ☏ 491 1215; www.thesmokehouse.com.my; incl breakfast r RM365, ste RM450-

710; 📶) This characterful old house, dating back to 1937 and located about 2km north of Tanah Rata along the road to Brinchang, looks as if it's been lifted straight from deepest Surrey, complete with a red British phone box outside. Rooms, which are decked out with heavy antique furniture, are more comfortable than luxurious, although they too possess their own particular English charm. The restaurant, specialising in English cuisine, does a good all-day afternoon tea (RM25 to RM33).

HILLVIEW INN   Guesthouse **$$**
(Map p98; ☏ 491 2915; www.hillview-inn.com; 17 Jln Mentigi, Tanah Rata; r RM70-140; @📶) Located in a three-storey home at the edge of town, this midrange-feeling guesthouse has a variety of rooms, both with and without attached bathroom, and supplemented with communal TV rooms and a ground-floor cafe. Rooms vary in size and amenities, so ask to see a few.

HOTEL DE'LA FERNS   Hotel **$$$**
(Map p98; ☏ 491 4888; www.hoteldelaferns.com.my; r RM380-580, ste RM680-1800; @📶) The type of multistorey mock-Tudor monstrosity that has come to define accommodation in the Cameron Highlands. Fortunately, the theme is relegated to the exterior, and inside you'll find large rooms decked out in an attractively subtle, yet modern theme.

Eating

KOUGEN   Japanese, International **$$**
(Map p98; 35 Jln Besar, Tanah Rata; mains RM13.90-20.90; ⏰ 11am-9pm) Run by an

Detour:
Kuala Kangsar

This easygoing town is an easy day trip from Ipoh or Taiping. Kuala Kangsar is the seat of sultan of Perak and, although the town centre is a scruffy jumble, the royal district is spacious and quiet. Don't miss several royal palaces, the **Masjid Ubudiah** (Ubudiah Mosque; Jln Istana; admission by donation; ⏱7am-6pm), a small but magnificent mosque designed by AB Hubbock, the architect of many of Ipoh's colonial edifices; and the **Malay College** (Jln Tun Abdul Razak), the first Malay school to provide English education for Malays destined for the civil service.

Frequent buses connect Kuala Kangsar to Ipoh and Taiping; the town is also on the Kuala Lumpur–Butterworth train line.

apparent Japanophile from KL, this new restaurant does a mix of traditional Japanese (sushi, tempura) and the not-so-traditional (lamb stew, minced beef and pork steak). All main dishes are served with rice and soup.

JASMINE CAFE International $$
(Map p98; 45 Jln Besar, Tanah Rata; mains RM7-33; ⏱noon-9pm; 🛜) Get ready for some cultural confusion here: Jasmine Cafe is a Dutch-themed restaurant that serves mostly Western-style food prepared by an ethnic Chinese chef. Against all odds it works, and dishes like the peppery chicken chop, particularly if accompanied by a glass of fresh strawberry juice, are some of the tastiest in town.

🛈 Getting There & Away

Tanah Rata's bus station, known as Terminal Freesia, is located at the eastern end of Jln Besar. Taxis also wait at Terminal Freesia. Full-taxi fares are RM140 to Ipoh, RM300 to KL and RM350 to Penang. For touring around, a taxi costs RM25 per hour.

TAIPING
📞05

Scratch Taiping's surface and you'll find one of Malaysia's most well-preserved colonial towns. Tourist brochures still boast of Taiping's '31 Firsts' for Malaysia, including the first museum; first railway; first newspapers in English, Malay and Tamil; and first zoo.

👁 Sights & Activities

FREE **MUZIUM PERAK** Museum
(Jln Taming Sari; ⏱9am-5.30pm Sat-Thu, 9am-12.25pm & 2.45-5.30pm Fri) Perak's State Museum is housed in an impressive colonial building. Correspondingly, it's the oldest museum in Malaysia, having opened in 1883 – a fact evidenced by the rather motley collection of stuffed animals in the Natural Life section.

ZOO TAIPING & NIGHT SAFARI Zoo
(www.zootaiping.gov.my; Jln Taman Tasik; adult/child RM12/8, night safari adult/child RM16/10; ⏱8.30am-6pm daily, night safari 8-11pm Sun-Fri & 8pm-midnight Sat) If they're not snoozing in the midday heat, you can see all manner of creatures, including elephants, tigers, Malayan sun bears and tapirs, lolling about. The zoo's **night safari**, billed as Malaysia's first, provides a better chance of seeing nocturnal animals beginning to stir, such as fishing bats, slow loris and big cats. It's located about 2km east of central Taiping; a taxi here will cost RM10.

TAMAN TASIK TAIPING Gardens
(Lake Gardens; Jln Kamunting Lama) Taiping is renowned for its beautiful 62-hectare gardens, built in 1880 on the site of an abandoned tin mine. The gardens owe their lush greenery to the fact that Taiping's annual rainfall is one of the highest in Peninsular Malaysia – hence the nickname 'Rain City'.

 **Sleeping**

SENTOSA VILLA Hotel $$
(✆805 1000; www.sentosa-villa.com; Jln 8; r
RM148-458, villa RM258-628; ❄ 🛜) Easily
the most appealing place to stay in
Taiping; the bad news is that you'll
need private transport to get here.
The attractive rooms are either in
the main structure or in a handful of
stand-alone and duplex wooden villas,
all located at the foot of Bukit Larut
(Maxwell Hill). Woods, walking paths
and running water lend the place a
rural, natural feel. Sentosa Villa is
located about 3km outside of town,
off the road that leads to Bukit Larut –
follow the signs.

 Eating

BISMILLAH RESTORAN Malay $
(138 Jln Taming Sari; mains from RM3; ◷7am-
5pm) Your typical *nasi kandar* (Indian/
Malaysian-style dishes served over rice)
restaurant found all over Malaysia; the
biryani here is particularly tasty.

ℹ️ **Getting There & Away**

Taiping's long-distance bus station, Kemunting
Raya, is 7km north of the town centre, at
Kemunting – hop on bus 8 (RM1.20, 6am to
8.30pm) to get to/from the local bus station, or
take a taxi (RM10) to the town centre.

Local buses leave from the local bus station
across the street from Masjid Daerah Taiping;
taxis depart from the Central Market.

Taiping's train station is 1km west of the town
centre, on the Kuala Lumpur–Butterworth line.

BUKIT LARUT (MAXWELL HILL)
♪05

Some 1019m above sea level, Bukit Larut
(Maxwell Hill) is Malaysia's oldest hill
station. It's not nearly as developed as
the Cameron Highlands, and while the
scenery is a little less dramatic, there's
more of a sense of what hill stations were

If You Like… Street Food

Despite being a heck of a lot smaller, Taiping
just about rivals George Town in the street-
food department.

1 KEDAI KOPI PRIMA
(cnr Jln Kota & Jln Manecksha; mains from RM3;
◷10am-midnight) This big, busy Chinese coffee shop
spills out onto the street in the evenings, with several
vendors selling a mix of Chinese and Malay dishes.
Big-screen TVs, music and endless crowds make for a
lively atmosphere.

2 PUSAT MAKANAN TAMAN TASIK
(Jln Maharaja Lela; mains from RM3; ◷24hr) A
busy hawker court/coffee shop with a good selection
of mostly Chinese stalls.

3 PUSAT PENJAJA TAIPING
(Jln Tupai; mains from RM3; ◷9am-11pm)
Open-air food court with a mix of vendors. Open at
lunch but busier at night.

originally about here: elegant bungalows,
quiet lanes, sweet-smelling gardens and
not much more noise than the wind in the
leaves.

Few people visit Bukit Larut; bungalows
here only accommodate around 70
visitors. However, during the school
holidays, all are full. Even if you don't stay,
Bukit Larut can be an excellent day trip.
Getting up to the hill station is half the
fun, and once there, you've got excellent
opportunities for walks and fine views
over Taiping far below.

Most visitors go up and back by Land
Rover (round-trip RM6; every hour on
the hour from 8am to 3pm; about 30
minutes) from the station at the foot of
the hill; a taxi here from Taiping should
cost RM10. The hill is also a favourite
with locals, who regularly walk up in the
mornings. It's a very scenic path, but
don't imagine this is some casual stroll –
you need to be fit to complete the 10km
walk, which can take as long as four
hours.

ROYAL BELUM STATE PARK

This state park in the northernmost corner of Perak is one of Peninsular Malaysia's largest stretches of virgin jungle. It's a green dream of a wilderness, constituting the Belum-Temengor Forest, and fairly seething with some of the nation's most dramatic megafauna: tapirs, tigers, sun bears, panthers and the endangered Sumatran rhino, whose preservation was one of the motivating factors behind gazetting the park.

Visiting the state park requires advance permission, which can be arranged by just about any hotel in the area at least one week in advance. Otherwise, the resorts listed here all offer various excursions into the jungle south of the park. Because much of the area was inundated after Temengor Dam was completed in 1972, all excursions are conducted by boat.

Sleeping & Eating

BELUM ECO RESORT   Resort **$$**
(☏ 012 524 9184; www.belumecoresort.com.my; all-inclusive 3-day/2-night package per person RM590) Be a guest of the Khong family on their own private island – previously a mountaintop before the Temengor Dam was built. Accommodation here is in a houseboat, bungalow or villa, and the fee includes boat transportation to and from the island, all meals, and excursions including a visit to an Orang Asli village and jungle trekking to a waterfall and rafflesia flower. Accommodation here is at the basic end of the spectrum.

BELUM RAINFOREST RESORT Resort **$$**
(☏ 791 6800; www.belumresort.com; r incl breakfast RM288-388; ❄ @ 🛜) A smallish resort of 76 rooms successfully combining industrial (textured concrete, brick) and natural (bamboo) elements. When we visited, a spa, a pool and additional rooms

Left: Market in Ipoh (p104), **Below:** Long-tailed macaque, Taman Negara (LEFT) CHERYL CHAN/GETTY IMAGES © (BELOW) ALTRENDO NATURE/GETTY IMAGES ©

were being built. As with the other resorts in the area, visits to the protected area and other outdoor pursuits can be arranged here (per person RM70 to RM351).

① Getting There & Away

The easiest transport option is to hop on any Kota Bharu–bound bus from Butterworth or Taiping; ask the driver to drop you off at Jeti Pulau Banting for the boat to Belum Eco Resort (p102). Other resorts are located near Hwy 76, which continues toward the Thai border and Kota Bharu; you'll be expected to pay the full fare to Kota Bharu.

FRASER'S HILL (BUKIT FRASER)

🎣09

Of all the hill stations, Fraser's Hill, around 100km north of Kuala Lumpur, retains the most colonial charm and attracts a fraction of the visitors of the Cameron Highlands. Situated across seven densely forested hills at a cool altitude of 1524m,

this quiet and relatively undeveloped place is best visited for gentle hikes and bird spotting. For more information see www.fraserhill.info.

◉ Sights & Activities

Fraser's Hill's main attraction is its abundant flora and fauna, in particular its birdlife. Some 265 species of birds have been spotted here, including the Malaysian whistling thrush, the Kinabalu friendly warbler, the brilliantly coloured green magpie, and the long-tailed broad-bill with its sky-blue chest. In June the hill station hosts its International Bird Race, in which teams of bird spotters compete to record the highest number of species. In the sports centre opposite the Puncak Inn, there's a Bird Interpretation Centre at the **golf clubhouse**; get the key from the staff at the Puncak Inn.

103

Detour:
Ipoh

Ipoh is one of Malaysia's more pleasant midsized cities, chock full of colonial architecture, faded tropical mansions, friendly folks and some of the country's best food. The elegant layout and design of the city's 'Old Town' speaks to the wealth once generated here from Kinta Valley tin mines; in its day, Ipoh was one of the wealthiest cities in Southeast Asia.

Today, the city can be approached as a worthwhile urban interlude, or as a convenient gateway to the Cameron Highlands. You can do a self-led tour, using the excellent Ipoh Heritage Trail Maps 1 and 2, available at Ipoh's **tourist information centre** (05-208 3155; Jln Bandaraya; 8am-5pm Mon-Fri & 10am-3pm Sat) or, if you're in town on a Saturday, you can join the **Ipoh Heritage Walk** (RM20; 8am-noon Sat), which sets out from the train station.

Sekeping Kong Heng (012-227 2745; www.sekeping.com/kongheng/home.html; Jln Bandar Timah; r RM200-800;), cleverly built over and around an ancient cafe, is a great place to stay. **Nasi Lemak Ayam Kampung** (43-45 Jln Ali Pitchay; mains RM5.50-30; 4.30pm-2.30am) is the place to come for fancy-pants – and delicious – *nasi lemak*.

It's easy to get to Ipoh by bus, train or long-distance taxi from major urban centres. **Firefly** (www.firefly.com.my) also commutes between Ipoh and Singapore. **Ipoh-Online** (www.ipoh-online.com.my) is a useful resource.

Pick up a leaflet from the Puncak Inn outlining various hikes, most pretty straightforward and signposted. You'll need to arrange a guide for the 5km-long Pine Tree Trail, which takes around six hours and crosses three mountain peaks, including 1505m Pine Tree Hill; **Mr Durai** (013-983 1633; durefh@hotmail.com), who charges around RM30 per hour, is a recommended guide.

Sleeping

There's plenty of accommodation but musty, damp rooms and cottages go with the territory. Many places charge 20% to 40% more on weekends and public holidays when you will need to book ahead. Rates typically include breakfast.

**YE OLDE SMOKEHOUSE
FRASER'S HILL** Hotel $$$
(362 2226; www.thesmokehouse.my; Jln Jeriau; d/ste from RM308/385) Exposed beams, log fires, four-poster beds and chintz – the Smokehouse goes for broke on its English-charm offensive. Even if you don't stay here, drop by for a well-made pie or roast at lunch or afternoon tea (from RM18) on the garden terrace. There's also a sister property in the Cameron Highlands.

**HIGHLAND RESTHOUSE HOLDINGS
BUNGALOWS** Bungalow $$
(362 2645; www.hrhbungalows.com;)
Check the website of this company for details about the range of rooms and bungalows at Fraser's Hill, starting from RM180 per room at the eight-bedroom Pekan bungalow, a well-kept property overlooking the golf course, to RM2000 for full hire of the four-bedroom Jerantut bungalow.

PUNCAK INN Hotel $$
(3622 007; puncakinn1@yahoo.com; r incl breakfast RM100, apt/bungalow RM120/300)
Newly renovated Puncak has the best-value rooms in Fraser's in a handy central

location. It also rents out studio, two- and three-bed apartments in the Fraser's Silverpark Resort, and four cottages, sleeping between four and 15 people.

Eating

HILL VIEW   Western, Chinese **$**
(Hawker's Stalls, Pine Tree Rd; mains from RM10; ⏱9.30am-9pm) Simple dishes are cooked up by a family who have run this stall for a couple of generations.

❶ Getting There & Away

The route to Fraser's Hill is via Kuala Kubu Bharu (KKB), which is connected to KL by train. A taxi from KKB to Fraser's Hill is one-way/return including waiting RM80/200, or from KL's Pudu Sentral bus station R150/300.

If driving yourself, note there's no petrol station in Fraser's Hill.

Penang

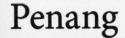

'Pearl of the Orient', Penang's nickname, conjures romantic images of Southeast Asia. Perhaps you see trishaws pedalling past watermarked Chinese shophouses, blue joss smoke and a sting of chilli in the air; or maybe it's gold-embroidered saris displayed in shop windows, and ornate temples next to mosques sending a call to the midday prayer. But really, whatever you're imagining, chances are that Penang is that reality. Add surprises like slick cafes, jungles and white beaches and you'll have an even sharper image.

Historically, Penang was the waterway between Asia's two halves and the outlet to the markets of Europe and the Middle East. As such, the island sits on the juncture of Asia's great kingdoms and colonial empires. Today the culture of this region, forged over decades of colonialism, commercial activity, hosting tourists and preserving heritage, is one of Malaysia's most tolerant, cosmopolitan and exciting, especially on the palate.

Rickshaw beside a traditional Chinese doorway, George Town (p120)
GAVIN HELLIER/GETTY IMAGES ©

Batu Ferringhi (p136)
DANIELLE GALI/GETTY IMAGES ©

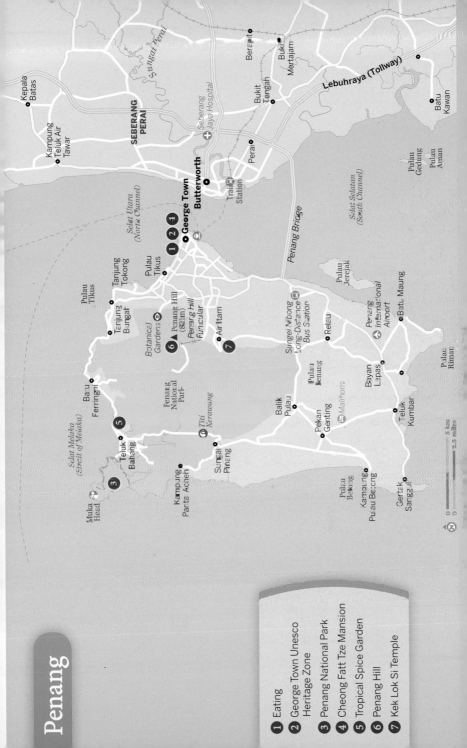

Penang

1. Eating
2. George Town Unesco Heritage Zone
3. Penang National Park
4. Cheong Fatt Tze Mansion
5. Tropical Spice Garden
6. Penang Hill
7. Kek Lok Si Temple

Kepala Batas
Kampung Teluk Air Tawar
SEBERANG PERAI
Sungai Perai
Bukit Tengah
Bukit Mertajam
Berapit
Lebuhraya (Tollway)
Batu Kawan
Pulau Gedung
Pulau Aman
Perai
Seberang Jaya Hospital
Train Station
Butterworth
George Town
Selat Utara (North Channel)
Tanjung Tokong
Pulau Tikus
Tanjung Bungah
Pulau Tikus
Botanical Gardens
Penang Hill (821m)
Penang Hill Funicular
Air Itam
Batu Ferringhi
Penang National Park
Titi Kerawang
Teluk Bahang
Muka Head
Kampung Parta Acheh
Sungai Pinang
Selat Melaka (Strait of Melaka)
Penang Bridge
Selat Selatan (South Channel)
Pulau Jerejak
Penang International Airport
Batu Maung
Sungei Nibong Long-Distance Bus Station
Relau
Pulau Betong
Mallborn
Pulau Betong
Balik Pulau
Pekan Genting
Bayan Lepas
Teluk Kumbar
Pulau Rimau
Kampung Pulau Betong
Gertak Sanggul

0   5 km
0   2.5 miles

Penang Highlights

① Culinary Penang

Penang is generally regarded as the region's gastro-nomic ground zero; some Kuala Lumpur residents make the four-hour drive for a single meal, and Singa-poreans pack out hotels on weekends. George Town's **hawker stalls** are a particular highlight. Above: Hokkien mee

Need to Know

TOP TIP Hawker stall vendors run flexible schedules, but avoid Mondays and Thursdays when many vendors tend to stay at home **For further coverage, see p129**

Culinary Penang Don't Miss List

BY BEE YINN LOW, FOOD WRITER,
WWW.RASAMALAYSIA.COM

1 CHINESE AND NONYA FOOD

Penang is the street food mecca of Malaysia and offers a wide variety of hawker food, from Chinese noodle dishes to Malay's banana leaf rice *(nasi lemak)* to Indian crepes such as *appam*. Penang was also a Straits settlement, so one can find delicious Nonya (Straits Chinese, or Peranakan) food here, too. Hawker dishes not to miss include *char kway teow*, flat rice noodles fried with prawn, cockles and Chinese sausage, served with fresh bean sprouts and chives; Hokkien mee, a noodle dish with a rich, shrimp based broth, and topped with shrimp, pork, sliced hard-boiled egg and fried shallots; Penang *asam* laksa, rice noodles in a spicy and sour fish broth, garnished with herbs and vegetables; and curry mee, noodles in spicy and aromatic curry broth with fried tofu puffs and cockles.

2 LORONG BARU

Also known by locals as New Lane, this nightly **hawker market** (p129) can always be relied on. Dishes to try are grilled stingray wrapped with banana leaf, or grilled curried squid, chicken wings, satay, *chee cheong fun* (steamed rice rolls with gooey shrimp paste) and *jiu hu eng chai* (cuttlefish with morning glory).

3 SEAFOOD

Because Penang is an island, fresh seafood such as shrimp, cockles and fish are staples of its cuisine. My favourite place to eat seafood is **Hai Boey** (☎013-488 1114; 29 MKY Pasir Belanda; mains RM8-50; ⊙lunch & dinner), a modest restaurant by the beach at Teluk Kumbar, a village at the south of Penang, about a RM60 taxi ride from George Town. The food is good and you can't beat the views, especially during sunset.

4 FRUITS & DRINKS

Penang offers some of the best durian in the region; it's absolutely creamy, rich and sweet. There are also many drinks served at local *kopitiam* (coffee shop). A drink particularly associated with the island is nutmeg juice, which you can get at any coffee shop.

George Town Unesco Heritage Zone

In 2008 the historic heart of George Town was declared a Unesco World Heritage Site for having 'a unique architectural and cultural townscape without parallel anywhere in East and Southeast Asia'. In general, the city has safeguarded its age-old feel while also reaping the benefits of a facelift. Below: Khoo Kongsi (p120); Top Right: Pinang Peranakan Mansion (p121); Bottom Right: Durian sellers on Love Lane

Need to Know

TOP TIP Value Your Built Heritage, available at George Town World Heritage Inc (www.gtwhi.com.my), is an entertaining guide to the town's shophouses **For further coverage, see p121**

2

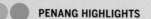

George Town Unesco Heritage Zone Don't Miss List

BY HOWARD TAN, PHOTOGRAPHER

1 CLANHOUSES

Penang has one of the densest concentrations of clan architecture found outside China. Arguably George Town's most impressive clanhouse is the **Khoo Kongsi** (p120).

2 STREET ART

Officially sponsored street art is not common in Malaysia, but in George Town it has been embraced by the community and provides a quirky counterpoint to the historic core. For the 2012 George Town Festival murals were commissioned from Lithuanian artist Ernest Zacharevic, who combines objects like bicycles (on Lebuh Armenian) and telephone booths with his paintings. The art has been a hit, with visitors constantly lining up to be photographed beside the Lebuh Armenian piece in particular. When it was vandalised in August 2012, locals quickly cleaned it up again.

3 CLAN JETTIES

The five **Clan Jetties** (p124) spread along the waterfront of Weld Quay represent a unique settlement of Chinese immigrants who share common historical, geographical and lineage origin. They're all that remains of George Town's waterfront community.

4 PINANG PERANAKAN MANSION

Pinang Peranakan Mansion (p121) is the island's best-kept mansion. Its sheer size and opulence are breathtaking. Every single room is decorated to a high standard with original antiques, giving it a real wow factor.

5 LOVE LANE, LORONG STEWART LANE & LEBUH ARMENIAN

Constructed between 1803 and 1810, these three streets are extremely historic and house some of the best examples of working shophouses in Penang today. Stamford Raffles lived on Love Lane for four years and Armenian St has Chinese military leader Chiang Kai-Shek's house, a number of excellent coffee shops and **88 Armenian Street**, an art complex that includes my photography gallery.

Hike to the Beach

At just 2300 hectares, **Penang National Park** (p133) is the smallest in Malaysia; it's also one of the newest, attaining national park status in 2003. It has some interesting and challenging trails through the jungle, a canopy walkway, and some of Penang's finest and quietest beaches. Hike up to **Muka Head** for sweeping coastal views.

3

Cheong Fatt Tze Mansion

4

Also known as the Blue Mansion because of its striking exterior paint job, **Cheong Fatt Tze Mansion** (p124) was the feng-shui-to-the-max home of a Hakka merchant trader with a rags to extraordinary riches story. Cheong Fatt Tze, known as the 'Rockerfeller of the East', did nothing by halves – the place melds Eastern and Western styles with eccentric abandon.

MO PEERBACUS/ALAMY ©

Spice Up Your Life

5

The **Tropical Spice Garden** (p136) is an oasis of tropical, fragrant fecundity. Ferns, bamboo, ginger and heliconias are among the lush vegetation and you might spot a giant monitor lizard or two. Its restaurant, **Tree Monkey**, is excellent, and the garden conducts regular cooking courses so you can learn how best to use all those tropical ingredients.

Ascend Penang Hill

6

Ride the funicular or hike up to **Penang Hill's** (p125) 821m summit for a spectacular view over the island and across to the mainland; its generally about 5% cooler here than at sea level. Atop the hill there are gardens, a simple food court, an exuberantly decorated **Hindu temple**, a **mosque** and **David Brown's** (p132), a colonial-style British restaurant where you can take afternoon tea.

Gain Buddha's Blessing

7

Kek Lok Si Temple (p125), the 'Temple of Supreme Bliss', is Malaysia's largest Buddhist temple and one of the most recognisable buildings in the country. Perpetually thronged with worshipers and tourists, the massive compex that took over two decades to build is presided over by a 36.5m-high bronze statue of Kuan Yin, goddess of mercy. Also here is a large Thai Buddha image donated by King Bhumibol of Thailand.

Penang's Best...

Museums & Historic Buildings

o **Khoo Kongsi** (p120) Learn about clanhouses at Penang's most ostentatious example.

o **Pinang Peranakan Mansion** (p121) Admire the gilded Straits Chinese interior decoration.

o **Penang Museum** (p124) Take a visual tour through the island's history.

o **Dr Sun Yat Sen's Penang Base** (p121) See where the doctor planned the 1911 Chinese revolution.

Heritage Hotels

o **Eastern & Oriental** (p128) The archetypal 19th-century colonial grand hotel.

o **23 Love Lane** (p127) Boutique property crafted from a mansion and former kitchen and stables.

o **Cheong Fatt Tze Mansion** (p129) An 'heirloom with rooms' and powerful *chi* energy.

o **Lone Pine Hotel** (p136) Relax in the hammocks strung between the pines shading this revitalised 1940s gem at Batu Ferringhi.

Local Eats

o **Lorong Baru** (New Lane, p129) Reliably good hawker stalls mixing standard faves with adventurous choices.

o **Teksen** (p129) Several steps up from the everyday delicacies of Chinatown.

o **China House** (p130) Cake-tastic cafe, restaurant and bar complex spanning a whole block.

o **Gurney Drive** (p129) Top-class collection of hawker stalls by the sea offering Malay and Western delicacies.

Urban Escapes

○ **Penang Hill** (p125) A number of roads and walking trails traverse the island's original hill station retreat.

○ **Botanical Gardens** (p126) Join locals practising t'ai chi, jogging, picnicking and even line-dancing in these lush gardens on the slopes of Penang Hill.

○ **Penang National Park** (p133) Picnic on Teluk Duyung (Monkey Beach) with numerous primates.

○ **Malihom** (p134) Serene hilltop hotel surrounded by jungle in the south of the island.

Need to Know

VITAL STATISTICS

○ **Area code** 📞04

ADVANCE PLANNING

○ **One month before** Book accommodation.

○ **One week before** Book Malay cooking course.

○ **One day before** Plan out where to eat and check on local festivals.

RESOURCES

○ **Visit Penang** (www.visitpenang.gov.my) Official website of state tourism body.

○ **iGeorge Town Penang** (www.igeorgetownpenang.com) Newsletter providing under-the-skin information on George Town.

○ **Tourism Penang** (www.tourismpenang.gov.my) Details of the island's multiple attractions.

GETTING AROUND

○ **Buses** Run by Rapid Penang (www.rapidpenang.com.my). Fares range from RM1.40 to RM4. Most originate at Weld Quay and also stop at Komtar along Jln Chulia.

○ **Car** Penang's a good place to rent a car, but reserve in advance for weekends and holidays. Rates start at around RM160 per day plus insurance.

○ **Motorcycle & Bicycle** Can be hired from many places in George Town or Batu Ferringhi, from RM20 per day for a bike and RM30 for a motorcycle.

○ **Taxi** You have to negotiate fares despite taxis having meters. Typical fares around George Town's centre range from RM6 to RM15.

○ **Trishaws** The ideal way to negotiate George Town's backstreets; cost around RM40 per hour.

BE FOREWARNED

○ **Dress** Shoes off and cover up for respectful visits to mosques and temples.

○ **Street Names** Many central George Town roads have both a Malay and an English name. In this book we use primarily the Malay name.

○ **Accommodation** During holidays, most notably Chinese New Year (January/February), hotels tend to fill up very quickly and prices can become ridiculously inflated; if you intend to stay at this time, book well in advance.

Penang Walking Tour

This walk around George Town's Unesco heritage zone will give you a glimpse of Penang's cultural grab bag: English, Indian, Malay, Baba-Nonya and Chinese.

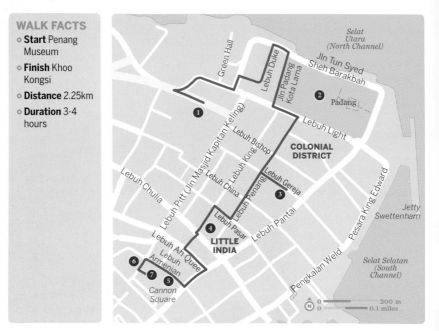

WALK FACTS
- **Start** Penang Museum
- **Finish** Khoo Kongsi
- **Distance** 2.25km
- **Duration** 3-4 hours

❶ Penang Museum & Supreme Court

Starting at Penang Museum, head west and then up to the waterfront, passing the Supreme Court built between 1901 and 1905; beside here on Lebuh Light is the Logan Memorial commemorating James Richardson Logan, advocate for nonwhites during the colonial era.

❷ Around the Padang

Walk up Lebuh Duke to the waterfront, then right and right again down Jln Padang Kota Lama past the green **padang** (grassy field) and grandiose architecture of the **City Hall** and **Town Hall**.

❸ Pinang Peranakan Mansion

Proceed left along Lebuh Light, then right on Lebuh Penang. A short detour along Lebuh Gereja finds the impressive, green-painted **Pinang Peranakan Mansion**, the old digs of Chung Keng Kwi, one of George Town's great Baba-Nonya merchant barons. After visiting this ornately decorated house, be sure to also check out the adjacent **ancestral hall** and the **temple**, which by comparison feels decidedly less flashy.

❹ Little India

Continue down Lebuh Penang into Little India and take a deep breath of all that spice; if it's around lunchtime, refuel with a curry. At Lebuh Pasar, head right past shops selling milky Bengali sweets, then left at Lebuh King to the intersection of Lebuh King and Lebuh Ah Quee, a literal example of Penang's cultural crossroads: to your south is a **Chinese assembly hall** and rows of fading **Chinese shopfronts**, to your north is a small **Indian mosque** and across the street is a large **Malaysian cafeteria**.

5 Lebuh Armenia

Left onto Lebuh Ah Quee, right on Jln Pantai, then right on Lebuh Armenia (if you want to go off-route to explore sidelanes and alleyways this is the time to do it). The street became a centre for Chinese secret societies and was one of the main fighting stages of 1867 riots that broke out between the societies. It's much more peaceful today and a very popular spot, not least for the street art mural of two kids on a bicycle that you'll find near the entrance to **Tuah Pek Kong**, home of the oldest Straits Chinese clan association in Penang.

6 Yap Kongsi & Khoo Kongsi

On the corner of Lebuh Armenia and Lebuh Pitt is the small 1924 Hokkien clanhouse **Yap Kongsi**, its outer alter decorated with symbols from the Taoist I Ching. Turn left and left again into Cannon Square to reach the magnificently ornate **Khoo Kongsi**, the most impressive *kongsi* in the city.

Penang In ...

ONE DAY

Explore George Town's heritage zone on a **walking tour**. Visit the **Khoo Kongsi** and **Pinang Peranakan Mansion**. Dine at hawker heaven **Lorong Baru** or superb Chinese eatery **Teksen**.

TWO DAYS

Ride the funicular up **Penang Hill**, and consider walking down through the lush **Botanical Gardens**. Join the afternoon tour of the **Cheong Fatt Tze Mansion**, then retire to the **Eastern & Oriental Hotel** for afternoon tea. Your culinary journey continues at **China House**.

THREE DAYS

Visit the **Kek Lok Si Temple** and Penang's other top temples. Enjoy more hawker delights with a sea breeze at **Gurney Drive**, then check into the **Lone Pine Hotel** at Batu Ferringhi.

FOUR DAYS

Relax on Batu Ferringhi's beach, or trek through the **Penang National Park** to find a quieter beaches with monkeys for company. Take a cooking class at the **Tropical Spice Garden**.

Colonial houses in George Town (p120)

Discover Penang

At a Glance

○ **George Town** (p120) The Unesco-protected heritage zone covers parts of Chinatown, Little India and the colonial district.

○ **Penang Hill & Around** (p125) A cool retreat from the sticky heat below, flanked by temples and botanical gardens.

○ **Batu Ferringhi & Around** (p136) Prime beach and resort strip, near to Penang National Park and the Tropical Spice Garden.

History

Little is known of Penang's early history. The island came under the control of the sultan of Kedah, but in 1771 the sultan signed the first agreement with the British East India Company, handing it trading rights in exchange for military assistance against Siam.

Fifteen years later Captain Francis Light, on behalf of the East India Company, took possession of Penang, which was formally signed over in 1791. Light permitted new arrivals to claim as much land as they could clear and this, together with a duty-free port and an atmosphere of liberal tolerance, quickly attracted settlers from all over Asia.

Penang briefly became the capital of the Straits Settlements (which included Melaka and Singapore) in 1826, until it was superseded by Singapore. After the Settlements were dissolved, Penang became a state of the Federation of Malaya in 1948 and one of independent Malaysia's 13 states in 1963.

With its free-port status withdrawn in 1969, Penang went through several years of decline, but over the next 20 years the island built itself up as one of the largest electronics manufacturing centres of Asia.

GEORGE TOWN

◉ Sights

Chinatown

KHOO KONGSI　　Historic Building
(Map p122; www.khookongsi.com.my; 18 Cannon Sq; admission adult/child RM10/1; ⏰9am-6pm)

Boardwalk at George Town's clan jetties (p124)
WILL TAN/GETTY IMAGES ©

The *kongsi,* or clanhouse, is a major node of overseas Chinese communities. Built by immigrants between the mid-1800s and the mid-1900s, these clanhouses created a sense of community, provided lodging and helped find employment for newcomers. Over time many clan associations became extremely prosperous and their buildings became more ornate; Khoo Kongsi is the most impressive one in Penang.

The Khoo, who trace their lineage back 25 generations, are a successful clan, and they're letting the world know. Stone carvings dance across the entrance hall and pavilions, many of which symbolise or are meant to attract good luck and wealth. Note the Sikh guardian watchman at the entrance. The interior is dominated by incredible murals depicting birthdays, weddings and, most impressively, the 36 celestial guardians (divided into two panels of 18 guardians each).

Khoo Kongsi was once more ostentatious; the structure caught fire on the night it was completed in 1901, an event put down to divine jealousy. The present *kongsi* dates from 1906.

KUAN YIN TENG   Buddhist Temple
(Temple of the Goddess of Mercy; Map p122; Lebuh Pitt (Jln Masjid Kapital Keling); ◷24hr) This temple is dedicated to Kuan Yin – the goddess of mercy, good fortune, peace and fertility. The temple, which was built in the early 19th century by the first Hokkien and Cantonese settlers in Penang, is not so impressive architecturally, but it's very central and popular with the Chinese community. It seems to be forever swathed in smoke from the outside furnaces where worshippers burn paper money, and from the incense sticks waved around inside. It's a very active place, and Chinese theatre shows take place on the goddess's birthday, celebrated on the 19th day of the second, sixth and ninth lunar months.

**DR SUN YAT SEN'S
PENANG BASE**   Museum
(Map p122; 120 Lebuh Armenian; admission RM3; ◷10am-5pm Mon-Sat) Dr Sun Yat Sen was

Unesco & George Town

For information on George Town's World Heritage status, stop by the **George Town World Heritage Inc. Headquarters** (Map p122; www.gtwhi. com.my; 116-118 Lebuh Acheh; ◷8am-1pm & 2-5pm Mon-Thurs, 8am-12.15pm & 2.45-5pm Fri), where you'll find displays and media about the city's architectural heritage. An excellent guide to the city's buildings that also covers many of the main sights is the *George Town World Heritage Site Architectural Walkabout,* available at the Penang Heritage Trust (p135).

the leader of the 1911 Chinese revolution, which overturned the Ching dynasty and established China as the first republic in Asia. He lived in George Town with his family for about six months in 1910. This house was not his residence but was the central meeting place for his political party. Today the structure serves as a museum documenting Dr Sun Yat Sen's time in Penang, and even if you're not interested in history, is worth a visit simply for a peek inside a stunningly restored antique shophouse.

Colonial District & Little India

**PINANG PERANAKAN
MANSION**   Museum
(Map p122; www.pinangperanakanmansion. com.my; 29 Lebuh Gereja; admission adult/child RM10/5; ◷9.30am-5.30pm Mon-Sat) This building rivals the Cheong Fatt Tze Mansion as the most stunning restored residence in the city. Every door, wall and archway is carved and often painted in gold leaf; the grand rooms are furnished with majestic wood furniture with intricate mother-of-pearl inlay. The house belonged to Chung Keng Quee, a 19th-century merchant, secret society leader and community pillar as well as being one of the wealthiest Baba-Nonyas of that era.

PENANG GEORGE TOWN

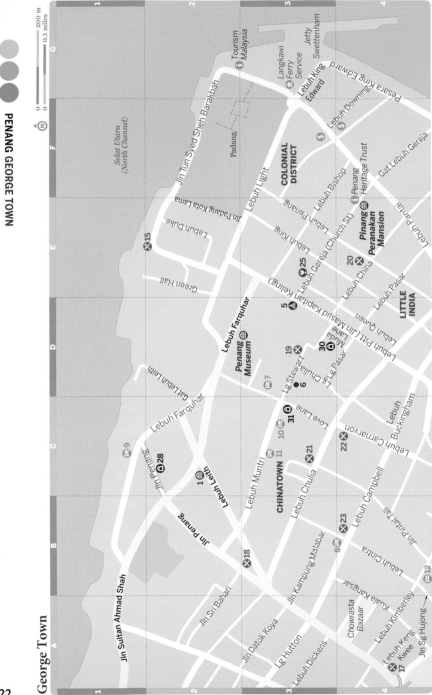

George Town

PENANG GEORGE TOWN

TRAVEL INK/GETTY IMAGES ©

Don't Miss Cheong Fatt Tze Mansion

This magnificent 38-room, 220-window mansion was built in the 1880s, commissioned by Cheong Fatt Tze, a Hakka merchant-trader who left China as a penniless teenager and eventually established a vast financial empire throughout east Asia. Rescued from ruin in the 1990s, the mansion blends Eastern and Western designs with louvred windows, art nouveau stained glass and beautiful floor tiles, and is a rare surviving example of the eclectic architectural style preferred by wealthy Straits Chinese of the time. The best way to experience the house, now a boutique hotel, is to stay here; otherwise hour-long guided tours give you a glimpse of the beautiful interior.

NEED TO KNOW

Map p122; www.cheongfatttzemansion.com; 14 Lebuh Leith; admission RM12; ⊙tours 11am, 1.30pm & 3pm Mon-Sat

PENANG MUSEUM   Museum
(Map p122; www.penangmuseum.gov.my; Lebuh Farquhar; admission RM1; ⊙9am-5pm Sat-Thu) This is one of the best-presented state museums in Malaysia. There are engaging exhibits on the customs and traditions of Penang's various ethnic groups, with photos, documents, costumes, furniture and other well-labelled displays. Upstairs is the history gallery, with a collection of early 19th-century watercolours by Captain Robert Smith, an engineer with the

East India Company, and prints showing landscapes of old Penang.

CLAN JETTIES   Neighbourhood
(Map p122; Pengkalan Weld) During the late 18th and early 19th centuries, Pengkalan Weld was the centre of one of the world's most thriving ports and provided plentiful work for the never-ending influx of immigrants. A community of Chinese grew up around the quay, with floating and stilt houses built along rickety docks; these

docking and home areas became known as the clan jetties.

Today the clan jetties are low-income areas with a jumble of dilapidated floating houses and planks, and are becoming popular tour bus stops. If you get here sans tour bus, it's a fun place to wander around with docked fishing boats, folks cooking in their homes and kids running around.

Penang Hill & Around

PENANG HILL Mountain
(www.penanghill.gov.my; funicular adult/child RM30/15, museum admission free; ⊙6.30am-7pm Mon-Fri & 6.30am-9pm Sat-Sun, funicular every 30min during opening hours) A cooler climate reigns at the summit of Penang's highest peak and, if the weather is playing ball, there are panoramic views.

Avoid weekends and public holidays when lines for the funicular can be horrendously long, with waits of up to 30 minutes; on weekdays queues are minimal. From the trail near the upper funicular station you can walk the 5.5km to the Botanical Gardens (Moon Gate) in about three hours. The easier 5.1km tarred jeep track from the top also leads

to the gardens, just beyond the Moon Gate.

From Weld Quay, Komtar or Lebuh Chulia, you can catch the frequent bus 204 (RM2). A taxi here from the centre of George Town will set you back about RM25.

KEK LOK SI TEMPLE Buddhist Temple
(⊙9am-6pm) Built by an immigrant Chinese Buddhist in 1890, Kek Lok Si is a cornerstone of the Malay-Chinese community, who provided the funding for its two-decade-long building (and ongoing additions).

To reach the entrance of the largest Buddhist temple in Malaysia, walk through a maze of souvenir stalls, past a tightly packed turtle pond and murky fish ponds, until you reach **Ban Po Thar** (Ten Thousand Buddhas Pagoda; admission RM2), a seven-tier, 30m-high tower. The design is said to be Burmese at the top, Chinese at the bottom and Thai in between. A **cable car** (one way/return RM2/4; ⊙8.30am-5.30pm) whisks you to the highest level, which is presided over by an awesome bronze statue of Kuan Yin, goddess of mercy.

View from Penang Hill

If You Like…
Buddhist Temples

Penang has an uncommonly diverse and burgeoning Buddhist community that embraces not only traditional Chinese Buddhism but also the Thai, Burmese, Sinhalese and Tibetan schools of Buddhist philosophy. In addition to the below, Penang's visit-worthy Buddhist temples include Kuan Yin Teng (p121), the oldest Chinese temple in Penang and the second oldest in the country, and Kek Lok Si Temple (p125).

1 WAT CHAYAMANGKALARAM
(Temple of the Reclining Buddha; Lorong Burma; admission free; ⏰7am-6pm) The Temple of the Reclining Buddha is a typically Thai temple with it sharp-eaved roofs and ceiling accents; inside it houses a 33m-long reclining Buddha draped in a gold-leafed saffron robe. It's located about 2.5km northwest of central George Town; a taxi here will cost RM15.

2 DHAMMIKARAMA BURMESE BUDDHIST TEMPLE
(Lorong Burma; admission free; ⏰7am-6pm) A rare instance of a Burmese Buddhist temple outside Burma (now Myanmar). This was Penang's first Buddhist temple, built in 1805; it has been significantly added to over the years. The temple is located about 2.5km northwest of central George Town; a taxi here will cost RM15.

3 WAT BUPPHARAM
(8 Perak Rd; admission free; ⏰8am-6pm) This Thai temple is home to the lifting Buddha, an allegedly 1000-year-old, gold-leaf-encrusted Buddha statue about the size of a well-fed house cat. As a seeker, kneel in front of the statue, pay respects to the figure with a clear mind and then ask, in your mind, the yes or no question you wish to have answered; ask also that you wish for the figure to become light for an affirmative answer. Try to lift the statue. To verify the answer, ask your question again, only this time ask that the statue become heavy. Lift again. When the statue is heavy it won't budge and when it's light it lifts off the platform like a butterfly.

There are several other temples in this complex, as well as shops and a **vegetarian restaurant** (mains from RM5; ⏰10am-7pm Tue-Sun).

A taxi here from the centre of George Town starts at about RM25, or you can hop on bus 204 to Air Itam (RM2).

BOTANICAL GARDENS Gardens
(www.penangbotanicgardens.gov.my; Waterfall Rd; ⏰5am-8pm) These 30-hectare gardens are also known as the Waterfall Gardens after the stream that cascades through from Penang Hill, and the Monkey Gardens for the many long-tailed macaques that scamper around. Don't be tempted to feed them: monkeys do bite, and there's a RM500 fine if you're caught. You'll also see dusky leaf monkeys, black giant squirrels and myriad giant bugs and velvety butterflies, which are all considerably more docile.

Once a granite quarry, the gardens were founded in 1884 by Charles Curtis, a tireless British plant lover who collected the first specimens and became the first curator. They are located about 8km outside of George Town. To get there, take bus 102 (RM2) from Komtar or Weld Quay; a taxi will cost at least RM25.

 ## Courses

NAZLINA'S SPICE STATION Cooking Course
(Map p122; ☎012 453 8167; www.penang-cooking-class.com; 71 Lg Stewart; class RM135; ⏰9am-1pm Tue-Sat) The bubbly and enthusiastic Nazlina leads instruction in local dishes ranging from *asam laksa* to prawn curry. Visit a morning market, grind your own supplies and have fun seeing how much work goes into Malaysian cuisine. Classes are held at the cooking school and, on Wednesdays, at the Eastern & Oriental Hotel (p128).

Tours

There's a huge variety of self-guided tours of George Town, from food tours to traditional trades to architecture – pick up a pamphlet of the routes at the tourist office or at the Penang Heritage Trust (p135). This NGO conducts a variety of walking tours of central George Town, including the 'Little India Experience' and the 'Heritage Trail'. Both last around three hours and cost RM60 – be sure to book at least a day in advance. The office also has free brochures with details of self-guided walks.

Another option is presented by the **Penang Global Ethic Project** (www.globalethicpenang.net/webpages/act_02b.htm), whose World Religion Walk takes you past the iconography and houses of worship of Christians, Muslims, Hindus, Sikhs, Buddhists and Chinese traditional religion.

There's also a free **tourist shuttle bus** (⏱6am-midnight), which runs between the Weld Quay and Komtar, winding its way through the colonial core of George Town. It's a good way to get a quick overview of the town, and you can get on and off at one of 19 stops.

Sleeping

George Town has all the accommodation possibilities you would expect in a big, bustling tourist city, from the grungiest hostels to the swankiest hotels, although it's worth noting that there's not a whole lot to choose from in the midrange. The Unesco-designated 'core zone' is home to several boutique hotels in heritage buildings.

23 LOVE LANE　　　　　Historic Hotel
(Map p122; ☎262 1323; www.23lovelane.com; 23 Love Lane; r incl breakfast 800-1200; ❄@ 🛜)
The 10 rooms here, which are found both in the main structure (a former mansion) or the surrounding buildings (former kitchen and stables), tastefully combine antique furniture and fixtures with modern design touches and artsy accents. There's lots of open spaces and high ceilings to catch the breezes, inviting communal areas, a peaceful aura, and service that compliments the casual, homey vibe.

STRAITS COLLECTION　　Historic Hotel
(Map p122; ☎262 7299; www.straitscollection.com; 89-95 Lebuh Armenia; ste RM450-490; ❄@ 🛜) If you've ever dreamed of living in a retro-chic restored Chinese shophouse, head here. Each residence is essentially a house (but no cooking facilities), artfully decorated with regional antiques, bright-coloured cushions and attractive original art. Each is different but all have some sort of unforgettable detail such as wooden

Kek Lok Si Temple (p125)
SIMON LONG/GETTY IMAGES ©

Japanese bathtubs or ancient sliding doors.

NEW ASIA HERITAGE HOTEL   Hotel $$
(Map p122; ☎ 262 6171; www.newasiahotel. com; 71 Lebuh Kimberly; r RM88-158; ❄ 🛜) As we were told by the gruff-but-friendly manager here, 'The most important thing about this hotel is that everything is the same in every room.' And he's right; the 24 rooms in this clean, well-run, comfortable midranger are similarly equipped with TV, air-con, and relatively attractive and functional furniture, although some rooms are slightly larger and have huge balconies. If you favour value rather style, this would be your best option in George Town.

MOON TREE 47   Hotel $$
(Map p122; ☎ 264 4021; 47 Lebuh Muntri; r RM80-120; ❄ 🛜) The main structure of this antique shophouse holds three rooms, all sharing a bathroom, while out back are three two-level suites (three additional family rooms were being built at research time), all with a funky, retro vibe and friendly service. It's perfect for young couples or solo travellers, although some older travellers or families might be put off by some of the hotel's rather rustic amenities and features.

CAMPBELL HOUSE   Historic Hotel
(Map p122; ☎ 261 8290; www.campbellhouse-penang.com; 106 Lebuh Campbell; r incl breakfast 270-550; ❄ @ 🛜) This former hotel, dating back to 1903, is seeing a new life as a thoughtful, sumptuous boutique. The European owners have employed their extensive experience in the luxury world to include amenities such as locally sourced, organic toiletries, beautiful Peranakan tiles in the bathrooms, Nespresso machines and high-quality mattresses.

EASTERN & ORIENTAL HOTEL   Luxury Hotel $$$
(E&O; Map p122; ☎ 222 2000; www.eohotels. com; 10 Lebuh Farquhar; ste incl breakfast RM350-2480; ❄ @ 🛜 ☒) One of the rare hotels in the world where historic opulence has gracefully moved into the present day. Originally established by the Sarkies brothers in 1885, today the hotel comprises the Heritage Wing, which includes the original domed lobby, and additional wings that date to the 1970s and 2001. A new wing was under construc-

Eastern & Oriental Hotel

tion at the time of research. The suites seamlessly blend European comfort with Malaysian style using hardwood antiques and sumptuous linens; those with a sea view are worth the extra outlay.

MUNTRI MEWS Historic Hotel **$$$**
(Map p122; ☏ 263 5125; www.muntrimews. com; 77 Lebuh Muntri; r RM300-360; ✳@🛜) This building's original owners would no doubt be shocked to learn that their former stablehouse (mews) is today an attractive boutique hotel. The nine rooms have an elegant minimalist feel, with each room boasting an inviting lounge area and a retro black-and-white tiled bathroom, but conspicuously at this price range, no wardrobe, minibar or safe.

**CHEONG FATT TZE
MANSION** Historic Hotel
(Map p122; ☏ 262 5289; www.cheongfatttze mansion.com; 14 Lebuh Leith; r RM420-800; ✳@🛜) Stay in the Blue Mansion, an 'heirloom with rooms', for the ultimate Eastern colonial experience. The house has near-perfect feng shui – even if you don't have a clue what feng shui is, once here you'll realise it's powerful stuff. Each room is uniquely themed and has a dreamy name like 'fragrant poem' or 'jolie', and represents a moment of Cheong Fatt Tze's life. A delicious courtyard breakfast is included in the price. Some guests say they have trouble sleeping here despite the wonderful energy, peace and quiet; old folks say it's the ghosts.

 Eating

People come to George Town just to eat. Even if you thought you were here for another reason, your priorities might change dramatically once you start digging into the Indian, Chinese, Malay and various hybrid treats available. Days revolve around where and what to eat, and three meals a day starts to sounds depressingly scant. And it's the same for locals, for whom eating out is a daily event.

Chinatown

TEKSEN Chinese **$$**
(Map p122; 18 Lebuh Carnavon; mains from RM10; ⏱noon-2.30pm & 6-9pm Wed-Mon) A recent 'branding and uplifting enterprise' has elevated this longstanding restaurant a couple steps up from Penang's typically gritty shophouse restaurants. There's a lengthy menu translated into English but we suggest you do as the locals do and

Right: Entrance to the Khoo Kongsi (p120); **Below:** Batu Ferringhi (p136)

(RIGHT) RICHARD I'ANSON/GETTY IMAGES ©: (BELOW) TRAVEL INK/GETTY IMAGES ©

ask the staff for the daily specials – this strategy rewarded us with some great soups, a tasty Malaysian-style stir-fry of morning glory and sambal, and a delicious dish of stir-fried roast pork. Highly recommended.

KEBAYA
Nonya **$$$**

(Map p122; ☎264 2333; www.seventerraces. com; Seven Terraces, Lebuh Stewart; 4-course menu RM100; ⏱7-10pm Tue-Sun) The restaurant attached to this splendid new hotel, both decorated with a gorgeous collection of antiques, offers an inspired contemporary spin on Nonya cuisine. The confit duck with five spice, plums and oranges is delectable – and don't miss the pandan-infused crème brulee.

CHINA HOUSE
International **$$$**

(Map p122; ☎263 7299; www.chinahouse. com.my; 153 & 155 Lebuh Pantai) Where do we start? This new complex of three co-joined heritage buildings features two

dining outlets; cafe/bakery **Kopi C** (www.chinahouse.com.my; China House, 153 & 155 Lebuh Pantai; mains from RM10; ⏱9am-midnight); two galleries; and a bar, Canteen (p134).

BTB (mains RM-38-68; ⏱dinner), the flagship dining venue, does a short but appetising menu of Middle Eastern- and Mediterranean-influenced dishes; think seared sea bass with Ras-el-Hanout spices, cauliflower puree and roasted pumpkin, pine nut and pomegranate dressing.

Courtyard Cafe (mains RM12-30; ⏱5pm-midnight) does a more casual burger and tapas menu. Whew.

KASHMIR
Indian **$$**

(Map p122; Oriental Hotel, 105 Jln Penang; mains RM6.90-54.90; ⏱lunch & dinner) Don't be fooled by this hotel-basement restaurant's cheesy 1970s, den-like interior; Kashmir serves some super delicious tandoori. Attentive service, an assertive Indian soundtrack and yes, cocktails complete the package.

GOH HUAT SENG   Chinese $$

(Map p122; 59A Lebuh Kimberley; hotpot RM40-80; ⏰5-9.30pm) With five decades under its belt, Goh Huat Seng continues to serve Teo Chew-style hotpot the old way: in charcoal-fired steamboats. Get some friends together and enjoy some communal dipping or, if you've got the language skills, order classic Teo Chew dishes from the restaurant's Chinese-language menu on the wall.

THO YUEN RESTAURANT   Chinese $

(Map p122; 92 Lebuh Campbell; dim sum RM1-5; ⏰6am-3pm Wed-Mon) Our favourite place for dim sum. It's packed with newspaper reading loners and chattering groups of locals all morning long, but you can usually squeeze in somewhere – as long as you arrive early. Servers speak minimal English but do their best to explain the contents of their carts to the clueless round-eye.

SKY HOTEL   Chinese $

(Map p122; Lebuh Chulia; mains from RM6; ⏰lunch) It's incredible that this gem sits in the middle of the greatest concentration of travellers in George Town, yet is somehow almost exclusively patronised (in enthusiastic numbers) by locals. It is incumbent on you to try the *char siew*

Little Penang Street Market

On the last Sunday of every month, the pedestrian section of upper Jln Penang hosts the **Little Penang Street Market** (Map p122; www.littlepenang.com.my; ⏰10am-5pm), selling Malaysian arts and crafts such as dolls, batik, pottery, T-shirts and painted tiles, as well as items like bottled chutney.

131

If You Like...
Afternoon Tea

Penang's English, Chinese and Indian legacies have left an appreciation for tea that remains strong today. More recent immigrants to George Town have imported an enviable Western-style cafe culture.

1 SUFFOLK HOUSE
(www.suffolkhouse.com.my; 250 Jln Ayer Itam; high tea for 2 RM68; ⏱2.30pm-6pm) For the ultimate English tea experience head to this 200-year-old Georgian-style mansion, where high tea, featuring scones and cucumber sandwiches, can be taken inside or in the garden. Suffolk House is located about 6.5km west of George Town; a taxi here will cost around RM15.

2 1885
(Map p122; 📞261 8333; Eastern & Oriental Hotel, 10 Lebuh Farquhar; English afternoon tea RM52; ⏱2-5pm) The Eastern & Oriental Hotel's (p128) main restaurant offers a daily English afternoon tea with scones, smoked salmon and, of course, cucumber sandwiches.

3 DAVID BROWN'S
(www.penanghillco.com.my; Penang Hill; afternoon tea RM34-78; ⏱9am-6pm) Located at the top of Penang Hill, this is yet another atmospheric destination for colonial-style high tea.

(barbequed pork), *siew bak* (pork belly), *siew cheong* (honey-sweetened pork) and roast duck.

JOO HOOI Hawker $
(Map p122; cnr Jln Penang & Lebuh Keng Kwee; mains from RM3; ⏱11am-6pm) The hawker centre equivalent of one-stop shopping, this cafe-style joint has all of Penang's best dishes in one location: laksa, *rojak* (, *char kway teow*, *lor bak* (deep-fried meats served with dipping sauces), *cendol* (shaved ice with palm sugar, coconut milk and jellies) and fresh fruit juices.

Colonial District & Little India

WELD QUAY SEAFOOD RESTAURANT Chinese $$
(Tree Shade Seafood Restaurant; Map p122; Pengkalan Weld; mains RM10-50; ⏱lunch & dinner Thu-Tue) Named for its location under a giant tree, this is where locals head for cheap and tasty seafood. Pick your aquatic protein from the trays out front, and the staff will fry, steam, soup or grill it up for you. Located directly across from the Weld Quay bus terminal.

MADRAS NEW WOODLANDS RESTAURANT Indian, Vegetarian $
(Map p122; 60 Lebuh Penang; set lunch RM5.25, mains from RM1.50; ⏱8.30am-10pm; 🅿) It draws you in with its display of Indian sweets outside (try the *halwa*), but once you experience the food you might not have room for dessert. Tasty banana-leaf meals and North Indian specialities are the mainstays, as well as the thickest mango lassi in town. The daily set lunch for RM5.25 might be Penang's greatest food bargain.

Outside the Heritage Zone

SEA PEARL LAGOON CAFE Chinese $$
(📞899 0375; off Jln Tanjong Tokong; dishes from RM8; ⏱11am-10pm Thu-Tue) On the surface, this somewhat gritty open-air place isn't much different than many of George Town's hawker cafes. But the view – tables looking out over the North Channel – and the food – salt roasted prawns, *ikan bakar* (fish grilled with sambal) and excellent satay – combine to make it one of our favourite places to eat outside the city centre. It's located 7km northwest of George Town, in Tanjong Toking next to Thai Pak Koong Temple; a taxi here costs about RM25.

NYONYA BREEZE Nonya $$
(50 Lorong Abu Siti; mains RM8.60-22; ⏱lunch & dinner Wed-Mon) Considered by many local Peranakans to serve the best Nonya food, this cafeteria-like place makes you feel at home while you sample exquisite

FRASER HALL/GETTY IMAGES ©

Don't Miss **Penang National Park**

The **office** (📞 881 3500; 🕐 8am-6pm) at the park entrance has a few maps and leaflets and can help you plan your day. Just across from the main park office is the **Penang Nature Tourist Guide Association** (PNTGA; 📞 881 4788; www.pntga.org) office; it offers guide services with a slew of options. It's best to reserve longer tours in advance with agencies around George Town or at your hotel.

The park entrance is a short walk from Teluk Bahang's main bus stop; a taxi from George Town will cost at least RM40. From here it's an easy 20-minute walk to the 250m-long canopy walkway, suspended 15m up in the trees from where you can hear water flowing from the mountain and get a view over the broccoli-headed park. From here, the easiest walk is the 20-minute stroll to Teluk Tukun beach where Sungai Tukun flows into the ocean. There are some little pools to swim in here. Following this trail along the coast about 25 minutes more brings you to the private University of Malaysia Marine Research Station and a nice beach to stop at for a rest.

From here it's another 45 minutes or so down the beach to Teluk Duyung, also called Monkey Beach, after the numerous primates who scamper about here on the beach on Muka Head, the isolated rocky promontory at the extreme northwestern corner of the island. On the peak of the head, another 15 minutes along, is an off-limits 1883 lighthouse and an Achenese-style graveyard. The views of the surrounding islands from up here are worth the sweaty uphill jaunt.

NEED TO KNOW

Taman Negara Pulau Pinang; admission free, canopy walkway adult/child RM7/5; 🕐 canopy walkway 10am-1pm & 2-4pm Sat-Thu

Detour:
Malihom

The serene retreat **Malihom** (☎04-226 4466; www.malihom.com; all-inclusive RM570-700; ❄@🛜🏊) comprises nine 100-year-old rice barns imported from Thailand and brought up to this 518m peak in the south of Penang where they have been restored to a cramped but comfortable state in a Balinese style. From the small complex there are 360-degree view over hills of jungle, the sea and several villages. The infinity pool is guarded by white Buddhas, the grounds are a perfect balance of shade, flowers and koi ponds, there's a conference room and yoga studio, and indoor hang-out areas perfect for sipping espresso or a glass of wine from the cellar, reading a book or watching movies. Basically you come here to completely relax because, aside from a few walks, mountain biking or fruit picking (it's amid a durian orchard), there's blissfully little to do.

The retreat is located off winding Rte 6 between Balik Pulau and Kampung Sungai Batu, staff will shuttle you up the steep hill at Malihom in their 4WD.

specialities like *kari kapitan* (chicken curry with coconut milk and kaffir lime) and *sambal* goreng (prawns, eggplant and cashews in chilli sauce). There's lots of daily specials and weekday lunchtime set meals (RM13.90).

Lorong Abu Siti intersects with Jln Burma about 500m northwest of Jln Transfer.

🍷 Drinking & Entertainment

CANTEEN
Bar

(Map p122; www.chinahouse.com.my; 183B Lebuh Victoria, China House; ⏰5pm-midnight) This is about as close as George Town comes to a hipster bar – minus the pretension. Canteen has an inviting artsy/warehouse vibe, there's live music from Thursday to Sunday, and great bar snacks available every night. Canteen is also accessible via China House's entrance on Lebuh Pantai.

B@92
Bar

(Map p122; 92 Lebuh Gereja; ⏰noon-late) Need a drinking buddy while in town? Resident Serbian Aleksandar is more than happy to oblige. Food, an eclectic music selection and friendly regulars make B@92 the kind of bar you wish you could throw in

your backpack and carry with you across Southeast Asia. Bring this guidebook, or ask about the origin of Aleks' skull ring, and you might just get a discount.

THAT LITTLE WINE BAR
Bar

(www.thatlittlewinebar.com; 54 Jln Chow Thye; ⏰5pm-midnight Mon-Sat) A cosy yet chic bar and lounge run by a German chef and his wife. Enjoy a selection of wine – glasses start at RM20 – and champagne cocktails. Accompany your drink with tapas (RM18 to RM60) and slightly heavier mains (RM28 to RM65).

Jln Chow Thye is located off Jln Burma, about 1.5km northwest of Jln Transfer; a taxi here will set you back about RM15.

QEII
Bar, Club

(Map p122; 8 Pengkalan Weld; ⏰6pm-1am Mon-Tue, 1pm-2am Wed-Sat, 3pm-2am Sun) QEII, with 360-degree views of the Straits of Malacca, serves passable pizza and better ambience; on Friday and Saturday nights, QEII transforms into a dance club.

🔒 Shopping

UNIQUE PENANG
Arts & Crafts

(Map p122; www.uniquepenang.com; 62 Love Lane; ⏰5pm-midnight Sun-Fri, 9pm-midnight Sat) This shophouse gallery features the work of the friendly young owners, Clovis and Joey, as well as the colourful paintings of the latter's young art students. As the couple point out, paintings are notoriously hard to squeeze in a backpack, so nearly all of the gallery's art is available in postcard size.

ROZANAS BATIK   Handicrafts
(Map p122; 81B Lebuh Acheh; ⏱11.30am-6.30pm) Tiny shop featuring the beautiful hand-made batik items of the eponymous owner. If you want to learn more, take a walk-in two-hour class in the adjacent studio (RM50 to RM 75).

SPRINGSFIELD   Arts & Crafts
(Map p122; 8 Muda Lane; ⏱9am-6pm) Pick up some hand-painted Peranakan tiles (made in Vietnam) at this boutique in a restored shophouse. There are few other interesting local-style knick-knacks available, and the profits go to help stray animals.

ℹ Information

Tourist Information

Penang Heritage Trust (PHT; ☎264 2631; www.pht.org.my; 26 Lebuh Pantai; ⏱9am-5pm Mon-Fri, 9am-1pm Sat) Information on the history of Penang, conservation projects and heritage walking trails.

Penang Tourist Guide Association (☎261 4461; www.ptga.my) Call or check the website to find a local tour guide.

Tourism Malaysia (☎262 0066; www.tourism.gov.my; 10 Jln Tun Syed Sheh Barakbah; ⏱8am-5pm Mon-Fri) George Town's main tourist information office gives out maps and bus schedules.

ℹ Getting There & Away

Air

Penang's **Bayan Lepas International Airport** (☎643 4411) is 18km south of George Town.

Boat

Several ferry providers, including **Langkawi Ferry Service** (LFS; ☎264 3088; www.langkawi-ferry.com; PPC Bldg, Pesara King Edward; ⏱7am-5.30pm Mon-Sat, 7am-3pm Sun), have merged and operate a shared ferry service to Langkawi (adult/child one way RM60/45, return RM115/85; 1¾ to 2½ hours) Boats leave at 8.30am and 8.15am. Boats return from Langkawi at 2.30pm and 5.15pm. Book a few days in advance to ensure a seat.

Getting To & From Butterworth

Butterworth, the city on the mainland bit of Penang (known as Sebarang Perai), is home to Penang's main train station and is the departure point for ferries to Penang Island. Unless you're taking the train or your bus has pulled into Butterworth's busy bus station from elsewhere, you'll probably not need to spend any time here.

The cheapest way to get between Butterworth and George Town is via the **ferry** (per adult/car RM1.20/7.70; ⏱5.30am-1am); the terminal is linked by walkway to Butterworth's bus and train stations. Ferries take passengers and cars every 10 minutes from 5.30 to 9.30pm, every 20 minutes until 11.15pm, and hourly after that until 1am. The journey takes 10 minutes and fares are charged only for the journey from Butterworth to Penang; returning to the mainland is free.

If you choose to take a taxi to/from Butterworth (approximately RM50), you'll cross the 13.5km Penang Bridge, one of the longest bridges in the world. There's a RM7 toll payable at the toll plaza on the mainland, but no charge to return.

Detour:
Tropical Spice Garden

Along the road to Teluk Bahang is the lush **Tropical Spice Garden** (📞881 1797; www.tropicalspicegarden.com; Jln Teluk Bahang; adult/child RM14/10, incl tour RM22/15; ⏱9am-6pm), offering over 500 species of flora, with an emphasis on spices. There is an excellent Thai restaurant, **Tree Monkey** (mains RM12.80-48.80; ⏱9am-11pm), on the premises, and the opportunity to partake in **cooking courses** (RM200; ⏱9am-1pm Mon-Sat). To get here, take bus 101 towards Teluk Bahang and ask to get off at the Spice Garden (RM2).

Bus

All long-distance buses to George Town arrive at the Sungei Nibong Bus Station, just to the south of Penang Bridge, while buses bound for Butterworth arrive at the Butterworth Bus Station. A taxi from Sungei Nibong to George Town costs RM25; a taxi from Butterworth can cost as much as RM50.

Buses to destinations in Malaysia can be boarded at Sungai Nibong and, more conveniently, the Komtar bus station; international destinations only at the latter. Note that transport to Thailand (except to Hat Yai) is via minivan; minivans are also an option in getting to the Cameron Highlands and the Perhentian Islands.

Train

Penang's train station is next to the ferry terminal and bus and taxi station in Butterworth. There are three daily trains to Kuala Lumpur (six hours, RM34 to RM67) and one in the opposite direction to Hat Yai in Thailand (four hours, RM26 to RM108); check with www.ktmb.com.my for the latest info on fares and schedules.

BATU FERRINGHI

For years, and no doubt aided by the tourism authorities, the lure of sun and sand at Batu Ferringhi was the main reason people came to Penang. In reality, the beach can't compare to Malaysia's best; the water isn't as clear as you might expect, swimming often means battling jellyfish, and the beach itself can be dirty, especially on weekends when hordes of day trippers visit. Still, it's the best easy-access beach stop on the island, and a pleasant break from the city.

The vast majority of the area's accommodation and restaurants are located along Jln Batu Ferringhi, the main strip, a short walk from the beach.

◉ Sights & Activities

There are plenty of **watersports** rental outfits along Batu Ferringhi's beach; they tend to rent **wave runners** (RM120 for 30 minutes), and offer **waterskiing** (RM60 for 15 minutes) and **parasailing** (RM80 per ride) trips.

After all this you might need a relaxing **massage**. All sorts of foot masseuses will offer you their services; expect to pay around RM40 for a 30-minute deep-tissue massage.

🛏 Sleeping

LONE PINE HOTEL  Resort $$$
(📞886 8686; www.lonepinehotel.com; 97 Jln Batu Ferringhi; incl breakfast r RM680-840, ste RM950-2940; ❄@🛜🏊) Dating back to the 1940s, the Lone Pine is one of Batu Ferringhi's oldest resorts. A 2010 remodel and expansion has given the hotel a new life, while still preserving many of its classier original aspects. The 90 rooms all have some perk, from personal plunge pools to private gardens. They also feel quite large, and are decorated with splashes of colour and attractive furniture. The grounds have a stately,

national park–like feel, with hammocks suspended between the pines (actually casuarina trees), and a huge saltwater pool as a centrepiece.

RASA SAYANG RESORT Resort **$$$**
(☎881 1966; www.shangri-la.com; Jln Batu Ferringhi; incl breakfast r RM1080-2130, ste RM1710-10,000; ❄ @ 🛜 🏊) Part of the Shangri-La chain, this is a vast and luxurious establishment – the island's only five-start resort – that feels like something out of a South Sea dream. Rooms are large and decorated with fine hardwood furniture, and cloud-like white duvets float on the beds; all have balconies and many have sea views. There's a yoga studio, tennis courts, a putting green and several restaurants. The hotel's Chi Spa is among the poshest on Penang.

HARD ROCK HOTEL Resort **$$$**
(☎881 1711; www.penang.hardrockhotels.net; Jln Batu Ferringhi; incl breakfast r RM700-1300, ste RM1300-4000; ❄ @ 🛜 🏊) If you can stomach the hyper-corporate vibe (and the unrelenting gaze of Beatles memorabilia), this resort – at research time, Batu Ferringhi's youngest – is a fun place to stay. There's a particular emphasis on family friendliness, and child-friendly pools, kid-friendly suites and teen-themed play areas (complete with pool table and video games) make

it an easy decision for anybody travelling with children.

 Eating

LONG BEACH Malay **$$**
(Jln Batu Ferringhi; mains from RM4; ⏱6.30-11.30pm) This buzzy hawker centre has the usual selection of Chinese noodle dishes, Indian breads and meat curries, and Malaysian seafood dishes.

Long Beach is located approximately in the centre of Batu Ferringhi's main strip, not far from the petrol station intersection.

TARBUSH Middle Eastern **$$$**
(www.tarbush.com.my; Jln Batu Ferringhi; mains RM12-55; ⏱10am-1am; ❄) Middle Eastern tourists and residents have brought their food to Batu Ferringhi, and Lebanese restaurants line the town's main strip. The best of the lot is most likely this branch of a KL restaurant empire. Look for the large seaside building topped with a fez.

ℹ Getting There & Away

Bus 101 runs from Weld Quay and from Komtar, in George Town, and takes around 30 minutes to reach Batu Ferringhi (RM4). A taxi to Batu Ferringhi from George Town will cost at least RM35.

Langkawi

Langkawi is synonymous with 'tropical paradise' – and with good reason. The archipelago's official title is *Langkawi Permata Kedah* (Langkawi, the Jewel of Kedah), no doubt inspired by the surrounding sparkling waters, relatively pristine beaches and lush jungle. The district's been duty free since 1986 and roping in tourists well before that. The beaches here are world famous for a reason: the sand is white and fine, the water is clear and there has been less development than in other Southeast Asian destinations. The ancient jungle on Pulau Langkawi can be explored from above, via the Panorama Langkawi cable car, or seen up close at one of the island's numerous waterfalls or on a guided jungle trek.

The Langkawi archipelago is part of Kedah province. Kedah's capital, Alor Setar, is the province's principal mainland attraction, while Perlis, Malaysia's tiniest state, is worth a detour for its Thai-border park Taman Negara Perlis.

Pelangi Beach, Pulau Langkawi
JOHN MILLER/GETTY IMAGES ©

Tanjung Rhu (p154)
RICHARD I'ANSON/GETTY IMAGES ©

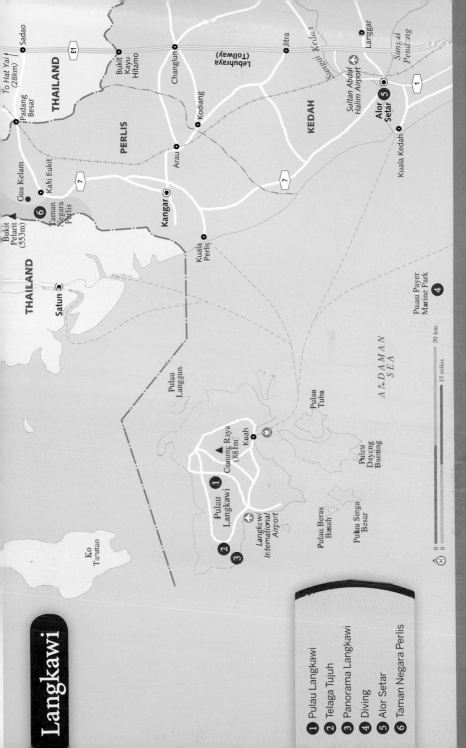

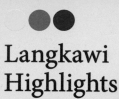

Langkawi Highlights

1

Pulau Langkawi

Pulau Langkawi is a living island as well as prime tourist territory. There's plenty to explore beyond the beach (of which there are many beautiful possibilities), including jungle-clad mountains, mangroves and freshwater rock pools. Above: Pantai Cenang (p154); Top Right: Pulau Dayang Bunting (p157); Bottom Right: Laksa at Bon Ton (p156)

Need to Know

BEST TIME TO VISIT November to March **TOP TIP** Langkawi has duty free status so is a good place to stock up on items like booze **For further coverage, see p150**

Pulau Langkawi Don't Miss List

BY NARELLE MCMURTRIE, RESORT OWNER

1 ISLAND LIFE
Langkawi is different from other beachy places in Southeast Asia because for its size it has very few hotels. In the last eight years only one five-star hotel has opened. So development is slow and this is the pace of life. Visitors have the opportunity to see a real island with people totally unaffected by tourism.

2 PULAU DAYANG BUNTING
Pulau Langkawi is a big island and you can easily spend several days exploring it. However, you should try and visit some of the other islands in the archipelago and this is easily done on island-hopping cruises or by chartering a boat. My favourite small island is **Pulau Dayang Bunting**. Apart from its famous lake, which is great for swimming, there are several deserted beaches sheltering in beautiful little coves with clear water.

3 EATING & DRINKING
My favourite lunch place is **Siti Fatimah** (p160). Normally 70 dishes on offer, buffet style, for approximately RM7 with a drink. They are not after the tourist dollar and serve from the heart – very genuine people. **Nam** (p159), the restaurant at **Bon Ton** (p156), has been going strong for 18 years. If you happen to be here for fasting month (Ramadan), you get to sample amazing home cooking from all the little stalls that appear from nowhere. **La Sal** (p161) is a good bar for sunset cocktails, surf and sand.

4 HIRE A CAR
This is the best way to explore the island and get to off-the-beaten-track places. The drive to the top of **Gunung Raya** (p151), the island's highest mountain, is spectacular – on a clear day you can see all the way to Thailand.

Cool off in Rock Pools

In Langkawi legend, **Telaga Tujuh** (p151, Seven Wells) is a playground for mountain fairies. These freshwater rock pools are found at the top of a waterfall inland from Langkawi's Pantai Kok. Slippery moss coating the rocks between the pools helps you slip from one to another – but take care as there's a 90m drop off the cliff from the final deep one.

Get High on Langkawi

The best reason for visiting the cheesy Oriental Village shopping mall is to board the cable car **Panorama Langkawi** (p150) for the thrilling 20-minute trip up 708m **Gunung Machinchang**. Spectacular views over the island and Andaman Sea are guaranteed. At the summit, walk across the single-span **suspension bridge**, 100m above old-growth trees, for a closer look at the jungle habitat.

Dive in a Marine Park

The **Pulau Payar Marine Park**, strung out like green jewels in teal, is the focus of Langkawi's diving and snorkelling expeditions (p154). Most trips come to 2km-long **Pulau Payar**, although you probably won't see the interior of the island — all the action centres on a diving platform and horseshoe-bend of coast. When the water's clear you don't even have to snorkel to be treated to some wonderful views of tropical fish.

Eat Fish-Head Curry

Alor Setar, Kedah's state capital, has a few things going for it, including a tall telecommunications tower you can take tours up, and attractive architecture around its central square. But the best reason for visiting is to savour the delicious fish-head curry conjured up at the **Muda Coffee Shop** (p165) — it may be one of tastiest meals you'll have in Malaysia.

Taman Negara Perlis

Head well of the beaten track to explore Perlis' wildlife-rich **state park** (p164), which contains Malaysia's only semi-deciduous forest. This is the only habitat in Malaysia for the stump-tailed macaque. White-handed gibbons and a rich array of birds can also be found here. With a guide you'll also be able to explore numerous cave systems.

Langkawi's Best...

Beaches

○ **Pantai Cenang** (p154) Langkawi's most developed and popular beach is a gorgeous strip of white sand.

○ **Pantai Tengah** (p154) A bit more upscale and less busy than Pantai Cenang.

○ **Pantai Kok** (p154) Fringing a beautiful bay encased by mountains and jungle.

○ **Tanjung Rhu** (p154) The sunsets here give 'stunning' new meaning.

Activities

○ **Island-hopping** (p157) The most popular day tour offered on Langkawi is a boat tour of the archipelago's smaller islands.

○ **Dev's Adventure Tours** (p155) Learn about Langkawi's natural environment from Dev and his well-qualified team of guides.

○ **Alun-Alun Spa** (p154) This Langkawi operation uses natural and organic products.

Local Eats

○ **Muda Coffee Shop** (p165) Yes, we're recommending that you eat steamed fish-head in Alor Setar. Yes, we think you'll love it.

○ **Siti Fatimah** (p160) Buffet-style restaurant that's a Langkawi standout for Malay food.

○ **Night markets** (p162) Eat your way around the island at this roving night market.

Resorts

- **Bon Ton & Temple Tree** (p156) Malay stilt houses and other vernacular architecture weave their charms at these twin resorts.
- **Ambong Ambong** (p157) Minimalist contemporary jungle retreat that's one of Langkawi's more sophisticated places to stay.
- **Tanjung Sanctuary** (p158) Deluxe duplex villas in a remote, wild Langkawi location
- **Tanjung Rhu Resort** (p159) Beautiful location and family friendly.

Left: Night market (p162) at Kuah; **Above:** Pantai Cenang (p154)

(LEFT) FELIX HUG/GETTY IMAGES ©; (ABOVE) MATTHEW MICAH WRIGHT/GETTY IMAGES ©

Need to Know

VITAL STATISTICS

- **Area code** ☎04

ADVANCE PLANNING

- **One month before** Book accommodation and flights.
- **One week before** Hire a car and book a dive trip.
- **One day before** Check where the night markets are happening.

RESOURCES

- **Langkawi Geopark** (www.langkawigeopark.com.my) Information on the island's natural areas.
- **Langkawi Online** (www.langkawi-online.com) A comprehensive source of island information.
- **My Langkawi** (www.mylangkawi.com) Another source of island info.
- **Visit Kedah** (www.visitkedah.com.my) Info on the state's tourism highlights.

GETTING AROUND

- **Car** Car hire is available at Langkawi airport and Kuah jetty. Rates start at around RM60 per day, but drop if you bargain. Elsewhere, a convenient place to rent cars or motorcycles is T-Shoppe, which has branches at Kuah, Pantai Cenang and Pantai Tengah.
- **Bicycle and motorbike** Motorbikes (RM35 per day) can be hired at stands all over Langkawi. A few places also rent mountain bikes for RM15 per day.
- **Taxi** As there is no public transport, taxis are the main way of getting around, but fares are relatively high.

BE FOREWARNED

- **Accommodation** During school holidays and the peak tourist season (approximately November to February), advance bookings are generally necessary for Langkawi's hotels.
- **Monsoon season** Shelve any notions of taking the ferry to Langkawi during the July to mid-September monsoon season; rough seas make it a guaranteed vomit-inducing experience.
- **Kuah** Save Langkawi's main port for a rainy day; there's little to do here other than shop.
- **Jellyfish** Watch out when swimming at Pantai Cenang.

Langkawi Itineraries

Be seduced by Langkawi's pleasures on a long week-end or combine the island with a couple of mainland stops on a five-day escape. Either way you'll want to return soon and for longer.

3 DAYS PULAU LANGKAWI TO PULAU DAYANG BUNTING
Relaxing Beach Break

Pick up your hire car at **(1) Langkawi Airport**. Having settled into your hotel, head to **(2) Pantai Cenang** and pick a sunbathing spot. If it's low tide and the sandbar appears walk across it to the island of Pulau Rebak Kecil. Otherwise book a massage at the spas in nearby **(3) Pantai Tengah**. Return to Pantai Cenang in the evening to enjoy sunset cocktails at the candlelit beach bars.

Make a circuit of the island; it's about 70km of excellent roads and can easily be completed in a day. Stop first at **(4) Pantai Kok** where you can hop on the Panorama

Langkawi cable car for a ride to the summit of Gunung Machinchang. Afterwards, follow the twisting road through the jungle to **(5) Teluk Datai**; enjoy lunch at either of the resorts here to gain access to their lovely beaches. Later in the afternoon, drive to the summit of **(6) Gunung Raya**, the highest point on the island.

Save a day to join an island-hopping cruise, making sure that it includes the lovely island of **(7) Pulau Dayang Bunting** where you can swim in a freshwater lake surrounded by craggy limestone cliffs.

5 DAYS

ALOR SETAR TO TAMAN NEGARA PERLIS

Exploring the Northwest

(1) Alor Setar, capital of the Kedah state, is a very Malay city with Thai influences noticeable in the temples scattered around town. A day here is sufficient to stroll the area around the grassy *padang* (town square) lined with a beautiful mosque, the sultan's palace and handsome colonial-era buildings. You can also take in the view across the city from the 88m-high observation deck in the Menara Alor Setar.

Move on to the busy fishing village **(2) Kuala Kedah** to catch one of the frequent ferries to **(3) Kuah**, Langkawi's main port. Spend three nights on the island chilling at one of its several appealing resorts or beach- and island-hopping. Alternatively, dig a bit deeper into island life by searching out the roving night markets and off-the-beaten-track villages for local eats. An early morning guided jungle hike or a boat trip through the mangroves is a fascinating way to learn about the native flora and fauna.

Return to the mainland on a ferry bound for **(4) Kuala Perlis**. From there arrange a taxi to **(5) Taman Negara Perlis**, a heavily forested state park whose visitor centre is 3km from the Thai-border village of Kampung Wang Kelian.

Gunung Machinchang (p151)

149

Discover Langkawi

PULAU LANGKAWI

Despite their immense drawing power, the 99 islands that make up the Langkawi archipelago have not been overdeveloped beyond recognition. Get just a little way off the main beaches and this is idyllic rural Malaysia, all *kampungs* (villages) and oil lamps. It's the kind of tropical island where there's no lack of spas, seafood restaurants and beach bars, but where the locals continue to go about their ways just as they have for generations.

The main island, Pulau Langkawi, is big – almost 500 sq km. Kuah, in the southeast corner of the island, is the main town and the arrival point for ferries, but it has scant attractions and the beaches are elsewhere.

 Sights

UNDERWATER WORLD   Aquarium
(Map p155; www.underwaterworld langkawi.com.my; Pantai Cenang; admission adult/child RM38/28; ⏲10am-6pm) Malaysia's largest aquarium, featuring 200 different species of marine and freshwater creatures. Some exhibits (especially the rainforest walk) are well executed; some feel like a tropical aquarium in need of a cleaning, but in general it's a great place for the kids.

ORIENTAL VILLAGE   Amusement Park
(Map p152; www.orientalvillage.my; Pantai Kok; ⏲most outlets 10am-7pm) Even if you're not into shopping, this Disneyland-like open-air mall is home to one of the island's most worthwhile attractions. **Panorama Langkawi** (Map p152; www.panoramalangkawi. com; ⏲10am-8pm Mon & Tue, noon-8pm Wed,

Panorama Langkawi
ANDY SELINGER/ALAMY ©

PAUL KENNEDY/GETTY IMAGES ©

Don't Miss Telaga Tujuh

If you've been splashing around in the ocean, why not add some variety to your life and lounge in some freshwater rock pools? Telaga Tujuh, located at the top of a waterfall inland from Pantai Kok, is a series of small pools connected by a thin trickle of refreshingly cool mountain water. The pools, also known as Seven Wells, are surrounded by thick jungle that is home to a family of cheeky (and somewhat intimidating – keep any food out of sight) monkeys, and also offer brilliant views of the island.

The smooth rut between the pools is slick enough to slide down, especially towards the bottom, but it's worth noting that over the years a few people have managed to slip past the partially gated edge of the falls, resulting in serious injury and even death.

NEED TO KNOW

Map p152; You can get here by rented car, motorbike or taxi; follow the main road 1km past Pantai Kok, then turn right at the T-intersection, continuing until the road dead-ends at a car park. From here it's a steady 10-minute climb through the rainforest (stay to the right) to the wells at the top of the falls.

10am-8pm Thu, 9.30am-8pm Fri-Sun) is a cable car that takes visitors on a vertiginous 20-minute trip to the top of the majestic Gunung Machinchang (708m). There are some incredible views along the way, and at the top you can walk across the **SkyBridge**, a single-span suspension bridge located 100m above old-growth jungle canopy. The park's other attractions include the overpriced **Langkawi Elephant Adventures** (Map p152; www.gajah.org; elephant rides for 2 adults & 1 child 5/15min RM80/200; ☺10.30am-1pm & 2-5.45pm); **Tiger! Tiger!** (Map p152; admission free; ☺10am-7pm), a tiger exhibit and gallery; and a handful of restaurants and souvenir shops.

GUNUNG RAYA   Mountain
The tallest mountain on the island (881m) can be reached by a snaking, paved road through the jungle. It's a spectacular drive to the top with views across the

Pulau Langkawi

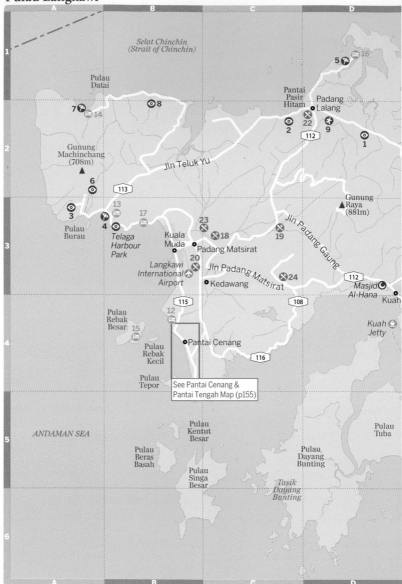

island and over to Thailand from a lookout point and a small teahouse (assuming there's no fog). Access to the mountain may occasionally be restricted by the government, and the gate at the foot of the mountain lowered.

AIR HANGAT   Hot Springs
(Map p152; ⊙8am-6pm) This village, located south of Tanjung Rhu, is known for its hot springs. Soak your feet for free or bathe in a private room for RM70 per hour. Massage is also available for RM80 per

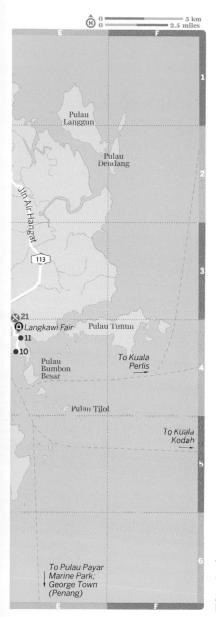

Pulau Langkawi

⊙ Sights
1 Durian Perangin D2
2 Kompleks Kraf Langkawi C2
3 Oriental Village A3
4 Pantai Kok B3
5 Tanjung Rhu D1
6 Telaga Tujuh A2
7 Teluk Datai A2
8 Temurun Waterfall B2

⊙ Activities, Courses & Tours
9 Air Hangat D2
10 East Marine E4
11 Langkawi Coral E4
    Langkawi Elephant Adventures .. (see 3)
    Panorama Langkawi ....(see 3)
    Tiger! Tiger! ....(see 3)

⊙ Sleeping
12 Bon Ton & Temple Tree B4
13 Danna B3
14 Datai Langkawi A2
15 Rebak Marina Resort B4
16 Tanjung Rhu Resort D1
17 Tanjung Sanctuary B3

⊙ Eating
18 Ashkin C3
    Nam ....(see 12)
19 Night Market (Jalan Makam
    Mahsuri Lama) C3
20 Night Market (Kedawang) B3
21 Night Market (Kuah) E3
22 Night Market (Padang Lalang) D2
23 Night Market (Padang Matsirat) C3
24 Siti Fatimah C3

⊙ Shopping
    Atma Alam Batik Art Village .... (see 18)

🏃 Activities & Tours

Boat Trips & Cruises
The pier near Tanjung Rhu is the main jumping-off point for the much-touted **boat trips** (⊙9am-5pm; RM250 per person) into the extensive mangrove forests that edge much of the northeastern coast of Langkawi. Boats can accommodate up to eight passengers, and options include stops at caves, fish farms and eagle watching. .

hour. The modern complex also holds occasional 'cultural shows' – contact Langkawi's tourist office to see if anything is lined up.

If You Like...
Beaches

You don't have to go far on Langkawi to find an idyllic seaside spot of sand.

1 PANTAI CENANG
(Map p155) This gorgeous 2km-long strip of white sand on the island's south coast is Langkawi's busiest and most developed beach, with abundant watersport options. A sandbar sometimes appears at low tide, allowing you to inspect local sea life – although watch out for jellyfish, which are common here.

2 TELUK DATAI
(Map p152) On the far northwestern corner of the island, the beaches at Teluk Datai are arguably some of the island's most beautiful and secluded, but are really only accessible if you're staying in one of the area's two luxury resorts.

3 TANJUNG RHU
(Map p152) Tanjung Rhu, on the north coast, is one of Langkawi's wider and better beaches, fronted by magnificent limestone stacks that bend the ocean into a pleasant bay. On clear days the sunsets here give stunning new meaning. The water is shallow, and at low tide you can walk across the sandbank to the neighbouring islands. Accommodation is provided by two upscale resorts.

4 PANTAI TENGAH
(Map p155) There are some big, all-inclusive resorts here, good restaurants and bars, and a few cheaper chalet clusters.

5 PANTAI KOK
(Map p152) Pantai Kok fronts a beautiful bay surrounded by limestone mountains and jungle. Unfortunately an outdoor shopping centre and the nearby harbour have left it feeling somewhat overdeveloped. There are a handful of equidistantly located upscale resorts around here, many with their own small strips of beach.

There are several **cruise operators** in Langkawi, nearly all of whom offer daily dinner, sunset and cocktail cruises. Boats depart from various piers across the island and bookings can be made through the operators or via travel agents.

During the monsoon season from July to mid-September, the seas are often too rough and unpredictable for many of the boat trips.

Diving & Snorkelling

EAST MARINE　　Diving & Snorkelling
(Map p152; ☎ 966 3966; www.eastmarine.com. my; Jln Pantai Dato Syed Omar, Royal Langkawi Yacht Club, Kuah; snorkelling/diving trips from RM230/RM250; ⏰8am-6pm) Probably the most reputable diving outfit on the island. East Marine conducts full-day diving and snorkeling excursions to Pulau Payar, as well as PADI certification courses starting at RM1300.

LANGKAWI CORAL　　Diving & Snorkelling
(Map p152; ☎ 899 8822; www.langkaw-icoral.com; 64 Jln Tanjung Tokong, Kuah; snorkelling/diving from RM300/455) Diving and snorkelling trips to Pulau Payar include a buffet lunch and some for sunbathing and fish-feeding. Langkawi Coral operate a stall at Kuah's ferry pier, open approximately 7am to 9pm.

Massages & Spas

The main strip along Pantai Tengah is home to the bulk of the island's spas. Massage treatments average about RM150 per hour, while facials and other treatments start at about RM60. Many of the following also offer complimentary transfer; call for details.

ALUN-ALUN SPA　　Spa
(Map p155; ☎ 955 5570; www.alunalunspa.com; ⏰11am-11pm) With three branches across the island, Alun-Alun is accessible and gets good reviews. The spa's natural/organic products are also available for purchase.

ISHAN SPA　　Spa
(Map p155; ☎ 955 5585; www.ishanspa.com; ⏰10am-8pm) The six spa suites here offer some pretty posh pampering

(air treatments, body scrubs and the like) in a space that screams traditional.

NITHI AYURVEDIC MASSAGE   Spa
(Map p155; ☎955 9078; www.langkawi-ay-urvedic-massage.com; Pantai Cenang; ☉10am-7pm) Customers rave about treatments like *shiro dhara*, where a continual flow of warm herbal oil is poured over your forehead as your head and shoulders are massaged. Treatments run from RM65 to RM195.

Nature & Adventure Tours

DEV'S ADVENTURE TOURS   Guided Tour
(☎494 9193; www.langkawi-nature.com; Pantai Cenang; tours RM100-220) Cycling, bird watching, mangrove excursions, jungle walks, culture tours... This outfit offers a fat menu of options, and its guides and

service get rave reviews. Booking is done online or by phone, and transportation is provided from most hotels.

LANGKAWI CANOPY ADVENTURES   Guided Tour
(☎012-466 8027; www.langkawi.travel; tours RM180-220) The main highlight here is 'air-trekking' through the rainforest canopy, with excursions divided into two levels of difficulty. Booking can be done by phone or online, and needs to be done at least a day in advance. You'll need to arrange a taxi to take you to the site – a 30-minute ride from most parts of the island – at Lubuk Semilang, in the middle of Pulau Langkawi.

Pantai Cenang & Pantai Tengah

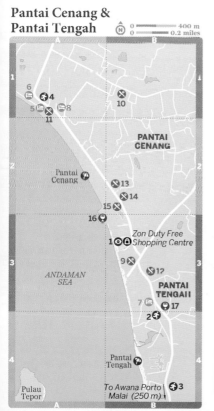

0   400 m
0   0.2 miles

ANDAMAN SEA

PANTAI CENANG

Pantai Cenang

Zon Duty Free Shopping Centre

PANTAI TENGAH

Pantai Tengah

Pulau Tepor

To Awana Porto Malai (250 m)

Pantai Cenang & Pantai Tengah

Sights
1 Underwater World B3

Activities, Courses & Tours
2 Alun-Alun Spa B4
3 Ishan Spa B4
4 Nithi Ayurvedic Massage A1

Sleeping
Ambong Ambong .... (see 3)
5 Beach Garden Resort A1
6 Casa del Mar A1
7 Frangipani B3
8 Sweet Inn A1

Eating
9 Hungry Monkey B3
10 Night Market (Bohor
Tempoyak) B1
11 Orkid Ria A1
12 Osteria B3
13 Putumayo B2
14 Red Tomato B2
15 Tomato B2

Drinking
Babylon .... (see 11)
16 Cliff A3
La Sal .... (see 6)
17 Little Lylia's Chill Out Bar B3
Yellow Café .... (see 15)

Sleeping

Despite the apparent variety, and perhaps due to the island's general isolation, accommodation on Langkawi doesn't have the same high standard as other beachy places in Southeast Asia. Sure, there are some amazing luxury resorts, but midrange places (and even many of the upscale ones) can feel lacklustre. There are relatively few budget-oriented hostels and dorms; Pantai Cenang is home to the bulk of them.

Pantai Cenang & Around

BON TON & TEMPLE TREE Boutique Hotel **$$$**
(Map p152; ☏955 1688; ❄@☎🛇) These two quasilinked boutique hotels are our favourite places on Langkawi, if not in the region. **Bon Ton** (www.bontonresort.com. my; villas incl breakfast RM650-1270) takes the form of eight Malay stilt houses perched over a grassy, coconut-palm-studded plot of land, each one decked out with dark wood and positioned to catch the breeze.

With its organic accents and traditional craftwork, it's somehow regal and rustic all at once. Next door, **Temple Tree** (www. templetree.com; r/villas incl breakfast RM670-1370) ups the stakes with a collection of antique structures relocated from various points in Malaysia. An imposing Chinese mansion, a wooden villa from Penang, colonial-style shophouses and other restored structures make up the stately, parklike compound. Linking both locations is a common thread of class, style, thoughtful service and – take this as a warning if you don't care to share your villa with Felix – cats.

BEACH GARDEN RESORT Hotel **$$**
(Map p155; ☏955 1363; www.beachgardenresort. com; r RM230-320; ❄☎🛇) An unabashedly old-school, yet clean 'n' cheery, resort-style place right on a relatively quiet patch of Pantai Cenang. All 12 rooms are decked out with the same aged furniture, and share access to a tiny pool and the resort's rustically inviting restaurant.

REBAK MARINA RESORT Resort **$$$**
(Map p152; ☏966 5566; www.rebakmarina.com; incl breakfast r RM1100-1450, ste 1750-2050; ❄@☎🛇) Lying just off Pantai Cenang, the small island of Rebak Besar plays host to this exclusive resort, which offers spacious and elegant chalets in beautifully landscaped grounds. It has all the facilities you would expect, including a gym, a spa, tennis courts and restaurants. Transfers from Langkawi airport are included in the price, and package deals strip a significant amount off the rates shown here.

CASA DEL MAR Boutique Hotel **$$$**
(Map p155; ☏955 2388; www.casadelmar-langkawi. com; ste incl breakfast RM1200-2100; ❄@☎🛇) This is a sumptuous,

Monkey in the forest by Telaga Tujuh (p151)
HOLGER LEUE/GETTY IMAGES ©

EYE UBIQUITOUS/ALAMY ©

Don't Miss Island-Hopping

Langkawi's most popular day trip is the island-hopping tour, offered by most tour and diving companies, and costing as little as RM25 per person. The operator **Coral Island** (www.coralisland.com.my) gets good reviews. Tours usually take in **Dayang Bunting** (Lake of the Pregnant Maiden), located on the island of the same name. It's a freshwater lake surrounded by craggy limestone cliffs and dense jungle, and it's good for swimming.

Other destinations include **Pulau Beras Basah**, sea stacks, sea caves and a cruise around mangroves for a look at the local eagles. You could also visit **Pulau Singa Besar**, with its resident population of mouse deer and crotchety monkeys.

vaguely Spanish-themed place on the quieter northern end of Pantai Cenang. Rooms are decked out with thoughtful design touches and techie amenities, as well as a small private garden or balcony. Various package deals are available, and rates can vary dramatically according to occupancy.

SWEET INN   Hotel $
(Map p155; 📞955 8864; r incl breakfast RM80-100; ❄️🛜) Super Sweet, actually: a cute orange building dotted with umbrella-shaded tables, plain rooms that manage to keep cool in the heat and a friendly common area where meeting fellow con-

gregants at the temple of backpacking is easy and breezy.

Pantai Tengah & Around

AMBONG AMBONG   Hotel $$$
(Map p155; 📞955 8428; www.ambong-among. com; ste incl breakfast RM685-1195; ❄️🛜🏊) This clutch of minimalist, contemporary structures on a jungly hillside results in a noteworthy and pleasing contrast. Choose between one of four inviting studio suites or one of the vast-feeling two-bedroom cottages; all are stylish and airy, have balconies overlooking the greenery, and a stay includes a complimentary massage. One of Langkawi's more sophisticated places to stay.

157

FRANGIPANI   Resort $$$

(Map p155; ☏ 952 0000; www.frangipanilang-
kawi.com; incl breakfast r RM700-1200, ste
RM1500-1800; ❄@🛜🏊) Friendly service,
genuine efforts towards ecological
conservation and the location right on a
quiet stretch of beach are the reasons to
stay at this vast resort, less so the slightly
cramped rooms.

Pantai Kok & Around

TANJUNG SANCTUARY   Resort $$$

(Map p152; ☏ 952 0222; www.tanjung
sanctuary.com.my; ste incl breakfast RM1000-
1300; ❄@🛜🏊) Wind through thick
jungle to emerge at a rocky headland and
this subtle, classy resort. The 16 duplex
villas are spacious and well appointed, but
we liked the resort's remote, almost wild
location, and the generous real estate
between villas. Recommended.

DANNA   Luxury Hotel $$$

(Map p152; ☏ 959 3288; www.thedanna.com; incl
breakfast r RM1400-1700, ste RM3000-20,000;
❄@🛜🏊) The imposing, colonial-
themed Danna seems intent on setting
a new standard for luxury on Langkawi.
Rooms are huge and come decked out
with attractive furniture and marble
floors, and the hotel boasts its own manufactured private island and Langkawi's
biggest hotel pool. The Danna has several
dining outlets of its own, but also has the
benefit of being next door to the dining
and nightlife options at Telaga Harbour
Park.

Teluk Datai

DATAI LANGKAWI   Resort $$$

(Map p152; ☏ 959 2500; www.thedatai.com.my;
incl breakfast r RM2300-3200, ste RM3300-
22,000; ❄@🛜🏊) Tucked into a jungly
corner in the far northwest of the island,
the Datai manages to feel both untamed
and luxurious. Choose between the spacious and modern rainforest or seafront
villas, all of which have access to a small
city's worth of amenities (spas, gyms,
yoga – the works), not to mention one of
the island's best beaches. A unique luxury
experience.

Left: Oriental Village (p150) and Gunung Machinchang; **Below:** Lagoon at Tanjung Rhu
(LEFT) RICHARD I'ANSON/GETTY IMAGES ©; (BELOW) RICHARD I'ANSON/GETTY IMAGES ©

Tanjung Rhu

TANJUNG RHU
RESORT Resort $$$
(Map p152; ☏959 1033; www.tanjungrhu.com. my; incl breakfast r RM1400-1600, ste RM1800-2800; ❄@☎☒) This beautifully situated resort has large and comfy rooms with balconies and great views of the limestone and green water at Tanjung Rhu. Service is a pleasant blend of competent and friendly, and the resort has a family-friendly vibe. The only real downside is its distance from virtually all of Langkawi's attractions, restaurants and nightlife.

 Eating

Pantai Cenang & Around

NAM International $$
(Map p152; ☏955 3643; mains RM30-74; ☺11am-11pm; ☑) At Bon Ton Resort (p156), Nam boasts a well-executed menu of fusion goodness, from char-grilled rack of lamb with roast pumpkin,

mint salad hummus and tomato jam, to a nine-course sampler of Straits Chinese cuisine. There are lots of veggie options, and at night, amid Bon Ton's starry jungle grounds, the setting is superb. Reservations recommended during peak season (December/January).

ORKID RIA Chinese $$$
(Map p155; dishes from RM12; ☺11.30am-3pm & 6-11pm) The place to go on Pantai Cenang for Chinese-style seafood. Fat shrimp, fish and crabs are plucked straight from tanks out front, and there's the added benefit of air-con. It don't come cheap though.

TOMATO Indian, Malay $
(Map p155; mains from RM4; ☺24hr) This, your typical Malaysian *kandar* (Indian-influenced dishes served over rice) joint, serves excellent rotis and a standard curry-rice Indian/Malay menu at all hours – take note, nighthawks.

159

If You Like...
Waterfalls

Langkawi's waterfalls are best viewed at the end of the monsoon season: late September and early October.

1 TEMURUN WATERFALL
(Map p152) In the northwest corner of the island and a brief walk from the main road, these falls are Langkawi's tallest. The turn-off is just east of a huge concrete archway spanning the road.

2 DURIAN PERANGIN
(Map p152) The waterfalls are located 3km off the 113 road, just south of Tanjung Rhu. The swimming pools, 10 minutes' walk up through the forest, are always refreshingly cool.

RED TOMATO   International $$
(Map p155; mains RM20-40; ⊙9am-11pm) The Red Tomato is run by expats who crank out some of the best pizza and pasta on the island. Of all the midrange places serving Western standards on the Cenang strip, this is probably your best bet.

PUTUMAYO   International $$
(Map p155; mains RM18-48; ⊙1-11pm) Excellent service (the waiter folds your napkin in your lap) amid a beautiful open-air courtyard. The cuisine ranges from across Asia, looping from Malaysia through Thailand to China; we highly recommend the fish cooked Nonya style.

Pantai Tengah & Around
HUNGRY MONKEY   Turkish $$
(Map p155; mains RM29-139; ⊙9.30am-11pm) Hungry Monkey features a cosy dining room, friendly service and a menu that extends far beyond döner kebab. We loved the Adana lamb kebab with eggplant dip which, like most dishes, was filling and tasty, and came served with a loaf of yeasty, home-made bread.

OSTERIA   Italian $$
(Map p155; mains RM25-56; ⊙noon-11pm) Favoured by local residents, this breezy, quasi open-air dining room serves wood-fired pizzas, home-made pasta and other Italian specialties. Osteria is at its sexy best when it's dark out, so consider a dinner visit.

Elsewhere on the Island
SITI FATIMAH   Malay $
(Map p152; Jln Kampung Tok Senik, Kawasan Mata Air; meals from RM5; ⊙8am-5pm Thu-Tue) Quite possibly Langkawi's most famous destination for Malay food – and for good reason. Food here is served buffet style, and it's up to you to choose from among the rich curries, grilled fish, dips, stir-fries and other dishes. The flavours are strong and the prices low. Siti Fatimah is located on Jln Kampung Tok Senik, the road that leads to Kota Mahsuri; most taxi drivers are familiar with the place.

ASHKIM   Turkish $$
(Map p152; ☏012-687 0494; Jln Padang Matsirat, Padang Matsirat; mains RM22-150; ⊙9.30am-11pm Mon-Sat, noon-11pm Sun) Run by an impossibly friendly Turkish-German couple, this is an unpretentious spot for homey Turkish and Mediterranean-style food. Expect kebabs, salads, mezze and fresh bread, much of which is made using imported ingredients. Ashkim is located on Jln Padang Matsirat, next door to the Atma Alam Batik Gallery; call for directions.

🍷 Drinking

As Langkawi is a duty-free island, it's arguably the best spot for booze in Malaysia. While you can get alcohol at many restaurants and hotels for half the price on the mainland, there are some decent beach-style bars here as well, most found along the southern end of Pantai Cenang.

LITTLE LYLIA'S CHILL OUT BAR   Bar
(Map p155; Pantai Cenang; ⊙9am-4am) This long-standing, chummy bar spills out on to Pantai Cenang until the late hours. The chairs and tables may be practically falling apart, but friendly service and a chilled-out vibe hold the place together.

CLIFF
Restaurant, Bar

(Map p155; www.thecliflangkawi.com; Pantai Cenang; ☺11am-11pm) Perched on the rocky outcrop that divides Pantai Cenang and Pantai Tengah, Cliff is located for a sunset cocktail. Expect a full bar, a good wine selection, and an eclectic dinner menu that spans from Europe to Malaysia (mains RM38 to RM68).

YELLOW CAFÉ
Restaurant, Bar

(Map p155; Pantai Cenang; ☺1pm-1am Tue-Sun) A fun, breezy place with tables right on the beach and a few imported beers Come between 4pm and 6pm when you can get two beers for the price of one.

BABYLON
Bar

(Map p155; Pantai Cenang; ☺4pm-1am) At a glance, this appears to be your typical beach reggae bar, but with a ful menu of cocktails, its own satay stall and two levels of seating, it emerges a bit more sophisticated than most.

LA SAL
Restaurant, Bar

(Map p155; www.casadelmar-langkawi.com; Casa del Mar, Pantai Cenang) Open-air restaurant/ cocktail bar with some creative drinks and a vague Euro vibe. Come evening,

tables in the sand and torchlight make La Sal a sexy sunset drink destination.

🛍 Shopping

If you haven't already noticed, Langkawi is a duty-free zone, and is a relatively cheap place to buy imported luxury goods, especially alcohol. The greatest conglomeration of duty-free shops is at the jetty in Kuah and at the southern end of Pantai Cenang, near Underwater World.

ATMA ALAM BATIK ART VILAGE
Handicrafts

(Map p152; www.atmaalam.com; Padang Matsirat; ☺9am-6pm) A huge handicraft complex with an emphasis on batik, all set to a funky karaoke-like soundtrack. Visitors can paint and take home their own swatch of batik for RM30. Atma Alam is located in Padang Matsirat, not far from the airport; most taxi drivers are familiar with it.

KOMPLEKS KRAF LANGKAWI
Handicrafts

(Map p152; www.malaysiacraft.com.my; Langkawi Craft Complex, Pantai Pasir Hitam; ☺10am-6pm)

Pantai Tengah (p154)

FELIX HUG/GETTY IMAGES ©

Don't Miss Langkawi's Roving Night Market

Local food can be a bit hard to find on Langkawi. Fortunately, for fans of Malay eats there's a rotating *pasar malam* (night market) held at various points across the island. It's a great chance to indulge in cheap, take-home meals and snacks, and is held from about 6pm to 10pm at the following locations:

Monday Jalan Makam Mahsuri Lama (Map p152), in the centre of the island, not far from the MARDI Agro Technology Park.

Tuesday Kedawang (Map p152), just east of the airport.

Wednesday & Saturday Kuah (Map p152), opposite the Masjid Al-Hana; this is the largest market.

Thursday Bohor Tempoyak (Map p155), at the northern end of Pantai Cenang.

Friday Padang Lalang (Map p152), at the roundabout near Pantai Pasir Hitam.

Sunday Padang Matsirat (Map p152), near the roundabout just north of the airport.

An enormous handicrafts centre where you can watch demonstrations of traditional crafts and buy any traditional Malaysian product or craft you can imagine. There are also a couple of on-site exhibitions devoted to local legends and wedding ceremonies. The complex is located in the far north of the island, virtually across from Pantai Pasir Hitam.

ⓘ Getting There & Away

Air

Langkawi International Airport (☎955 1311) is located in the west of the island at Padang Matsirat. It's well stocked with ATMs, exchange booths, car-rental agencies, travel agencies and, by the time you read this, a Tourism Malaysia office.

Boat

All passenger ferries operate from Kuah's busy ferry terminal. Several ferry providers, including **Langkawi Ferry Service** (LFS; ☎966 9439; www.langkawi-ferry.com), have merged and operate a shared ferry service to George Town, Penang. Other destinations include the following:

DESTINATION	TIME (HR)	FARE (RM, ADULT/ CHILD)	FREQUENCY
Kuala Perlis	1	18/13	Every 1½hr, 7.30am-6.30pm
Kuala Kedah	1½	23/17	Hourly, 7.30am-6.30pm
Satun (Thailand)	1½	30/23	9am, 1pm & 5.15pm
Ko Lipe (Thailand)	1½	118	9.15am (Oct-May only)
George Town	2½-3	60/45	2.30pm & 5.15pm

ALOR SETAR

◉ Sights

Some impressive buildings front the *padang* including the **Balai Besar** (Royal Audience Hall; Jln Sultan Muhaman Jiwa) state ceremonial building; the royal museum **Muzium Diraja** (Royal Museum; Jln Raja; ⊘9am-5pm Sat-Thu, 9am-12.30pm & 2.30-5pm Fri) and the **State Art Gallery** (Jln Sultan Muhaman Jiwa; ⊘9am-5pm).

MASJID ZAHIR Mosque
(Jln Sultan Muhaman Jiwa; ⊘7am-7pm) Masjid Zahir, Kedah state mosque, is one of the largest and most beautiful mosques in Malaysia. Built in 1912, it has a classical beauty, more of an apparition from *The Thousand and One Nights* than a smoothed-out modern Malaysian mosque. The building encloses the cemetery of Kedah warriors who fought the Thais in 1821.

Masjid Zahir

DANIELLE GALI/CORBIS ©

Detour:
Taman Negara Perlis

The small state park of Taman Negara Perlis, in the northwest of the state, runs for 36km along the Thai border, covering about 5000 hectares. It comprises the **Mata Ayer** and **Wang Mu** forest reserves, and the **Nakawan Range**, the longest continuous range of limestone hills in Malaysia.

Park highlights include its numerous cave systems – especially **Gua Wang Burma**, which has intriguing limestone formations – and Malaysia's only semideciduous forest.

The nearest town is Kaki Bukit from which a winding mountain road leads to the tiny village of Kampung Wang Kelian. The modern wooden chalets in the **park visitor centre** (☏945 7898; admission RM2; ☺9am-noon & 2-5pm), at Wang Kelian, 2km from the Thai border, are very comfortable. There's no restaurant, but staff can prepare food. Hire guides at the visitor centre (RM40 for four hours).

There is no public transport to the park. Buses to Kaki Bukit run from Kangar's local bus station every two hours from 8.45am to 6.45pm (RM4.20). A taxi to the park from Kangar will cost at least RM50.

FREE MUZIUM NEGERI Museum
(Lebuhraya Darul Aman; ☺10am-5pm Sat-Thu) The State Museum is 2km north of the *padang*. The small collection includes early Chinese porcelain, artefacts from archaeological excavations at Lembah Bujang and dioramas of royal and rural Malaysian life. A taxi from the town centre costs RM10.

MENARA ALOR STAR Tower
(Telekom Tower; www.menaraalorstar.com.my; Lebuhraya Darul Aman; admission adult/child RM10/5; ☺9am-10pm) If the Petronas Towers weren't enough for you in KL, the second-tallest tower in the country is the Menara Alor Star, which at 165.5m high is by far the tallest structure in town. A glass-sided lift will take you to the observation deck for good views of Alor Setar and the surrounding countryside.

WAT SIAM NIKRODHARAM Buddhist Temple
(Jln Stadium; ☺7am-4pm) Although Alor Setar has weathered Thai occupation, its main Buddhist community is Chinese in heritage. Thus the presence of this cross-cultural wat (Buddhist temple): typically Thai with its stupas and fire-in-the-lotus

imagery, yet scattershot with Chinese Buddhist saints, of import to the Chinese donors who funded the construction of this complex.

🛏 Sleeping

HOLIDAY VILLA Hotel **$$**
(☏734 9999; www.holidayvilla.com.my; 162 Jln Tunku Ibrahim; incl breakfast r RM300-440, ste RM630-2800; ❀@🛜🏊) This towering hotel adjoining the City Point Plaza shopping mall is easily the best place in town. It has spacious, tastefully furnished rooms with all the amenities, and a range of facilities, including a gym, a pool and a spa.

NEW REGENT Hotel **$$**
(☏731 5000; info.newregent@yahoo.com; 1536 Jln Sultanah Badlishah; incl breakfast r RM140-200, ste RM280; ❀🛜) A 2012 makeover has the exterior and lobby of this long-standing hotel looking downright sexy. The rooms, however, although clean, functional and relatively attractive, still carry traces of the slightly more utilitarian hotel that it used to be.

Eating

MUDA COFFEE SHOP　　　Chinese **$**
(111 Jln Pekan China; mains RM3-20; ⏲8pm-1am
Sat-Thu) We should start by making it clear
that this place is for adventurous eaters
only: the grumpy/indifferent staff don't
speak much English, and the highlight is
a dish of steamed fish head. But oh what
a fish head. Accompanied with *or mee*
(noodles fried with dark soy sauce) and
a beer, it was frankly one of the tastiest
meals we had in Malaysia.

KIM BEE CHEW　　　Malay **$**
(Jln Tunku Ibrahim; mains from RM5; ⏲breakfast
& lunch) Chinese coffee shop that's also
home to a popular *nasi kandar* vendor;
expect fragrant yellow rice topped with a
variety of rich curries.

ℹ Getting There & Away

Air

Sultan Abdul Halim Airport is 11km north of
town just off the Lebuhraya.

Bus

The tiny local bus station handles frequent
departures to Kuala Kedah (one hour, RM3), for
ferry access to Langkawi, from 7am to 10pm.

Ferry Warning

During the monsoon season, from
July to mid-September, you may
want to shelve any notions of taking
the ferry to Langkawi. During this
time of year, the seas are typically
very rough and the ferry ride (in
reality a large speedboat) can be a
terrifying experience.

The main bus terminal, Shahab Perdana, is
4km north of the town centre. A taxi there costs
RM10.

Train

The **train station** (Jln Stesyen) is southeast of the
town centre; check with www.ktmb.com.my for
the latest info on fares and schedules.

Getting Around

There is an informal **taxi stand** on Jln
Tunku Ibrahim. A taxi to/from the airport
costs RM20. The town centre is accessible on foot.

The Perhentians & the East Coast

Malaysia's east coast is beautiful, with many a lovely beach and bucolic *kampung* (village) well worth visiting. But what brings folks back to the region time and again are the tantalising islands offshore. 'Paradise' barely does these gems justice, though that'll likely be the word that comes to mind when you first lay eyes on the white sands and swaying palms of the Perhentians or Pulau Kapas. Snorkellers and scuba divers will find the coral and marine life beneath the azure waves second to none.

Inland, exchange the turtle-dotted lagoons and horseshoe bays of the islands for the lush green-blues of Tasik Kenyir, vine-shrouded in its jungle womb.

Cultural travellers, meanwhile, will find in cities like Kota Bharu and Kuala Terengganu a distinctively Malay vibe that's managed to remain fairly undiluted despite the nation's headlong rush to prosperity.

Kite-maker in Kota Bharu (p178)

167

Masjid Tengku Tengah Zaharah (p186)
PATRICE HAUSER/GETTY IMAGES ©

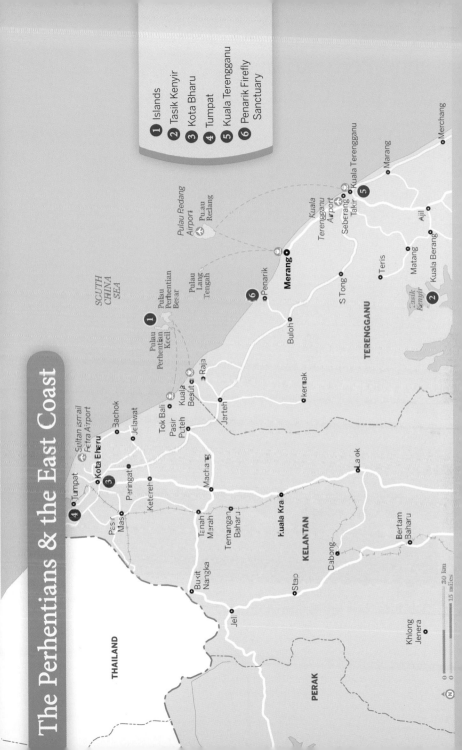

The Perhentians & the East Coast

THAILAND

PERAK

KELANTAN

TERENGGANU

SOUTH
CHINA
SEA

1 Islands
2 Tasik Kenyir
3 Kota Bharu
4 Tumpat
5 Kuala Terengganu
6 Penarik Firefly
  Sanctuary

Sultan Ismail
Petra Airport

Kuala
Terengganu
Airport

Kuala Terengganu

Pulau Redang
Airport

Pulau
Redang

Pulau Perhentian Besar
Pulau Perhentian Kecil

Pulau Lang Tengah

Penarik

Merang

Marang

Merchang

Ajil

Kuala Berang

Matang

Teris

S Tong

Buloh

Tasik
Kenyir

Seberang
Takir

Tumpat
Kota Bharu
Bachok
Jelawat
Paringat
Ketereh
Machang
Pasir Puteh
Tok Bali
Kuala Besut
Raja
Jerteh
Kemak

Pasir Mas

Tenah Merah
Temangan Baharu
Kuala Kra
La ok
Cabong

Bukit Nangka
Stap
Jeli
Bertam Baharu

Khlong Jenera

30 km
15 miles

N

The Perhentians &
the East Coast Highlights

1

Islands, Diving & Snorkelling

The aquamarine waters that lap at the east coast islands teem with tropical fish and corals that make them a magnet for diving and snorkelling enthusiasts. Among the rainbow array of sea creatures, you may spot turtles, stingray, parrotfish and black-tip reef sharks.

Top Right: Pulau Redang (p183); Bottom Right: Pulau Kapas (p185)

Need to Know

BEST TIME TO VISIT April to October **TOP TIP** Bring plenty of cash as there are no banks or ATMs on the islands **For further coverage, see p181.**

Islands, Diving & Snorkelling Don't Miss

BY DAVE HOGAN JR, TRAVEL WRITER,
HTTP://BLOG.MALAYSIA-ASIA.MY

1 PULAU PERHENTIAN

These islands have always been a popular destination for both locals and overseas travellers. Many budget-style to moderate resorts are available on **Perhentian Besar** and **Perhentian Kecil** islands. Activities include diving, snorkelling and just relaxing. There are no roads or vehicles so everyone moves around via foot or boat here. Chances of spotting turtles while snorkelling are high and there are many excellent scuba diving spots. One of my favourite places to stay is **Coral View Island Resort** (p184) on Perhentian Besar. It's run by a local Malay family, has some pretty interesting features and is located in between two beaches with a great view.

2 REDANG ISLAND MARINE PARK

There are nine islands gazetted as part of the **Redang Island Marine Park**, all accessible from **Pulau Redang** (p183). One of my favourite for snorkelling is **Pulau Pinang**, a beautiful island with no resorts, chalets or villages. When I came here the skies were amazingly blue with puffy white clouds, and I was in awe when I saw how clear the waters were. Tours from Pulau Redang will bring you here but I just hired a boat for RM250 per day and the friendly boatman took me anywhere I wanted to go. Just 15ft from the beach, coral fishes swim freely with snorkellers and everywhere I looked in the waters there were shoals of colourful fishes swimming about happily.

3 PULAU KAPAS

Serene on the weekdays, this tiny **island** (p185), half an hour by boat from Marang, becomes overrun with day trippers on holidays and long weekends, and actually shuts down during the monsoon season (November to March). Just offshore, even smaller **Pulau Gemia** has just one place to stay, the **Gem Wellness Spa & Island Resort**, where there's a green turtle hatchery.

Tasik Kenyir

The construction of the Kenyir Dam in 1985 flooded some 2600 sq km of jungle, creating Southeast Asia's largest manufactured **lake** (p190), with clumps of wild overgrowth gasping over the water's surface. Fishing is a popular activity and the lake is surprisingly rich in species, including *toman* (snakehead), *buang* (catfish), *kelah* (a kind of carp), *kelisa* (green arowana) and *kalui* (giant gouramy).

Kota Bharu

A logical overnight stop between Thailand and the Perhentians, **Kota Bharu** (or KB as it's known locally, p178) is a good base for exploring Kelantan on physical and cultural levels, as the state's villages are within day-tripping distance, and its crafts and culture are present in the city itself. Tour the museums around the central **Padang Merdeka** and you'll come away a semi-expert in Malay culture and history. Traditional spinning top at Kota Bharu's Gelanggang Seni (p181, Cultural Centre)

Tumpat

North of Kota Bharu, the **Tumpat district** (p183) is Malaysia's culturally porous hinterland, neither wholly Malay nor Thai, with a dash of Chinese culture thrown in for good measure. Buddhist temples are numerous and include **Wat Phothivihan**, one of the largest such temples in Southeast Asia. Wesak Day (a celebration of Buddha's life, usually held in April or May) is a particularly good time to visit.

Kuala Terengganu

With seafood-heavy local cuisine and good transport links, the state capital of **Kuala Terengganu** (p186) is worth a day or two in between the islands and jungles. Wander around the compact Chinatown, go craft shopping and head slightly out of town to explore the state museum **Kompleks Muzium Negeri Terengganu** (p188); there's a cluster of traditional houses here that's worth the price of admission alone. Komplex Muzium Negeri Terengganu

Penarik Firefly Sanctuary

In the mangroves around the coastal Terengganu town of **Penarik** (p189) you can view the unusual sight of thousands of fireflies blinking in near-perfect synchronisation, a phenomenon unique to the area. Sex-crazed entomologists naturally suspect mating habits. The fireflies are best viewed on the darkest of nights (so not at full moon); the boat trip through the ghostly and ethereal mangrove forest is unforgettable.

The Perhentians & the East Coast's Best...

Beaches

○ **Long Beach** (p182) *The* spot if you want to party on Pulau Perhentian Kecil, this is arguably the island's most attractive beach.

○ **Teluk Kerma** (p183) Also on Kecil, but more isolated and home to only one resort.

○ **Main Beach** (p181) Pulau Perhentian Besar's top sand strip with a great family vibe.

Temples & Mosques

○ **Wat Phothivihan** (p183) Contemplate nirvana in front of a 40m-long reclining Buddha statue in the Tumpat district.

○ **Masjid Tengku Tengah Zaharah** (p186) Admire the Moorish beauty of this 'floating mosque' outside Kuala Terengganu.

○ **Taman Tamadu Islam** (p189) This miniature architecture park of famous Islamic landmarks also houses the full-sized glass and steel Crystal Mosque.

Local Cuisine

○ **Night Market** (p180) Say *'Suka pedas'* ('I like it hot') to eat as the locals do at this Kota Bharu institution.

○ **Santai Restaurant** (p182) Tuck into the best seafood BBQ on the Perhentians.

○ **West Lake Eating House** (p180) Serves some of the tastiest Chinese food on the east coast.

Need to Know

Craft Markets & Shops

o **Central Market, Kota Bharu** (p180) One of Malaysia's most colourful and active; head upstairs for brassware and batik.

o **Wanisma Craft & Trading** (p189) For batik dyed fabrics and brasswork crafted on the spot.

o **Kraftangan Malaysia** (p189) Admire the intricate silver and gold thread patterns of *kain songket* (handwoven fabric).

VITAL STATISTICS
o **Area code** ✎09

ADVANCE PLANNING

o **One month before** Book accommodation and buy discount flights to Kota Bharu.

o **One week before** Book your dive trip.

o **One day before** Check on local festivals and traditional culture shows.

RESOURCES
o **Ping Anchorage** (www.pinganchorage.com.my) This acclaimed tour-company's site provides an abundance of travel ideas.

o **Perhentian Island** (www.perhentian.com.my) Comprehensive details on what to do on the islands.

o **Tourism Terengganu** (http://tourism.terengganu.gov.my) Official state tourism site.

GETTING AROUND
o **Boat** Speedboats will take you out to the islands, although less so during the rainy season (November to Februrary).

o **Bus** A good way to get between urban centres along east-coast and inland destinations.

o **Taxis & shared taxis** Faster and with more flexible options than the bus.

o **Train** From Tumpat, just across the Thai border, the 'jungle railway' runs through Kuala Krai, Gua Musang, Kuala Lipis and Jerantut, the access point for Taman Negara. The nearest station to Kota Bharu is Wakaf Baharu.

BE FOREWARNED
o **Dive trips** Book your trip directly through a dive shop.

o **Rainy season** The monsoon season here runs from November to February; during this time many island operations shut down.

o **Drownings** Look out for the rip tides of Pulau Perhentian Kecil's Long Beach.

o **Sunbathing** This is a conservative Malay region so no topless sunbathing for women.

o **Mosques** Dress respectfully (shoes off, shoulders and legs covered) if you visit a mosque.

o **Cash** There are no banks or ATMs on the islands – bring plenty of cash.

Left: Crystal Mosque, Taman Tamadu Islam (p189);
Above: Pulau Perhentian (p181)

175

The Perhentians & the East Coast Itineraries

Grab some rays and snorkel for two days on the Perhentians if you're in a hurry; with more time to spare, savour the coast then journey inland to Tasik Kenyir.

3 DAYS

KOTA BHARU TO PULAU PERHENTIAN
Perhentian Pop Over

Fly to **(1) Kota Bharu**. In this devoutly Muslim city you can learn about its Malay heritage and traditions at the various museums around Padang Merdeka – the best one is in the Istana Jahar. Time your stay for a Monday, Wednesday or Saturday between February and September and you should be able to see free cultural performances, including displays of local martial arts and shadow puppet plays, at the Gelanggang Seni.

Colourful traditional markets selling food and crafts are another highlight of Kota Bharu; make sure you dine with locals on the best and cheapest Malay food at the night market.

Take an early morning taxi to **(2) Kuala Besut** where speedboats wait to make the 40-minute shuttle out to the Perhentians, a pair of islands that tick all the boxes marked paradise. Base yourself on **(3) Pulau Perhentian Besar** where you can relax on the relatively quiet beaches fringing Teluk Dalam, or go hiking through the dense jungle.

Spend a day beach-hopping around **(4) Pulau Perhentian Kecil** and going on a diving or snorkelling trip. End the day with sundowners and a meal at vibey Long Beach.

6 DAYS

PENARIK TO TASIK KENYIR
East Coast Essence

Fresh off the boat from the Perhentians In **(1) Kuala Besut**, head south by taxi to the sleepy coastal village of **(2) Penarik**. During the day you can enjoy the windswept beaches and chill out at Terrapuri Heritage Village, an eye-candy resort made up of painstakingly restored antique houses. The real magic comes after nightfall, on the tour boats that float through the ethereal mangroves illuminated by thousands of fireflies.

Continue south to **(3) Merang**, the jumping-off point for **(4) Pulau Redang**; booking a package is the best deal for visiting this blissfully pretty island sporting several comfortable resorts and quiet beaches. At the heart of a marine park, it's also a great diving and snorkelling destination.

Explore the scattered attractions around **(5) Kuala Terengganu**. The city itself offers Islamic hospitality, Malay friendliness and a picturesque Chinatown. Highlights include the Kompleks Muzium Negeri Terengganu, and the centuries-old boat-building techniques still practised at Pulau Duyung.

Turn inland and spend a day and a night at **(6) Tasik Kenyir**, Southeast Asia's largest manufactured lake, dotted with over 300 islands.

Pulau Perhentian Besar (p181)

Discover the Perhentians & the East Coast

Central Market (p180), Kota Bharu
PAUL KENNEDY/GETTY IMAGES ©

KOTA BHARU

Kota Bharu (KB) has the energy of a midsized city, the compact feel and friendly vibe of a small town, superb food and a good spread of accommodation. Kelantan's villages are within day-tripping distance, and its crafts and culture are present in the city itself.

 Sights

ISTANA JAHAR — Museum
(Royal Ceremonies Museum; Map p179; Jln Istana; adult/child RM3/1.50; ⏱8.30am-4.45pm Sat-Thu) An achingly beautiful chocolate-brown building, dating back to 1887, houses displays focusing on Kelatanese ritual and crafts, from detailed descriptions of batik-weaving to the elaborate ceremonies that once marked the life of local youth.

ISTANA BATU — Museum
(Royal Museum; Map p179; Jln Istana; adult/child RM2/1; ⏱8.30am-4.45pm Sat-Thu) This museum was once the crown prince's palace. The richly furnished rooms give a surprisingly intimate insight into royal life.

 Tours

Most hostels organise tours for their guests. Apart from city tours possible itineraries include the following:

- two-day/three-night expeditions into the jungle around Gua Musang (RM250 to RM350)

- boat trips up small local rivers into sleepy fishing villages where silk kites are made by candlelight (RM60 to RM80)

Kota Bharu

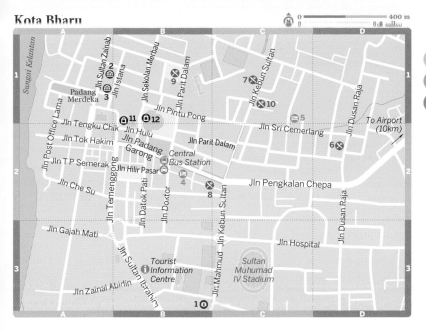

Kota Bharu

⦿ Sights

1	Gelanggang Seni	B3
2	Istana Batu	A1
3	Istana Jahar	A1

⊟ Sleeping

4	KB Backpackers Lodge	B2
5	Zeck's Traveller's Inn	C1

⊗ Eating

6	Four Seasons	D2

7	Medan Selera Kebun Sultan Food Court	C1
8	Nasi Air Hideng Pok Sen Food Court	B2
9	Night Market	B1
10	West Lake Eating House	C1

⦿ Shopping

11	Bazaar Buluh Kubu	B1
12	Central Market	B1

○ two-hour tours of the Tumpat temples (RM75)

○ half-day craft tours (RM90 to 115).

 **Sleeping**

ZECK'S TRAVELLER'S INN   Homestay **$**
(Map p179; ☑743 1613; 7088-G Jln Sri Cemerlan; dm/s/d from RM10/15/25, air-con 45-60; ✱@🛜) Zeck and Miriam ('call me mama') Zaki's home is located in a peaceful nook north of the city centre, with an attractive little garden to lounge about in and light meals and drinks always at hand. Friendly and social, this family-owned and -run place is a great way to get a feel for genuine Malaysian *kampung* (village) life in the heart of Kota Bharu.

**KB BACKPACKERS
LODGE**   Budget Hotel, Hostel **$**
(Map p179; ☑019-944 5222, 748 8841; www.kb-backpackers.com.my; 1872-D Jln Padang Garong; dm/r from RM8/20; ✱@) KB's rooms are only so-so (the bigger the better is the rule). But owner Pawi is so helpful and a

179

If You Like…
Quick Eats

In KB you can eat well (and cheaply) without ever setting foot into a restaurant.

1 NIGHT MARKET
(Map p179; Jln Pintu Pong) Stalls are set up here around 5pm and stay open past midnight. Specialities include *ayam percik* (marinated chicken on bamboo skewers) and *nasi kerabu* (rice with coconut, fish and spices), blue rice, squid-on-a-stick and *murtabak* (pan-fried flat bread filled with everything from minced meat to bananas).

2 NASI AIR HIDENG POK SEN FOOD COURT
(Map p179; Jln Padang Garong) Offers Malay specialities, a self-serve buffet, coffee, iced beverages and screenings of movies in an open-air setting.

3 MEDAN SELERA KEBUN SULTAN FOOD COURT
(Map p179; ✆746 1632; Jln Kebun Sultan; mains from RM3; ⏱lunch & dinner) Try Chinese dishes like claypot chicken rice and *kway teow* (rice-flour noodles). Also serves beer.

wealth of information, and the vibe at his hostel is so internationally chill in the way that made us love backpacking in the first place, that it more than makes up for it.

 Eating

WEST LAKE EATING HOUSE   Chinese $
(Map p179; Jln Kebun Sultan; mains from RM5; ⏱10am-8pm; ✐) Don't let the plain-looking decor and plastic chairs fool you. West Lake may well serve some of the tastiest Chinese fare in eastern Malaysia, thanks to a particularly talented chef who works ceaselessly in the tiny kitchen.

FOUR SEASONS   Chinese $$
(Map p179; www.fourseasonsrestaurant.com.my; 5670 Jln Sri Cemerlang; mains from RM15; ⏱lunch & dinner) The Four Seasons is packed nightly with locals enjoying

seafood dishes like claypot prawn and dry cuttlefish with mango salad. Sold by weight, the house speciality, deep-fried soft-shell crab, should only set you back about RM40 for two people.

Shopping

Batik, *kain songket* (cloth brocaded with gold and silver), silverware, wood-carving and kite-making factories and shops are dotted around town.

CENTRAL MARKET   Market
(Pasar Besar Siti Khadijah; Map p179; Jln Hulu; ⏱6am-6pm) One of the most colourful and active markets in Malaysia. At its busiest first thing in the morning, and has usually packed up by early afternoon. Downstairs is the produce section, while upstairs stalls selling spices, brassware, batik and other goods stay open longer.

BAZAAR BULUH KUBU   Handicrafts
(Map p179; Jln Hulu; ⏱Sat-Thu) The bazaar is a good place to buy handicrafts such as batik, traditional Malay clothing and jewellery.

ℹ Getting There & Away

Air
Flights take off from Sultan Ismail Petra Airport , 8km outside of the city centre.

Bus
Most buses operate from the central bus station. A few buses also leave from Lembah Sireh Bus Station near the Kota Bharu Tesco. Since these change from time to time it's best to ask your guesthouse or the tourist information centre where your bus leaves from.

Car
Hire cars from Hawk (✆773 3824; Sultan Ismail Petra Airport).

Taxi
The taxi stand is on the southern side of the central bus station. Avoid the unlicensed cab drivers who will pester you here and elsewhere around town, and take an official taxi as these are cheaper and safer.

Train

The nearest station is Wakaf Baharu. KTM has a ticket office (counter 5) at Kota Bharu's Jln Hamzah bus station.

PULAU PERHENTIAN

The Perhentians are a tropical paradise, boasting waters simultaneously electric teal and crystal clear; jungles thick and fecund, and beaches with sand so white from a distance it might pass for snow. Most people come to snorkel, dive or do nothing at all.

There are two main islands: Kecil ('Small'), popular with the younger backpacker crowd, and Besar ('Large'), with higher standards of accommodation and a quieter, more relaxed ambiance. The quick hop between the two costs around RM20.

While you can usually find a beach party, the Perhentians are a long way from having a Thai-style party atmosphere. Alcohol is available at many restaurants.

Activities

Hiking

On Kecil, the jungle track between Long Beach and Coral Bay is an easy, signposted 15-minute walk. A longer track runs mostly along the shore between Coral Bay and Pasir Petani.

Besar has excellent hiking, including a long and hilly track cutting nothwest from Teluk Dalam to perhaps the best beach on the islands, a beautiful half-moon bay with good coral around on either side,

Sleeping & Eating

Besar

MAIN BEACH

REEF CHALETS Chalet **$$**
(Map p182; ✆691 1762, 019-981 6762; chalets RM100-290; ❄🛜) An absolute find, this family-owned chalet resort offers 12 beautiful chalets set along the beach and surrounding a beautifully maintained jungle garden featuring feather-soft grass and trees filled with lemurs, monkeys, birds and bats.

ABDUL'S CHALETS Chalet **$$**
(Map p182; ✆019-912 7303; www.abdulchalet. com; s/d from RM80/260; ❄🛜) Humble Abdul's has undergone a fairly substantial renovation since our last visit; Abdul's still has fan-cooled huts for RM80, but now there's a bevy of higher-grade accommodation, from Garden View chalets with air-con for RM150 up to a full air-con, seaview family room for RM240 and sea-view suites (with TV to compete with the sea view) for RM260.

TELUK DALAM

FLORA BAY RESORT Chalet **$$**
(Map p182; ✆691 1666; www.florabayresort. com; r RM60-210; ❄@🛜) The aptly named Flora Bay (flowers abound!) has a variety of options at the back of the beach, ranging from hill-view fan huts for RM60 to 'deluxe' air-con beach chalets for 210.

Flora 2 (Map p182), an extension of Flora Bay, is a little further along the beach, with a smaller range of pretty much identical chalets, but only Flora 1 has wireless.

Kecil

LONG BEACH

BUBU RESORT   Resort $$$
(Map p182; ☎03-2142 6688, in KL; www.bubu-resort.com.my; Long Beach; r from RM415; ❄ ☎)
At the northern end of the bay, this top-

end option offers 38 rooms in a modern, three-storey setting overlooking Long Beach itself and a gorgeous restaurant in *palapa* style (open-sided, with a thatched roof made of dried palm leaves). **Santai Restaurant** is the highest-end eatery on Kecil, serving – in our opinion – the best seafood BBQ in eastern Malaysia.

D'ROCK GARDEN RESORT   Chalet $$
(Map p182; ☎0123 252162; Long Beach; d with/without bathroom from RM120/45, deluxe r

Pulau Perhentian

Pulau Perhentian

🛏 Sleeping
1 Abdul's Chalets B4
2 Bubu Resort A2
3 Chalets @ The World Cafe A2
4 Coral View Island Resort B3
5 D'Lagoon Chalets A1

6 D'Rock Garden Resort A2
7 Flora 2 .... C4
8 Flora Bay Resort C4

🍴 Eating
9 Reef Chalets B3

Detour:
Tumpat's Temples

North of Kota Bharu, the Tumpat district is dotted with numerous Buddhist temples. The best way of getting around is to hire a local tour guide.

At Kampung Jambu the massive **Wat Phothivihan** offers a 40m-long reclining Buddha statue, smaller shrines, a canteen and a resthouse for pilgrims.

Wat Kok Seraya, about 1km outside Chabang Empat, houses a modest standing female Buddha. While the temple's architecture is Thai, the female Buddha is more Chinese.

Continuing north about 4km towards Tumpat, you will come to **Wat Pikulthong**, housing an impressive gold mosaic standing Buddha.

Near Kampung Bukit Tanah the 'floating temple' **Wat Maisuwankiri** is a richly decorated dragon boat surrounded by a channel of murky water. Inside the preserved body of a former abbot is kept on somewhat morbid public display.

RM325) Cheaper rooms are fan cooled, and only the deluxe have hot showers. The position of the huts (even the cheaper ones) overlooking the long sweep of Long Beach is fabulous.

CHALETS @ THE WORLD
CAFE   Chalet $$$
(Map p182; ☎016 260 3540; chalet d from RM450; ✲ 🖥) The six air-conditioned chalets have private terraces, hot-water showers and huge, comfortable beds. Even if you're not staying here, it's worth a visit to the World Cafe, a *palapa* restaurant sitting on the beach and serving coffee, cocktails and an eclectic mix of European foods.

TELUK KERMA

D'LAGOON CHALETS   Hut $
(Map p182; ☎019-985 7089; Teluk Kerma; camp site RM10, dm RM20, chalet RM60; tr RM150) The folks at D'Lagoon have taken full advantage of their position as the bay's sole spot to create something right out of Peter Pan. Accommodation ranges from a longhouse with dorm beds to simple chalets on stilts to a honeymoon treehouse. Among the activities on offer are snorkelling, shark- and turtle-watching trips, jungle hikes to remote beaches, and the island's only zip line.

🛈 Getting There & Away
Speedboats (adult/child RM70/35 return, 30-40mins) run several times a day between Kuala Besut and the Perhentians from 8.30am to 5.30pm, although you can expect delays or cancellations if the weather is bad or if there aren't enough passengers. The boats will drop you off at any of the beaches.

In the other direction, speedboats depart from the islands daily at about 8am, noon and 4pm. It's a good idea to let the owner of your guesthouse know a day before you leave so they can arrange a pick-up. If the water is rough or tides are low you may be ferried from the beach on a small boat to your mainland-bound craft; you'll have to pay around RM3 for this.

PULAU REDANG

Redang's position within a marine park lends itself to excellent diving and snorkelling, and you can easily lose yourself in between the golden sunlight, cackling jungle and lapping waves. Unfortunately, it's difficult to visit outside of package tours, which tend to be regimented affairs with arrival lectures and set times for meals, snorkelling and 'leisure'.

There is a RM5 conservation fee for entering the marine reserve, usually payable at your resort.

MICHAEL AW/GETTY IMAGES ©

Don't Miss Diving & Snorkelling

There are coral reefs off both Besar and Kecil and around the nearby uninhabited islands, Pulau Susu Dara in particular. The best bets for snorkelling off the coast are the northern end of Long Beach on Kecil, and the point in front of **Coral View Island Resort** (Map p182; ☏ 697 4943; www.coralviewislandresort.com; r/ste from RM140/550; ❄ @) on Besar. You can swim out to a living coral reef right in front of Tuna Bay Island Resort on Besar. Most chalets organise snorkelling trips for around RM40 per person (more or less depending on the size of the group) and also rent out equipment.

For scuba divers there are several operations on both islands; prices are pretty uniform. At the time of research, open-water certification went from RM850 to RM1100, while dives cost around RM80 to RM125, with discounts for multiple dives. Many operators run dive excursions out to Pulau Redang.

Sleeping & Eating

Tour companies sell packages for all the Perhentians' resorts, and several resorts have offices in Kuala Terengganu.

CORAL REDANG ISLAND RESORT
Resort $$

(☏ 630 7110; www.coralredang.com.my; s/d chalets per night from RM239/319; ❄) This resort towards the northern end of the beach has undergone a major renovation. A wide variety of snorkelling/diving packages starting at RM585/785 per person are on offer at the attached dive centre, including equipment, all meals and two nights' accommodation (based on two people sharing a room) .

REDANG HOLIDAY BEACH VILLA
Villa $$

(☏ 624 5500; www.redangholiday.com; r from RM399, garden/seaview chalet 499/549; ❄ 🛜) This welcoming villa features a series of smart duplex chalets climbing the rocks (chalets S13 and S14 have the best outlooks).

ℹ️ Getting There & Away

Package tours include boat transfer to the island. Independent travellers can hitch a ride on one of the resort boats (adult/child RM100/50), but in the high season (April to September) room-only deals will be scarce. Ferries run from the string of jetties along the river in Merang. Ferries also run from Shahbandar jetty in downtown Kuala Terengganu, but are less frequent and must generally be arranged via your resort. A schedule for all resort ferries can be found at www.redang.org/transport.htm.

Redang's airport is near the Berjaya Redang Beach Resort; Berjaya Air (☎630 8866; www.berjaya-air.com) has daily flights to Kuala Lumpur, Kuala Terengganu and Singapore.

PULAU KAPAS

Pretty Pulau Kapas has something for everybody. Practically all accommodation is concentrated on three small beaches on the west coast, but you can walk or kayak to quieter beaches if you're so inclined.

🤸 Activities

Kapas is a snorkelling paradise, with the best coral on the less accessible beaches on the northern end and around tiny Pulau Gemia. North of Gemia, a sunken WWII Japanese landing craft, now carpeted in coral, is a popular dive site.

Resorts here can arrange snorkelling and diving trips. The only dive shop on Kapas is **Aqua-Sport Divers** (☎019-983 5879; www.divekapas.com); it charges RM110/180 for one/two dives, including equipment. Trips out to the Japanese wreck are RM150, and snorkelling costs RM30 for a session.

🛏️ Sleeping & Eating

KAPAS TURTLE VALLEY   Resort $$
(☎013-354 3650; www.kapasturtlevalley. com; bungalow incl breakfast RM170-360 ; 🛜)

❤️ If You Like...
Beaches

With an abundance of amazing beaches, your biggest dilemma on the Perhentians may well be choosing the right one.

1 **LONG BEACH**
(Map p182; Pasir Panjang; Kecil) The Perhentians' prettiest beach and the partiest vibe, but can sometimes feel a bit over-touristed.

2 **CORAL BAY**
(Map p182; Aur Bay; Kecil) Most of the resorts on this sheltered beach within walking distance of Long Beach are open year-round. Coral Bay is more rocky than sandy, and an ongoing construction boom threatens to diminish the quaintness of this once-quiet spot.

3 **MAIN BEACH**
(Map p182; Besar) A good selection of accommodation and a long stretch of white sand that's almost as lovely (and less prone to currents) as Long Beach. There's more of a family vibe happening on the big island than elsewhere.

4 **TELUK DALAM**
(Map p182; Besar) This circular bay has white-sand beaches and excellent accommodation in all budget ranges. There are a few good restaurants, and good snorkelling spots on the bay's western edge.

Located in a nook on the Kapas' southern end, Sylvia and Peter's Turtle Valley Resort is a hidden gem. The couple's eight bungalows – all beautifully furnished and festooned with colourful local batiks – sit over a quiet, protected white-sand beach perfect for swimming, lounging and even snorkelling. There's an excellent on-site restaurant.

ℹ️ Getting There & Away

Boats (return RM40) leave from Marang's main jetty. MGH Boat Service (☎013-915 9748) offers discounted tickets for groups of six or more. Be sure to arrange a pick-up time when you purchase your ticket. You can usually count on morning departures at around 8am and 9am.

KUALA TERENGGANU

A microcosm of Malaysia's economic explosion, Kuala Terengganu is surprisingly attractive despite the number of newly built (with petro-wealth), sterile-looking skyscrapers. There's a boardwalk, a couple of decent beaches, a few old *kampung*-style houses hidden among the high rises, and one of Eastern Peninsular Malaysia's prettiest Chinatowns. A couple of the best sights are a few kilometres outside the city.

◉ Sights

CHINATOWN Neighbourhood
(Map p187) Tiny (but more picturesque for its small size) Chinatown is the most interesting area to explore. There are atmospheric, watermarked buildings and faded alleyways clotting this small neighbourhood, which is centred on Jln Kampung Cina (also known as Jln Bandar). The oldest Chinese temple in the state, **Ho Ann Kiong** (Map p187), is a compact explosion of vibrant red and gold dating from the early 1800s.

CENTRAL MARKET Market
(Map p187; Jln Sultan Zainal Abidin) For fish so fresh it's still in its death flop, look for the boats docking at the central market. Besides indulging your piscatorial fix, there's a good collection of batik and *kain songket*.

**MASJID TENGKU TENGAH
ZAHARAH** Mosque
The most famous religious structure in the state is the 'Floating Mosque', located 4.5km southeast of Kuala Terengganu. It's not really floating, just set on a man-made island, but its white, traditional Moorish design is beautifully blinding in the strong daylight, and warmly enchanting as the sun sets. Bus 13 from Kuala Terengganu will drop you outside (RM1).

Tours

Popular tours include day trips to Tasik Kenyir (from RM189), river cruises and packages to Pulau Redang. Going in groups reduces individual rates. Recommended operators include **Ping Anchorage** (Map p187; 🖉 626 2020; www.

Reclining Buddha at Wat Phothivihan, Tumpat (p183)

Kuala Terengganu

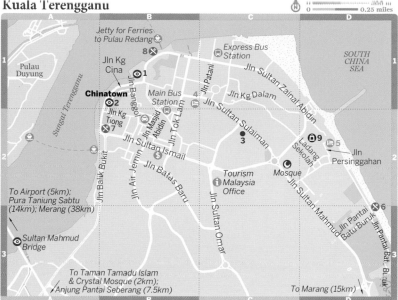

Kuala Terengganu

pinganchorage.com.my; 77A Jln Sultan Sulaiman)
and **Heritage One Stop Travel & Tours**
(Map p187; ☏ 631 6468; www.heritageonestop.
com.my; Blok Teratai, Jln Sultan Sulaiman).

Sleeping

PRIMULA BEACH RESORT   Resort $$
(Map p187; ☏ 622 2100; www.primulahotels.
com; Jln Persinggahan; s/d/ste RM280/280/650;
✱@☎) This seafront hotel with spa-
cious, attractively furnished rooms
includes some outstanding suites with

four-poster beds and multiple balconies.
It has a few very good restaurants and the
best coffee bar in town.

**PING ANCHORAGE
TRAVELLERS' INN**   Budget Hotel $
(Map p187; ☏ 626 2020; www.pinganchorage.
com.my; 77A Jln Sultan Sulaiman; r RM25-65;
☎) Spread over two floors above the
travel agency of the same name, Ping is
a budget standby. Rooms are clean and
tidy, with more expensive ones offering
air-conditioning and large windows. The
inn's antique-filled rooftop cafe, which

187

Don't Miss **Kompleks Muzium Negeri Terengganu**

Exhibits at Terengganu's state museum range from the historically interesting (a Jawi – traditional Malay text – inscription that essentially dates the arrival of Islam to the nation) to the mildly bizarre (a wildlife exhibit featuring taxidermy that's seen better decades) to corporate propaganda (an exhibit touting the goodness of the oil industry). The museum comprises a series of interconnected buildings on 26 hectares of land; the complex of traditional houses that fronts the grounds is worth the price of admission. English signage is sparse, however. To get here, take minibus 10 (RM1), marked 'Muzium/Losong', from Kuala Terengganu's main bus station. A taxi will cost RM20.

NEED TO KNOW

Terengganu State Museum Complex; ☎ 622 1433; http://museum.terengganu.gov.my; adult/child RM15/10; ⏰ 9am-5pm Sat-Thu

---

serves beer and food with a spectacular view of the city, is worth a visit.

 **Eating & Drinking**

Fish plays a big role in local cuisine, but the real local speciality is *kerepok*: a grey concoction of deep-fried fish paste and sago, usually moulded into sausages. The beachfront **night market** (Map p187) every Friday evening is a great place to sample *kerepok*, satay and sweets.

T. HOMEMADE CAFE Chinese, Malay $
(Map p187; Jln Kampung Cina; mains from RM5; ⏰lunch & dinner) Right next to the Chinatown gate, this place is actually a sort of cooperative conglomeration of a few food stalls in a shared space; you can get Chinese and Malay dishes here, as well as clay pots and refreshing, homemade juices.

TERAPUNG PUTERI Malay $
(Map p187; Jln Sultan Zainal Abidin; mains from RM5; ⏰lunch & dinner) This busy Malay

restaurant is perched on stilts, *kampung*-style, on the seafront next to the jetty. There's a huge menu, with fish, prawns and crab featuring heavily, as well as local items, such as *kerepok,* and a few Western dishes.

🔒 Shopping

Batik and *kain songket* are particularly good buys.

KRAFTANGAN MALAYSIA Handicrafts
(📞622 6458; ⏰9am-5pm Sun-Thu) About 4.5km south of town, this outlet sells high-quality *kain songket* costing as much as RM12,000 for 2.5 sq m.

**WANISMA CRAFT &
TRADING** Handicrafts
(Map p187; 📞622 3311; 32 Ladang Sekolah; ⏰9.30am-6.30pm) You can watch the stilled craftspeople at this batik-dyeing and brass workshop.

ℹ️ Getting There & Away

Air
Malaysia Airlines (📞662 6600; www.malaysiaairlines.com) and AirAsia (📞32 171 9333; www.airasia.com) both have direct flights to KL. Firefly (📞7845 4543; airport) offers flights to Singapore, and Berjaya Air (📞630 2228; www.berjaya-air.com) flies to Redang. All have offices inside the Kuala Terengganu airport.

Bus
Head to the express bus station for long-distance services.

Taxi
The main taxi stand is near the local bus station, but taxis can be found throughout the city. Some long-distance taxis leave from Jln Masjid Abidin.

ℹ️ Getting Around

A taxi to the airport costs around RM28. Local buses leave from the main bus station.

The Heritage City Shuttle Town Bus goes to all of the major sites in and around town and runs

Detour:
Taman Tamadu Islam

Touted as the world's first 'Islamic civilisation park', **Taman Tamadu Islam** (📞627 8888; www.tti.com.my; admission RM15; ⏰10am-7pm Mon-Thu, 9am-7pm Fri-Sun), 2.5km west of Kuala Terengganu, is essentially a series of miniature models of famous Islamic landmarks from across the world, including Jerusalem's Dome of the Rock and Mecca's Masjid al-Haram. The highlight of the park is the Crystal Mosque. Widely considered among the world's most beautiful mosques, it features a particularly striking steel, glass and crystal exterior. The Heritage Bus runs here, and a taxi will cost around RM15.

through the main bus station on an hourly basis for RM1 per trip.

Taxis around town cost a minimum of RM5. There are also a few bicycle rickshaws plying their trade through town. Prices are highly negotiable.

PENARIK

With its windswept beach and charmingly low-key population of farmers and fisher folk, the village of Penarik is as lovely a spot for a taste of coastal Malaysian culture as you could wish for. But for something truly magical, stick around until the sun goes down and charter a boat to take you down the Penarik river for a journey through the **Penarik Firefly Sanctuary**, where, on certain nights (the darker the better) you'll be treated to thousands of fireflies blinking in near-perfect synchronisation.

Sleeping

TERRAPURI HERITAGE VILLAGE Resort **$$$**
(☏624 5020; www.terrapuri.com; house RM399-RM1099; ⏰minimum 2 nights; 🛜🏊)
To step onto the beautifully manicured grounds of Terrapuri Heritage Village is like entering a set-piece for a film about the lives of Sultans of yore. Meaning 'Land of Palaces', Terrapuri is equal parts restoration museum and resort. It features 29 classically furnished antique houses laid out to resemble Terengganu palace circa 1850 (though all fully equipped with modern amenities). The land on which Terrapuri sits is equally regal, flanked by the South China Sea (with stunning views of Pulau Perhentian, Lang Tengah and other islands) on one side and the Setiu Wetland mangrove river on the other. By night, the flashing of fireflies is reflected in Terrapuri's long swimming pool, and during the summer months visitors may see ocean-going green turtles laying their eggs on the sandy shore.

Terrapuri offers delicious traditional meals and a wide variety of activities. Full details are available on the website.

ⓘ Getting There & Away

Buses from Kuala Terengganu to Kuala Besut will let you off at the Penarik mosque for RM6. From the other direction, buses from Kota Bharu to Kuala Terengganu are RM15. Taxis from either city are also available.

TASIK KENYIR

Tasik Kenyir (Lake Kenyir) and its 340 islands constitute Terengganu's most popular inland tourism destination. If you're looking to spend a relatively luxurious night in the local jungle, which houses some 8000 species of flowers, this is the spot for you.

◎ Sights

Waterfalls, **caves** and **fish farms** are among Kenyir's prime attractions. These can be reached by boat, as part of day

Left: Tasik Kenyir; **Below:** *Wayang kulit* (shadow puppet, p343), Kota Bharu
(LEFT) T L CHUA PHOTOGRAPHY/GETTY IMAGES ©; (BELOW) MOON YIN LAM/ALAMY ©

trips from the lake's main access point, Pengkalan Gawi. Perhaps more interesting are trips up the rivers that empty into the lake. Among these, a journey up **Sungai Petuang**, at the extreme northern end of the lake, is a highlight of a Kenyir visit.

Sleeping & Eating

Most accommodation is in resort chalets or floating longhouse structures built over the lake. Resorts usually offer meals and boat transport from Pengkalan Gawi.

PETANG ISLAND RESORT   Resort $$
(☎ 822 1276, 822 2176; http://pirkenyir.webs.com; dm/r/ste RM30/90/250; ❄ ☀) On its own little island in the middle of the lake, this is a quiet retreat with a choice of comfortably furnished single- or double-storey chalets and longhouse rooms. Chalets have kitchens if you want to cook for yourself, but there's a good restaurant here, too.

LAKE KENYIR RESORT   Resort $$$
(☎ 666 8888; www.lakekenyir.com; r/villa/ste from RM380/440/1200; ❄ ☎ ☀) Formerly known as Kenyir Lakeview Resort, this peaceful resort – the most glamorous property on the lake – has spacious and well-equipped chalets with balconies overlooking the water or the rainforest. There's a restaurant serving a bountiful variety of Malay and Western dishes and very inviting lounge with a great view of the lake. The resort also has tennis courts, a gym, and plenty of organised activities.

ℹ Getting There & Away

The main access point is the jetty at Pengkalan Gawi on the lake's northern shore. A taxi from Kuala Terengganu should cost around RM120. Your best bet is to book an all-inclusive package from an agency in Kuala Terengganu.

191

Pulau Perhentian (p181)
VIRGINIE BLANQUART/GETTY IMAGES ©

Melaka, Johor & Tioman

Melaka (p194)

This historic city offers much to see including a Chinatown with Unesco World Heritage status.

Johor Bahru (p208)

Cheek by jowl with Singapore but more affordable, Malaysia's southern gateway has cleaned up its act.

Pulau Tioman (p212)

An island paradise that's one of Malaysia's top diving and beach destinations.

Melaka

HIGHLIGHTS

1 **Food** (p203) Eat Chinese dim sum for breakfast, Nonya food for lunch and Pakistani tandoori for dinner.

2 **Chinatown** (p199) Wander through this historic district or take a trishaw tour.

3 **Jonker's Walk Night Market** (p205) Browse the trinket and snack stalls at this lively weekend shopfest.

4 **Baba-Nonya Heritage Museum** (p199) Learn about the city's multicultural past.

Melaka street food
ANSHU AJITSARIA/GETTY IMAGES ©

Melaka

🔊07

Melaka's Chinatown was granted Unesco World Heritage Site status in 2008 and this sealed the city's claim as one as Malaysia's hottest tourist destinations. The development that has ensued is mind-boggling. Unfortunately, 'preserving heritage' has often been translated here into gaudy, cartoon-like shop signs, night market street vendors selling cheap trinkets rather than authentic Melakan items and big-name businesses like the Hard Rock Cafe building giant, new buildings right on the historic riverfront.

The charm in Chinatown still lingers however, and is best represented by its resident artists, cooks and creative trishaws. With the oldest functioning mosque, Catholic church and Buddhist temple in the country, the city today (as it has for centuries) exudes a tolerance that accepts visitors of every creed and always promises to show them a good time. And all the modern action still blends in with the gorgeous surrounding Peranakan, Portuguese and Dutch architecture.

It's easy to feel the town's old magic (and get a seat at the more popular restaurants) on the quiet weekdays but during the weekends there are so many photo-snapping tourists (mostly from Malaysia and Singapore) that the whole town can feel like front row at a rock concert.

History

Founded by Parameswara, a Hindu prince from Sumatra, located halfway between China and India, and with easy access to the spice islands of Indonesia, Melaka attracted merchants from all over the East and became a favoured port.

In 1405 the Chinese Muslim Admiral Cheng Ho arrived in Melaka bearing gifts from the Ming emperor and the promise of protection from Siamese enemies. Chinese settlers followed, who mixed with the local Malays to become known as the Baba and Nonya, the Peranakans or Straits Chinese. By the time of Parameswara's death in 1414, Melaka was a powerful trading state. Its position was consolidated by the state's adoption of Islam in the mid-15th century.

In 1509 the Portuguese came seeking the wealth of the spice and in 1511 Alfonso de Albuquerque forcibly took the city. Under the Portuguese, the fortress of A'Famosa was constructed, and missionaries strove to implant Catholicism. The city passed into Dutch hands after an eight-month siege in 1641 and the Dutch ruled Melaka for about 150 years.

When the French occupied Holland in 1795, the British (as allies of the Dutch) temporarily assumed administration of the Dutch colonies. In 1824 Melaka was permanently ceded to the British.

Melaka, together with Penang and Singapore, formed the Straits settlements, the three British territories that were the centres for later expansion into the peninsula. However, under British rule Melaka was eclipsed by other Straits settlements and then superseded by the rapidly growing commercial importance of Singapore. Melaka returned again to being a quiet backwater, patiently awaiting its renaissance as a tourist drawcard.

 Sights

Historic Town Centre & Chinatown

This area has a ridiculous number of museums clustered along Jln Kota. A few such as the **Islamic Museum** (Map p196; admission RM1; 9am-5.30pm Wed-Sun), the **Architecture Museum** (Map p196; admission RM2; 9.30am-5pm Tue-Sun), which focuses on local housing design, and the **Muzium Rakyat** (People's Museum; Map p196; adult RM2; 9am-5.30pm Wed-Mon), which covers everything from *gasing uri* (top-spinning) to mutilation for beauty, are worth visiting if you have time on your hands.

STADHUYS   Historic Building
(Town Sq; Map p196; 282 6526; admission adult/child RM5/2; 9am-5.30pm Sat-Thu, 9am-

12.15pm & 2.45-5.30pm Fri) Melaka's most unmistakable landmark and favourite trishaw pick-up spot is the Stadthuys, the imposing salmon-pink town hall and governor's residence. It's believed to be the oldest Dutch building in the East, built shortly after Melaka was captured by the Dutch in 1641, and is a reproduction of the former Stadhuis (town hall) of the Frisian town of Hoorn in the Netherlands.

Housed inside the Stadthuys is the nicely presented **History & Ethnography Museum** (Map p196; guided tours 10.30am & 2.30pm Sat & Sun), and also part of the complex is the mildly interesting **Literature Museum** (Map p196), focusing on Malaysian writers. Admission to both museums (as well as the **Governor's House** (Map p196) and the **Democratic Government Museum** (Map p196)) is included in the admission price to Stadthuys.

PORTA DE SANTIAGO   Ruin
(A'Famosa; Map p196; Jln Bandar Hilir) A quick photo stop at this fort is a must for anyone visiting Melaka. Porta de Santiago was built by the Portuguese as a fortress in 1511. The Dutch were busy destroying the bulk of the fort when forward-thinking Sir Stamford Raffles came by in 1810 and saved what remains today.

In 2006, work on the Menara Taming Sari revolving tower uncovered another part of the famous wall. The revolving tower was relocated further inland, the remains of the fortress walls were reconstructed and are now home to the 13m high **Melaka Malay Sultanate Water Wheel** (Map p196) replica. The original wheel would have been used to channel the river waters for the large number of traders swarming Melaka during the 15th and 16th centuries.

ST PAUL'S CHURCH   Ruin
(Map p196) St Paul's Church is a breezy sanctuary reached after a steep flight of stairs. Originally built by a Portuguese captain in 1521, the church offers views over Melaka from the summit of Bukit St Paul. The church was regularly visited by St Francis Xavier, and following his death

Melaka City

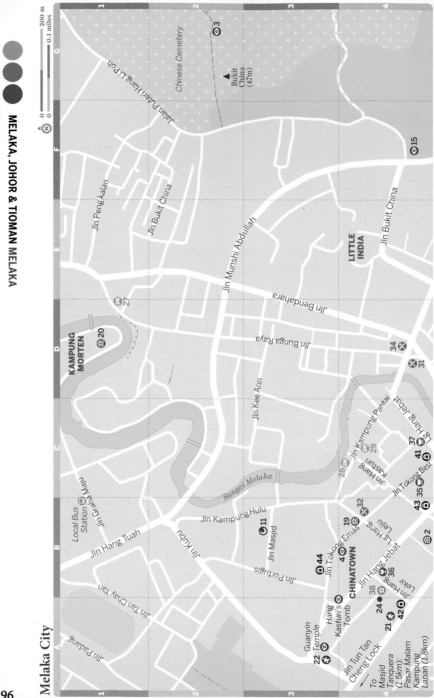

Chinese Cemetery

Bukit China (47m)

KAMPUNG MORTEN

LITTLE INDIA

CHINATOWN

Local Bus Station

Sungai Melaka

Jln Padang
Jln Tan Chay Yan
Jln Hang Tuah
Jln Graha Maju
Jln Peng Kalan
Jalan Puteri Hang Li Poh
Jln Bukit China
Jln Munshi Abdullah
Jln Bendahara
Jln Bunga Raya
Jln Kee Ann
Jln Kampung Hulu
Jln Kampung Pantai
Jln Hang Kasturi
Jln Tokong Besi
Lg Hang Jebat
Jln Tokong Emas
Jln Hang Lekiu
Jln Hang Jebat
Jln Hang Lekir
Jln Tun Tan Cheng Lock
Jln Kubu
Jln Portugis
Jln Masjid
Jln Bukit China

Guanyin Temple 22
Hang Kasturi's Tomb
11
44
4 19
32
29
28
24
21 42
38 36
2
43 35
41 37
31 34
27
20
3
15

To Masjid Tanquera (1.5km);
Pasar Malam Kampung Lapan (1.8km)

N
0   200 m
0   0.1 miles

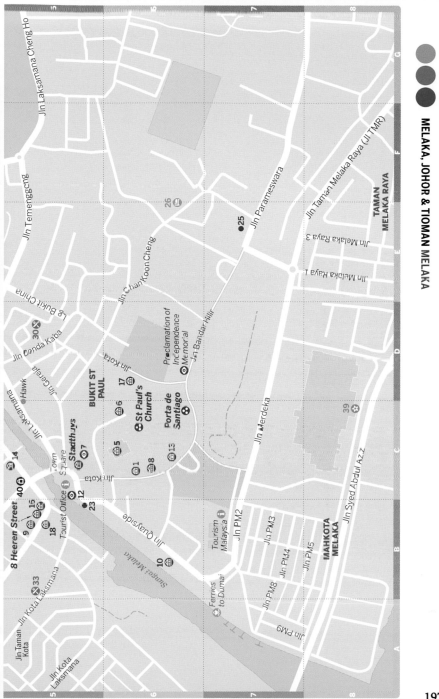

Jln Laksamana Cheng Ho

Jln Temenggong

Jln Paramesvara

Jln Taman Melaka Raya (Jl TMR)

TAMAN
MELAKA RAYA

Jln Melaka Raya 3

26

25

Jln Melaka Raya 1

Jln C'han Koon Cheng

Lg Bukit China

Jln Banda Kaba

30

Jln Gereja

Proclamation of
Independence
Memorial

Jln Kota

Jln Bandar Hilir

BUKIT ST
PAUL

Hawk

Jln Laksamana

17

6

St Paul's
Church

Porta de
Santiago

Jln Merdeka

39

Stadthuys

7

5

1

8

13

Town
Square

Jln Kota

14

40

Tourist Office

12

23

9

16

15

18

Jln Quayside

Tourism
Malaysia

Jln PM2

Jln PM3

Jln Syed Abdul Aziz

MAHKOTA
MELAKA

10

Jln PM4

Jln PM5

33

Sungai Melaka

Ferries
to Dumai

Jln PM8

Jln PM9

Jln Taman
Kota

Jln Kota
Laksamana

Melaka City

in China the saint's body was temporarily interred here for nine months before being transferred to Goa, where it remains today. Visitors can look into his ancient tomb (surrounded by a wire fence) in the centre of the church and a marble statue of the saint gazes wistfully over the city.

When the Dutch completed their own Christ Church in 1590 at the base of the hill, St Paul fell into disuse. Under the British a lighthouse was built and the church eventually ended up as a storehouse for gunpowder. The church has been in ruins for more than 150 years.

SULTANATE PALACE   Museum
(Map p196; Jln Kota; admission RM3; ◷9am-6pm) Housing a cultural museum, this wooden replica of the palace of Mansur Shah, the famous sultan who ruled Melaka from 1456 to 1477, is based on descriptions of the original palace from *Sejarah Melayu* (*Malay Annals;* a chronicle of the establishment of the Malay sultanate and 600 years of Malay history), and is built entirely without nails.

MARITIME MUSEUM & NAVAL MUSEUM
Museum

(Map p196; Jln Quayside; admission RM5; ☺9am-5.30pm Sun-Thu, 9am-9pm Fri & Sat) Housed in a huge recreation of the *Flor de la Mar,* a Portuguese ship that sank off the coast of Melaka, the Maritime Museum merits a visit. Clamber up for a detailed examination of Melaka's history, picked out by rather faded and dated props. The museum continues in the building next door with more absorbing exhibits featuring local vessels, including the striking *Kepala Burung* (a boat carved like a feathered bird) plus an assortment of nautical devices.

8 HEEREN STREET
Historic Building

(Map p196; 8 Jln Tun Tan Cheng Lock; admission free; ☺11am-4pm Tue-Sat) This 18th-century Dutch-period residential house was restored as a model conservation project. The project was partially chronicled in the beautifully designed coffee-table book *Voices from the Street,* which is for sale at the house along with other titles. You can also pick up an *Endangered Trades: A Walking Tour of Malacca's Living Heritage* (RM5) booklet and map for an excellent self-guided tour of the city centre.

BABA-NONYA HERITAGE MUSEUM
Museum

(Map p196; ☎283 1273; 48-50 Jln Tun Tan Cheng Lock; adult/child RM10/5; ☺10am-12.30pm & 2-4.30pm Wed Mon) Touring this traditional Peranakan townhouse takes you back to a time when women hid behind elaborate partitions when guests dropped by, and every social situation had its specific location within the house. The captivating museum is arranged to look like a typical 19th-century Baba-Nonya residence. The highlight is the tour guides, who tell tales of the past with a distinctly Peranakan sense of humour.

CHENG HOON TENG TEMPLE
Chinese Temple

(Qing Yun Ting or Green Clouds Temple; Map p196; 25 Jln Tokong; ☺7am-7pm) Malaysia's oldest traditional Chinese temple (dating from 1646) remains a central place of worship for the Buddhist community in Melaka. Notable for its carved woodwork, the temple is dedicated to Kuan Yin, the Goddess of mercy. Across the street from the main temple is a **traditional opera theatre**.

MASJID KAMPUNG HULU
Mosque

(Map p196; cnr Jln Masjid & Jln Kampung Hulu) This is the oldest functioning mosque in Malaysia and was, surprisingly, commissioned by the Dutch in 1728. The mosque is made up of predominantly Javanese architecture with a multitiered roof in place of the standard dome; at the time of construction, domes and minarets had not yet come into fashion.

Chinatown

Chinatown is the heart of Melaka and is by far the most interesting area to wander around. Stroll along **Jln Tun Tan Cheng Lock**, formerly called Heeren St, which was the preferred address for wealthy Baba (Straits-born Chinese) traders who were most active during the short-lived rubber boom of the early 20th century.

The centre street of Chinatown is **Jln Hang Jebat**, formerly known as Jonker St (or Junk St Melaka), that was once famed for its antique shops but is now more of a collection of clothing and crafts outlets and restaurants. On Friday, Saturday and Sunday nights, the street is transformed into the **Jonker's Walk Night Market** (p205).

Finally, the northern section of **Jln Tokong** (also known as Harmony St) houses a mosque, a Chinese temple and a handful of authentic Chinese shops.

Melaka's Art Galleries

Almost hidden between the gaudy trinket shops and humble local businesses are an array of eclectic art galleries that make for a lovely day of browsing. Opening hours are erratic but many try to be open from 10am to 6pm and most close on Wednesday.

Paku Pakis Collection (Map p196; 21 Jln Tukang Besi) Go here for Leong Hock Khoon's Baba-Nonya–inspired art that ranges from realism to modern and stylised.

Shih Wen Naphaporn Artist Studio (Map p196; 14 Jln Tuna Tan Cheng Lock) A husband and wife duo. Chiang Shiwen is Melaka born and creates Cubo-futuristic works while Thai Naphapone Phanwiset uses fish, fruit and the female form as her muse in marvelous neutral-toned pieces.

Tham Siew Inn Artist Gallery (Map p196; 49 Jln Tun Tan Teng Lock) Than Siew works mostly with watercolours while his son makes traditional stone Chinese stamps to order (from RM60).

Kim Hai Gallery (Map p196; 42 Jln Tun Tan Cheng Lock) Kim Hai paints apples to create mosaics of colour.

Titi Art Gallery (Map p196; 4 Jln Tokong) Gallery owner Titi Kawok paints village and fishing landscapes as modern images.

Around the City Centre

BUKIT CHINA Cemetery
(Map p196) More than 12,500 graves, including about 20 Muslim tombs, cover the 25 grassy hectares of this serene hill. Since the times of British rule there have been several attempts to acquire Bukit China for road widening, land reclamation or development purposes. Fortunately, **Cheng Hoon Teng Temple** (p199), with strong community support, has thwarted these attempts.

In the middle of the 15th century the sultan of Melaka imported the Ming emperor's daughter from China as his bride, in a move to seal relations between the two countries. She brought with her a vast retinue, including 500 handmaidens, to Bukit China and it has been a Chinese area ever since. **Poh San Teng Temple** (Map p196) sits at the base of the hill and was built in 1795. To the right of the temple is the **King's Well** (Map p196), a 15th-century well built by Sultan Mansur Shah.

VILLA SENTOSA Historic Building
(Peaceful Villa; Map p196; ☎282 3988; entry by donation; ⏰flexible but around 9am-6pm) A highlight of a visit to the area is viewing this 1920s Malay *kampung* (village) house on Sungai Melaka. A member of the family will show you around the house and its collection of objects including Ming dynasty ceramics and a 100-year-old copy of the Quran. Most of all, it's an opportunity to wander through a genuine *kampung* house and chat with your charming host.

Activities

Cookery Courses
NANCY'S KITCHEN Cooking
(Map p196; ☎283 6099; 15 Jln Hang Lekir; per person RM100 per) Nancy of this near legendary Nonya **restaurant** (p203) teaches recommended cookery classes on request. Reserve well in advance.

WOK & WALK
Cooking

(Map p196; ☎Hotel Equatorial 282 8333; Hotel Equatorial; per person 2-day packages from RM340) Nonya cooking workshops include six signature dishes and packages can include a stay at Hotel Equatorial and meals at the hotel restaurant.

PERANAKAN CULINARY JOURNEY
Cooking

(☎289 8000; www.majesticmalacca.com; Majestic Malacca Hotel, 188 Jln Bunga Raya; per person RM285) Learn about each ingredient and the history of each dish in a gorgeous kitchen with a master Peranakan chef at the Majestic Malacca Hotel.

Massage & Reflexology

It seems that reflexology centres have opened up on every corner in Melaka. If you have specific ailments – anything from migraines to water retention – many will create a special treatment for you. There are also ear candles, fire cupping, body scrubs and more. A one-hour massage at these types of places is usually RM60 while a half-hour foot massage costs RM30.

BIOSSENTIALS PURI SPA
Spa

(Map p196; ☎282 5588; www.hotelpuri.com; Hotel Puri, 118 Jln Tun Tan Cheng Lock; spa services from RM80; ⊗Thu-Mon) This international-calibre spa in a sensual garden has a delicious menu of treatments including steams, body wraps, scrubs, facials and a variety of massages.

MASSA SUTRA
Massage

(Map p196; ☎016-662 503; www.massasutra.com; 20 Jln Kubu; 1hr massage RM60) We can say with conviction that Chris Loh is a master masseur (using Thai or Zen techniques).

 ## Tours

Historic walking tours are offered through several hotels. Particularly recommended are the ones led by Pek Choo Ho at the **Majestic Malacca** (p202) hotel.

Boat Trips

MELAKA RIVER CRUISE
Boat Tour

(Map p196; RM15) Frequent 40-minute riverboat trips (minimum eight people) along the Melaka River depart from two locations: the 'Spice Garden' on the corner of Jln Tun Mutahii and Jln Tun Sri Lanang in the north of town, and the quay near the Maritime Museum. Cruises don't go further than 9km upriver past Kampung Morten and old *godowns* (river warehouses). There's also a hop-on, hop-off day pass for RM30.

Bike Tours

ECO BIKE TOUR
Bike Tour

(☎019-652 5029; www.melakaonbike.com; per person RM100, minimum 2 people) Explore the fascinating landscape around Melaka with Alias on his three-hour bike tour through 20km of oil-palm and rubber-tree plantations and delightful *kampung* communities surrounding town.

Tricked-out Trishaws

Nowhere else in Malaysia will you find such a wild and crazy collection of trishaws. Outrageously kitsch, the favourite decorations are plastic flowers, baby doll heads, religious paraphernalia, tinsel, Christmas lights and a sound system. While taking a ride in one of these things might be the most 'I'm a tourist' thing you do in Malaysia, it's good fun and supports an industry that is dying nearly everywhere else in the country. As a spectator, keep an eye out for Singaporean tourists hiring out trishaws en masse: the effect, with several '80s hits blaring at the same time, cameras snapping and all that glitzy decoration, turns the streets of Melaka into a circus-like parade.

MALACCA NIGHT CYCLING   Bike Tour
(☎016-668 8898; RM25-25) Touring Melaka
at night takes the bite off the heat of the
day and it's a pleasant time to cycle and
see the city. Tours leave nightly at 8.30pm
and last two to three hours.

🛏 Sleeping

So many new places are opening up in
Melaka that accommodation options are
particularly vulnerable to change. Rooms
have private showers and dorms have
shared bathrooms, unless otherwise
stated.

Chinatown is the best area of the city
to stay although it can get both busy and
noisy.

**45 LEKIU & THE
STABLE**   Private House **$$$**
(Map p196; ☎012-623 4459; www.45lekiu.com;
45 Lg Hang Lekiu (45 Lekiu), No D Jln Hang Kas-
turi; 45 Lekiu weekdays/weekends RM999/1099,
The Stable weekdays/weekends RM300/360;
❄️🛜🏊) These gorgeous restoration
projects are in two different locations –
when you stay at either, the whole house
is yours and both have basic cooking
facilities. 45 Lekiu is the more upscale of
the two, with four extremely comfortable
stories of big old beams and exposed
original brick work all within a clean, mod-
ern decor. It also has a lap pool.

**RIVER VIEW
GUESTHOUSE**   Guesthouse **$**
(Map p196; ☎012-327 7746; riverviewguest-
house@yahoo.com; 94 & 96 Jln Kampung Pantai;
dm RM20, r RM45-70; ❄️🛜) Bordering the
ambient riverfront promenade, this im-
maculate guesthouse is housed in a large
heritage building. There's a big shared
kitchen and common area and the hosts
begin your stay with a handy map of town
and directions to all their favourite sights
and restaurants.

The owner's overflow property,
Rooftop Guesthouse (Map p196; 39 Jln
Kampong Pantai), is almost as nice but
doesn't offer the riverfront perk.

HOTEL PURI   Hotel **$$**
(Map p196; ☎282 5588; www.hotelpuri.com; 118
Jln Tun Tan Cheng Lock; r RM164-564; ❄️🛜)
One of Chinatown's gems, Hotel Puri is an
elegant creation in a superb old renovated Peranakan mansion. Its elaborate
lobby, decked out with beautiful old cane
and inlaid furniture, opens to a gorgeous
courtyard garden. Standard rooms
have butter-yellow walls, crisp sheets,
satellite TV, wi-fi and shuttered windows.
There's an on-site spa (**Biossentials Puri
Spa**, p201), and breakfast, taken in the
courtyard or air-conditioned dining area,
is included.

MAJESTIC MALACCA   Hotel **$$$**
(Map p196; ☎289 8000; www.majesticma-
lacca.com; 188 Jln Bunga Raya; r RM410-2000;
❄️@🛜🏊) Melaka's most elegant hotel
is an interesting mix: the lobby is in a
1920s colonial Chinese mansion while
the bulk of the hotel is in a tasteful
modern building behind. Rooms con-
tinue with this old and new theme with
hardwood floors, sheer ivory-coloured
drapes and heritage-style wood furnish-
ings – yet all are very modern in their
level of comfort.

Of course the place is stacked with
amenities including a small swimming
pool, a gym, a top-notch spa and stellar
service.

APA KABA HOME & STAY   Guesthouse **$**
(Map p196; ☎283 8196; www.apakaba.hostel.
com; 28 Kg Banda Kaba; r incl breakfast RM40-
90; ❄️🛜) Nestled in a quiet and authentic
Malay *kampung* that seems to magically
float in a bubble in the heart of town, this
homestay-style guesthouse is in a simple
yet beautiful old Malay house complete
with creaky wood floors, louvred shutters
and bright paint.

You can chill out in the enormous
garden (look for ripe mangos) or take a
stroll out the back gate through tiny lanes
that meander into Chinatown.

HOTEL EQUATORIAL   Hotel **$$$**
(Map p196; ☎282 8333; www.equatorial.com;
Jln Parameswara; r RM300-1000; ❄️🛜🏊)
While it's a bit frayed around the edges,

somehow this adds to the old charm of this centrally located hotel. Good discounts online can cut prices nearly in half for an excellent value. Service is well mannered and the overall presentation is crisp. There's a swimming pool, a ladies-only pool, a quality fitness centre, a tennis court and wi-fi access.

It's worth upgrading to one of the deluxe rooms (RM500), which have either balconies or heaps of extra room space.

🍴 Eating

Melaka's food mirrors the city's eclectic, multicultural DNA. Peranakan cuisine (Nonya or Straits Chinese; prepared here with a salty Indonesian influence) is the most famous type of cooking here, but there's also Portuguese Eurasian food, Indian, Chinese, Indonesian and more.

PAK PUTRA RESTAURANT Pakistani **$$**
(Map p196; 56 Jln Taman Kota Laksmana; tandoori from RM8; ☾dinner, closed every other Mon) This fabulous Pakistani place cooks up a variety of meals and seafood in clay tandoori ovens perched on the footpath. Apart from the tandoori try the *taw prawns* (cooked with onion, yoghurt and coriander, RM11) or mutton rogan josh (in onion gravy with spices and chilli oil, RM9). Everything is so good that dinner conversation is often reduced to oohs and ahs of gustatory delight.

NANCY'S KITCHEN Nonya **$**
(Map p196; 15 Jln Hang Le-kir; meals RM10; ☾11am-5.30pm Wed-Mon) In a town already known for its graciousness, this home-cooking Nonya restaurant is our favourite for friendly service. If you want an intimate meal,

head elsewhere. The server is as chatty and full of suggestions as they come, and will have you making conversation with the other handful of customers in no time. It's like a happy dinner (or lunch) party with particularly good food. Try the house speciality, chicken with candlenut (a large white nut used to make a mild, creamy sauce). Still hungry? Nancy also offers **cooking courses** (p200).

CAPITOL SATAY Melakan **$**
(Map p196; 🕿 283 5508; 41 Lg Bukit China; meals around RM8) Famous for its *satay celup* (a Melaka adaptation of satay steamboat), this place is usually packed and is one of the cheapest outfits in town. Stainless-steel tables have bubbling vats of soup in the middle where you dunk skewers of okra stuffed with tofu, sausages, chicken, prawns and bok choy. Side dishes include pickled eggs and ginger.

SELVAM Indian **$**
(Map p196; 🕿 281 9223; 3 Jln Temenggong; meals around RM8; 🍴) This is a classic banana-leaf restaurant always busy with its loyal

Porta de Santiago (p195)
ANDERS BLOMQVIST/GETTY IMAGES ©

band of local patrons ordering tasty and cheap curries, roti and tandoori chicken sets. Even devout carnivores will second-guess their food preferences after trying the Friday-afternoon vegetarian special with 10 varieties of veg.

LOW YONG MOW   Chinese $

(Map p196; ☎282 1235; Jln Tokong; dim sum RM1-8; ⏱5am-noon, closed Tue) Famous Malaysia-wide for large and delectably well-stuffed *pao* (steamed pork buns), this place is Chinatown's biggest breakfast treat. With high ceilings, plenty of fans running and a view of Masjid Kampung Kling, the atmosphere oozes all the charms of Chinatown. It's great for early-bus-departure breakfasts and is usually packed with talkative, newspaper-reading locals by around 7am.

 **Drinking**

Unlike much of Malaysia, Melaka is studded with watering holes. On Friday, Saturday and Sunday nights **Jonker's Walk Night Market** (p205) in Chinatown closes down Jln Heng Lekir to traffic and the handful of bars along the lane become a mini street party with tables oozing beyond the sidewalks and live music.

GEOGRAPHÉR CAFE   Bar

(Map p196; ☎281 6813; www.geographer.com.my; 83 Jln Hang Jebat; ⏱10am-1am Wed-Sun) This ventilated, breezy bar with outside seating and late hours, in a prewar corner shophouse, is a godsend. Seat yourself with a beer amid the throng and applaud long-time resident artist and musician Mr Burns as he eases through gnarled classics. A tasty choice of local and Western dishes and laid-back but professional service rounds it all off.

CHENG HO TEA HOUSE   Tea House

(Map p196; Jln Tokong; ⏱10am-5pm) In an exquisite setting that resembles a Chinese temple garden courtyard, relax over a pot of fine Chinese tea (from RM15) or take a tea appreciation course with owner and tea connoisseur, Pak.

ZHENG HO TEA HOUSE   Tea House

(Map p196; ☎016-764 0588; 3 Jln Kuli; tea ceremony for four people RM20) The best place in town for tea ceremony, this place is humble but the family are simply lovely and it

Chinatown (p199)

Jonker's Walk Night Market

Melaka's weekly shopping extravaganza **Jonker's Walk Night Market** (Map p196; Jln Hang Jebat; ⊙6-11pm Fri-Sun) keeps the shops along Jln Hang Jebat open late while trinket sellers, food hawkers and the occasional fortune teller close the street to traffic. It has become far more commercial, attracting scores of Singaporean tourists over the years, but it is an undeniably colourful way to spend an evening shopping and grazing.

Besides the official Hainan Food Street, there are also hawker stalls along Jln Hang Jebat and on Jln Tokong where it meets Jln Portugis. Sample fried dumplings on a stick and quaff sugarcane juice, fresh fruit juices, soy milk and chestnut or chrysanthemum tea. Also don't miss the performance by Kung Fu master Dr Ho Eng Hui (southern end of Jln Hang Jebat; around 6.30pm to 9pm Friday and Saturday); he eats fire, throws knives and pummels his finger into a coconut.

just feels good to be here. There are also a few rooms for rent upstairs (from RM130 including one home cooked meal).

⭐ Entertainment

MIXX Club
(Map p196; 2nd fl, Mahkota Arcade, Jln Syed Abdul Aziz; cover charge RM10; ⊙10pm-late Tue-Sat) Melaka's hottest new club has two parts: Paradox, a laser-lit warehouse-style venue where international DJs spin techno and electronic beats, and Arris, which has a garden area and live bands. It ain't Kuala Lumpur but for Melaka this place is very hip. Cover is charged on Friday and Saturday nights only (when the place gets VERY crowded) and includes one drink.

ELEVEN Club
(Map p196; 11 Jln Hang Lekir) This is *the* place to go if you want to get your groove on in Chinatown. Yes there's hip heritage lounge-style seating and Eurasian food, but head here after around 11pm (weekends in particular) and resident DJs spin their best and the dance floor fills. It has been dubbed Melaka's only gay bar but it's a very relaxed scene and you'll find all sorts hanging out.

Shopping

Taking time to browse Chinatown's eclectic mix of shops is an activity in itself. Melakan favourites include Nonya beaded shoes, Nonya 'clogs' (with a wooden base and a single plastic-strip upper), antiques (know your stuff and haggle aggressively), Southeast Asian and Indian clothing, handmade tiles, charms, crystals and more. Peek into the growing array of silent artists studios, where you might see a painter busy at work in a back room.

ORANGUTAN HOUSE Fashion
(Map p196; 59 Lg Hang Jebat; ⊙10am-6pm Thu-Tue) All shirts are the work of local artist Charles Cham and have themes ranging from Chinese astrology animals to rather edgy topics (at least for Malaysia) such as 'Use Malaysian Rubber' above a sketch of a condom. Other branches are at **96 Jln Tun Tan Cheng Lok** (Map p196; www. charlescham.com; ⊙closed Tue) and **12 Jln Hang Jebat** (Map p196; www.charlescham. com; ⊙closed Thu).

WAH AIK SHOEMAKER Shoes
(Map p196; 56 Jln Tokong) Raymond Yeo continues the tradition begun by his grandfather in the same little shoe-

ANDERS BLOMQVIST/GETTY IMAGES ©

maker's shop that has been in his family for generations. The beaded Nonya shoes here are considered Melaka's finest and begin at a steep but merited RM300. Tiny silk bound-feet shoes (from RM90) are also available.

🛈 Information

Tourist Information

Tourism Malaysia (☎283 6220; Jln Mahkota; ⊙9am-10pm) At the Menara Taming Sari tower; has very knowledgeable, helpful staff.

Tourist Office (☎281 4803; www.melak.gov.my; Jln Kota; ⊙9am-1pm & 2-5.30pm) Diagonally across the square from Christ Church.

🛈 Getting There & Away

Air

Melaka International Airport is 20km north of Melaka in Batu Berendam. **Firefly** (www.fireflyz. com.my) offers flights between Melaka and KL's Subang Airport (twice weekly) and Penang (one flight Wednesday).

Bus

Melaka Sentral, the huge, modern long-distance bus station, is inconveniently located opposite a huge branch of Tesco off Jln Tun Razak, in the north of town.

A taxi into town should cost RM20, or you can take bus 17 (RM1.40).

You can buy bus tickets in advance from downtown Melaka (not a bad idea on busy weekends or if you have a plane to catch) at **Discovery Cafe** (Map p196; 3 Jln Bunga Raya) – it charges RM5 for the service.

Car

Car-hire prices begin at around RM150 per day. If driving, Melaka's one-way traffic system requires patience. Try **Hawk** (☎283 7878; 52 Jln Cempaka), north of town.

Taxi

Taxis leave from the long-distance bus station. Taxi rates: Johor Bahru (RM250), Mersing (RM300), KL (RM170) and KL airport (RM160).

Train

The nearest **train station** (☎441 1034) is 38km north of Melaka at Tampin on the main north–south line from KL to Singapore. Taxis from Melaka cost around RM60 or take the Tai Lye bus (RM5, 1½ hours), which leaves every half-hour from Melaka Sentral.

ⓘ Getting Around

Melaka is small enough to walk around or, for the traffic-fearless, you can rent a bike for around RM3 per hour from guesthouses around Chinatown. A useful service is town bus 17, running every 15 minutes from Melaka Sentral to the centre of town, past the huge Mahkota Parade shopping complex, to Taman Melaka Raya and on to Medan Portugis.

Taking to Melaka's streets by trishaw is a must – by the hour they should cost about RM40, or RM15 for any one-way trip within the town, but you'll have to bargain.

Taxis should cost around RM15 for a trip anywhere around town with a 50% surcharge between 1am and 6am.

Johor Bahru

HIGHLIGHTS

❶ **Heritage District** (p208)
Discover JB's surprisingly charming waterfront and colonial backstreets.

❷ **Royal Abu Bakar Museum** (p208)
Admire the sultan's treasures in his Victorian-style palace.

❸ **Food** (p209) Join savvy Singaporeans tucking into bargain-priced, supremely tasty Malaysian dishes.

Sultan Abu Bakar Mosque (p209)

Johor Bahru
🔊 07

After years of being criticised as a dirty, chaotic border town, Johor's capital Johor Bahru (JB) has been repaved and re-planted and is suddenly a lively, appealing place to hang out. Even the sketchy watch salesmen and down-and-out sidewalk lurkers who congregated along Jln Tun Abdul Razak have been swept away by an increased police presence. Just off this main drag you'll find bustling food hawkers, interesting old architecture and wide, clean sidewalks. The city still has more crime compared with most Malaysian towns, but there's a real urban buzz and some surprisingly cosmopolitan corners to explore.

JB is connected to Singapore by road and rail across a 1038m-long causeway, across which Singaporeans flood for shopping and excitement on weekends and holidays. However, other than just for changing trains, planes or buses, few foreign travellers linger here although it has great potential as a budget base for Singapore.

◉ Sights

HERITAGE DISTRICT   Architecture
Wandering around the heritage area between Jln Ibrahim and Jln Ungku Puan is a real highlight of JB. Walk past colourful, old shophouses filled with sari shops, barbers, Ayurvedic salons, gorgeous temples, and old-style eateries.

ROYAL ABU BAKAR MUSEUM   Museum
(🔊 223 0555; Jln Ibrahim; adult/child US$7/3; ⏰9am-5pm Sat-Thu, ticket counter closes 4pm) The marvellous Istana Besar, once the Johor royal family's principal palace, was built in Victorian style by Anglophile sultan Abu Bakar in 1866. It was opened as a museum to the public in 1990 and displays the incredible wealth of the sultans. It's now the finest museum of its kind in Malaysia, and the 53-hectare palace grounds (free entry) are beautifully manicured.

At the time of research the museum was getting an extensive, two-year remodel, but will no doubt have reopened by the time you're reading this, with the – possibly increased – entrance fee payable in ringgit.

SRI RAJA MARIAMMAN DEVASTHANAM
Hindu Temple

(4 Jln Ungku Puan) This beautiful Hindu temple, with ornate carvings and devotional artwork, and a tall, brightly painted *gopuram* (tower) entrance way, is the heart of JB's Hindu community.

SULTAN ABU BAKAR MOSQUE
Mosque

(Jln Gertak Merah) The stunning white-washed walls and blue-tiled roofing of the Sultan Abu Bakar features a mix of architectural influences, including Victorian. It was built between 1892 and 1900 and is quite rightly hailed as one of the most magnificent mosques in the area. Sadly, non-Muslims cannot enter the building itself.

CHINESE HERITAGE MUSEUM
Museum

(42 Jln Ibrahim; RM10; ⊙9am-5pm Tue-Sun) Well-laid-out exhibits chronicling the history of Chinese immigrants in this part of the Malay peninsula. Learn how the Cantonese brought their carpentry skills here, while the Hakkas traded in Chinese medicines and the Hainanese kickstarted a trend in coffeeshops, which lasts to this day.

Sleeping

The main zone of cheap and low-bracket midrange hotels clusters on and around the relatively ambient Jln Meldrum, in the centre of town. More midrange business-oriented hotels hover in the lively area around KSL Mall, where you'll find tons of good eating options and shopping.

Many hotels inflate prices on Friday, Saturday and Sunday by about 10%.

THISTLE JOHOR BAHRU
Hotel $$

(✆222 9234; www.thistle.com.my; Jln Sungai Chat; r from RM240; ❄@☎⛱) Overlooking the Straits of Johor, the hotel is the poshest city option this side of the Causeway. It's in a class above the rest with marble bathrooms, a lovely curving swimming

Stay Alert!

Although travelling in JB is generally safe, visitors should be alert to motorcycle-riding bag-snatchers and, as in any city, avoid walking alone down dark alleyways. If you have any troubles call the **police hotline** (✆225 6699).

pool and and airy, light ambiance but the location near Danga Bay is a little out of the way. Thistle is located about 4km from the town centre, just off the main road, Jln Lingkaran Dalam.

MELDRUM HOTEL
Hotel $

(✆227 8988; www.meldrumhotel.com; 1 Jln Siu Nam; dm RM40, s/d with shared bathroom RM70/80, r with bathroom from RM90; ❄☎) All options here are air-conditioned, clean, spacious and freshly painted, and the rooms have TVs, free drinking water and kettles. It's worth upgrading to a RM100 superior room with attached bathrooms and free wi-fi – these are downright plush. Dorms are cramped, air-conditioned and filled mostly with local men.

GRANDEUR PALM RESORT
Resort $$$

(✆599 6000; www.palmresort.com; Jln Persiaran Golf; r from RM472; ❄@☎⛱) Only a three-minute drive from Senai International Airport (28km from central JB), this resort is a far cry from the city's hubbub. Alongside the elegant accommodation there are nearly unlimited activities available from golf to paintball, an Olympic-sized pool and ATV trails. Afterwards chill out at the on-site Le Spa.

Eating

Whatever you think of JB, you can't complain about the food. The streets here (try the area around KSL City Mall) sizzle with some of the country's best seafood, as well as local specialities including a local, curry-heavy version of laksa.

ROOST JUICE & BAR   International $$
(Jln Dhoby; mains RM8-28, juice from RM7.90;
⊙12-4pm & 6pm-midnight Mon-Sat, 6pm-
midnight Sun) JB's most chillable spot uses
recycled wood, bottles and more to create
a cafe-bar that feels like someone's (very
hip) living room. And the food's great, too.
Try the Hainese noodles, fish 'n' chips,
mutton ribs or Nonya fish fillets and finish
it off with fresh juice or a cold beer. The
same folks also run **Roost Repurposed
Recycled**, an excellent salad and frozen
yogurt cafe just a few doors down.

**HIAP JOO BAKERY &
BISCUIT FACTORY**   Bakery $
(13 Jln Tan Hiok Nee; rolls & cakes RM1-4;
⊙8am-6pm) For over 80 years this little
bakery has baked delicious buns, cakes
and biscuits in a charcoal oven just as
the founder had done before in his native
Hainan. The coconut buns and bread rolls,
ready by 12.30pm, are sold out by 3pm.

ANNALAKSHMI   Indian $
(☑227 7400; 39 Jln Ibraham; set meals by dona-
tion; ⊙11am-3pm Mon-Fri; ✈) A classy and
authentic vegetarian Indian restaurant
run by volunteers of the Temple of Fine
Arts, with the motto of 'eat what you want
and give as you feel'.

Legoland

Got kids? Opened in September
2012, Southeast Asia's first **Legoland**
(☑597 8888; www.legoland.com.my;
Medini, Nusajaya; adult/child/senior
RM140/110/110; ⊙10am-6pm) offers 31
hectares of fun with over 40 rides
and attractions. Nearly everything
is hands on, and it's not just about
the bricks. Expect to crawl around,
pull yourself up a tower with ropes,
ride a dragon-coaster and shoot
lasers at mummies. The centrepiece
is Miniland, in which regional
landmarks like the Petronus Towers
are built in miniature.

RESTORAN NILLA   Indian $
(Jln Ungku Puan & Jln Trus; mains from RM2;
⊙7am-10pm; ✈) An excellent banana leaf
place with two nearby outlets – the other is
just around the corner, on Jln Ungku Puan.
For some of the best chicken you've ever
had, ask for the 'vegetarian chicken.' It's
tofu but it's so good you'll hardly believe it.

**MEDAN SELERA
MELDRUM WALK**   Food Stall $
(Medan Selera Meldrum; meals from RM3; ⊙din-
ner) Every late afternoon, the little food
stalls crammed along this alley (parallel
to Jln Meldrum) start frying up everything
from *ikan bakar* to the local curry laksa.
Wash down your meal with fresh sugar-
cane juice or a Chinese herbal jelly drink.

🍷 Drinking

THE ZON   Bars, Clubs
(☑221 9999; The Zon Ferry Terminal) Three
words: duty-free booze. About 10 bars
and clubs surround the courtyard of this
happening spot. Hip **Roost** (p210) has an
outlet here for drinking in funky recycled
decor while Dolce and Cabana are prob-
ably the most fun places for dancing.

ⓘ Information

**Tourism Malaysia & Johor Tourist Information
Centre** (☑223 4935; www.johortourism.com.my;
CIQI Immigration Complex & 3rd fl, Jotic Bldg, 2
Jln Air Molek; ⊙9am-5pm Mon-Sat)

Tourism Malaysia has two offices in JB, the
most convenient being the one at the CIQ
Complex, right after you pass immigration from
Singapore.

ⓘ Getting There & Away

Air

JB is served by the **Senai International Airport**
(p211) in Senai, 32km northwest of JB.

Bus

Larkin bus station is a frantic sprawl of hawker
stalls, restaurants, clothes shops and other
outlets as well as numerous bus companies.

Johor Bahru to Singapore

From JB Sentral you can clear immigration and take a bus or taxi across the Causeway to Singapore. From central JB, board your bus after clearing Malaysian immigration just before the Causeway – you can buy yours tickets onboard. There are also frequent buses between JB's Larkin bus station, 5km north of the city, and Singapore's Queen St bus station. Most convenient is **Causeway Link** (www.causewaylink.com.my; from JB/Singapore RM2.50/S$2.40, 6.30am to midnight, every 10 minutes).

Registered taxis to Singapore depart from the Plaza Seni Taxi Terminal in the centre of town (RM60 to Orchard Rd or Queen St terminal).

Alternatively, **Trans Star Cross Border Coaches** (from JB/Singapore RM7/S$7; every hour 5am-9pm) run between the Kotaraya 2 Terminal in Johor Bahru and Singapore's Changi International Airport.

For details on doing the trip in the opposite direction see p261.

Taxi

JB's main long-distance taxi station (☎223 4494) is at the Larkin bus station, 5km north of town; there's a handier terminal on Jln Wong Ah Fook. Destinations include Melaka (RM280), KL (RM460) and Mersing (RM160). Prices are per person for a 4-person taxi.

Train

Three daily express trains leave from the sparking JB Sentral train station in the CIQ complex, running to KL (6.30am, 2.56pm and 8.25pm). The line passes through Tampin (for Melaka), Seremban, KL Sentral, Tapah Rd (for Cameron Highlands), Ipoh, Taiping and Butterworth. The line bifurcates at Gemas so you can board the 'jungle train' for Jerantut (for Taman Negara), Kuala Lipis and Kota Bharu.

ⓘ Getting Around

To/From Senai International Airport

JB's Senai International Airport (☎599 4500; www.senaiairport.com), 32km northwest of town, is linked to the city centre by regular shuttle buses (RM8, 45 minutes) that run from the bus station at Kotaraya 2 Terminal. A taxi between the airport and JB is RM60, taking 30 to 45 minutes, depending on traffic.

Bus

Local buses operate from several stops around town, the most convenient being the stop in front of Public Bank on Jln Ah Fook. From Larkin bus station bus 39 goes into central JB (RM1.80)

Car

Car hire in JB is considerably cheaper than in Singapore, but check that the hire firm allows cars to enter Singapore. Car hire prices begin at around RM153 per day; prices are inclusive of insurance and tax. Many rental companies hire cars from Senai International Airport.

Hawk Car Rental (☎224 2849; Suite 221, 2nd fl, Pan Global Plaza, Jln Wong Ah Fook)

Taxi

Taxis in JB have meters, and drivers are legally required to use them. Flagfall is RM3, with an average trip costing RM10. Taxis can be hired at around RM35 per hour for sightseeing.

Pulau Tioman

HIGHLIGHTS

1 **Beach-hopping** (p214) The hardest part of your Tioman adventure may well be deciding which is your favourite beach.

2 **Diving and snorkelling** (p215) Take your pick from 20-odd dive sites including famous wreck dives.

3 **Hiking** (p212) A great way to view wildlife is to hit the trails criss-crossing the island.

Mukut (p214)
DOUG MEIKLE DREAMING TRACK IMAGES/GETTY IMAGES ©

Pulau Tioman
♫09

Beautiful Tioman has a near-Polynesian feel to it, with its heavy-lidded hibiscus flowers, steep green peaks and turquoise, coral-rich waters. At 20km long and 11km wide, the island is so spacious that your ideal holiday spot is surely here somewhere. But of course this is no secret: the island attracts around 190,000 visitors annually looking for their dream beach. Fortunately holidaymakers are absorbed subtly and the island retains an unspoiled feel, with pristine wildernessand friendly, authentic village life.

A short stretch of road runs along the western side of the island from Berjaya Tioman Beach, Golf & Spa Resort to the northern end of Tekek, where it is interrupted by steps before continuing as a path to the end of Air Batang (known as ABC). A winding, newly paved road links Tekek with the dozy east-coast idyll of Juara.

Tekek is Tioman's largest village and its administrative centre. The airport is here, as well as the island's only cash machine. Bear in mind that everything stocked in shops on Tioman is shipped over from the mainland and tends to be expensive (except beer and tobacco), so stock up on essentials before you arrive.

◉ Sights & Activities

Hiking

Jungle-filled Tioman offers plenty of excellent hikes to keep the intrepid landlubber exhausted and happy. You'll see more wildlife here than in most of Malaysia's national parks, including black giant squirrels, long-tailed macaques, brush-tailed porcupines and – if you're out with a torch at dawn or dusk and incredibly lucky – the endangered, nocturnal binturong (bear cat).

Be wary of entering the jungle after around 4.30pm, as it's easy to get lost in the dark.

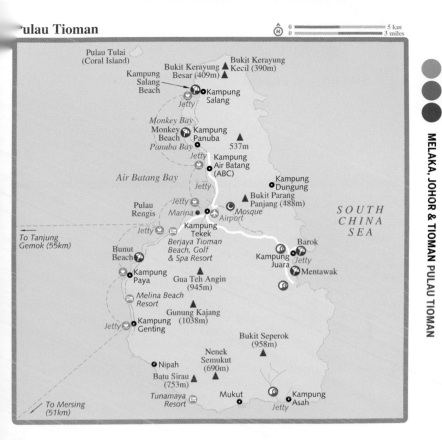

Tekek to Juara

This 7km jungle walk offers an excellent feel for the richness of the spectacular interior, not to mention the added bonus of bringing the hiker to beautiful Juara at hike's end. While the walk isn't too strenuous, parts of it are steep, and hiking in tropical heat can be taxing. Carry plenty of water; if you lose the trail, follow the power lines overhead.

You'll find signs for the jungle walk about 1km north of the main jetty in Tekek. You can also walk along the recently paved road to Juara, a longer and somewhat less satisfying hike. A car back from Juara will cost around RM90.

ABC to Salang

The 3.5km ABC to Salang Trail, which runs inland from the coast, is short but can be difficult. The trail isn't well marked, but it does lead to some excellent empty beaches. Climb up to Bamboo Hill Chalets at the northern end of ABC bay for a 10-minute hike over the next headland to Panuba Bay. From there it's another 40 minutes through the rainforest to Monkey Beach, before the trail continues from the far end of the beach across the next headland to the white-sand beach at Monkey Bay. From here, it's a long, steep climb over the headland to Salang.

Tekek to Berjaya Tioman

An easier 30-minute hike heads south from Tekek to Berjaya Tioman, either by the road or by rock-hopping around the headland at low tide. From there you can walk through the golf course; just before the telecommunications tower there is a trail to the deserted beach of Bunut. From the end of the beach, the occasionally faint trail continues over the headland to Paya.

🛏 Sleeping & Eating

From Salung to Mukut, all towns and beaches with accommodation are serviced by regular ferries from Mersing. Ferries to Juara run only when tidal conditions allow, and even then only when enough people are going to make it worth the captain's while.

Budget accommodation largely comprises small wooden chalets and longhouse rooms (all in poor condition), typically with a bathroom, fan and a mosquito net. More expensive rooms have air-con and hot showers. Most operations have larger family rooms

Choosing a Slice of Paradise

The options, counter-clockwise from North to South are:

Salang The most backpacker-esque of Tioman's *kampung*. Come to snorkel off nearby Coral Island, look for monstrous monitor lizards that lurk in the inky river than runs through the village centre. Stay for the beach parties

Air Batang (ABC) Slightly more upscale than Salang, ABC has a good choice of restaurants and accommodation, though the beach isn't all that spectacular.

Tekek Tioman's commercial hub is a good central location from which to explore the rest of the island, and the beach on the southern end of town is lovely.

Kampung Paya With two moderately priced resorts offering all-inclusive packages, Paya is more popular with Singaporean students and the organised-tour set looking to snorkel off Paya beach.

Genting The beach here is fairly built up, but is surrounded by a local village with an appealing *kampung* atmosphere. A good spot for meeting local fisherman.

Nipah Blissful, isolated Nipah Beach is a long strip of white with an unusual stripe of black sand running through it. A river mouth at the southern end creates a deep blue swimming hole that's bordered on one side by a large, flat knuckle of sand with a volleyball pitch. This is the place to come to hang in a hammock, snorkel, or hike in the jungle. The waters of Nipah are home to phosphorescent seaweed, and actually glow at night.

Mukut On the southern tip of Tioman, Mukut may be the loveliest – and most secluded – village on the island. The beach is a tad less amazing than the one in Juara, but this is made up for by the prettiness of the town itself, with its traditional homes and flower-lined paths.

Juara It's the hardest to get to, but Juara has the best surfing beach in Tioman and enough restaurants and accommodation to make it well worth the trip. It's the sole place to stay on the east coast of the island and hovers in a constant sleepy state of remote-hideaway bliss. There are two long stretches of wide white sandy beach here (separated by a small hill and boulder outcrop). The northern half of the beach (called Barok) is where most accommodation is found, while the southern strip (known as Mentawak) is near-deserted and kicks up some of the country's best surfing waves during the monsoon. Turtles nest on both beaches and the area has been proclaimed a 'green zone' by the Sultan of Johor. This means it is protected from development, including the building of any big new resorts.

REINHARD DIRSCHERL/GETTY IMAGES ©

Don't Miss Diving & Snorkelling

Many come to Tioman solely to dive – the underwater world around the island offers some of the best (and most accessible) diving and snorkelling in Malaysia. It's also one of the few places in the country where you have a good chance of seeing pods of dolphins.

There is good snorkelling off the rocky points on the west coast of the island, particularly those just north of ABC, but the best snorkelling is around nearby Pulau Tulai, better known as Coral Island. Snorkelling equipment for hire is easy to find (masks and snorkels are typically RM10 per day) at many places around the island.

There are plenty of excellent dive centres on Tioman, and PADI courses are priced competitively. Expect to pay about RM1000 for a four-day PADI open-water course and RM100 for fun dives.

for those with children, and many have restaurants.

Tekek

SWISS COTTAGE RESORT   Resort $$
(☏419 1642; www.swiss-cottage-tioman.com; longhouse d fan/air-con RM100-120, garden-/ sea-view chalets RM130-150, sea-view bungalows RM180; ❄️ 🛜) This resort is clearly operated by creative folk. The rooms to nab here are the sea-view chalets (RM180), which have breezy bamboo and wood interiors alongside colourfully painted walls and comfy deck furniture. Other options are nestled in a shady back garden,

including the newly renovated beachside bungalow. The onsite chill-out spot is the perfect place to hang out after diving with the folks at the also onsite **Tioman Dive Centre** (www.tioman-dive-centre.com).

CORAL REEF HOLIDAYS   Longhouse $$
(☏419 1868; dm RM25, dm incl breakfast RM45, air-con longhouse s/d/tr RM130/160/160; ❄️ 🛜) Adik and Hasnizah's lovely beachfront longhouse has rooms facing the sea, all with individually crafted stonework, raised platform beds, air-conditioning and colour televisions. The couple also offer air-conditioned and fan cooled dorms,

Tioman's Resorts

Tioman has a number of resorts ranging from merely high-end to the downright extravagant. All have exclusive beaches and private jetties. Book a package deal in advance, either through a travel agent or through their websites. Note that many of these resorts offer amazing deals (up to 50% off listed price) during the monsoon season (November to February)

Melina Beach Resort (☏ 419 7080; www.tioman-melinabeach.com; chalets for 4/5/6/8 people incl breakfast RM200-495; ❄ 🛜) Melina is located on a remote beach of photogenic boulders and white sand. Each sleeping option is unique, creatively designed from wood, thatch and Plexiglas to create a certain Crusoe chic – the most interesting is a tree house that hovers right over the beach. Meals are served at the resort or you can walk for 20 minutes to Genting and try the restaurants there. The owners have set up a successful turtle hatchery, and plenty of activities are organised to keep folks entertained; there's also a beachside bar and BBQ. The relaxed atmosphere attracts lots of families.

Panuba Inn Resort (☏ 419 1424, 07-799 6348; www.panubainn.com; 3-days 2-nights per person from RM355; ❄ 🛜) Peaceful Panuba Inn, over the headland from ABC, has a pier and restaurant and 30 chalets built on a hill overlooking the bay. Rooms all face the sea, ranging from simple fan affairs to chalets with hot shower, air-con and plenty of mod-cons.

Berjaya Tioman Beach, Golf & Spa Resort (☏ 419 1000; www.berjayaresorts. com/tioman; d RM407-1800; ❄ 🛜 🏊) Berjaya is the biggest resort on Tioman. Its accommodation ranges from chalets and suites to entire villas, not to mention standout attractions including tennis, a football pitch, a kid's playground, donkey rides and an arcade. There's two swimming pools (one with great water slides), four restaurants and a beach bar.

and operate an excellent restaurant serving Western and local food.

Air Batang (ABC)

Internet in ABC is spotty; a few guesthouses have wireless, and **Mokhtar's Place** (per hr RM10; ⊙ 9am-10.30pm) has a small internet cafe that isn't always open during posted hours.

ABC CHALET   Chalet $
(☏ 419 1154; d chalets RM50-150; ❄ 🛜) Swing on a hammock overlooking the sea at this lovely section of beach at the north end of ABC. Accommodation is spread over pleasant, well-tended grounds, with a couple of chalets almost on the beach. The large, pricier chalets come with hot water showers, air-con, sea views,

a freezer, and tea- and coffee-making facilities.

BAMBOO HILL CHALETS   Chalet $$$
(☏ 419 1339; bamboosu@tm.net.my; chalets RM90-140; @ 🛜) These six well-kept chalets are in a stupendous location, perched on rocks on the northern end of the beach, surrounded by bougainvillea and humming cicadas alongside a waterfall and pool. They are almost always full, so call ahead.

Salang

SALANG INDAH RESORT   Resort $$
(☏ 419 5015; chalets from RM60-185; ❄ @)
An expanse of chalets seemingly sprawls forever at this resort complex. Most rooms aren't in tip-top condition, but if

you look at several you'll probably find one to your liking. The most interesting are the Popeye-like chalets on stilts over the sea (RM120). The mosque-like restaurant acts as a hub of sorts and serves everything from cheeseburgers to cheap local-style seafood (dishes around RM8). There's also a bar, a shop and internet access (RM10 per hour).

ELLA'S PLACE
Chalet $

(419 5004; chalets RM60-120; ❄) There's usually a lounge-able patch of sand at this cute-as-a-button family-run place at the quiet northern end of the beach. There are 10 clean chalets (some with air-con) and a small café.

Juara

All the places to stay in Juara overlook the magnificent beach; a few places hire out kayaks (RM15 per hour), surfboards (RM20 per hour) and fishing rods (RM15 per hour).

BUSHMAN
Chalet $

(419 3109; matbushman@hotmail.com; chalets fan/air-con RM50/80; ❄ 🛜) Nabbing one of Bushman's five new varnished wood chalets, with their inviting wicker-furnished terraces, is like winning the Juara lottery – reserve in advance! The location is right up against the boulder outcrop and a small river that marks the end of the northern beach. Bushman's little cafe serves breakfast, lunch and dinner, and is a wondrously languorous place to chill out.

BEACH HUT
Hostel $

(012-696 1093; timstormsurf@yahoo.au; camp sites with tent for 2 RM15, dm/chalets RM15/45-55) By the time you read this, Tim and Izan's Beach Hut will have moved 100m north to a brand new location on Matawa beach. If the old spot (a long-time Lonely Planet favourite) is anything to go by, the new establishment will incorporate the same colourful eco-friendly building techniques, including shell mobiles, strategically placed driftwood and Bollywood fabrics run riot. Beachside tent and sleeping bag accommodation will still be available and, of course, surf lessons (RM60 per hour) with surf legend Tim Brent will remain on offer. The social, lounge-able Tube Café will also migrate to the new spot.

Salang (p214)

JOCHEN SCHLENKER/GETTY IMAGES ©

Nipah

NIPAH BEACH TIOMAN   Chalet **$**
(☎ 019-735 7853; chalets from RM70) Young,
friendly host Abbas runs these rustic
chalets on stilts by the water's edge. They
sit so close to the beach that the sound
of waves lapping at the stairs will soothe
you to sleep.

Mukut

MUKUT CORAL RESORT   Chalet **$**
(☎ 07-799 2612, 07-799 2535; r/chalets
RM25/88; ❄️) Traditional village-style chalets (all with air-con and hot water, some
with TV) are set in a marvellous location
beside Mukut's jetty. There's a sea-view
restaurant serving Chinese and Western
food.

❶ Information

Tioman's sole cash machine is in Tekek across
from the airport and takes international cards.
It's been known to run dry, so consider getting
cash in Mersing. Travellers cheques can be
cashed at the Berjaya Tioman Beach, Golf &
Spa Resort and there's a moneychanger at the
airport.

❶ Getting There & Away

Air

Berjaya Air (☎ 419 1309, in KL 03-7846 8228, in
Singapore 02-6481 6302; www.berjaya-air.com)
Has daily flights to/from KL and Singapore.

Boat

Mersing in Johor is the main access port for
Tioman. **Island Connection Tours** (☎ 799
2535; return RM70) has an office in Mersing.
Other operators sell tickets by the jetty for
the same price. Boats run from early morning
until late afternoon, stopping at Genting,
Paya, Berjaya Tioman, Tekek, ABC and Salang,
returning in the reverse order on the return trip.
Decide where you want to get off and tell the
ticket inspector. On weekends and holidays it's
a good idea to buy your tickets in advance since
the boats fill quickly.

Boat departures during the monsoon season
(November to February) can be erratic, with
sailings become more regular during the low
monsoon months (January and February).

Ferries also depart for Tioman from the **Tanjung
Gemok ferry terminal** (☎ 413 1997; return

Golf course, Pulau Tioman

Getting to Juara

Juara is trickier to reach than other spots on Tioman, but oh so worth it. Though the paving of the Tekek–Juara road has technically made Juara more accessible, most taxi drivers still charge the same exorbitant (RM90 to RM120 per vehicle) pre-paved price for the 15-minute trip. A taxi boat from ABC will set you back RM150.

Though the town has a fine jetty, the east coast waves that attract surfers has thus far kept Juara from enjoying the same regular ferry service as towns on the west coast (though the Mersing Ferry sometimes stops here for four or more travellers).

Your best bet for getting here is to arrange transit with one of the hotels. If you're the hardy sort, hiking over from Tekek is definitely an option.

RM70), 35km north of Mersing near Endau. This route is useful if coming from the north. Call ahead and make sure the ferries are running before you arrive.

ℹ Getting Around

Typical sea taxi fares from Telek are: Salang (RM30), ABC/Panuba (RM25), Paya Beach (RM30), Genting (RM30), Nipah (RM75) and Juara (RM105). Most chalets can arrange boat charter. Expect to pay around RM600 for a full day on a boat, and expect waters to be far rougher on the Juara side of Tioman.

If you have the time, you can explore some of the island on foot. Bicycles can be hired at guesthouses on all the main beaches (RM5 per hour).

Though the road from Tekek to Juara is now paved, most operators still are trying to get the pre-paved price of RM90 to RM120 for the relatively short ride. Bargain hard!

Singapore

Love it or loathe it, Singapore is hard to ignore. It's a long-haul stopover staple and Southeast Asia's overachiever. It's also the perfect antidote to the region's trademark grit. But if you think Singapore is little more than endless malls and regulations, get set for a rethink. In recent years the city-state has been revamping itself as Asia's new 'it kid', subverting staid stereotypes with cutting-edge architecture, dynamic museums and hip boutiques. Some of the world's hottest creatives have set up shop on these steamy streets, including New York celebrity chefs and fashion-forward local designers.

Beyond the new and the hyped is a well-worn brew of Chinese, Malay, Indian and Western traditions, of hypnotic temples, gut-rumbling food markets and pockets of steamy jungle. Admit it: Asia's uptight geek is just a little cooler than you ever gave it credit for.

Singapore skyline
REBECCA ANG/GETTY IMAGES ©

Singapore

MALAYSIA

JOHOR BAHRU

Johor Bahru

Strait of Johor

SEMBAWANG

Border Crossing

Sembawang

WOODLANDS

Admiralty

Sungei Buloh Wetland Reserve

Woodlands

Neo Tiew Rd

KRANJI

Marsiling

Kranji

NEE SOON

Sarimbun Reservoir

Lim Chu Kang Rd

Kranji Reservoir

Seletar Expwy

Mandai Rd

④

Old Upper Thomson Rd

Murai Reservoir

Yew Tee

Woodlands Rd

Upper Seletar Reservoir

Choa Chu Kang

Bukit Timah Expwy

CHOA CHU KANG

Lower Peirce Reservoir

Poyan Reservoir

Kranji Expwy

Upper Bukit Timah Rd

Upper Peirce Reservoir

Bukit Batok Rd

Bukit Gombak

Central Catchment Nature Reserve

⑦

MALAYSIA

SINGAPORE

Border Crossing

Tengeh Reservoir

Restricted Zone

Pan Island Expwy

Jln Boon Lay

Lakeside

Bukit Batok

MacRitchie Reservoir

Lornie Rd

Border Crossing

Boon Lay

Chinese Garden

Jurong East

Bukit Timah Rd

Botanic Gardens

Joo Koon

Pioneer

Bukit Timah Rd

TUAS

International Rd

Tuas Cres

Jln Ahmad Ibrahim

Jurong Pier Rd

Pandan Reservoir

Clementi

Holland Village

Farrer Park

JURONG

Tuas Rd

Pioneer Rd

Dover

Boona Vista

Pulau Damar Laut

West Coast Hwy

Kent Ridge Park

See Orchard Road Map (p244)

Strait of Jurong

(Formerly Torumlau Retan Laut)

Queenstown

Redhill

Ayer Rajah Expwy

Haw Par Villa

PASIR PANJANG TERMINAL

Pasir Panjang

Mt Faber Cable Car Station

Jurong Island

Labrador Park

Harbour Front

Sebarok Channel

Pulau Ular

Pulau Bukum

Pulau Hantu

Sisters' Islands (Pulau Subar Darat & Pulau Subar Laut)

Pulau Sudong

Pulau Semakau

Pulau Sakeng

Pulau Sebarok

Strait of Singapore

MALAYSIA

0   5 km
0   2.5 miles

Strait of Johor

Pulau Seletar

YISHUN

Khatib

Lower Seletar Reservoir

Pulau Punggol Barat

Seletar Airport

Pulau Punggol Timor

Punggol Point

Punggol

JL KAYU

Punggol Rd

Punggol

PUNGGOL

Pulau Serangoon

Noordin Beach

Mamam Beach

Pulau Ubin

Pulau Tekong Kechil

Pulau Tekong

Yio Chu Kang

Central Expwy

Ang Mo Kio

Ang Mo Kio Ave 3

Ang Mo Kio Ave 1

SERANGOON

Marymount

Bishan

Braddell

Toa Payoh

Sengkang

Buangkok

HOUGANG

Hougang

Lorong Chuan

Kovan

Serangoon

Tampines Rd

Tampines Expwy

PASIR RIS

Tampines Rd

TAMPINES

Tampines

Pasir Ris Park

LOYANG

Pasir Ris

Simei

SIMEI

Pulau Ketam

Pulau Ubin Ferry Terminal

Changi Point

Changi Point Ferry Terminal

Loyang Rd

CHANGI

Changi Beach Park

Singapore Changi Airport

Changi Airport

Upper Changi East Rd

Expo

Changi Rd

Changi Coast Rd

PAYA LEBAR

Potong Pasir

Serangoon

KIM CHUAN

Paya Lebar

Bedok Reservoir

Simei Ave

Xilin Ave

BEDOK

Bedok

Tanah Merah

Novena

See Little India & Kampong Glem Map (p242)

3

Newton

5

Fiong Bahru

6

1

2

Aljunied

Eunos

Kallang

Lavender

KATONG

Kembangan

See Colonial District & the Quays Map (p231)

East Coast Parkway

Marina Bay

See Chinatown & the CBD Map (p240)

Pulau Brani

Keppel Harbour

Sentosa Island

Lazarus Island (Pulau Sakijang Pelepah)

Kusu Island (Pulau Tembakul)

St John's Island (Pulau Sakijang Bendera)

Strait of Singapore

❶ Marina Bay
❷ Eating
❸ Little India
❹ Singapore Zoo
❺ Shopping
❻ Museums
❼ Jungle Hikes

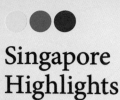

Singapore Highlights

Above: Helix Bridge (p233); Top Right: Gardens by the Bay; Bottom Right: Fullerton Hotel (p247)

① Marina Bay

Singapore's central skyline has been forever transformed with the development of **Marina Bay**. Let your eyeballs [sw]ing from the soaring towers of the CBD to the incred[ible] [a]rchitecture of **Marina Bay Sands** (p233) and the [Garde]ns **by the Bay** (p235). Above: Helix Bridge (p233); Top Right: [Gardens] at the Gardens by the Bay; Bottom Right: Fullerton Hotel (p247)

Need to Know

DO AS THE LOCALS
DO Enjoy superior hawker food at Gluttons Bay, next to Esplanade – Theatres on the Bay **TOP TIP** See the sights from a river cruise **For further coverage, see p234**

Don't Miss Marina Bay

BY YU-MEI BALAMSINGCHOW, WRITER

1 ARCHITECTURE

Marina Bay came up over the last decade as part of a grand government plan to create a new purpose-built precinct for business, living and leisure – and it shows in the stunning architecture. The already iconic **Esplanade – Theatres on the Bay** (p235) complex has been eclipsed by the Moshe Safdie–designed **Marina Bay Sands** (p**233**); its three 55-storey towers are connected by a sky terrace that looks like a giant spaceship coming into dock. There's a viewing deck up there, as well as the see-or-be-seen **Ku De Ta** bar, or you can take a turn in the nearby **Singapore Flyer**, the world's largest Ferris wheel (for now).

2 GARDENS BY THE BAY

Futuristic, 50m high 'supertrees' dominate the 101-hectare **Gardens by the Bay** (p235), the glitzy botanical showpiece that sprawls over the southern waterfront of Marina Bay. The gardens include two giant air-cooled conservatories for flowers and plants from the Mediterranean, semi-arid tropical and cooler mountain regions. Up in the supertrees – which collect rainwater, produce solar power and act as venting ducts for the conservatories – there's a suspended walkway where you can get lovely views of the gardens and waterfront.

3 COLLYER QUAY

Amid all this reinvention some fragments of old Singapore remain. **Collyer Quay**, where immigrants once used to disembark, has been revamped and former port offices turned into elegant restaurants. Check out historic **Clifford Pier** and the rooftop bars at **Customs House**, or admire the neo-classical architecture of the **Fullerton Hotel** (p247).

Culinary Singapore

Singapore is one of the world's top dining destinations, and the locals' obsession with all things edible borders on the fanatical. Everyone is a self-proclaimed expert on where to find the food and you can easily find their opinions and photos online. Below: Chicken-rice set; Top Right: Glutton's Bay food court at Esplanade – Theatres on the Bay (p235); Bottom Right: Singapore food store

Need to Know

TOP TIPS At hawker centres join the longest queues and look for stalls decorated with accolades **For further coverage, see p248**

2

Don't Miss Culinary Singapore

BY DR LESLIE TAY, FOOD WRITER,
WWW.IEATISHOOTIPOST.SG

1 HAWKER CENTRES & MARKETS

At hawker centres you'll find many unique Singaporean dishes which have evolved from the cuisines of China, Malaysia, Indonesia and India. Park your airs and graces: here it's all about queuing up for your food, sharing tables and using plastic spoons and disposable chopsticks. At the more popular places you'd be well advised to *chope* (reserve) a seat first and have a companion save it while you browse the stalls. If you want to eat like a local, then head for **Maxwell Road Hawker Centre** (p249) or Smith St, where you can find a plethora of stalls selling local delights such as chicken-rice, fish soup and more. If you want to see where the locals buy their produce, head for the **Tekka Centre** (p250), or Geylang Serai in Singapore's east. You will find a great concentration of Indian and Malay cuisines at these two markets respectively.

2 HAUTE CUISINE

Singapore had fancy dining spots long before the integrated resorts (casino complexes at Marina Bay and Sentosa) upped the stakes by signing up international culinary talents including Tetsuya Wakuda, Guy Savoy and Daniel Boulud. The prices at these star chef restaurants are equally extravagant, which can leave you wondering about value for money. If you want a more reasonably priced white tablecloth experience, reliable recommendations include **Jaan** (p248), **Iggy's** (p251) and **Au Jardin Les Amis** (p251). Haute hawker cuisine, including souped up versions of local favourites like *bak kut teh* (pork stew) and Hokkien mee (noodles), can be found atop the Marina Bay Resort at **Sky on 57**.

3 FOOD TOURS & COOKING CLASSES

The best way to get handle on the local food scene is join a food tour. **Betel Box Tours** (www.betelbox. com) runs a Thursday night food walk around the eastern Singapore neighbourhood of Joo Chiat – this is a backpackers' favourite. **Food Safari Tours** (www. makansutra.com) has itineraries that cover different themes and areas of the island. For a more hands-on experience there's also several excellent cooking classes.

227

Explore Little India

The most atmospheric of Singapore's historic quarters (p238) is as close as it gets to Singapore of the old chaotic days. The five-foot ways of the shophouses spill over with aromatic spices and colourful products. The deity-festooned temples flicker with thousands of ghee candles. In 2014 the new **Indian Heritage Centre** will open at the corner of Campbell Lane and Clive St. *Gopuram* (entrance tower), Sri Veeramakaliamman Temple

3

4

Animal Close Encounters

Singapore's amazing **zoo** (p245) is one of the few places outside of Borneo or Sumatra where you can stand under trees with orangutans a few feet above your head. The open-air enclosures allow for both freedom for the animals to roam and unobstructed visitor views. Observe nocturnal creatures like leopards and Malayan tigers at the **Night Safari** (p245) next door. White tigers at Singapore Zoo

Shop Till You Drop

RICHARD I'ANSON/GETTY IMAGES ©

5

Mall-heavy, chain-centric Orchard Rd is Singapore's retail queen, though it's only one of several retail hubs. For computers and electronics, hit specialist malls like **Funan Digita-Life Mall** (p256), **Sim Lim Square** (p258) and the **Mustafa Centre** (p258). **Kampong Glam** is also famous for its perfume traders, as well as for hip, independent fashion boutiques on **Haji Lane** (p257). Good places for antiques include Dempsey Hill and Chinatown. Sim Lim Square

SONY

TP

LM

LJ

WA1

SONY
Digital Home

A New Style
in Home Living

Packard

CLAUS VEDFELT/GETTY IMAGES ©

6

Magnificent Museums

Another thing Singapore does supremely well is museums. The **National Museum of Singapore** (p234) is a colourful, intimate journey, peppered with historical artefacts, personal accounts, and evocative reconstructions that span everything from ancient Malay royals to colonial era back-stabbing, 20th-century rioting and reinvention, hawker food, fashion and film. Also well worth visiting are the **Asian Civilisations Museum** (p234) and the **Peranakan Museum** (p235). Asian Civilisations Museum

7

Jungle Hikes

Jungle? In Singapore? Believe it or not the island offers a surprising number of green pockets. The **Bukit Timah Nature Reserve's** (p259) unbroken forest canopy shelters numerous surviving species of Singapore's native wildlife, including monkeys, pythons and birds. Also check out the **Southern Ridges** (p243), 9km of trails through shaded parks and across spectacular suspended walkways. Bukit Timah Nature Reserve

SINGAPORE HIGHLIGHTS **229**

Singapore's Best...

Urban Escapes

o **Singapore Botanic Gardens** (p239) Free classical-music concerts are held regularly here and its a lovely spot for a meal or picnic.

o **Fort Canning Park** (p235) A wonderfully cool retreat from the hot downtown streets below.

o **Pulau Ubin** (p251) A rustic island getaway that offers a glimpse of *kampung* (village) life.

o **Sentosa** (p241) Singapore's playground offers Universal Studios, an aquarium, a mega-casino and beach-side cocktails.

Religous Buildings

o **Thian Hock Keng Temple** (p238) The gates are Scottish and the tiles Dutch at this historic Chinatown temple.

o **Sultan Mosque** (p239) Gold-domed focal point of Kampong Glam.

o **Sri Mariamman Temple** (p238) Every October hosts the Thimithi festival, during which devotees hot-foot it over burning coals. Ouch.

o **St Andrew's Cathedral** (p235) The grounds make a lovely place for a picnic or siesta on the grass.

Hawker Food

o **Maxwell Road Hawker Centre** (p249) Chicken-rice is famous here; the late hours are also a bonus.

o **Chomp Chomp Food Centre** (p248) Join locals at this central island hawker heaven.

o **Old Airport Road Food Centre** (p248) An out-of-centre hawker gem.

o **Tekka Centre** (p250) Little India's wet market has a fab hawker selection.

o **Lau Pa Sat** (p250) Touristy but in a fabulous iron structure shipped from Glasgow in 1894.

Drinking

Lantern Bar (p252) Atop the Fullerton Bay Hotel with knockout views of Marina Bay.

New Asia (p251) Dazzling decor, 70th-floor views and a dance floor.

Brewerkz (p252) Microbrewery happiness at Clarke Quay.

Tippling Club (p253) Cocktail creativity in Montigrey Hill.

Tanjong Beach Club (p254) Sip cocktails with the body-beautiful crowd on Sentosa.

Left: Sultan Mosque (p239); **Above:** Singapore Botanic Gardens (p239)

Need to Know

VITAL STATISTICS
- **Country code** 65

ADVANCE PLANNING
- **One month before** Book accommodation and reserve tables at top restaurants.

- **One week before** Book tickets online for Gardens by the Bay and Baba House.

- **One day before** Check for local events and festivals. Prepare your system to gorge on local eats.

RESOURCES
- **Visit Singapore** (www. visitsingapore) Official tourism-board site.

- **Singapore.SG** (www. sg.com) General info.

- **Sistic** (www.sistic.com. sg) One stop shop for show and concert tickets.

GETTING AROUND
- **Mass Rapid Transit (MRT)** The local subway is the most convenient way to get around from 6am till midnight. Get a tap-and-go EZ-link electronic travel card to use on MRT trains and local buses; these can be purchased at all MRT stations.

- **Buses** Go everywhere the trains do and more. Great for views.

- **Taxis** Fairly cheap by global city standards. Flag one down or go to taxi stands (the best options are at busy places like Orchard Rd).

BE FOREWARNED
- **Accommodation** Book well in advance (and be prepared to pay more) for weekends, public holidays and big events like the Formula One Night Race.

- **Visas** Citizens of most countries are granted 30-day visas on arrival by air or overland (though some others may get 14-day visas). The exceptions are Myanmar, India, Pakistan, most Middle Eastern countries and the Commonwealth of Independent States.

- **Taxis** Good luck getting one in the rain or at driver shift change-over times (around 4pm). Watch out for hefty surcharges during peak hours and from midnight to 6am.

Singapore Walking Tour

You'll experience colonial and contemporary Singapore on this walk. It's a visual history lesson on the city's evolution, beginning at the hotel named for its founder and ending at 21st-century wonder Marina Bay Sands.

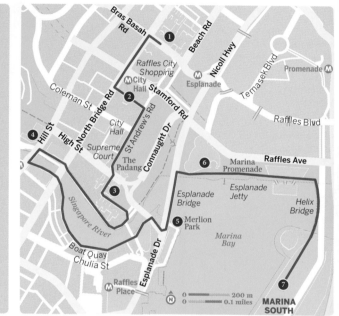

WALK FACTS

- **Start** Raffles Hotel
- **End** Marina Bay Sands
- **Distance** 4km
- **Time** Four to five hours

❶ Raffles Hotel

Start at Singapore's most famous hotel, in business since 1887. Wander around the cavernous lobby and shopping arcade (on the 3rd floor you'll find the **Raffles Hotel Museum**) before heading out along North Bridge Rd.

❷ St Andrew's Cathedral, City Hall & the Supreme Court

Turn left into the magnificent **St Andrew's Cathedral**; this building dates from 1862 after lightning damaged the original 1838 building twice. Pop out the opposite side on St Andrew's Rd.

Continue past **City Hall** and the **old Supreme Court**; both are in the process of being converted into the **National Art Gallery** (www.nationalartgallery.sg), due to open in 2015. Nearby is the **new Supreme Court**, with its unmistakable spaceship design.

❸ Victoria Theatre & Concert Hall

Below where St Andrew's Rd curves to the left you'll find a group of colonial-era buildings including the **Victoria Theatre & Concert Hall** and **Old Parliament House**, in front of which you'll see the **original Raffles statue**, which once stood at the Padang.

Old Hill Street Police Station & Boat Quay

Hang a right and continue along the northern bank of the **Singapore River**. The picturesque building with the multicoloured window frames, on the corner of Hill St, is the **old Hill Street Police Station**, which currently houses the Ministry of Communication & the Arts (MICA) and several good art galleries. Cross the road at Hill St and head towards the river. This stretch is **Boat Quay**, once Singapore's centre of commerce, remaining an important economic area into the 1960s. By the mid-1980s many of the shophouses were in ruins. Declared a conservation zone by the government, the area has reinvented itself as an entertainment district packed with restaurants and bars.

5 Merlion Statue

Follow the river further east to the point where it reaches **Marina Bay**. In **Merlion Park** here you find the famous **Merlion statue**. This legendary-looking figure, part lion and part fish, was actually designed for the Singapore Tourism Board in 1964.

6 Esplanade – Theatres on the Bay

Head north along the **Esplanade Bridge** towards **Esplanade – Theatres on the Bay**. This S$600-million arts complex has been compared to flies' eyes, melting honeycomb and two upturned durians. In fact, the building's aluminium shades reference Asian reed-weaving geometries and maximise natural light.

7 Helix Bridge & Marina Bay Sands

Head east along the **Marina Promenade** till you get to the **Helix Bridge**, its twisting shape inspired by the structure of DNA. The footbridge offers a great vantage point for photos across **Marina Bay**. Ahead lies your last stop, **Marina Bay Sands**: this stunning contemporary building houses a casino, a hotel and a full range of shopping and entertainment options.

Singapore In ...

ONE DAY

Gain some cultural insight at the city's top museums. Posh nosh at **Flutes at the Fort**, then check out Chinatown's temples. Dine at **Blue Ginger** and slurp mojitos at **La Terrazza**.

TWO DAYS

Breakfast at Little India's **Ananda Bhavan** or the **Tekka Centre** and shop at the **Mustafa Centre**, then mall-hop **Orchard Rd** or browse **Haji Lane**. Head to **Singapore Zoo** before 'going wild' at the **Night Safari**.

THREE DAYS

Take an early-morning stroll along the **Southern Ridges** before catching the cable car to **Sentosa**. Lounge on one of the beaches then hit the rides at **Universal Studios**.

FOUR DAYS

Catch a bumboat to **Pulau Ubin** for a jungle cycle. On the way back, drop into the **Old Airport Road Hawker Centre** for a cheap Singaporean feast. End the night at **Lantern Bar** or party at **Clarke Quay**.

Siloso Beach, Sentosa Island (p

Discover Singapore

History

Singapore has hardly looked back since Sir Thomas Stamford Raffles stepped into the mud in 1819 hell-bent on making the island a bastion of the British Empire. Despite a few ups and downs – invasion by the Japanese in WWII and getting booted out of the nascent federation of Malaysia in 1965 – the island has prospered in its role as a free-trade hub for Southeast Asia.

◉ Sights

Colonial District, the Quays & Marina Bay

NATIONAL MUSEUM OF SINGAPORE Museum

(Map p236; www.nationalmuseum.sg; 93 Stamford Rd; adult/child S$10/5; ⊙history gallery 10am-6pm, living galleries 10am-8pm; MDhoby Ghaut) Imaginative, prodigiously stocked and brilliantly designed, Singapore's National Museum is good enough to warrant two visits. Staid exhibitions are ditched for lively, multimedia galleries that bring Singapore's action-packed bio to vivid life.

ASIAN CIVILISATIONS MUSEUM Museum

(Map p236; www.acm.org.sg; 1 Empress Pl; adult/child S$8/4, half price after 7pm Fri; ⊙1-7pm Mon, 9am-7pm Tue-Thu, Sat & Sun, 9am-9pm Fri; MRaffles Pl) This remarkable museum houses Southeast Asia's most comprehensive collection of pan-Asian treasures. Its 11 beautifully curated galleries explore the history, cultures and religions of Southeast Asia, China, the Asian subcontinent and Islamic West Asia, with

Gardens by the Bay
SIVAKUMAR SATHIAMOORTHY/GETTY IMAGES ©

...lennia of ancient carvings, weaponry, ...ttering jewels and textiles.

PERANAKAN MUSEUM Museum
(Map p236; www.peranakanmuseum.sg; 39 Armenian St; adult/child S$6/3, admission 7-9pm Fri free; ☉1-7pm Mon, 9.30am-7pm Tue-Sun, to 9pm Fri; Ⓜ City Hall) Stylish, interactive and thoroughly engrossing. Explore 10 thematic galleries for an insight into both traditional and contemporary Peranakan culture, from marriage and folklore, to fashion and food. Artefacts include exquisite textiles, furniture and engaging multimedia displays.

SINGAPORE ART MUSEUM Museum
(SAM; Map p236; ☎6332 3222; www.singapore artmuseum.sg; 71 Bras Basah Rd; adult/student & senior S$10/5, admission free 6-9pm Fri; ☉10am-7pm Sat-Thu, to 9pm Fri; Ⓜ Bras Basah) SAM showcases mostly modern and contemporary Southeast Asian from painting and sculpture, to site-specific installations and video art. Round the corner, the art museum's newer extension, **8Q SAM** (Map p236; www.singart.com/8qsam; 8 Queen St; admission free with SAM ticket; ☉10am-7pm Sat-Thu, to 9pm Fri; Ⓜ City Hall or Bras Basah), delivers quirky installations, interactivity and (more) contemporary creations.

GARDENS BY THE BAY Park
(www.gardensbythebay.org.sg; 18 Marina Gardens Drive; admission free, adult/child conservatories S$28/15, skyway S$5/3; ☉5am-2am, conservatories & skyway 9am-9pm, last ticket sales conservatories 8pm, skyway 8pm Mon-Fri, 7pm Sat & Sun; Ⓜ Bayfront) Catapulting nature into the future, Gardens by the Bay is the latest blockbuster attraction at Marina Bay and Singapore's newest botanic gardens. Highlights include soaring, sci-fi 'supertrees' and futuristic conservatories housing plants from endangered habitats.

RAFFLES HOTEL Historic Building
(Map p236; www.rafffleshotel.com; 1 Beach Rd; Ⓜ City Hall) Birthplace of the Singapore Sling, and featured in novels by Joseph Conrad and Somerset Maugham, the grand old Raffles started life in 1887 as a 10-room bungalow fronted by the (since land-filled) beach.

FORT CANNING PARK Park
(Map p236; Ⓜ Dhoby Ghaut) When Raffles rolled into Singapore in 1819, locals steered clear of Fort Canning Hill, then called Bukit Larangan (Forbidden Hill), out of respect for the sacred shrine of Sultan Iskandar Shah, ancient Singapura's last ruler. Today, you can glimpse 14th-century Javanese artefacts at the park's archaeological dig, get a natural high in the park's spice garden, and snoop around WWII bunkers at the **Battle Box Museum** (Map p236; www.legendsfortcanning. com/fortcanning/battlebox.htm; 2 Cox Tce; adult/child S$8/5; ☉10am-6pm, last entry 5pm; Ⓜ Dhoby Ghaut).

ESPLANADE – THEATRES ON THE BAY Arts Centre
(Map p236; ☎6828 8377; www.esplanade. com; 1 Esplanade Dr; ☉10am-6pm, box office noon-8.30pm; Ⓜ Esplanade) Poster-boy for contemporary Singapore, this arts complex offers a nonstop program of international and local performances, some great restaurants and free outdoor performances.

ST ANDREW'S CATHEDRAL Church
(Map p236; www.livingstreams.org.sg; 11 St Andrew's Rd; ☉9am-5pm Mon-Sat; Ⓜ City Hall) Singapore's sugar-white wedding-cake cathedral has a 63.1m-tall tower, towering naves and lovely stained glass above the west doors.

Chinatown & the CBD

FREE **BABA HOUSE** Museum
(Map p240; ☎6227 5731; www.nus.edu.sg/cfa/ museum; 157 Neil Rd; ☉1hr tours 2pm Mon, 6.30pm Tue, 10am Thu, 11am Sat; Ⓜ Outram Park) You need to book ahead to visit Baba House, but the guided tour of this faithfully restored Peranakan heritage home is well worth the effort. It's furnished as it was in the 1920s, and its knowledgeable tour guides weave tales of affluent Peranakan life with every detail, including the secret peepholes through which shy Nonya ladies could spy on guests in the central hall.

2

Colonial District & the Quays

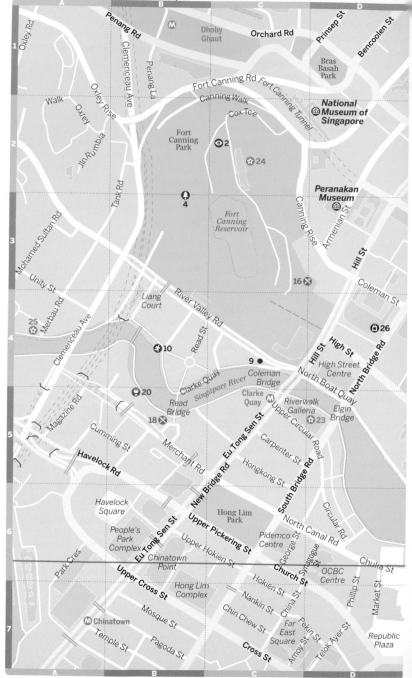

Oxley Rd

Penang Rd

Dhoby Ghaut

Orchard Rd

Prinsep St

Bencoolen St

Clemenceau Ave

Penang La

Walk

Oxley Rise

Oxley

Fort Canning Rd

Fort Canning Tunnel

Canning Walk

Cox Tce

Bras Basah Park

National Museum of Singapore

Jln Rumbia

Fort Canning Park

2

24

Tank Rd

Peranakan Museum

Armenian St

Mohamed Sultan Rd

4

Fort Canning Reservoir

Canning Rise

Unity St

Merbau Rd

Liang Court

River Valley Rd

Hill St

Coleman St

25

Clemenceau Ave

16

26

Read St

High St

Magazine Rd

10

Clarke Quay

Coleman Bridge

9

Hill St

High Street Centre

North Boat Quay

North Bridge Rd

North Bridge Rd

20

Read Bridge

Singapore River

Clarke Quay

Riverwalk Galleria

Elgin Bridge

18

Eu Tong Sen St

Upper Circular Road

23

Cumming St

Merchant Rd

Carpenter St

Havelock Rd

New Bridge Rd

Hongkong St

South Bridge Rd

Circular Rd

Havelock Square

Upper Pickering St

Hong Lim Park

North Canal Rd

People's Park Complex

Eu Tong Sen St

Upper Hokien St

Pidemco Centre

George St

Chulia St

Park Cres

Chinatown Point

Church St

Singapore

OCBC Centre

Upper Cross St

Hong Lim Complex

Hokien St

China St

Phillip St

Market St

Chinatown

Mosque St

Chin Chew St

Nankin St

Far East Square

Pekin St

Telok Ayer St

Republic Plaza

Temple St

Pagoda St

Cross St

Amoy St

5

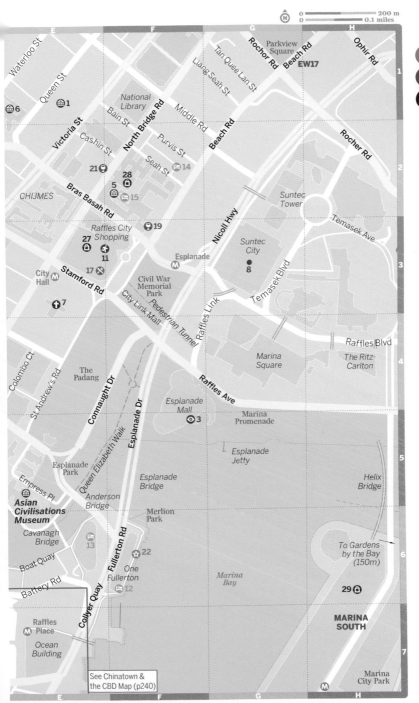

0   200 m
0   0.1 miles

Waterloo St

Queen St

6

1

Victoria St

National Library

Bain St

North Bridge Rd

Middle Rd

Purvis St

Beach Rd

Tan Quee Lan St

Liang Seah St

Rochor Rd

Parkview Square

Beach Rd

EW17

Ophir Rd

Rochor Rd

Cashin St

Seah St

14

21

28

5

15

CHIJMES

Bras Basah Rd

Suntec Tower

Temasek Ave

Raffles City Shopping

27

19

11

17

Esplanade

Suntec City

8

Temasek Blvd

City Hall

Stamford Rd

7

Civil War Memorial Park

City Link Mall

Pedestrian Tunnel

Nicoll Hwy

Raffles Link

Marina Square

Raffles Blvd

The Ritz-Carlton

Colombo Ct

St Andrew's Rd

The Padang

Connaught Dr

Esplanade Dr

Raffles Ave

Esplanade Mall

3

Marina Promenade

Esplanade Park

Queen Elizabeth Walk

Esplanade Bridge

Esplanade Jetty

Helix Bridge

Empress Pl

Anderson Bridge

Merlion Park

Asian Civilisations Museum

Cavanagh Bridge

Fullerton Rd

13

22

To Gardens by the Bay (150m)

Boat Quay

Battery Rd

One Fullerton

12

Marina Bay

29

MARINA SOUTH

Raffles Place

Ocean Building

Collyer Quay

See Chinatown & the CBD Map (p240)

Marina City Park

Colonial District & the Quays

**THIAN HOCK KENG
TEMPLE**   Hindu Temple

(Map p240; 158 Telok Ayer St; ⏰7.30am-5.30pm; Ⓜ Chinatown, Tanjong Pagar, Raffles Pl) Chinatown's most important Hokkien temple is often a haven of tranquillity. Built between 1839 and 1842, it was once the favourite landing point of Chinese sailors, before land reclamation pushed the sea far down the road.

**BUDDHA TOOTH
RELIC TEMPLE**   Buddhist Temple

(Map p240; www.btrts.org.sg; 288 South Bridge Rd; ⏰7am-7pm, relic viewing 9am-6pm; Ⓜ Chinatown) Consecrated in 2008, this huge, five-storey Buddhist temple houses what is reputedly the left canine tooth of the Buddha. While its authenticity is contested, the relic enjoys VIP status inside a 420kg solid-gold stupa (BYO binoculars) in a dazzlingly ornate 4th-floor room.

**SRI MARIAMMAN
TEMPLE**   Hindu Temple

(Map p240; 244 South Bridge Rd; ⏰7am-noon & 6-9pm; Ⓜ Chinatown) Originally built in 1823, then rebuilt in 1843, Singapore's oldest Hindu temple is most famous for its explosively colourful *gopuram* (entrance tower) featuring deliciously kitsch statues of Brahma the creator, Vishnu the preserver and Shiva the destroyer.

Little India & Kampong Glam

**SRI VEERAMAKALIAMMAN
TEMPLE**   Hindu Temple

(Map p242; 141 Serangoon Rd; ⏰5.15am-12.15pm & 4-9.15pm; Ⓜ Little India) Little India's most colourful, bustling temple is dedicated to the goddess Kali, usually depicted wearing a necklace of skulls and disembowelling unfortunate humans. The temple is at its most evocative during each of the four daily *puja* (prayer) sessions.

ABDUL GAFOOR MOSQUE   Mosque

(Map p242; 41 Dunlop St; MLittle India) Completed in 1910, the Abdul Gafoor mosque serves up a storybook fusion of Moorish, southern Indian and Victorian architectural styles. Look out for the elaborate and unique sundial crowning its main entrance, each of its 25 rays decorated with Arabic calligraphy denoting the names of 25 prophets.

SRI SRINIVASA
PERUMAL TEMPLE   Hindu Temple

(Map p242; 397 Serangoon Rd; ⊘5.45am-noon & 5-9pm; MFarrer Park) Dedicated to Vishnu, this temple dates from 1855 but the striking, 20m-tall *gopuram* is a S$300,000 1966 addition. Inside is a statue of Vishnu, his companions Lakshmi and Andal, and his bird-mount Garuda.

SULTAN MOSQUE   Mosque

(Map p242; www.sultanmosque.org.sg; 3 Muscat St; ⊘9am-noon & 2-4pm Sat-Thu, 2.30-4pm Fri; MBugis) Singapore's largest mosque was originally built in 1825 with the aid of a grant from Raffles and the East India Company, as a result of Raffles' treaty with the Sultan of Singapore that allowed him to retain sovereignty over the area. A hundred years later in 1928, the original mosque was replaced by the present magnificent building.

Orchard Road & Around

SINGAPORE BOTANIC
GARDENS   Garden

(☎6471 7361; www.sbg.org.sg; 1 Cluny Rd; Garden admission free, National Orchid Garden adult/senior/child S$5/1/free; ⊘5am-midnight, National Orchid Garden 8.30am-7pm, last entry 6pm; ☐7, 105, 123, MBotanic Gardens) Located 2km west of Orchard Rd, Singapore's 52-hectare Botanic Gardens are an urban Xanax, complete with lakes, rare rainforest, symphony stage and themed gardens.

The National Orchid Garden is home to over 1000 species and 2000 hybrids of orchids, around 600 of which are on display – the largest showcase of tropical orchids on Earth. Look out for the *Vanda*

❤ # If You Like...
Spas & Massage

Massage, beauty treatments and reflexology are regulation Singaporean indulgences. Every mall seems to have a spa or massage joint of some sort, so you're never too far from an overhaul.

1 WILLOW STREAM
(Map p236; ☎6339 7777; www.willowstream.com/singapore; Level 6, Fairmont Hotel, 80 Bras Basah Rd; massage treatments from S$149; MCity Hall) Plunge pools, jacuzzis, and aromatic steam rooms await at this luxe oasis. There are 11 types of massage (including 'travel recovery' and 'shoppers relief' options).

2 PEOPLE'S PARK COMPLEX
(Map p240; 1 Park Rd; ⊘10am-9.30pm; MChinatown) This no-frills Chinatown mall is packed with cheap massage places ready to vie for your body parts (opt for the busier ones). Our favourite is **Mr Lim Foot Reflexology** (Map p240; 03-53 & 03-78, People's Park Complex).

3 KENKO WELLNESS SPA
(Map p240; www.kenko.com.sg; 199 South Bridge Rd; reflexology per 30min $36, body massage per 60min S$91; ⊘10am-10pm; MChinatown) Kenko is the McDonalds of Singapore spas, with branches throughout the city, but there's nothing drive-through about its foot reflexology, romantic couples' sessions (S$328 per 2 ½ hour session) or Chinese and Swedish massage (if you're after something forceful, go Chinese).

Miss Joaquim, Singapore's national flower, which Agnes Joaquim discovered in her garden in 1893.

EMERALD HILL
ROAD   Historic Neighbourhood

(Map p244; MSomerset) Take refuge from retail on Emerald Hill Rd, a heritage-lauded street lined with some of Singapore's finest terrace houses. Special mentions go out to No 56 (built in 1902, and one of the earliest buildings here), Nos 39 to 45 (with unusually wide frontages and a grand Chinese-style entrance gate) and

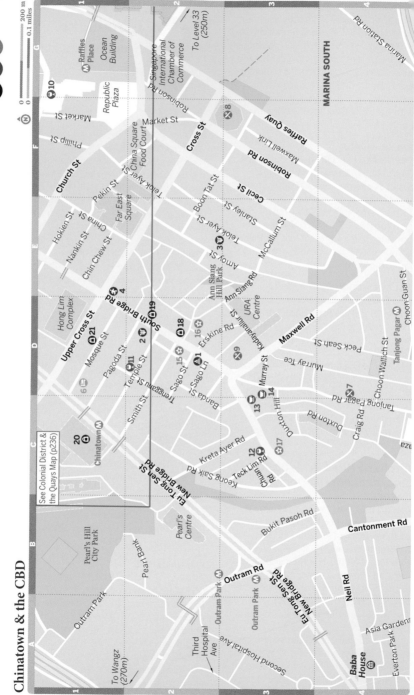

Chinatown & the CBD

See Colonial District & the Quays Map (p236)

To Wangz (270m)

Pearl's Hill City Park

Pearl Bank

Outram Park

Third Hospital Ave

Second Hospital Rd

Outram Park Ⓜ

Outram Rd

Eu Tong Sen St New Bridge Rd

Neil Rd

Asia Gardens

Baba House

Everton Park

Pearl's Centre

Bukit Pasoh Rd

Cantonment Rd

Hong Lim Complex

Upper Cross St

Mosque St

Pagoda St

Temple St

Smith St

Trengganu St

Sago St

Sago Ln

Banda St

Kreta Ayer Rd

Keong Saik Rd

Teck Lim Rd

Chin Cheng Rd

Eu Tong Sen St New Bridge Rd

South Bridge Rd

Nankin St

Hokien St

China St

Chin Chew St

Pekin St

Far East Square

Telok Ayer St

China Square Food Court

Church St

Phillip St

Market St

Cross St

Market St

Robinson Rd

Boon Tat St

Stanley St

Cecil St

McCallum St

Amoy St

Ann Siang Hill Park

Ann Siang Rd

URA Centre

Kadayanallur St

Erskine Rd

Maxwell Rd

Murray St

Duxton Hill

Duxton Rd

Craig Rd

Tanjong Pagar Rd

Peck Seah St

Murray Tce

Choon Wallich St

Tanjong Pagar Ⓜ

Choon Guan St

Marina Station Rd

MARINA SOUTH

Robinson Rd

Maxwell Link

Raffles Quay

Raffles Place Ⓜ

Ocean Building

Republic Plaza

Singapore International Chamber of Commerce

To Level 33 (250m)

Chinatown Ⓜ

Pearl's Centre

Raffles Quay

200 m
0.1 miles

Ⓝ

Ⓖ 10

Ⓖ 20

Ⓖ 8

Ⓖ 21

Ⓖ 4

Ⓖ 2

Ⓖ 11

Ⓖ 1

Ⓖ 3

Ⓖ 9

Ⓖ 6

Ⓖ 7

Ⓖ 12

Ⓖ 13

Ⓖ 14

Ⓖ 15

Ⓖ 16

Ⓖ 17

Ⓖ 18

Ⓖ 19

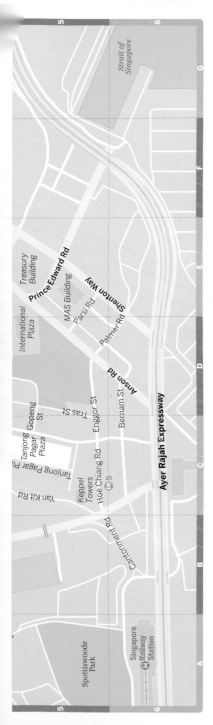

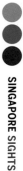

Chinatown & the CBD

◎ Top Sights
Baba House A4

◎ Sights
1 Buddha Tooth Relic Temple...............D2
2 Sri Mariamman Temple D2
3 Thian Hock Keng Temple....................E2

⊕ Activities, Courses & Tours
4 Kenko Wellness Spa.............................E1
Mr Lim Foot Reflexology............(see 20)

⊜ Sleeping
5 Klapsons C6
6 Wink Hostel...D1

⊗ Eating
7 Blue Ginger D4
8 Lau Pa Sat...F3
9 Maxwell Road Hawker Centre.............D3

⊝ Drinking
10 1 Altitude G1
11 Backstage Bar......................................D2
La Terrazza .... (see 16)
12 Tantric Bar...C3
13 Tea Chapter...C3
14 Yixing Xuan Teahouse.........................D3

⊛ Entertainment
15 Chinese Theatre Circle........................D2
16 Screening Room D2
17 Taboo C3

⊜ Shopping
18 Eu Yan Sang..D2
19 Far East Legend D2
20 People's Park Complex........................C1
21 Utterly Art D1

Nos 120 to 130 (with art deco features dating from around 1925).

At the Orchard Rd end of the hill is a cluster of buzzing bars housed in beautiful shophouse renovations, among them handsome Latino Que Pasa (p253).

Sentosa Island & Mt Faber

There is a small entrance fee to enter Sentosa Island, but it varies depending on which form of transport you choose. If you walk across from the VivoCity shopping mall, the fee is S$1. If you catch the Sentosa Express monorail (which leaves from Level 3 of VicoCity), it's S$3.50. If you ride the cable car, the fee is included in the cable car ticket price.

Once on the island, it's easy to get around, either by walking, taking the Sentosa Express (7am to midnight),

riding the free 'beach tram' (shuttling the length of all three beaches, 9am to 11pm, to midnight Friday and Saturday) or by using the free three colour-coded bus routes that link the main attractions

Little India & Kampong Glam

Little India & Kampong Glam

◎ Sights
1 Abdul Gafoor Mosque B3
2 Sri Srinivasa Perumal Temple C1
3 Sri Veeramakaliamman Temple B2
4 Sultan Mosque C4

◎ Sleeping
5 Albert Court Village Hotel A3
6 Wanderlust B3

◎ Eating
Ah-Rahman Royal Prata .... (see 8)
Ananda Bhavan .... (see 8)
7 Bismillah Biryani B3

8 Tekka Centre A3
9 Warong Nasi Pariaman C4

◎ Drinking
10 Zsofi Tapas Bar B3

◎ Shopping
11 Celebration of Arts A3
12 Dulcetfig C4
13 K.I.N. C4
14 Little Shophouse D4
15 Mustafa Centre B2
16 Sifr Aromatics D4
17 Sim Lim Square B4

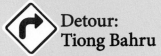

Detour:
Tiong Bahru

Those with finely tuned hipster radars will most likely end up in Singapore's Tiong Bahru neighbourhood. Yet Singapore's latest epicentre of cool is more than just idiosyncratic boutiques, bars and cafes – it's also a rare heritage gem. Distinctly low-rise, the area was Singapore's first public housing estate and its streetscapes of whitewashed, 'walk-up' art deco apartments are an unexpected architectural treat.

For a taste of pre-gentrification, dive into the **Tiong Bahru Market & Food Centre** (83 Seng Poh Rd; M Tiong Bahru), old school right down to its orange-toned exterior, the neighbourhood's original hue. The upstairs hawker centre is home to cultish **Tiong Bahru Roasted Pig** (02-38, Tiong Bahru Market & Food Centre; ⌚7.30am-7.30pm) and **Jan Bo Shui Kueh** (02-05, Tiong Bahru Market & Food Centre; ⌚6.30am-10.30pm), the latter famous for its amazing *chwee kueh* (steamed rice cake topped with diced preserved radish).

For new-school cool, hit Yong Siak St. It's here that you'll find coffee geek mecca **40 Hands** (www.40handscoffee.com; 78 Yong Siak St; ⌚8.30am-6.30pm Tue & Sun, 8.30am-10pm Wed & Thu, 8.30am-11pm Fri & Sat; M Tiong Bahru), fantastic independent bookshop **BooksActually** (www.booksactually.com; 9 Yong Siak St; ⌚11am-6pm Mon, 11am-9pm Tue-Fri, 10am-9pm Sat, 10am-6pm Sun; M Tiong Bahru) and worldly design store **Strangelets** (www.strangelets.sg; 7 Yong Siak St; M Tiong Bahru).

(7am to 11pm, to 12.30am Friday and Saturday).

UNIVERSAL STUDIOS Amusement Park (www.rwsentosa.com; Resorts World; adult/child/senior S$74/54/36; ⌚10am-7pm) The top-draw attraction at Resorts World, Universal Studios' booty of rides, roller coasters, shows, shops and restaurants, are neatly packaged into fantasy world themes based on your favourite Hollywood films. One of the highlights is the pair of 'dueling roller coasters' in Sci-fi City, said to be the tallest of their kind in the world.

MARITIME EXPERIENTIAL MUSEUM Museum (www.rwsentosa.com; Resorts World; adult/child museum S$5/2, theatre S$6/4; ⌚10am-7pm Mon-Thu, 10am-9pm Fri-Sun, Typhoon Theatre closes 1hr earlier) Explore the intriguing history of the maritime Silk Route at this interactive, state-of-the-art museum. While the 360-degree Typhoon Theatre is a slight let-down (think 10 minutes of computer-generated wizardry, wind machines and bad acting), the Maritime Archaeology in Southeast Asia exhibition is genuinely engrossing, with fascinating information on the conservation of shipwreck artefacts.

UNDERWATER WORLD Aquarium (☎6275 0030; www.underwaterworld.com.sg; behind Siloso Beach, adult/child S$25.90/17.60, ⌚10am-7pm) Seadragons and wobbling medusa jellyfish are mesmeric, while stingrays and 10ft sharks cruise inches from your face as the travolator transports you through the Ocean Colony's submerged glass tubes. Entry includes admission to next door **Dolphin Lagoon**, where Indo-Pacific humpbacked dolphins perform with seals several times daily (check times online).

MT FABER PARK & CABLE CAR Park (www.mountfaber.com.sg; cable car one-way adult/child S$24/14 ; ⌚park 8.30am-2am, cable car 8.30am-9.30pm; M HarbourFront) Standing proud (if not tall) at 116m on the southern fringe of the city, Mt Faber forms the centrepiece of Mt Faber Park, and the climax to a walk along the **Southern**

Ridges (www.nparks.gov.sg; admission free; Ⓜ Pasir Panjang, then 15min walk to Reflections at Bukit Chandu). The most spectacular way to reach the top is on the cable car, which connects Sentosa and HarbourFront to a cluster of slick hilltop bars and restaurants. Alternatively, take bus 409 (weekends only, midday to 9pm) or walk. It's a short but steep climb through secondary rainforest, dotted with strategically placed benches, pavilions and lookout posts as well as some splendid colonial-era black-and-white bungalows.

 Tours

The Singapore Tourism Board books a range of tours and publishes a handful of free, self-guided walking-tour brochures.

Harbour & River Cruises

IMPERIAL CHENG HO DINNER CRUISE   Boat Tour
(🖉 6533 9811; www.watertours.com.sg; adult/child daytime cruises S$29/16, dinner cruises $57/31; Ⓜ Marina Bay) Three daily tours from Marina South to Sentosa or Kusu

Orchard Road

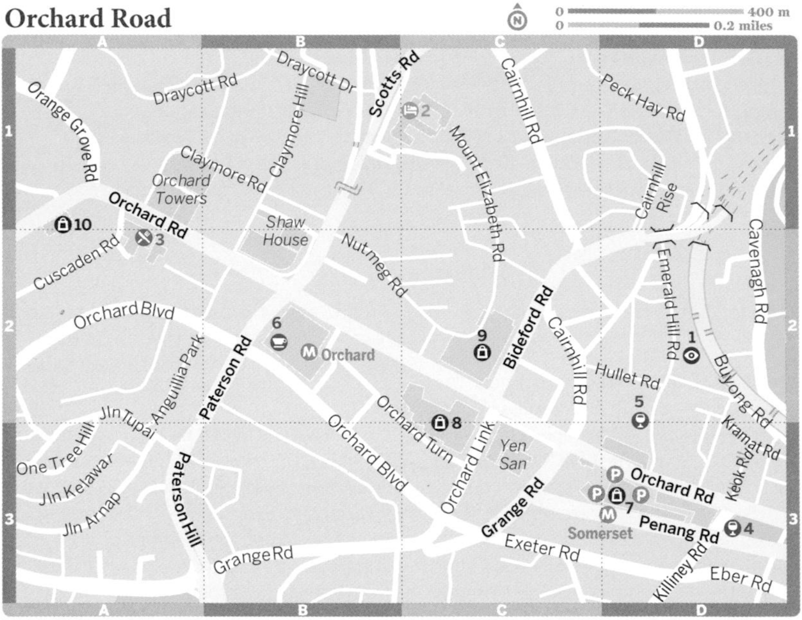

[Map of Orchard Road with streets including Orange Grove Rd, Draycott Rd, Draycott Dr, Scotts Rd, Cairnhill Rd, Peck Hay Rd, Claymore Rd, Claymore Hill, Orchard Towers, Orchard Rd, Shaw House, Nutmeg Rd, Mount Elizabeth Rd, Cairnhill Rise, Cavenagh Rd, Cuscaden Rd, Orchard Blvd, Paterson Rd, Bideford Rd, Cairnhill Rd, Emerald Hill Rd, Buyong Rd, Kramat Rd, Keng Rd, Hullet Rd, Anguilla Park, Jln Tupai, One Tree Hill, Jln Kelawar, Jln Arnap, Paterson Hill, Orchard Turn, Orchard Link, Orchard Blvd, Yen San, Orchard Rd, Grange Rd, Exeter Rd, Somerset, Penang Rd, Killiney Rd, Eber Rd, Grange Rd. Markers: 10, 3, 6, Orchard, 9, 8, 1, 5, 7, 4, 2]

Orchard Road

KIMBERLEY COOLE/GETTY IMAGES ©

Don't Miss Singapore Zoo, Night Safari & River Safari

Even if you're not a zoo fan, Singapore Zoo should leave you purring. Set on a peninsula jutting into the Upper Seletar Reservoir, its 28 lushly landscaped hectares feel like an oasis. Cages are ditched for 'open concept' enclosures, and there is a range of engaging child-friendly shows and feeding sessions. Attractions like the 'The Great Rift Valley of Ethiopia' enclosure convey entire ecosystems: animal, mineral, vegetable and human. Visitors can stand behind a window in 'Ethiopia' and watch 50 shameless red-bummed baboons doing things that Singaporeans still get arrested for. You can get around the zoo on foot or by tram (adult/child S$5/2.50), and the zoo's 15-minute reservoir boat ride offers a relaxing interlude.

The adjacent Night Safari offers a very different type of after-dark thrill. The park's moats and barriers seem to melt away in the darkness, giving you the feeling of travelling through a mysterious jungle filled with over 120 species of animals, including lions and leopards. While you can walk around the three trails, the best experience is on the tram tour (adult/child S$10/5).

The latest addition to this zoological wonderland is the River Safari, a S$160 million, 12-hectare wildlife park that recreates the ecosystems of eight iconic world rivers. It houses 150 plant varieties and 300 animal species including giant pandas.

To save money, consider buying a combined Zoo and Night Safari ticket. After the Night Safari catch a return bus by 10.45pm to ensure you make the last train from Ang Mo Kio (11.30pm). Otherwise, there's a taxi rank out the front. Expect to pay around S$20 for a taxi ride back to central Singapore.

NEED TO KNOW

80 Mandai Lake Rd, Zoo & Night Safari combined ticket adult/child S$42/28, M Ang Mo Kio, then 138; Singapore Zoo www.zoo.com.sg, adult/child S$22/15, 8.30am-6pm; Night Safari www.nightsafari.com.sg; adult/child S$35/23; 7.30pm-midnight, restaurants & shops from 6pm; River Safari www.riversafari.com.sg, 9am-6pm

If You Like...
Cooking Classes

Cooking classes generally run from two to four hours. Many are hands-on; some are instruction only. Check websites or call first for bookings and schedules.

1 COOKERY MAGIC
(☎ 6348 9667; www.cookerymagic.com; 117 Fidelio St; 3hr classes from S$100; Ⓜ Eunos, then 🚌 28) Ruqxana conducts standout Asian-cooking classes in her own home. She also conducts classes in an old *kampung* home on the island of Pulau Ubin.

2 PALATE SENSATIONS COOKING SCHOOL
(☎ 6478 9746; www.palatesensations.com; Chromos 01-03, 10 Biopolis Rd; 3hr courses from S$100; Ⓜ Buona Vista) Both novices and serious foodies head here to hone their skills with top-notch chefs. Standard courses run for three hours and are wonderfully hands-on, with themes spanning anything from Malay festival foods, to classic Punjab cuisine and German Yuletide treats.

Island on a hulking replica of the *Cheng Ho* junk. The food may not be spectacular, but the views are.

DUCK TOUR   Tour
(Map p236; ☎ 6338 6877; www.ducktours.com.sg; adult/child S$33/23; Ⓜ Esplanade) A one-hour romp in the 'Wacky Duck', a Vietnam War amphibious curio, departing from Suntec City. Check out the city's sites from the road then hit the water for a harbour cruise. A good one for the kids.

HIPPO RIVER CRUISE   Boat Tour
(Map p236; ☎ 6338 6877; www.ducktours.com.sg; adult/child S$18/13, day pass S$23/17; Ⓜ Clarke Quay) This 30-minute open-top boat ride departs from Clarke Quay every 25 minutes. A day pass allows you to hop on/off at nine stops along the Singapore River.

SINGAPORE RIVER CRUISE   Boat Tour
(Map p236; ☎ 6336 6111; www.rivercruise.com. sg; adult/child from S$17/10; Ⓜ Clarke Quay)

Jump on a traditional bumboat and sail up and down the Singapore River on these 40- and 60-minute tours from the Merlion at the river mouth upstream to the city's famous quays.

Sleeping

Sleeping in Singapore is expensive, although hostel rooms can be had for as little as S$20 a night. Most midrange hotels are more about location than quality, while at the other end of the scale, many of Singapore's luxury digs offer history, cutting-edge design, or resort-style lushness.

Daily rates can fluctuate significantly at most midrange and top-end hotels, where room rates are about supply and demand. Be aware that top hotels usually add a 'plus plus' (++) after the rate they quote you. The two pluses denote service charge and GST, which together amounts to an extra 17% on your room rate. Prices quoted below are net prices ('net' includes taxes and the service charge).

Colonial District & the Quays

RAFFLES HOTEL   Hotel $$$
(Map p236; ☎ 6337 1886; www.raffleshotel.com; 1 Beach Rd; ste from S$1400; ✳ @ 🛜 🏊; Ⓜ City Hall) For colonial-era luxury, it's hard to beat this 125-year-old icon. Rooms feature spacious parlours, verandahs, lazily swirling ceiling fans and a Singapore sling from the Long Bar, while the rooftop pool, rambling gardens and historic bars offer perfect backdrops for languid posing.

NAUMI   Boutique Hotel $$$
(Map p236; ☎ 6403 6000; www.naumihotel. com; 41 Seah St; r incl breakfast S$340-400; ✳ @ 🛜 🏊; Ⓜ Esplanade, City Hall) Naumi is dressed so sharply in glass and steel you could get cut just by looking. It balances cool looks with lots of silk and leather and fluffy pillows. The small rooftop infinity pool offers jaw-dropping views across to neighbouring Raffles Hotel.

FULLERTON HOTEL

Hotel $$$

(Map p236; ☎6733 8388; www.fullertonhotel.com; 1 Fullerton Sq; r incl breakfast from S$515; ❄@🛜☎; MRaffles Pl) Occupying what was once Singapore's magnficent, Palladian-style general post office, the lavish Fullerton offers elegant, conservative rooms, with muted tones and views of the inner atrium, waterfront or skyline. Pool aficionados will swoon over the 25m showpiece pool, complete with river and skyline views. Close by, sister property **Fullerton Bay Hotel** (Map p236; ☎6333 8388; www.fullertonbayhotel.com; 80 Collyer Quay; MRaffles Place) serves up flashy bay-facing rooms at similar rates.

Chinatown

WANGZ

Boutique Hotel $$

(☎6595 1388; www.wangzhotel.com; 231 Outram Rd; r S$228-408; ❄@🛜; MOutram Park) This curvaceous boutique newcomer sits just west of Chinatown in trendy enclave Tiong Bahru. Each of its 41 rooms is smart and modern, sexed up with contemporary local art, sublimely comfortable beds, iPod docking stations and sleek bathrooms.

KLAPSONS

Boutique Hotel $$$

(Map p240; ☎6521 9000; www.klapsons.com; 15 Hoe Chiang Rd; r from S$290; ❄@🛜; MTanjong Pagar) New-kid Klapsons delivers modernist-inspired luxury and stunning design features (reception is in a steel sphere suspended above a pool of water). Rooms are beautifully textured and individually designed, each with soft goose-down bedding, showpiece showers and a personal Nespresso machine.

WINK HOSTEL

Hostel $

(Map p240; ☎6222 2940; www.winkhostel.com; 8 Mosque St; s/d pod S$50/90; ❄@🛜; MChinatown) Centrally located in a restored Chinatown shophouse, flashbacker favourite Wink combines hostel and capsule-hotel concepts. Instead of bunks, dorms feature private, sound-proof 'pods', each with comfortable mattress, coloured mood lighting, adjacent locker and enough room to sit up in.

Little India

WANDERLUST

Boutique Hotel $$

(Map p242; ☎6396 3322; www.wanderlusthotel.com; 2 Dickson Rd; r incl breakfast from S$232; ❄@🛜; MBugis) Wanderlust is genuinely

Raffles Hotel

If You Like...
Hawker Food

Once you've ploughed through Singapore's central hawker centres, head further out to where the real street-food geeks click their sticks.

1 CHOMP CHOMP FOOD CENTRE
(20 Kensington Park Rd; ⊙stalls vary; MToa Payoh, then ☐73) Despite its privileged status as (arguably) Singapore's best hawker centre, this evening option in Serangoon Gardens in the centre of the island gives off a chilled, convivial vibe.

2 OLD AIRPORT ROAD FOOD CENTRE
(Block 51 Old Airport Rd; ⊙10am-late; MMountbatten) You'll find a few more out-of-towners here than at Chomp Chomp, but the grub is no less authentic. The Hokkien mee (noodles) at **Na Sing Hokkien Fried Mee** (Stall 01-32; dishes from S$3; ⊙11am-7pm) are obligatory, while other winners include sweet'n'savoury *rojak* (salad of pineapple, cucumber, you tiao, turnip, crushed peanuts and homemade *rojak* sauce) from **Toa Payoh Rojak** (Stall 01-108; dishes from S$3; ⊙noon-8pm Mon-Sat).

boutique, with highly imaginative, individually designed rooms – think monochromatic 'Pantone' rooms, comic-book 'Mono' rooms', and 'Whimsical' rooms with themes like 'tree' and 'space'. Extra perks include excellent service, a funky French noshery and free wifi.

ALBERT COURT VILLAGE HOTEL Hotel **$$**
(Map p242; ☑6339 3939; www.stayvillage.com; 180 Albert St; r from S$200; ❄@☎; MLittle India) This splendid, colonial-era hotel, a short walk south of Little India, offers top-notch service and rooms with all the standard mod cons, including a choice of fan or air-con. The promotional rates go as low as S$150, with the best deals to be had online.

Orchard Road

GOODWOOD PARK HOTEL Hotel **$$$**
(Map p244; ☑6737 7411; www.goodwood parkhotel.com; 22 Scotts Rd; r from S$328; ❄@☎≋; MOrchard) A venerable slumber spot dating back to 1900, the Goodwood Park is both classic and elegant. Rooms include artful black-and-white photos of Singapore, plush furnishings and tastefully hidden TVs and minibars.

Sentosa Island

CAPELLA SINGAPORE Resort **$$$**
(☑6591 5000; www.capellahotels. com/singapore; 1 the Knolls; d S$700; ❄@☎≋) The Capella Singapore resort is arguably the crème de la crème of Sentosa's, possibly even Singapore's, accommodation options, with majestic whitewashed colonial architecture, lavish pools and gardens, and beautifully appointed rooms, villas and manors.

 Eating

Colonial District & the Quays

JAAN French **$$$**
(Map p236; ☑9199 9008; www.jaan.com.sg; Swissôtel the Stamford, 2 Stamford Rd; 7-course menu S$238, with wine parings S$398; ⊙lunch Mon-Sat, dinner daily; MCity Hall) Perched 70 floors above Singapore, chic, intimate Jaan is home to young-gun French chef Julien Royer and his show-stopping Gallic creations; think wild langoustine with fregola sarda, grey chanterelle, rosemary-smoked organic egg and black Périgord truffle. The set 7-course menu is a revelation. Always book ahead, and request a window seat overlooking Marina Bay Sands for a bird's-eye view of the nightly lightshow.

FLUTES AT THE FORT International **$$$**
(Map p236; ☑6338 8770; www.flutes.com.sg; Fort Canning Park, entrance via 23B Coleman St; mains S$38-48; ⊙lunch & dinner Mon-Sat, 10am-5pm Sun; MCity Hall) In a 1908 bun-

galow on the edge of Fort Canning Park, fine-dining Flutes seduces with its lush setting, attentive service and imaginative mod-Oz flavours.

JUMBO SEAFOOD Chinese **$$**
(Map p236; ☎6532 3435; www.jumboseafood. com.sg; 30 Merchant Rd, at 01-01/02 Riverside Point; dishes from S$8, chilli crab around S$48 per kg; MClarke Quay) If you're lusting for chilli crab, indulge right here. The gravy is sublimely sweet and nutty, with just the right amount of chilli. Make sure to order some yeasty, fried *man-tou* buns to dip with. While all of Jumbo's outlets have the dish down to an art, this one has the best riverside location. One kilo of crab is enough for two.

Chinatown & CBD

BLUE GINGER Peranakan **$$**
(Map p240; ☎6222 3928; www.theblueginger. com; 97 Tanjong Pagar Rd; mains S$10-30; MTanjong Pagar) A perennial favourite, famed for its beautifully cooked Peranakan food, a unique cuisine fusing Chinese and Malay influences. Savour rich, spicy, sour flavours in Blue Ginger's signature *ayam panggang* (grilled chicken in coconut and spices). Other winners include the soulful *bakwan kepiting* (minced pork and crabmeat ball soup) and *sambal terong goreng* (spicy fried eggplant). Bookings recommended.

MAXWELL ROAD HAWKER CENTRE Hawker **$**
(Map p240; cnr Maxwell Rd & South Bridge Rd; ☺individual stalls vary; ☒; MChinatown) One of Chinatown's most accessible hawker centres, Maxwell Rd is a user-friendly spot to chomp and slurp on Singapore street-food classics. While stalls slip in and out of favour with fickle Singaporeans, enduring favourites include **Tian Tian Hainanese Chicken Rice** (Stall 10; chicken-rice S$3; ☺11am-8pm Tue-Sun), **Maxwell Fuzhou Oyster Cake** (Stall 5; oyster cake S$1.50; ☺9.30am-8.30pm Mon-Sat), and **Fried Sweet Potato Dumpling** (Stall 76; snacks from S$0.50; ☺1-8pm Wed-Mon).

Tea Culture

For soothing cultural enlightenment, slip into one of Chinatown's atmospheric teahouses. Start at **Yixing Yuan Teahouse** (Map p240; www.yixingxuan-teahouse. com; 30/32 Tanjong Pagar Rd; 45min demonstration S$20; ☺10am-9pm Mon-Sat, 10am-7pm Sun; MTanjong Pagar), where reformed corporate banker Vincent Low explains everything you need to know about sampling different types of tea. Demonstrations with tastings last around 45 minutes to two hours (S$20 to S$40).

Once you know your green tea from your oolong, duck around the corner to **Tea Chapter** (Map p240; www.tea-chapter.com.sg; 9-11 Neil Rd; tea from $5; ☺11am-10.30pm Sun-Thu, 11am-11pm Fri & Sat; MChinatown), where Queen Elizabeth dropped by for a cuppa in 1989. If you don't know the tea-making drill, the waiter will give you a brief demonstration. Downstairs, all manner of tea paraphernalia are precariously balanced on display shelves and can be purchased.

If you're on Orchard Rd, drop into upmarket tea purveyor **TWG Tea** (Map p244; www.twgtea.com; 02-20 ION Orchard, 2 Orchard Rd; ☺10am-10pm; MOrchard), which peddles over 800 varieties of tea from around the world. Savour the flavour with a few tea-infused macaroons (the bain de roses is divine). You'll find other outlets at **Takashimaya** (www.takashimaya-sin.com; Ngee Ann City, 391 Orchard Road; MOrchard) and the Shoppes at Marina Bay Sands (p256) mall.

LAU PA SAT   Food Stall
(Map p240; 18 Raffles Quay; ☉24hr; M Raffles Place) Steamed dim sum, chilli crab and sizzling satay under a magnificent wrought-iron structure.

Little India & Kampong Glam

WARONG NASI PARIAMAN   Malay, Indonesian $
(Map p242; 📞6292 2374; 738 North Bridge Rd; dishes S$2.60-4.60; ☉7.30am-2.30pm Mon-Sat; M Bugis) With fans including former Malaysian prime minister Dr Mahathir Mohamad, this threadbare *nasi padang* stall is the stuff of legend. Don't miss the *belado* (fried mackerel in a slow-cooked chilli, onion and vinegar sauce), delicate beef rendang or *ayam bakar* (grilled chicken with coconut sauce). Get here by 11am to avoid the hordes, and be warned... it mostly sells out by 1pm.

TEKKA CENTRE   Hawker $
(Map p242; cnr Serangoon & Buffalo Rds; dishes S$3-5; ☉7am-11pm; 🍴; M Little India) Queue up for biryani, mutton curries, roti prata and *teh tarik* (pulled tea) at Little India's

most famous hawker hangout. Foodies flock to the legendary **Ah-Rahman Royal Prata** (Map p242; stall 01-248; murtabak S$4-5; ☉7am-10pm), whose *murtabak* (roti prata filled with mutton, chicken or vegetables) are so incredibly good that even Singapore's president is a fan. If you're undecided, go for the chicken *murtabak* with cheese.

BISMILLAH BIRYANI   Indian $
(Map p242; 50 Dunlop St; kebabs from S$4, biryani from S$6; ☉noon-8pm; M Little India) Head here for Singapore's best biryani. While the mutton biryani is the speciality – and it *is* special – even that is surpassed by the mutton sheekh kebab, which is a melt-in-the-mouth revelation. Most of the best stuff is history before 8pm.

ANANDA BHAVAN   Indian, Vegetarian $
(Map p242; Block 663, 01-10 Buffalo Rd; dishes S$3-5; ☉6.30am-10.30pm; M Little India) This super-cheap chain restaurant is a top spot to sample South Indian breakfast staples like *idly* and *dosa* (spelt 'thosai' on the menu). It also does great-value thali, some of which are served on banana leaves.

Esplanade – Theatres on the Bay (p235)

Detour: Pulau Ubin

Pulau Ubin feels worlds apart from mainland Singapore and its tower blocks. Indeed, it's the perfect day-trip getaway, coloured with unkempt expanses of jungle and tin-roofed buildings that ooze a sleepy *kampong* (village) vibe.

Bumboats (one way S$2.50, bicycle surcharge S$2; ⊘varies, usually 6am-9pm) to Pulau Ubin depart from Changi Point Ferry Terminal in Changi Village. There's no timetable: boats depart when 12 people are ready to go, dropping passengers off at **Pulau Ubin Village**. Food outlets aside (expect to pay between S$20 and S$40 for chilli crab), Pulau Ubin Village is the place to rent bikes (around S$5 to 10 per day for adults and S$2 for kids). For the sake of your booty, opt for a mountain bike. While you can't get maps of the island, there are signboards dotted around the place, though it's fun to simply trundle off on your bike and see where the road takes you.

If you only have time for one part of Pulau Ubin, make it the **Chek Jawa Wetlands** (⊘8.30am-6pm). Located on the eastern end of the island, its 1km coastal boardwalk takes you out over the sea before looping back through the mangrove swamp to the 20m-high **Jejawi Tower** and its stunning views. You can't bring your bike into the reserve so make sure the one you've rented comes with a bike lock so you can lock it securely to the bike stands at the entrance.

Orchard Road & Botanic Gardens

Burrow into most Orchard Rd malls and you'll find great value food courts.

IGGY'S　　　　International $$$
(Map p244; ☐6732 2234; www.iggys.com.sg; Level 3, Hilton Hotel, 581 Orchard Rd; lunch S$85, dinner S$195-275; ⊘lunch Mon-Fri, dinner Mon-Sat; ☑; ⓜOrchard) Arguably Singapore's best restaurant, where Japanese and European sensibilities mesh together in a tasting menu of epic proportions. The wine list is as impressive as it is extensive and there is a dedicated vegetarian tasting menu.

AU JARDIN LES AMIS　　　French $$$
(☐6466 8812; www.lesamis.com.sg; Cluny Rd, EJH Corner House, Singapore Botanic Gardens; set dinner menus from S$200; ⊘dinner daily, lunch Fri, brunch 11.30am-1.30pm Sun; ⓜBotanic Gardens) If you plan on seducing someone, look no further – think romantic colonial-era bungalow, Botanic Gardens backdrop, and decadent French fare. Daily dinner aside, there's a lunchtime sitting on Fri-days (two/three courses S$58/70) and a Sunday brunch (S$88). Book ahead.

🍷 Drinking

Singapore's bar scene is a kicking mix of designer rooftop lounges and cocktail dens, Euro-centric wine bars, microbreweries and hipster-approved coffee roasters. Popular drinking hubs include Boat Quay and Clarke Quay, Chinatown's trendy Club St, Ann Siang Hill and Duxton Hill precincts, sheesha-scented Kampong Glam and heritage-listed Emerald Hill Rd.

Unless otherwise stated, bars open around 5pm until at least midnight Sunday to Thursday, and through to 2am or 3am on Friday and Saturday.

Colonial District & the Quays

NEW ASIA　　　　　　　Bar
(Map p236; Swissôtel the Stamford, 2 Stamford Rd; ⊘3pm-1am Sun-Tue, to 2am Wed & Thu, to 3am Fri & Sat; City Hall) Martinis demand dizzying skyline views and few deliver

♥ If You Like...
Rooftop Bars

Singapore takes full advantage of its balmy weather at these al-fresco drinks parties atop buildings, offering spectacular nightscape views. Call three days in advance to be sure of a reservation.

1 LANTERN BAR
(Map p236; ☎6597 5299; Fullerton Bay Hotel, 80 Collyer Quay; ⏰8am-1am Sun-Thu, 8am-2am Fri & Sat; M Raffles Place) With a dress circle position on Marina Bay and surrounding a glittering mosaic pool, Lantern Bar is a seductive melange of frangipani trees, skyscraper views, DJ-spun house and well-mixed libations.

2 LOOF
(Map p236; www.loof.com.sg; 03-07 Odeon Towers Building, 331 North Bridge Rd; M City Hall) Loof cheekily gets its name from the Singlish mangling of the word 'roof'. Up here, City Hall district views are paired with smooth tunes, retro-Asian bar snacks, and regionally inspired libations.

3 LA TERRAZZA
(Map p240; ☎6221 1694; www.screeningroom. com.sg; Level 4, 12 Ann Siang Rd; M Chinatown) The Chinatown-meets-CBD panorama from this hugely popular rooftop bar, part of the **Screening Room film complex** (Map p240; www.screeningroom.com. sg; 12 Ann Siang Rd; Chinatown), are superb. Hunt down a comfy couch, kick off the shoes and have a shouting-into-each-other's-ears conversation over nostalgic '80s and '90s tunes.

4 ZSOFI TAPAS BAR
(Map p242; www.tapasbar.com.sg; 68 Dunlop St; M Little India) It's all about the rooftop here, a wonderful and highly unusual space for this part of town, and big enough to (nearly) always find a seat on. Drinks are anything but cheap – expect to pay at least S$12 for a beer – but every one of them comes with free tapas.

like this sleek bar-club hybrid, perched 71 floors above street level. Style up and head in early to watch the sun sink, then strike a pose on the dance floor. The S$25

cover charge on Friday and Saturday includes one drink... but with views like these, who's counting?

RAFFLES HOTEL Bar
(Map p236; www.raffles.com; 1 Beach Rd; M City Hall) Yup, it's a cliché, but still, few visit Singapore without at least stopping off for drinks at one of the bars in the famous Raffles Hotel. Ditch the **Long Bar** (Map p236; ⏰11-12.30am Sun-Thu, 11-1.30am 1am Fri & Sat) and its overpriced Singapore Slings and chill out Raj-style at the much more appealing **Bar & Billiard Room** (Map p236; ☎6412 1816; ⏰11am-midnight Tue-Sat; City Hall). Alternatively, rehydrate below rattling palms at the **Raffles Courtyard bar** (⏰11am-10.30pm).

BREWERKZ Brewery
(Map p236; www.brewerkz.com; 01-05 Riverside Point Centre, 30 Merchant Rd; ⏰noon-midnight Sun-Thu, noon-1am Fri & Sat; M Clarke Quay) The first among Singapore's crop of microbreweries and still the biggest and arguably the best. The beers are uniformly superb, from the hugely popular India Pale Ale to the quirkier seasonal fruit beers, with a solid choice of American comfort grub to soak it all up. Best (or worst) of all, the earlier you arrive, the cheaper the drinks.

Chinatown & the CBD
1 ALTITUDE Bar
(Map p240; www.1-altitude.com; lvl 63, 1 Raffles Place; admission S$25 (S$30 after 9pm), incl 1 drink; M Raffles Pl) Fancy sipping cocktails perched on a cloud? This is the next best thing. Occupying the 63rd floor of the soaring 1 Raffles Place skyscraper, it's a seductive combo of smooth lounge tunes, swaying palms and the twinkling sprawl of Singapore and beyond. Dress up (no shorts or flip-flops) and don't forget your camera.

LEVEL 33 Brewery
(www.level33.com.sg; Level 33, Marina Bay Financial Tower 1, 8 Marina Blvd; ⏰noon-midnight Sun-Thu, noon-2am Fri & Sat; M Raffles Pl) Brews with a view is what you get at the

ION Orchard Mall (p258)

DAN HERRICK/GETTY IMAGES © ARCHITECT: BENOY

world's highest 'urban craft brewery'. While the food doesn't quite match the loftiness of its locale, the house-brewed blonde lager, pale ale, porter and stout go down as smoothly as the view over Marina Bay.

TANTRIC BAR Gay
(Map p240; 78 Neil Rd; ⊙8pm-3am Sun-Fri, 8pm-4am Sat; MOutram Park, Chinatown) Complete with palm-fringed courtyard, Tantric is Singapore's hottest gay drinking hole. Especially heaving on Friday and Saturday nights, it's a hit with preened locals and eager expats, who schmooze and cruise to Gaga, Kylie and K-pop. Lushes shouldn't miss Wednesday nights, where S$20 gets you two martinis.

BACKSTAGE BAR Gay
(Map p240; www.backstagebar.moonfruit.com; 13A Trengganu St; MChinatown) While most of the look-at-me pretty boys head to Tantric Bar (p253) and Taboo (p255), less pretentious types gravitate here. Sit on the balcony to chat and flirt with local lads, or just sit back and watch the Chinatown action below. Entrance on Temple St.

Orchard Road

QUE PASA Wine Bar
(Map p244; 7 Emerald Hill Rd; MSomerset) This wine bar channels old España with its tin lamps, strung chilli and *El Pais* wallpaper. It also boasts an astute wine list – the perfect match for succulent bites like anchovy bread. Que Pasa's location on buzzing, heritage-handsome Emerald Hill Rd is nothing short of *fabuloso*.

KPO Bar
(Map p244; www.imaginings.com.sg; 1 Killiney Rd; ⊙3pm-1am Mon-Thu, 3pm-2am Fri & Sat; MSomerset) Housed in a renovated postmaster's house, trendy KPO is as well known for its philatelic pedigree as it is for the luxury wheels of its see-and-be-seen evening clientele. Style up, order a cocktail, and scan the gorgeous rooftop terrace for your prospective ride home.

Dempsey Road

TIPPLING CLUB Cocktail Bar
(www.tipplingclub.com; 8D Dempsey Rd; ⊙6pm-late Mon-Fri, noon-3pm & 6pm-late Sat; ☐7, 77, 106, 123, 174) Forest-fringed Tippling Club takes mixology to new heights. Savour the brilliance in cocktails like 'Wake Me

Up, F*ck Me Up' (VSOP cognac, fresh espresso and mole bitters), or 'Smoky Old Bastard' (a large whisky served in a glass tube filled with smoke made from dried orange powder and flavoured with maple syrup and banana). Not cheap (cocktails from S$21), but worth it.

REDDOT BREWHOUSE Brewery
(wwwreddotbrewhouse.com.sg; 25A Dempsey Rd; ⊙noon-midnight Mon-Thu, noon-2am Fri & Sat, 10am-midnight Sun; 🚌7, 77, 106, 123, 174) This microbrewery, tucked away in a quiet part of Dempsey Hill, is Valhalla for beer fiends. Seven brews on tap include a green pilsner, its alien tinge coming from the spirulina used in the brewing process. Food options are generally mediocre, so kick back on the deck and focus on the liquid gold.

Sentosa Island

TANJONG BEACH CLUB Bar
(www.tanjongbeachclub.com; Tanjong Beach; ⊙11am-11pm Tue-Thu, 10am-11pm Fri & Sat) Don't fancy swimming at the beach?

Cool down in the infinity pool at this stylish beach bar–restaurant. Aside from Sundays, the place is remarkably quiet, making it an ideal getaway from the madding Sentosa crowds.

 **Entertainment**

Chinese Opera
CHINESE THEATRE
CIRCLE Chinese Opera
(Map p240; 🖉6323 4862; 5 Smith St; Ⓜ China-town) Every Friday and Saturday at 8pm, this not-for-profit opera group delivers a brief talk (S$20, in English) on Chinese opera, followed by a 45-minute performance from an opera classic. Lychee tea and teacakes are included in the price and bookings are recommended. Search for Chinese Theatre Circle on Facebook.

Clubs
Most clubs have cover charges of around S$15 to S$40, often including at least one

Left: Fort Canning Park (p235) and the city skyline; Below: Peranakan terrace house (LEFT) GAVIN HELLIER/GETTY IMAGES ©; (BELOW) KEVIN CLOGSTOUN/GETTY IMAGES ©

drink; women usually pay less (or even nothing!).

ZOUK
Club

(www.zoukclub.com; 17 Jiak Kim St; ⊙Zouk 10pm-late Wed, Fri & Sat, Phuture & Velvet Underground 9pm-late Wed, Fri & Sat, Wine Bar 6pm-2am Tue, to 3am Wed & Thu, to 4am Fri & Sat) Singapore's hottest club is well known for its prolific DJs, massive dance floor and five bars. The complex is also home to alfresco Zouk Wine Bar, avant-garde Phuture, and boudoir-inspired Velvet Underground, hung with Andy Warhol and Keith Haring originals.

HOME CLUB
Club

(Map p236; www.homeclub.com.sg; B1/06 the Riverwalk, 20 Upper Circular Rd; ⊙7pm-3am Tue-Fri, 7pm-4am Sat; MClarke Quay) Home Club enjoys serious cred with music buffs. The resident nights kick some serious 'A', with playlists spanning house, electro, and retro, to drum and bass and psy-trance. The venue is also known for its credible live pop and rock acts, and its Tuesday comedy night.

BUTTER FACTORY
Club

(Map p236; www.thebutterfactory.com; 02-02 One Fullerton, 1 Fullerton Rd; ⊙10pm-4am Wed, Fri & Sat; MClarke Quay) At 8000 sq ft, Butter Factory is as huge as it is slick. Street art on the walls of **Bump**, the hip hop, rhythm and blues room, betrays its young and overdressed crowd. **Fash** is its chilled-out 'art' bar, and walls are plastered with colourful pop-art reminiscent of underground comics (yes, the ones you hid from mum).

TABOO
Gay

(Map p240; www.taboo.sg; 65/67 Neil Rd; ⊙8pm-2am Wed & Thu, 10pm-3am Fri, 10pm-4am Sat; MOutram Park, Chinatown) After drinks at Tantric (p253), cross the street and hit the dance floor at the hottest gay dance club on the scene. Expect the requisite line-up of shirtless gyrators,

255

If You Like... Discounts

Singapore isn't a bargain destination but there are a few ways to cut costs:

○ Travellers arriving on Singapore Airlines or Silk Air are entitled to discounts at selected hotels, shops, restaurants, and attractions by presenting their boarding pass. See www.singaporeair.com/boardingpass for details.

○ Children receive up to 50% discount at many tourist attractions, and children six and under are sometimes admitted free. Discounts are often available to visitors over 60. Present your passport or ID with your date of birth on it.

○ The National Heritage Board's **3 Day Museum Pass** (www.nhb.gov.sg/WWW/3daymuseumpass.html; adult/family S$20/50) offers unlimited admission to eight city museums, including the Asian Civilisations Museum, National Museum of Singapore and Singapore Art Museum. Passes can be purchased at the museums.

dance-happy straight women and regular racy themed nights.

Theatre & Dance

SINGAPORE REPERTORY THEATRE Theatre
(Map p236; ☎6733 8166; www.srt.com.sg; DBS Arts Centre, 20 Merbau Rd; Ⓜ Clarke Quay) The bigwig of the Singapore theatre scene has a repertoire spaning Shakespeare, modern Western classics and contemporary works from Singapore, Asia-Pacific and beyond. Although based at the DBS Arts Centre, productions are also held at Esplanade – Theatres on the Bay (p235) and Fort Canning Park (p235).

SINGAPORE DANCE THEATRE Dance
(Map p236; ☎6338 0611; www.singaporedance theatre.com; 2nd fl, Fort Canning Centre, Cox Tce; Ⓜ Dhoby Ghaut) Traditional ballet and contemporary works is what you'll get from Singapore's world-class dance company. The group's Ballet under the Stars season at Fort Canning Park is justifiably popular.

🛍 Shopping

Colonial District, the Quays & Marina Bay

FUNAN DIGITALIFE MALL Electronics
(Map p236; www.funan.com.sg; 109 North Bridge Rd; Ⓜ City Hall) The tech mall of choice for people who prefer to pay a bit more for branded products and cast-iron guarantees. **Challenger Superstore** (www.challenger.com.sg; Level 6, Funan DigitaLife Mall; ⏰10am-10pm) is the best one-stop shop for all IT desires. For cameras, visit family-run **John 3:16** (Map p236; 05-46, Funan DigitaLife Mall; ⏰12.30-9.30pm Mon-Sat).

SHOPPES AT MARINA BAY SANDS Mall
(Map p236; www.marinabaysands.com; 10 Bayfront Ave; Ⓜ Bayfront, Marina Bay) You'll find all the 'It' brands at this giant, glossy mall, including runway royalty Prada and Miu Miu. Clued-up fashionistas shop at unisex **Society of Black Sheep** (Map p236; www.societyofblacksheep.com; B1-64, Shoppes at Marina Bay Sands, Bayfront Ave; Ⓜ Promenade, Bayfront, Marina Bay). You'll also find an ice-free skating rink, celebrity nosh spots, and a floating Louis Vuitton store.

RAFFLES CITY Mall
(Map p236; www.rafflescity.com.sg; 252 North Bridge Rd; Ⓜ City Hall) One of Singapore's best malls, buzzing Raffles' includes a three-level branch of the excellent **Robinsons** department store, global fashion brands such as **Topshop**, **agnès b** and **Kate Spade**, a good selection of children's clothes and toys, the **Ode to Art** gallery, as well as a satisfying booty of food-court stalls and restaurants for flagging shopaholics.

RAFFLES HOTEL ARCADE Mall
(Map p236; www.raffles.com; 328 North Bridge Rd; Ⓜ City Hall) Part of the hotel complex, stylish Raffles Hotel Arcade is firmly upmarket, with designer clothes and accessories, watchmakers, galleries, wine sellers and similarly refined places gently tempting you into credit-card wantonness.

BRIAN HARTSHORN/ALAMY ©

Don't Miss Haji Lane

Fashion fiends in search of fresher, lesser-known labels flock to Haji Lane, a pastel-hued strip in Kampong Glam lined with hipster-approved, one-off boutiques. **Dulcetfig** (Map p242; www.dulcetfig.wordpress.com; 41 Haji Lane; ⏰12.30-9pm Mon-Thu, 12.30-10pm Fri & Sat, 1-8pm Sun; M Bugis) sets female fashion bloggers into overdrive with its cool local and foreign frocks and accessories, which includes high-end vintage bags and jewellery. Fashion-literate guys should check out minimalist **K.I.N** (Map p242; 51 Haji Lane; ⏰1-8pm Mon-Sat, 3-7pm Sun; M Bugis), where vintage-inspired shirts from Gitman Bros and design-centric bags from Makr sit beside K.I.N's own street chic, preppy-cool threads and shoes.

Chinatown

UTTERLY ART   Art
(Map p240; www.utterlyart.com.sg; Level 3, 20B Mosque St; ⏰noon-8pm Mon-Sat, noon-5.30pm Sun; M Chinatown) This small, welcoming art gallery is an excellent introduction to Singapore's contemporary art scene. It's mostly paintings, although they exhibit sculpture and ceramics on occasion, and roughly half of the stuff on show is the work of Singaporean artists.

FAR EAST LEGEND   Antiques, Handicrafts
(Map p240; 233 South Bridge Rd; ⏰11.30am-6.30pm; M Chinatown) Squeeze inside this cluttered bolthole for an excellent collection of furniture, lamps, handicrafts, statues and other *objets d'art* from all over Asia. Expect anything from dainty porcelain snuff boxes to ceramic busts of Chairman Mao. The owner is usually willing to 'discuss the price'.

EU YAN SANG   Chinese Medicine
(Map p240; www.euyansang.com; 269 South Bridge Rd; ⏰8.30am-7pm Mon-Sat; M Chinatown) Get your *qi* back at this venerable peddler of Chinese medicines and tonics. You can consult a herbalist (from S$12), or get off-the-shelf remedies such as instant bird's-nest (to tone the lung) or deer's-tail pills (to invigorate the kidneys). Most remedies also come with English instructions.

257

Little India & Kampong Glam

SIFR AROMATICS — Perfume

(Map p242; www.sifr.sg; 42 Arab St; ☺11am-8pm Sun-Thu, 11am-9pm Fri & Sat; MBugis) This Zen-like perfume laboratory belongs to third-generation perfume maker Johari Kazura, whose exquisite concoctions include the heady East (50ml S$140), a blend of oud, rose absolute, amber and neroli. Perfumes range from S$80 to S$300 for 50ml, while vintage perfume bottles range from S$60 to S$2000.

SIM LIM SQUARE — Electronics, Mall

(Map p242; www.simlimsquare.com.sg; 1 Rochor Canal Rd; ☺11am-8pm; MBugis) If you know what you're doing, there are real bargains to be had at this computer and electronics mega mall. The untutored, however, are more likely to be taken for a ride, so check the price at three vendors before bargaining hard.

LITTLE SHOPHOUSE — Handicrafts

(Map p242; 43 Bussorah St; ☺10am-6pm; MBugis) In his little workshop-cum-store, craftsman Robert Sng handbeads riotously colourful Peranakan slippers. Starting at around S$300, each pair takes two months to complete, with many admirers simply framing the shoe covers as works of art in themselves. Beadwork aside, you can also stock up on Peranakan-style tea sets, crockery, vases, handbags and jewellery.

CELEBRATION OF ARTS — Handicrafts

(Map p242; 2 Dalhousie Lane; ☺9am-9.30pm; MLittle India) Dive into this treasure trove for beautiful Indian ornaments, statues, lampshades, cushions, bedspreads, furniture and pashmina shawls. Several larger items aren't displayed, so if you're looking for something in particular, ask the friendly owner.

MUSTAFA CENTRE — Department Store

(Map p242; www.mustafa.com.sg; 145 Syed Alwi Rd; ☺24hr; MFarrer Park) As much cultural rite of passage as shopping experience, Mustafa's narrow aisles and tiny nooks have everything from electronics and clothing to cheap DVDs and gold. There are also moneychangers, a supermarket packed with Indian spices and pickles, and – on Sundays – half the population of Singapore.

Orchard Road

ION ORCHARD MALL — Mall

(Map p244; www.ionorchard.com; 430 Orchard Rd; MOrchard) Curvaceous, high-tech and striking, Ion is Singapore's hottest (and most photogenic) mall, packed with both high-end couture and more affordable 'It' labels like Paul Frank, G-Star, and True Religion. Shopped out? Recharge in the brilliant basement food court. The adjoining 56-storey tower comes with a top-floor observation deck, ION Sky (www.ionsky.com.sg; ticket counter

Buddha Tooth Relic Temple (p238)

Detour: Bukit Timah Nature Reserve

Singapore's steamy heart of darkness is this 164-hectare tract of undeveloped primary rainforest clinging to Singapore's highest peak, Bukit Timah (163.63m). Five walking trails weave through the **reserve** (☏1800-468 5736; www.nparks.gov. sg; 177 Hindhede Dr; ⊙6am-7pm, visitors centre 8.30am-5pm; 🚌171 or 🚌75 to Bukit Timah Shopping Centre), taking from 35 minutes to two-hours return, while cyclists can peddle over 6km of bike trails circumnavigating the forest – pick up a trail map from the visitors centre.

The most popular and easiest of the walking trails is the concrete-paved route straight to the summit, though you should leave time to explore the less busy side trails. The steep paths are sweaty work, so take plenty of water, embalm yourself in mosquito repellent, and don't feed the monkeys no matter how politely they ask.

The park's entrance is about 1km north of Bukit Timah Shopping Centre, along Hindhede Dr.

level 4; adult/child S\$16/8; ⊙10am-noon & 2-8pm).

NGEE ANN CITY · Mall
(Map p244; www.ngeeanncity.com.sg; 391 Orchard Rd; MOrchard) Housed in a downright ugly, brown-hued marble and granite building, Ngee Ann City redeems itself with seven floors of retail pleasure, where can't-afford luxury brands compete for space with the likes of **Kinokuniya** (Map p244; www.kinokuniya.com.sg; 03-09/10/15), Southeast Asia's largest bookstore, and Japanese department store Takashimaya, home to the mouthwatering **Takashimaya Food Village** (Map p244; B2, Takashimaya Department Store, Ngee Ann City, 391 Orchard Rd; snacks from S\$1; ⊙10am-9.30pm; MOrchard).

313 SOMERSET · Mall
(Map p244; www.313somerset.com.sg; 313 Orchard Rd; MSomerset) Hugely popular 313 has a great location above Somerset MRT Station and houses a cool, youthful mix of High St favourites like **Zara**, **Uniqlo**, **Mango**, **GUESS** and much-loved localwomen's label **M)phosis**. You'll also find music stores, restaurants, cafes, and the always-busy Apple shop **EpiCentre**. Coffee lovers can get a decent fix at **Oriole Café & Bar**, just outside the west entrance.

PARAGON · Mall
(Map p244; www.paragon.com.sg; 290 Orchard Rd; MSomerset) Even if you don't have a Gold Amex, strike a pose inside the Maserati of Orchard Rd malls. The Shop Directory reads like a Vogue index: **Burberry**, **Bulgari**, **Gucci**, **Hermès**, **Jimmy Choo**... Thankfully, mere mortals with a passion for fashion have a string of options here, too, including **Miss Selfridges**, **Calvin Klein Jeans**, **Banana Republic** and **Diesel**.

TANGLIN SHOPPING CENTRE · Mall
(Map p244; www.tanglinsc.com; 19 Tanglin Rd; ⊙9.30-9pm; MOrchard) This retro mall is *the* place for rugs, carvings, ornaments, jewellery, paintings, furniture and the like. The fascinating **Antiques of the Orient** (Map p244; www.aoto.com.sg; 19 Tanglin Rd, 02-40, Tanglin Shopping Centre; ⊙10am-6pm Mon-Sat, 11am-4pm Sun; MOrchard) is housed here, featuring wonderful old books, photographs and genuinely ancient maps from all parts of Asia. You'll also find **Select Books** (Map p244; www.selectbooks.com. sg; 03-15, Tanglin Shopping Centre; ⊙9.30am-6.30pm Mon-Sat, 10am-4pm Sun), an Asian book specialist, as well as some decent Asian-food options.

Detour:
MacRitchie Reservoir

Most people come to **MacRitchie Reservoir** (☎1800-4717 300; www.nparks.gov.sg; Lornie Rd; ⏰7am-7pm, Treetop Walk 9am-5pm Tue-Fri, 8.30am-5pm Sat & Sun, closed Mondays; Ⓜ Toa Payoh, then ☐157) for the excellent 10km walking trail that circumnavigates the reservoir, with much longer walking trails skirting the water's edge and snaking through parts of the surrounding forest. You'll almost certainly encounter monkeys (long-tailed macaques) in the forest and may be lucky enough to spot one of the huge monitor lizards that dart around the shallows of the reservoir with frightening speed.

The most popular place to aim for is Treetop Walk, the highlight of which is traversing a 250m-long suspension bridge, perched 25m up in the forest canopy. Trails then continue through the forest and around the reservoir, sometimes on dirt tracks, sometimes on wooden boardwalks.

It takes three to four hours to complete the main circuit. Young kids will have fun paddling on the submerged boardwalk, off to the left of the service centre in the small, landscaped MacRitchie Reservoir Park.

ⓘ Getting There & Away

Singapore Transport Connections

DESTINATION	AIR	BUS	TRAIN
Kuala Lumpur	1hr/from S$30	4-5hr/ from S$20	6-7hr/ from S$34
Penang	1hr 20min/ from S$40	9-10hr/ from S$45	9hr/ from S$60

Air

Most planes will land at one of the three main terminals or the Budget Terminal at Changi Airport (p364), located around 20km east of the city centre. Regularly voted the world's best airport, Changi Airport is vast, efficient and amazingly well organised. Among its many facilities you'll find free internet, courtesy phones for local calls, foreign-exchange booths, medical centres, left luggage, hotels, showers, a gym, a swimming pool and, of course, plenty of shops.

Land

The Causeway linking Johor Bahru (JB) with Singapore handles most traffic between the countries. Trains and buses run from all over Malaysia straight through to Singapore, or you can get a taxi or bus to/from JB. There's also a crossing called the Second Link linking Tuas, in western Singapore, with Geylang Patah in Malaysia – some buses to Melaka and Malaysia's west coast head this way. If you have a car, tolls on the Second Link are much higher than the Causeway.

Buses

Buses run frequently from Singapore into Malaysia, some continuing to Thailand. If you are travelling beyond Johor Bahru in Malaysia, the simplest option is to catch a bus straight from Singapore, though there are more options and lower fares travelling from JB.

While long-distance bus terminals include Queen Street Bus Terminal (cnr Queen & Arab Sts) and Lavender St Bus Terminal (cnr Lavender St & Kallang Bahru), a large number of buses depart from the Golden Mile Complex (5001 Beach Rd), where you'll also find a plethora of bus agencies selling tickets (shop around). You can also book online at www.busonlineticket.com.

Taxi

There are shared long-distance taxis to Johor Bahru, Malaysia, from the Queen St Bus Terminal (p260). Share taxis to Johor Bahru are about S$12 per person, with a maximum of four passengers per taxi, though prices may vary according to the queue at the immigration checkpoint.

Train

Singapore is the southern terminus for the Malaysian railway system, Keretapi Tanah Malayu (KTM; www.ktmb.com.my).

Malaysia has two main rail lines: the primary line going from Singapore to Kuala Lumpur, Butterworth, Alor Setar and then into Hat Yai, Thailand; and a second line branching off at Gemas and going right up through the centre of the country to Tumpat, near Kota Bharu on the east coast.

The art deco railway station in Singapore was closed for private redevelopment in 2011. The KTM train to Malaysia now runs out of the Woodlands Train Checkpoint (11 Woodlands Crossing; ☐170, Causeway Link from Queen St).

Three express trains depart every day to Kuala Lumpur roughly around 8am, 1pm and 10.30pm, and take six and seven hours; check the website for connecting train timings. You can book tickets either at the station or via the KTM website (www.ktmb.com.my).

The luxurious Eastern & Oriental Express (☎6395 0678; www.orient-express.com) departs Singapore on the 42-hour, 1943km journey to Bangkok before heading onwards to Chiang Mai and Nong Khai (for Laos). Don your linen suit, sip a gin and tonic, and dig deep for the fare: it ranges from S$3737 per person in a double compartment to S$7462 for the presidential suite. You can go as far as Kuala Lumpur or Butterworth (Penang) for a lower fare.

Singapore to Johor Bahru, Malaysia

The easiest way to cross the border is on the Singapore–Johore Express bus (S$2.40; one hour, every 15 minutes from 6.30am to 11pm), which departs from the Queen St Bus Terminal in Little India. The quickest way is to catch the MRT to Kranji, then bus 160 to the border.

The cheapest (and slowest) way is on bus 170 (S$1.90, every 10 to 15 minutes from 5.20am to 12.10am), which also leaves from Queen St Bus Terminal. Try to avoid crossing back into Singapore on Sunday nights, when traffic is hellish.

For details on doing the trip in the other direction, see p211.

Sea

The following main ferry terminals run services to Malaysia and/or Indonesia.

Changi Point Ferry Terminal (☎6546 8518; Ⓜ Tanah Merah, then ☐2)

Harbourfront Cruise & Ferry Terminal (☎6513 2200; www.singaporecruise.com; Ⓜ HarbourFront)

Tanah Merah Ferry Terminal (☎6513 2200; www.singaporecruise.com; Ⓜ Tanah Merah, then ☐35)

Malaysian Borneo

The natural beauty of Malaysian Borneo is quite simply gut-wrenching. The states of Sabah and Sarawak are blessed with deep green jungle, craggy mountains and shockingly blue seas that all seems to collide into one moving, magnificent vista. It's a land for adventure enthusiasts and yet, we must stress, not only adventure enthusiasts. Many treks around national parks, for example, really consist of vigorous hikes – jaunts you want to be fit to attempt, but don't need to be in Olympic shape to finish. Visits to longhouse communities and dipping into the urban buzz of the capital cities Kuching and Kota Kinabalu are also part of the package.

The diving in eastern Sabah – some of the best in the world – is easily accessible to beginners. And anyone can sit on a boat and appreciate the majesty of spotting prowling civets, doe-eyed loris and great ginger orangutans in the wild.

Pinnacles (p317), Gunung Mulu National Park

Waterfront market in Kota Kinabalu (p274)
PAUL KENNEDY/GETTY IMAGES ©

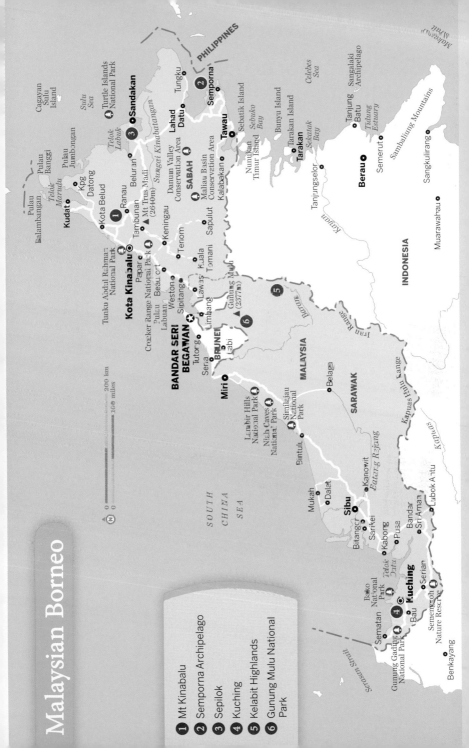

Malaysian Borneo

1 Mt Kinabalu
2 Semporna Archipelago
3 Sepilok
4 Kuching
5 Kelabit Highlands
6 Gunung Mulu National Park

Malaysian Borneo Highlights

AARON MCCOY/GETTY IMAGES ©

1 Mt Kinabalu

Although it rose from the depths below some nine million years ago, **Mt Kinabalu** is in geological terms still young – and growing by about 5mm a year. On a clear day you can see the Philippines from the summit, which can be reached on an adventurous two-day hike. Above: One of Mt Kinabalu's peaks; Top Right: *Via ferrata* (p282); Bottom Right: Bornean treepie

Need to Know

TOP TIP Do an overnight climb if you want a view from the summit, as the mountain is usually thoroughly wreathed in fog by mid-morning **For further coverage, see p280**

Mt Kinabalu Don't Miss List

BY QUEK I-GEK, MOUNTAIN CLIMBER
AND TOUR DIRECTOR

1 VIA FERRATA

According to the Guinness Book of World Records, the *via ferrata* (p282) on Mt Kinabalu is the highest 'iron road' in the world. The two courses are designed for anyone who is able to scale Mt Kinabalu and wants to take the experience to even greater heights. The Low's Peak Circuit at 3776m above sea level and including thread-like tightrope walks and swinging planks may look scary but it's a safe and controlled environment. Note that you need to be pretty fit to climb Kinabalu in the first place: the terrain makes it feel like squeezing five days of hiking into a 38-hour trek.

2 FLORA

Mt Kinabalu is a botanical paradise, designated a Centre of Plant Diversity and a Unesco listed World Heritage Site. The wide range of habitats supports an even wider range of natural history, and over half the species growing above 900m are unique to the area.

Among the more spectacular flowers are orchids, rhododendrons and the *Insectivorous nepenthe* (pitcher plant'). Park HQ is surrounded by dipterocarp forest (rainforest); creepers, ferns and orchids festoon the canopy, while fungi grow on the forest floor. Between 900m and 1800m there are oaks, laurels and chestnuts, while higher up there's dense rhododendron forest. On the windswept slopes above Laban Rata vegetation is stunted; sayat-sayat is a common shrub. The mountain's uppermost slopes are bare of plant life.

3 WILDLIFE

Deer and monkeys are no longer common around park HQ, but you can see squirrels, including the handsome Prevost's squirrel and the mountain ground squirrel. Tree shrews can sometimes be seen raiding rubbish bins. Common birds are Bornean treepies, fantails, bulbuls, sunbirds and laughing thrushes, while birds seen only at higher altitudes are the Kinabalu friendly warbler, the mountain blackeye and the mountain blackbird. You can also see colourful butterflies and the huge green moon moth.

Legendary Diving

The islands in the **Semporna Archipelago** (p**292**), adrift in the Celebes Sea, are graced with white sand and swaying palms. Around them drift the rainbow-coloured boats of copper-skinned Sea Gypsies. But no one comes this way for islands – rather it is the ocean and everything beneath it, that appeals. This is one of the best diving destinations in the world and includes the stunning submerged pinnacle of **Sipadan** (p293). Clownfish

② Sepilok Orang-Utan Rehabilitation Centre

Orang-utans (the name means 'jungle man') are the only species of great ape found outside of Africa. Less than 15,000 now exist in the wild. Orphaned or injured orang-utans are brought to the Sepilok **centre** (p287) to be rehabilitated and returned to forest life. Chances are high that at the centre's two daily feeding times you will have an encounter with these loveable bundles of ginger fun.

Urban Sophistication

Learn about the white rajahs in Borneo's most sophisticated and stylish city. **Kuching** (p294) offers an atmospheric old town, a romantic waterfront, fine cuisine for all budgets and chic nightspots that would be right at home in London or New York. But the biggest draw is what is nearby: some of Sarawak's finest natural sites, like **Bako National Park** (p304), are easy to visit on day trips.

4

5

Chill out in the Highlands

At 1500m above sea level, the **Kelabit Highlands** (p319) are one of the best spots in Malaysia to enjoy clean, cool air while trekking from longhouse to longhouse on mountain trails. The forests around Bario are a great place to spot pitcher plants, butterflies and even hornbills. Don't leave before sampling the area's famous aromatic rice and sweeter-than-sweet pineapples. Pitcher plant

6

Caves & Pinnacles

Among the remarkable features of **Gunung Mulu National Park** (p315) are its highest peak, Gunung Mulu, and a series of spectacular 'show caves' inhabited by millions of bats. In between are rugged karst mountains, deep gorges with crystal-clear rivers, and a mosaic of habitats supporting incredibly diverse wildlife. Mulu's most famous trekking attraction is the **Pinnacles** (p317), razor-sharp limestone spires jutting out of the jungle. Pinnacles

Malaysian Borneo's Best...

Wildlife Encounters

o **Borneo Sun Bear Conservation Centre** (p286) Near the Orang-Utan Rehabilitation Centre, this is another excellent reason to visit Sepilok.

o **Bako National Park** (p304) Top location for spotting proboscis monkeys.

o **Sungai Kinabatangan** (p288) Orang-utans and other wild animals can be seen along Sabah's longest river.

o **Danum Valley** (p291) Herds of pygmy elephants, orang-utans and a multitude of bird life.

Market Shopping

o **Night Market, Kota Kinabalu** (p278) The city's waterfront market is a place of delicious contrasts.

o **Satok Weekend Market** (p298) The air is heady with the aroma of fresh herbs and piles of tropical fruits.

o **Main Bazaar, Kuching** (p299) Best place to browse for handmade Dayak crafts.

o **Sibu Central Market** (p311) Malaysia's largest fruit and vegie market.

Indigenous Culture

o **Kelabit Highlands** (p319) Trek from longhouse to longhouse.

o **Sarawak Museum** (p300) A must-visit for anyone interested in Borneo's peoples, cultures and habitats.

o **Sabah Museum** (p275) The best place for an introduction to Sabah's ethnicities and environments.

o **Sarawak Cultural Village** (p306) A living museum centred on seven traditional dwellings.

Need to Know

Rainforest Canopy

○ **Gunung Mulu National Park** (p315) Reserve ahead for this 480m-long skywalk through the forest canopy.

○ **Ulu Temburong National Park** (p298) A delicate aluminium walkway hangs 60m above the forest floor.

○ **Danum Valley** (p291) Swinging bridges traverse a 107m-long section of forest.

○ **Rainforest Discovery Centre** (p286) Eight towers suspended a thrilling canopy walkway.

Left: Orang Ulu man at Sarawak Cultural Village (p306); **Above:** Night Market (p274), Kota Kinabalu
(LEFT) ANDERS BLOMQVIST/GETTY IMAGES ©;
(ABOVE) GERMAN/GETTY IMAGES ©

○ **One month before** Book accommodation, flights and a dive trip to Sipadan.

○ **One week before** Arrange trekking guides.

○ **One day before** Check weather conditions and their effect on flight schedules.

RESOURCES

○ **Sabah Tourism** (www.sabahtourism.com) Official state tourism site.

○ **Sabah Parks** (www.sabahparks.org) Sabah's national parks.

○ **Sarawak Tourism** (www.sarawaktourism.com) Official state tourism site.

○ **Sarawak Forestry** (www.sarawakforestry.com) Sarawak's national parks.

GETTING AROUND

○ **Flights** It can be remarkably cheap to fly and sometimes it's the only practical way to reach remote destinations such as the Kelabit Highlands and Gunung Mulu National Park.

○ **Boat** In some trackless areas, Sarawak's Batang Rejang for example, this is the only ride in town. 'Flying coffins' – 60-seat speedboats – are the norm.

○ **Bus** Provides links between major cities and towns, but doesn't cover more remote areas and can be slow.

○ **Car** Enables maximum flexibility but can be a major hassle because of poor or nonexistent road signage, dilapidated vehicles and a dearth of proper maps.

BE FOREWARNED

○ **Advance booking** Crucial for park accommodation and guided treks during the July to September high season and major public holidays such as Chinese New Year.

○ **Weather** Avoid making boat trips during the November to January rainy season – there can be rough seas and swollen rivers.

○ **Buses** Ask your hotel owner to ring ahead to check times, because transport is sometimes halted due to flooding caused by heavy rains.

Malaysian Borneo Itineraries

A couple of Sabah's top attractions, including Mt Kinabalu, can be squeezed into a five-day trip. A week will allow a more leisurely trip around some of Sarawak's touristic highlights.

5 DAYS

KOTA KINABALU TO SEPILOK
Mountains & Monkeys

Sample the highs and Low's of Sabah in this itinerary that takes in Malaysia's highest peak and some of the jungle's most famous inhabitants. Fly into **(1) Kota Kinabalu**, the state's modern capital. A visit to the atmospheric and visceral – and sometimes whiffy – night market will truly get you into the Southeast Asian swing of things.

Make it an early night as you'll be up at dawn the next day, arriving with plenty of time at **(2) Kinabalu National Park** for your overnight assault on Mt Kinabalu, the roof of Borneo. The 4095m summit is named Low's Peak, after Sir Hugh Low, the British colonial secretary who recorded the first official colonial ascent on the mountain in 1851. At the mountain's base enjoy easier trails and the cultivated Mountain Garden.

Strike out east from Kinabalu National Park to **(3) Sepilok**, home of Sabah's next top tourist attraction: the Sepilok Orang-Utan Rehabilitation Centre. The ginger-haired orang-utans often (but not always) swing on through at the feeding times at 10am and 3pm. While in the area also check out the excellent Rainforest Discovery Centre and the Borneo Sun Bear Conservation Centre, a new facility that cares for 27 rescued bears.

7 DAYS

KUCHING TO MIRI
Urban & Jungle Pleasures

Spend your first day in **(1) Kuching** immersed in the city's kaleidoscopic mix of cultures and cuisines. Explore the shophouses of Chinatown, ride a tiny passenger ferry to the English Renaissance–style Fort Margherita and take a sunset stroll along the Waterfront Promenade. If it's Saturday, don't miss the colourful Satok Weekend Market.

Spend a half-day spotting orang-utans at **(2) Semenggoh Nature Reserve**, then drive further inland to the longhouse of **(3) Annah Rais**, where you can stay overnight. The next day take a boat to **(4) Bako National Park**, keeping an eye out for proboscis monkeys, macaques

and pitcher plants as you hike around the peninsula. Either spend the night in the park or return to Kuching.

Fly from Kuching to **(5) Sibu** for an adventurous river boat in a 'flying coffin' up the Batang Rejang to **(6) Kapit,** the main upriver settlement. Return the next day and board another plane to **(7) Miri** where you can connect with a flight to **(8) Gunung Mulu National Park**. In this World Heritage Site hire a guide to lead you to the amazing show caves and book your place for the thrilling hike across the canopy walkway.

Discover
Malaysian Borneo

Mangrove forest, Bako National Park (p304)
ANDREW WATSON/GETTY IMAGES ©

SABAH
Kota Kinabalu

We realise you almost certainly didn't come to Sabah for the urban scene, but you have to book permits somewhere, you need to sleep after climbing Mt Kinabalu/diving in Sipadan/exploring the jungle etc, and you need some place to connect to onward travel, and KK, as everyone calls it, is a good place (sometimes the only place) to do all of the above. The centre is walkable. The population is a spicy mix of expats, Chinese, indigenous Kadazan and, of course, Malays. The food is good – surprisingly good, even, given that you're in Malaysia's hinterlands.The nightlife is fun, a testament to Sabah's laidback approach to life, although admittedly there aren't too many bars. The only real downside is out of control construction: KK desperately seems to want to answer the question, 'How many empty malls can we build in one city?' Past this one demerit, though, it's hard not to love this town.

◎ Sights & Activities

NIGHT MARKET Market
(Map p276; Jln Tun Fuad Stephens; ⊙late afternoon-11pm) KK's main market is huddled beneath the imposing Le Meridien and divided into two main sections: the southwest end is given over mostly to produce, while the northeast end (the area around the main entrance) is a huge hawker centre (p278) where you can eat your way right through the entire Malay gastronomy. A fish-and-food market extends to the waterfront;

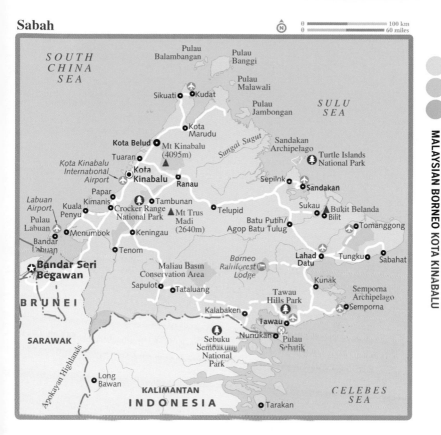

the closer you get to the ocean the more the scent of salt water, death, blood and spices envelops you – an oddly intoxicating experience.

SABAH MUSEUM
Museum

(☎088-253199; www.museum.sabah.gov.my; Jln Muzium; admission RM20; ⊗9am-5pm Sat-Thu; P) This fine museum is slightly south of the city centre, on the hilly corner of Jln Tunku Abdul Rahman and Jln Penampang. It's centred on a modern four-storey structure inspired by the longhouses of the Rungus and Murut tribes, and the main building houses good permanent collections of tribal and historical artefacts including ceramics, and exhibits of flora and fauna – some dusty, others well presented (including a centrepiece whale skeleton).

👉 Tours

KK has a huge number of tour companies. Head to Wisma Sabah – this office building is full of agents and operators.

GOGOSABAH
Tours

(Map p276; ☎088-316385, 088-317385; www.gogosabah.com; Lot G-4, Ground fl, Wisma Sabah, Jln Tun Razak) This fantastic tour company does a great job of booking just about anything, anywhere in Sabah. It's especially excellent for motorbike rentals – staff will help map out some of the choicest areas for exploration in Sabah. It also offers car rentals and a serviced apartment too. It's a good go-to organisation for package tours, but can also help independent travellers out with logistics, itineraries and information.

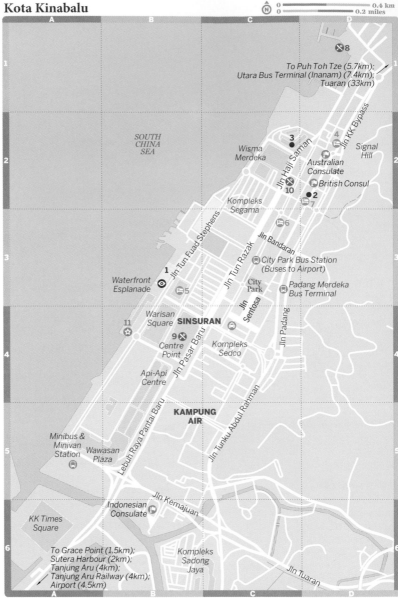

KK HERITAGE WALK Walking Tour (www.kkheritagewalk.com; RM200; ⏱walks 9am Tue & Thu) This two-hour tour, which can be booked through any of KK's many tour operators (just ask at your hotel front desk), explores colonial KK and its hidden delights. Stops include Chinese herbal shops, bulk produce stalls, a *kopitiam* (coffee shop), and Jln Gaya (known as Bond St when the British were in charge).

Kota Kinabalu

🖋 STICKY RICE   Tours

(📞088-250588; www.stickyricetravel.com) Besides having a great name, the Sticky Rice guys are extremely helpful, knowledgable about Borneo and committed to natural immersion, community engagement and independent travel.

🖋 ADVENTURE ALTERNATIVE
BORNEO   Nature

(Map p276; 📞019-802 0549; www.adventure alternativeborneo.com; 97 Jln Gaya) Adventure Alternative specialises in getting Sabah visitors off the beaten/package-tour path, and is an excellent resource for independent travellers, especially those who are interested in sustainable and responsible tourism.

 Sleeping

SARANGNOVA HOTEL   Hotel $$

(Map p276; 📞088-233750; www.sarangnova. com; 98 Jln Gaya; s/d from RM120/170) It's hard to miss this fascinating hotel: there's a conceptual, woodsy slat fixture attached to the front. The rooms are just as distinctive as the exterior, seeing as they're themed after Borneo's birds. No, no feathers on the walls or anything, but the attractively minimalist decor is offset by gallery-style portraits of local avian life; this includes some picture compositions that are downright Warhol-ian.

HOTEL EDEN 54   Boutique Hotel $$

(Map p276; 📞088-266054; www.eden54.com; 54 Jln Gaya; r RM119-179; ❄🛜) This smart choice would likely cost five times what it does were it plopped in the West. Fortunately this Eden's contrasting solid dark and light colours, geometric design sensibility and immaculate furniture have turned up in Kota Kinabalu. A fine choice for flashpackers, couples, even families. One warning: the cheapest rooms are windowless, and should be avoided.

RAINFOREST LODGE   Hotel $$

(Map p276; 📞088-258228; www.rainforest lodgekk.com; Jln Pantai; dm/s/d/ste from RM40/115/135/165; ❄@🛜) Located in the swinging centre of the 'Beach St' complex, the Rainforest is all of a stairward stumble from some of KK's best nightlife. Rooms are refreshingly chic, a nice mix of modern and Sabah-tribal style, and many have cool balconies that look onto the Beach St parade below. Just be warned: it gets loud at night.

LE MERIDIEN KOTA KINABALU   Hotel $$$

(Map p276; 📞088-322222; www.starwoodho tels.com; Jln Tun Fuad Stephens; r from RM300; P❄🛜♨) 'If you can't undercut 'em, outclass 'em' seems to be the motto at KK's most central five-star venture, which just reeks of luxury, from the incredible views from the pool deck to the flat-screen TVs and DVD players.

If You Like...
Hawker Food

The best food in KK is found at its hawker stalls. You really shouldn't be worried about sanitation, but assuage your fears by looking for popular stalls, especially those frequented by families.

1 NIGHT MARKET
(Map p276; off Jln Tun Fuad Stephens; meals from RM2; ⏱5pm-11pm) The best, cheapest and most interesting place in KK for dinner. Vegetarian options available.

2 CENTRE POINT BASEMENT FOOD COURT
(Map p276; Basement fl, Centre Point Shopping Centre, Jln Pasar Baru; mains RM3-10; ⏱11am-10pm) Your ringgit will go a long way at this popular and varied basement food court in the Centre Point mall.

3 GRACE POINT
(Grace Point; mains RM2-8; ⏱11am-3pm) Take bus 15 out near Tanjung Aru for some local grub at this Kota Kinabalu (KK) mainstay. The development is actually quite chic compared to the smoke-swathed food courts in the city centre – KKers joke that the public bathrooms here are Borneo's nicest (and it's true!).

 Eating

City Centre
MOON BELL   Chinese $$
(Map p276; ☎019-8611 605; 33 Jln Haji Saman; mains RM15-35; ⏱11am-9pm, closed Mon; ❄) Never had Xinjiang cuisine? This is the food of China's northwest frontier: spicy, rich and meaty. Moon Bell, run by a superlatively friendly Chinese granny, blows us away with spicy eggplant fried in a sweet, caramelised lacquer of dark sauce, gamey roast lamb, crispy-skinned duck and hearty clay hotpots. It's best to come here with a big group and eat family-style, just as all the locals do.

ALU-ALU CAFE   Seafood $$
(Map p276; Jessleton Point; mains from RM10-30; ⏱10.30am-2.30pm & 6.30am-10pm; ❄) Technically part of the **Gayana Eco Resort** (☎088-380390; www.gayana-eco-resort.com; villas from RM1200; ❄🛜🏊), Alu-Alu sources its ingredients from Borneo Eco-Fish, an organisation dedicated to harvesting and distributing seafood from sustainable sources – no shark fin here. Moral mission aside, Alu-Alu is legitimately delicious. It takes the Chinese seafood concept to new levels, lightly breading fish chunks and serving them drowned in a mouth-watering buttermilk sauce, or simmering amid diced chillies. Even the vegetables, simply steamed with a side of pungent garlic, are a main event as opposed to an afterthought.

Drinking & Entertainment

Get ready for loads of karaoke bars and big, booming nightclubs, clustered around the Waterfront Esplanade, KK Times Sq, where the newest hot spots are congregating, and Beach St, in the centre of town, a semi-pedestrian street cluttered with bars and eateries.

EL CENTRO   Bar
(Map p276; 32 Jln Haji Saman ; ⏱5pm-midnight, closed Mon) This fantastic spot, which doubles as a **restaurant** (Map p276; 🛜), is the traveller's hangout you've been looking for: cool, Asian-mod decor, soft lighting, good music that isn't the same recycled pop every other Malaysian bar plays, and a general sense of chilled ease that makes it easy to met other wanderers and form new friendships. The drinks are stupid strong, and it hosts impromptu quiz nights, costume parties and live-music shows.

BED   Club
(Map p276; ☎251901; Waterfront Esplanade) It's big, it's crowded, it's cheesy – chances are you'll end up in Bed one night. Yes, get those bed puns ready, as well as your

dancing shoes and patience for a *lot* of hip Chinese and locals in outfits that are alternatively slinky/shiny/skimpy. Bands play from 9pm, followed by DJs till closing.

ℹ Getting There & Away

Air

KK is well served by **Malaysia Airlines** (📞1300-883 000, 088-515555; www.malaysiaairlines.com; 1st fl, Departure Hall, KKIA; 🕙5.30am-7.30pm) and **AirAsia** (📞03-21719333; www.airasia.com; Ground fl, Wisma Sabah, Jln Gaya) within Malaysia and internationally. **Jetstar** (www.jetstar.com) and **Tiger Airways** (www.tigerairways.com) both offer flights to Singapore.

Bus & Minivan

Several different stations around KK serve a number of destinations, including Brunei. In general, buses heading east depart from Inanam (Utara Terminal; 9km north of the city) while those heading north and south on the west coast leave from Padang Merdeka Bus Station (also called Wawasan or 'old bus station') at the south end of town. Local buses (RM1.80) from Wawasan can take tourists to Inanam if you don't want to

splurge on the RM20 taxi. Have your hotel call ahead to the bus station to book your seat in advance. Same-day bookings are usually fine, although weekends are busier than weekdays.

Taxi

Share taxis operate from Padang Merdeka Bus Station. Several share taxis do a daily run between KK and Ranau, passing the entrance road to the Kinabalu National Park office. The fare to Kinabalu National Park is RM25 or you can charter a taxi for RM100 per car (note that a normal city taxi will charge around RM200 for a charter).

ℹ Getting Around

To/From the Airport

The international airport is in Tanjung Aru, 7km south of central KK. Please note that the two terminals of Kota Kinabalu International Airport (KKIA) are not connected – they feel like two different airports. Most airlines operate out of Terminal 1, but an increasing amount of carriers, including Air Asia, depart from Terminal 2. City bus 2 and bus 16A (RM1.50) service Terminal 2 and can be boarded at City Park station downtown. Minibuses (RM3) leave from City Park station

Food court

TOM COCKREM/GETTY IMAGES ©

for Terminal 1 (look for city bus 1 to access this terminal in the future). Public transport runs from 6am to 7pm daily. Taxis heading from terminals into town operate on a voucher system (RM38) sold at a taxi desk on the terminal's ground floor. Taxis heading to the airport should not charge over RM40 if you catch one in the city centre.

Car

Major car-rental agencies have counters on the 1st floor at KKIA and branch offices elsewhere in town. Manual cars start at around RM120 to RM140 per day and most agencies can arrange chauffeured vehicles as well.

Minivans

Minivans operate from several stops, including Padang Merdeka Bus Station and the car park outside Milimewa Superstore. They circulate the town looking for passengers. Since most destinations in the city are within walking distance, it's unlikely that you'll need to catch a minivan, although they're handy for getting to the airport or to KK Times Sq. Most destinations within the city cost RM1 to RM2.

Taxi

Expect to pay roughly between RM7 to RM10 for a ride in the city centre. Taxis can be found throughout the city and at all bus stations and shopping centres. There's a stand by Milimewa Supermarket (near the intersection of Jln Haji Saman and Beach St) and another 200m southwest of City Park.

Mt Kinabalu & Kinabalu National Park

Mt Kinabalu is ubiquitous in Sabah: it graces the state's flag and is a constant presence at the edge of your eyes, catching the clouds and shading the valleys. It is only when you give the mountain your full attention that you realise how special this peak, the region's biggest tourist attraction, truly is.

The 4095m peak may not be a Himalayan sky-poker, but Malaysia's first Unesco World Heritage Site is by no means an easy jaunt. The main trail up is essentially a very long walk up a very

Left: Water village on Mabul (p292); **Below:** Harlequin gliding tree frog, Danum Valley (p291) (LEFT) FOTOTRAV/GETTY IMAGES ©; (BELOW) CHRIS MATTISON/GETTY IMAGES ©

steep hill, past alpine jungle and sunlit moonscapes, with a little scrabbling thrown in for good nature. If you don't feel up to reaching the mountain top, its base has some worthy attractions, including a large network of nature trails.

That said, the main detriment to climbing is not the physical challenge, but the cost. Things are expensive within Mt Kinabalu National Park. Bottled water costs four or five times what it goes for in KK and Sutera Sanctuary Lodges has a monopoly on accommodation. You'll have to decide if you want to accept these fees, because they are basically the cost of climbing the mountain.

Orientation & Information

Kinabalu National Park HQ is 88km by road northeast of KK and set in gardens with a magnificent view of the mountain. At 1588m the climate is refreshingly cool compared to the coast; the average temperatures are 20°C in the day and 13°C at night.

On the morning of your arrival, pay your park entry fee, present your lodging reservation slip to the Sutera Sanctuary Lodges office to receive your official room assignment, and check in with the Sabah Parks office to pay your registration and guide fees. Advance accommodation bookings are essential if you plan on climbing the mountain.

Permits, Fees & Guides

A park fee, climbing permit, insurance and a guide fee are *mandatory* if you intend to climb Mt Kinabalu. All permits and guides must be arranged at the **Sabah Parks office** (☺7am-7pm), which is directly next door to the Sutera Sanctuary Lodges office, immediately on your right after you pass through the main gate of the park. Pay all fees at park HQ before you climb and don't ponder an 'unofficial' climb as permits (laminated cards worn on a string necklace) are scrupulously checked at

281

NORA CAROL/GETTY IMAGES ©

Don't Miss **Via Ferrata**

Mountain Torq (www.mountaintorq.com) has dramatically changed the Kinabalu climbing experience by creating an intricate system of rungs and rails crowning the mountain's summit. Known as *via ferrata* (literally 'iron road' in Italian), this alternative style of mountaineering has been a big hit in Europe for the last century.

After ascending Kinabalu in the traditional fashion, participants use the network of levers to return to the Laban Rata rest camp along the mountain's dramatic granite walls. Mountain Torq's star attraction, the **Low's Peak Circuit** (RM550; minimum age 17), is a four-to-five-hour scramble down metres upon metres of sheer rock face. This route starts at 3800m, passing a variety of obstacles before linking up to the Walk the Torq path for the last part of the journey.

Those who don't want to see their heart leaping out of their chest should try the **Walk the Torq** (RM400; minimum age 10) route. This two-to-three-hour escapade is an exciting initiation into the world of *via ferrata,* offering dramatic mountain vistas with fewer knee-shaking moments.

two points you cannot avoid passing on the way up the mountain. Virtually every tour operator in KK can hook you up with a trip to the mountain; solo travellers are often charged around RM1400. It's possible, and a little cheaper, to do it on your own – but plan ahead.

All visitors entering the park are required to pay a **park entrance fee**: RM15 for adults and RM10 for children under 18. A **climbing permit** costs RM100/RM40 for adults/children. **Climbing insurance** costs RM7 per person. **Guide fees** for the summit trek cost RM100. Climbers ascending Kinabalu along the Mesilau trail will pay an extra RM10 (small group) or RM20 (large group) for their guide. Your guide will be assigned to you on the morning you begin your hike. If you ask, the park staff will try to attach individual travellers to a group so that guide fees can be shared. Couples can expect to be given their own guide. Ask for a guide who speaks English – he or she (usually he) might point out a few interesting specimens of plant life. The path up the mountain is pretty straightforward, and the guides walk behind the slowest member of the group, so think of them as safety supervisors rather than trailblazers.

All this does not include at least RM415 for room-and-board on the mountain at Laban Rata. With said lodging, plus buses or taxis to the park, you're looking at spending over RM800 for the common two-day, one-night trip to the mountain. That said, you *can* do a one-day hike if you show up at the park entrance when it opens (7am) and are judged physically fit by a ranger. But there are two catches. First, when we say you need to be fit, we mean *fit*. Two, and more worryingly, there are rumours the park will discontinue allowing one-day hikes in the future.

Optional extra fees include a taxi ride from the park office to the Timpohon Gate (RM16.50 per vehicle, one-way, four-person maximum), a climbing certificate (RM10) and a porter (RM102 per trip to the summit or RM84 to Laban Rata) who can be hired to carry a maximum load of 10kg

Equipment & Clothing

No special equipment is required to successfully summit the mountain; however, a headlamp is strongly advised for the predawn jaunt to the top – you'll need your hands free to climb the ropes on the summit massif. Expect freezing temperatures near the summit, not to mention strong winds and the occasional rainstorm. Don't forget a water bottle,

which can be refilled at unfiltered (but potable) tanks en route.

Climbing Mt Kinabalu

If you're doing a two-day/one-night ascent of the mountain, you'll want to check in at park headquarters at around 9am (8.45am at the latest for *via ferrata* participants) to pay your park fees, grab your guide and start the ascent (four to six hours) to Laban Rata (3272m) where you'll spend the night before finishing the climb. On the following day you'll finish scrambling to the top at about 2.30am in order to reach the summit for a breath-taking sunrise over Borneo.

A climb up Kinabalu is only advised for those in adequate physical condition. It's all uphill and you will negotiate several obstacles along the way, including slippery stones, blinding humidity, frigid winds and slow-paced trekkers. There are rest shelters *(pondok)* at regular intervals, with basic toilets and tanks of unfiltered (but potable) drinking water.

There are two trail options:

Yellow rhododendron, Kinabalu
National Park

Timpohon Trail The best option for first timers; it's shorter, easier (but by no means easy!) and more convenient from the park headquarters (an hour's walk or short park shuttle ride; RM16.50 one way per vehicle, four-person maximum). If you are participating in Mountain Torq's *via ferrata,* you are required to take the Timpohon Trail in order to reach Laban Rata in time for your safety briefing at 4pm.

Mesilau Trail Offers second-time climbers (or fit hikers) the opportunity to really enjoy some of the park's natural wonders. This trail is less trodden so the chances of seeing unique flora and fauna are higher.

Walks Around the Base

It's well worth spending a day exploring the marked trails around park headquarters; if you have time, it may be better to do it before you climb the mountain, as chances are you won't really feel like it afterwards. There are various trails and lookouts.

Some interesting plants, plenty of birds and, if you're lucky, the occasional mammal can be seen along the **Liwagu Trail** (6km), which follows the river of the same name. When it rains, watch out for slippery paths and legions of leeches.

At 11am each day a **guided walk (per person RM3)** starts from the Sabah Parks office and lasts for one to two hours. If you set out from KK early enough, it's possible to arrive at the park in time for the guided walk.

Sleeping

The sleeping options located at the base of the mountain, all operated by Sutera Sanctuary Lodges (p285), are overpriced compared to sleeping spots just outside the park.

LABAN RATA (ON THE MOUNTAIN)

Camping is not allowed on the mountain, and thus access to the summit is limited by access to the huts on the mountain at Laban Rata (3272m). This *must* be booked in advance, the earlier the better. In order to have any hope of clear weather when you reach the summit, you must arrive around dawn, and the only way to do this is by spending a night at Laban Rata. If you attempt a one-day ascent starting around 7am, by the time you get to the

Resthouse at Laban Rata

TRAVELSCAPE IMAGES/ALAMY ©

summit it will almost certainly be clouded over or raining.

Sutera Sanctuary Lodges

(☎088-308470, 088-318888; http://suterasanctuarylodges.com.my; Lot G15, ground fl, Wisma Sabah) in Kota Kinabalu operates almost all of the accommodation here, but space is limited. Be mindful that travellers often report frustration with booking huts on the mountain – claiming the booking system is disorganised and inefficient, the huts are often full, or aren't full when they're told they are. Bookings can be made online (but only if you book at least two nights), in person or over the phone – our experience was that it was best to book at Sutera's offices in KK if you haven't done so in advance.

The most common sleeping option is the heated dormitory (bedding included) in the Laban Rata Resthouse, which sells for RM485 per person. Twin shares are available for RM920. Three meals are included in the price. Non-heated facilities surrounding the Laban Rata building are also available for RM415 per person (meals included).

The other option at Laban Rata is to stay at **Pendant Hut**, which is owned and operated by **Mountain Torq** (pricing is on par with Sutera). All guests sleeping at Pendant Hut take two of three meals at Sutera's cafeteria, and are required to participate in (or at least pay for) the *via ferrata* circuit. Pendant Hut is slightly more basic (there's no heat, although climbers sleep in uberwarm sleeping bags). However, there's a bit of a summer-camp vibe here while Laban Rata feels more like a Himalayan orphanage.

OUTSIDE KINABALU PARK

WIND PARADISE
Yurt $$

(☎088-714563, 012-820 3360; http://windparadise2011.blogspot.com/; Jln Mesilau, Cinta Mata, Kundasang; d from RM170, 4-person yurt RM300; P) There are elements of Wind Paradise that resemble just another (albeit well-executed) Mt Kinabalu resort: lodge-y rooms with attractive hard-wood floors and an odd mix of modern, minimalist furniture and rather garish bedsheets. Then there are the yurts,

the traditional tent used by Mongolian nomads. Almost all lodging comes with great views over the alpine jungle that surrounds Mt Kinabalu.

D'VILLA RINA RIA LODGE
Lodge $$

(☎088-889282; www.dvillalodge.com.my; dm/r RM30/120; @) This charming lodge is run by friendly staff that maintain cute, cosy rooms and a dining area that overlooks a lovely view over the mountain ranges/thick clouds of afternoon fog, depending on the mercy of the weather gods.

 Eating

Laban Rata (On the Mountain)

At Laban Rata the cafeteria style restaurant in the **Laban Rata Resthouse** has a simple menu and also offers buffet meals coordinated with the usual climbing times. Most hikers staying at Laban Rata (either in one of Sutera's huts or at Pendant Hut) have three meals (dinner, breakfast and lunch) included in their accommodation packages. It is possible to negotiate a price reduction if you plan on bringing your own food (boiling water can be purchased for RM1 if you bring dried noodles). Note: you will have to lug said food up to Laban Rata. Buffet meals can also be purchased individually – dinner costs RM45.

Park Headquarters (At the Base)

RESTORAN KINABALU BALSAM
Cafeteria $$

(dishes RM5-15; ⊙6am-10pm, to 11pm weekends) The cheaper and more popular of the two options in the park is this canteen-style spot directly below the park HQ. It offers basic but decent Malaysian, Chinese and Western dishes at reasonable prices. There is also a small but well-stocked shop in Balsam selling tinned and dried foods, chocolate, beer, spirits, cigarettes, T-shirts, bread, eggs and margarine.

 Getting There & Away

It is highly advised that summit-seekers check in at the park headquarters by 9am, which means if you're coming from KK, you should plan to leave by 7am, or consider spending the night somewhere near the base of the mountain.

Bus

Express buses (RM25) leave KK from the Utara Terminal bus station every hour on the hour from 7am to 10am and at 12:30pm, 2pm and 3pm and leaves at the same times in the reverse directions; minivans (RM15) leave from the same area when full. A shuttle bus (RM40) also runs from the Pacific Sutera (9am), the Magellan Sutera (9.10am) and Wisma Sabah (9.20am) to Kinabalu National Park HQ, arriving at 11.30am (RM40). In the reverse direction, it leaves Kinabalu National Park HQ at 3.30pm.

Taxi

Share taxis leave KK from Inanam and Padang Merdeka Bus Stations (RM150 to RM200).

Jeep

Share jeeps park just outside of the park gates and leave when full for KK (RM150) and Sandakan (RM400); each jeep can hold around five passengers, but they can be chartered by individuals.

Sepilok

The orang-utan is the associative species of Sabah, despite the fact the living space of the beast shrinks annually. The most reliable place to see this primate is the little hamlet of Sepilok, which sees almost as many visitors as the granite spires of Mt Kinabalu. Those who have time to stick around will also uncover several scenic nature walks, a sanctuary for the adorable sun bear and a couple of great places to call home for a night or two.

Sights & Activities

BORNEO SUN BEAR CONSERVATION CENTRE
Animal Sanctuary
(BSBCC; ☎089-534491; www.bsbcc.org.my; Jln Sepilok; RM30; ◷9am-4pm) The sun bear is the smallest of the world's bear species, as well as one of the most threatened. The BSBCC, at the time of research, cared for some 27 rescued sun bears. The pretty little beasts lumber and play in open-air forest enclosures; visitors can peek in on their activity from an expertly crafted walkway system. Please note the centre's admissions and opening times may change, as it was not officially open at the time of writing.

RAINFOREST DISCOVERY CENTRE (RDC)
Nature Reserve
(☎089-533780; www.forest.sabah.gov.my/rdc; adult/child RM10/5; ◷8am-5pm) The RDC, about 1.5km from the Sepilok Orang-Utan Rehabilitation Centre (SORC, p287), offers an engaging graduate-level education in tropical flora and fauna. A series of eight canopy towers connected by walkways give you a bird's-eye view of the green rooftops of the trees, by far the most rewarding element of a trip here. You can also book night walks, which afford the chance to spot nocturnal animals like tarsiers and wild cats.

It's best to get there either at 8am or 4pm, as wildlife tends to hibernate during the sweltering hours in the middle of the day. This is a good spot to while away time between feedings at SORC.

Sleeping & Eating

PAGANAKAN DII
Boutique Hotel $$
(☎089-532005; www.paganakandii.com; dm/chalets RM30/150; ❄☏) Chic design details made from recycled materials, crisp white linens, smooth wooden chalets, views into a jungle seemingly sliced out of Eden and friendly staff will have you thinking the owners surely left a zero off the price tag. Overall, staying here is a great reason to get stuck in Sepilok. Transfers to the Sepilok Rehabilitation Centre are included in the price. Book early.

SEPILOK FOREST EDGE RESORT
Resort $$
(☎089-533190, 089-533245; www.sepilok-forestedge.com; Jln Rambutan, Sepilok Mile 14;

PETER PTSCHELINZEW/GETTY IMAGES ©

Don't Miss Sepilok Orang-Utan Rehabilitation Centre (SORC)

One of only four orang-utan sanctuaries in the world, SORC occupies a corner of the Kabili-Sepilok Forest Reserve about 25km north of Sandakan. The centre was established in 1964; it now covers 40 sq km and has become one of Sabah's top tourist attractions, second only to Mt Kinabalu. While thousands of people see orang-utans during feeding time at Sepilok, the creatures are, after all, wild animals and their movements aren't guaranteed. On the bright side, there are two major feeding times a day, so if you miss them in the morning, you can always try again in the afternoon.

Feedings are at 10am and 3pm and last 30 to 50 minutes. The morning feeding tends to be more tour-group heavy, so try the afternoon for a quieter experience.

A worthwhile 20-minute video about Sepilok's work is shown five times daily (9am, 11am, noon, 2.10pm and 3.30pm) in the auditorium opposite opposite reception.

If you want to explore the sanctuary further, several walking trails lead into the forest; register at the visitor reception centre to use them.

NEED TO KNOW

📞089-531180; soutan@po.jaring.my; Jln Sepilok; daily admission RM30, camera fee RM10; ⏱9-11am & 2-3.30pm, walking trails 9am-4.15pm

dm/d/chalets from RM40/80/220; ❄🛋) This fine resort grew out of the excellent Labuk B&B, which is still technically part of the Forest Edge property. Serviceable dorm and double rooms are located in a pretty long house, but it's the chalets that are the property's pièce de résistance. The comfortable cabins are peppered across an obsessively maintained acreage (think golf course).

SEPILOK NATURE RESORT   Resort $$$
(☎089-674999, 089-673999; http://se-pilok.com; r from RM280; ❄@) This is
as luxurious as Sepilok gets – the full
five-star tropical treatment. Run by the
very exclusive Pulau Sipadan Resort &
Tours, these rattan-accented chalets are
exquisitely decked out and have private
verandahs overlooking scrumptious
gardens and a shaded lagoon. The on-
site restaurant cooks the best Western
food in Sepilok (not that there's a lot of
competition).

ℹ Information

Sepilok is located at 'Batu 14' – 14 miles (23km)
from Sandakan which has an airport and is
connected to KK and other major Sabah towns by
frequent buses.

It's best to get money in Sandakan, but an ATM
had been installed in a Petronas Station on the
road between Sandakan and Sepilok. The next-
closest ATM is in Sandakan Airport.

ℹ Getting There & Away

Bus

Bus 14 from Sandakan (RM3) departs hourly
from the city centre. If coming from KK, board
a Sandakan-bound bus and ask the driver to let
you off at 'Batu 14'. You will pay the full fare, even
though Sandakan is 23km away.

Taxi

If you are coming directly from Sandakan, a taxi
should cost no more than RM45 (either from the
airport or the city centre).Taxi 'pirates', as they're
known, wait at Batu 14 to give tourists a ride into
Sepilok. It's RM3 per person for a lift. Travellers
spending the night can arrange a lift with their
accommodation if they book ahead of time.
Walking to the SORC is also an option – it's only
2.5km down the road.

Van

You can usually organise a pick-up (in a shared
minivan from the Kinabatangan operators) from
Sepilok after the morning feeding if you are
planning to head to Sungai Kinabatangan in the
afternoon.

Sungai Kinabatangan

The Kinabatangan River is Sabah's
longest: 560km of water so choco-
latey brown it would pose a serious
safety risk to Augustus Gloop.
It coils like the serpents that
swim its length far into the
Borneo interior. Riverine
forest creeps alongside
the water, swarming
with wildlife. Lodges
are set up all along the
banks, while homestay
programs pop up with
the frequency of local
monkeys. Dozens of tin
boats putter along the
shores offering tourists
the opportunity to have
a close encounter with

Sepilok Nature Resort

ANDERS BLOMQVIST/GETTY IMAGES ©

Don't Miss Homestays On the Kinabatangan

Homestay programs are popping up with increasing frequency in Sukau, Bilit and other villages, giving tourists a chance to stay with local Orang Sungai – 'people of the river' – and inject money almost directly into local economies.

Our favourite homestay in the region is in the village of Abai. The villagers love hosting guests and, to the degree they can, chatting with you and generally forming cross-cultural bonds (the levels of English are admittedly not great). Expect to be asked to participate in the local village volleyball matches! This homestay is best arranged through Adventure Alternative Borneo (p277) in Kota Kinabalu, which maintains direct contact with the villagers. As a rule, homestays are booked through program coordinators who then place you with individual families.

a rhinoceros hornbill or perhaps a doe-eyed orang-utan.

River cruise/accommodation packages are exceedingly popular with dozens of lodges vying for trade. A 'three-day/two night' stint usually involves the following: arrive in the afternoon on day one for a cruise at dusk, two boat rides (or a boat/hike combo) on day two, and an early-morning departure on day three after breakfast. When booking ask about the cost of pick-up and drop off, as this is usually extra.

Sleeping & Eating

LAST FRONTIER RESORT   Resort $$$
(☏016-676 5922; www.thelastfrontierresort. com; 3-day, 2-night packages RM550; ✳ @ 🛜)
Getting to the Last Frontier is a good first step towards better cardiac health: the only hilltop lodge in the Kinabatangan region sits high, high up (538 steps!) on a hill overlooking the flood plains. Sadly a Sherpa is not included in the rates. What you do get is excellent fusion cuisine in the on-site cafe **Monkey Cup** (this place

is owned by a Belgian-Malaysian couple – anyone want *frites mit/avec nasi lemak*?), gorgeous views of the river, well-crafted, simple chalets and a host of trekking options.

SUKAU RAINFOREST LODGE   Lodge $$$

(088-438300; www.sukau.com; 3-day, 2-night packages RM1750; ❄ 🛜) The Rainforest Lodge participates in tree-planting projects aimed at reviving degraded portions of riverine forest, aims to reduce use of plastics and is pioneering the use of quiet electric motors on its river cruises (which utilise boats made of recycled materials). All this is well and good, but the sleeping experience is lovely as well: swish but unpretentious longhouses dotted into the jungle, situated around a lovely common space stuffed with gongs, tiki torches and *bubu* (local fish traps), welcome guests after their riverine adventures. Don't miss the 440m annotated boardwalk in the back that winds through the canopy.

NATURE LODGE KINABATANGAN   Lodge $$

(088-230534, 013-863 6263; www.nature-lodgekinabatangan.com; 3-day, 2-night packages dm/chalet RM380/415) Located just around the river bend from Bilit, this charming jungle retreat is a decent choice for backpacker budgets. The campus of bungalows is divided into two sections: the Civet Wing caters to penny-pinchers with dorm-style huts, while the spiffed-up Agamid Wing offers higher-end twin-bed chalets. Neither sleeping experience will blow you away: mattresses are thin and the rooms get dank after the rains, so don't expect luxury. The activity schedule, on the other hand, is fantastic: the three-day, two-night packages include three boat tours, three guided hikes *and* all meals, which is as good value as you'll find in these parts.

❶ Getting There & Away

Transfers are usually arranged with your lodging as part of your package, but you can save by arriving independently. Arrange transport from any of the drop-off points with your tour operator or with a local minivan.

Sungai Kinabatangan

ANDREW WATSON/GETTY IMAGES ©

Detour:
Danum Valley Conservation Area

This pristine rainforest covering some 440sq km of central Sabah is currently under the protection of **Yayasan Sabah** (Sabah Foundation; www.ysnet.org.my), a semi-governmental organisation tasked with both protecting and utilising the state's forest resources. Locals say that at any given time there are over a hundred scientists doing research in the Danum Valley. Tourists are less frequent visitors, but they are here, and you should count yourself lucky if you join their ranks.

There are only two places to stay: the very luxurious resort **Borneo Rainforest Lodge** (BRL; ☎088-267637, 089-880207; www.borneonaturetours.com; d standard/deluxe 3-day, 2-night packages per person RM2390/2690) or the budget-priced **Danum Valley Field Centre** (DVFC; ☎088-326300, 088-881688; rmilzah@gmail.com; resthouse r & board from RM180, camping RM30; ❄), where the main priority is accommodating scientists as opposed to, well, you. See the website of the **South East Asia Rainforest Research** (www.searrp.org) for more information on research occurring in the valley.

Living here are orang-utans, tarsiers, sambar deer, bearded pigs, flying squirrels, gibbons and pygmy elephants (to name a few). However, Danum is a jungle, and you may spend your entire time without spotting much wildlife.

The Danum Valley is only accessible by authorised private vehicle. If you do not want to spend the night in Lahad Datu, the closest town to the reserve, it is recommended you take the 6.25am MASwings flight from KK.

Bus & Minivan

From KK, board a Tawau- or Lahad Datu-bound bus and ask the driver to let you off at 'Sukau Junction,' also known as 'Meeting Point' – the turn-off road to reach Sukau. If you are on a Sandakan-bound bus, make sure your driver remembers to stop at the Tawau-Sandakan junction – it's called 'Batu 32' or 'Checkpoint' (sometimes it's known as Sandakan Mile 32).

From Sepilok or Sandakan, expect to pay around RM20 to reach 'Batu 32', and around RM30 if you're on a Sandakan–Tawau bus and want to alight at 'Meeting Point'.

A minivan ride to 'Meeting Point' from Lahad Datu costs RM20. When buying your bus tickets remember to tell the vendor where you want to get off so you don't get overcharged.

Car

If you are driving, note that the Shell petrol station on the highway at Sukau Junction (at the turn-off to Sukau) is the last place to fill up before arriving at the river. The road to Sukau is pretty smooth, but as you get closer to Bilit you'll start running into some dirt patches. It is possible to get to Bilit via 2WD – just drive carefully, especially if it's been raining.

Semporna

Semporna the-town is the mainland stopping point before Semporna-the-archipelago and all your diving/snorkelling fantasies. Unless you're lucky enough to get here early in the morning, there's a good chance you'll be sticking around overnight.

Scuba is the town's lifeline, and there's no shortage of places to sign up for it. Operators are clustered around the Semporna Seafront, while other companies have offices in KK. Due to the high volume of interest, it is best to do your homework and book ahead – diving at Sipadan is limited to 120 persons per day.

Sleeping & Eating

If you have to overnight in Semporna, your options are limited – but not dire. If you've already signed up with a scuba operator ask them about sleeping discounts.

Various *kedai kopi* (coffee shops) line the 'Semporna Seafront', while restaurants at the Seafest Hotel complex offer Chinese seafood. Sample the *nasi lemak* or *korchung* (rice dumplings) – Semporna is well known for these two dishes.

SIPADAN INN   Hotel **$**
(☎089-781766; www.sipadaninn-hotel.com; Block D, Lot No 19-24, Semporna Seafront; s/d from RM84/95) If you're on a budget, this is one of the better spots in Semporna. The bright white rooms are military clean, without a speck of dust, and it's a stone's throw from most of the dive centres.

SEAFEST HOTEL   Hotel **$$**
(☎089-782333; www.seafesthotel.com; Jln Kastam; r RM90-260; ❀) The jauntily dubbed Seafest is six storeys of bay-view, business-class comfort at the far end of the 'Semporna Seafront' neighbourhood. It's affiliated with Seafest fishery, so check the restaurant's catch of the day. Suites aren't really worth the extra ringitt.

ⓘ Getting There & Away

Air
The nearest airport to Semporna, served by flights from KK and Kuala Lumpur (KL), is at Tawau, roughly 28km from town. A private taxi from here to Semporna costs RM90, while Tawau–Semporna buses (RM15) will stop at the airport if you ask the driver nicely. Buses that do not stop at the airport will let you off at Mile 28, where you will have to walk a few (unshaded) kilometres to the terminal. Remember that flying less than 24 hours after diving can cause serious health issues, even death.

Bus
The 'terminal' hovers around the Milimewa supermarket not too far from the mosque's looming minaret. All buses run from early morning until 4pm (except the KK bus, which leaves at around 7am or 7pm) and leave when full.

Semporna Archipelago

The Semporna Islands are loosely divided into two geographical sections: the northern islands (protected as Tun Sakaran Marine Park) and the southern islands. Both areas have desirable diving – Sipadan is located in the southern region, as is Mabul and Kapalai. Mataking and Sibuan belong to the northern area. If you are based in Semporna you'll have a greater chance of diving both areas, although most people are happy to stick with Sipadan and its neighbours.

◉ Sights & Activities

Although Sipadan outshines the neighbouring sites, there are other reefs in the marine park that are well worth exploring. The macro-diving around **Mabul** (or 'Pulau Mabul') is world famous. The submerged sites around **Kapalai**, **Mataking** and **Sibuan** are also of note.

A three-dive day trip costs between RM250 and RM500 (some operators include park fees, other do not – make sure to ask), and equipment rental (full gear) comes to about RM50 or RM60 per day. Cameras (around RM100 per day) and dive computers (around RM80 per day) are also available for rent at most dive centres. Top-end resorts on Mabul and Kapalai offer all-inclusive package holidays (plus a fee for equipment rental).

A three-day Open Water course will set you back at least RM950. Advanced Open Water courses (two days) cost the same, and Divemaster certification runs for around RM2500.

Sleeping & Eating

Sleeping spots are sprinkled across the archipelago with the majority of options clustered on Mabul (Sipadan's closest neighbour). No one is allowed to stay on Sipadan. Note that prices rise in August

REINHARD DIRSCHERL/GETTY IMAGES ©

Don't Miss **Sipadan**

Located 36km off Sabah's southeast coast, Sipadan (also called 'Pulau Sipadan') is the shining star in the Semporna Archipelago's constellation of shimmering islands. The elliptical islet sits atop a stunning submerged pinnacle and famed near-vertical walls. This underwater beacon is a veritable way station for virtually all types of sea life, from fluttering coral to school-bus-sized whale sharks.

Roughly a dozen delineated dive sites orbit Semporna – the best known the aptly named **Barracuda Point**, where streamers of barracuda collide to form impenetrable walls of undulating fish. The west side of the island features technicolour walls that tumble down to an impossibly deep 2000m.

While it is possible to rock up and chance upon an operator willing to take you to Sipadan the following day, we strongly suggest that you book in advance. The government issues 120 passes (RM40) to Sipadan each day (this number includes divers, snorkellers and day trippers). No matter which operator you choose, you will likely be required to do a non-Sipadan intro dive unless you are a Divemaster who has logged a dive in the last six months. Permits to Sipadan are issued by day (and not by dive) so make sure you are getting at least three dives in your package.

and September. Nondivers are charged at different rates than divers.

At almost all of the places listed, you are tied to a set schedule of three to five meals broken up by roughly three diving (or snorkelling) trips per day. Meals are included; drinks are always extra, although tea and coffee are often gratis.

MABUL BEACH RESORT   Resort $$
(☎089-785372; www.scuba-junkie.com; dm RM95, r RM225-375; ❄ 🛜) Owned and operated by Scuba Junkie, this spot is all the rage with the flashpacker crowd. Chalets with en suite bathrooms, porches and polished wood floors make for some posh digs priced (relatively) within the top of the budget range. Note the room prices

are for single occupancy – rooms all have two beds, and are cheaper if rented out by two.

MABUL WATER BUNGALOW Resort **$$$**
(088-486389; www.mabulwaterbungalows.com; 3-day, 2-night dive packages from US$1016, nondivers US$606; ❄ 🛜) This gorgeously executed series of seaside chalets cum Balinese shrines is the best upmarket option on Mabul. Rooms are effortlessly opulent, and the resort's only suite features a waterfall in the bathroom, a dock and glass floors revealing the starfish-strewn sea floor.

BORNEO DIVERS MABUL RESORT Resort **$$$**
(088-222226; www.borneodivers.net; per person single/tw RM765/1148; ❄ @ 🛜) The oldest dive centre in the region features a horseshoe of semidetached mahogany bungalows. Open-air pavilions with gauzy netting punctuate the perfectly manicured grounds. Wi-fi is available in the dining room.

❶ Information

Consider stocking up on supplies (sunscreen, mozzie repellent etc) before heading into the archipelago. Top-end resorts have small convenience stores with inflated prices. ATMs are nonexistent, but high-end resorts accept credit cards (Visa and MasterCard). Wi-fi is available at most resorts, but service tends to be spotty.

The closest decompression chamber (089-783100) is at the Semporna Naval Base.

❶ Getting There & Around

Boat

All transport to the marine park goes through Semporna. Your accommodation will arrange any transport needs from Semporna or Tawau airport (sometimes included, sometimes for an extra fee – ask!), which will most likely depart in the morning. That means if you arrive in Semporna in the afternoon, you will be required to spend the night in town.

SARAWAK
Kuching

Borneo's most stylish and sophisticated city brings together a kaleidoscope of cultures, crafts and cuisines. The bustling streets – some very modern, others with a colonial vibe – amply reward visitors with a penchant for aimless ambling. Chinese temples decorated with dragons abut shophouses from the time of the white rajahs, a South Indian mosque is a five-minute walk from stalls selling half-a-dozen Asian cuisines, and a landscaped riverfront park attracts families out for a stroll and a quick bite.

Kuching's other huge asset is its day-trip proximity to a dozen first-rate nature sites.

State Assembly Building (p297)
RICHARD I'ANSON/GETTY IMAGES ©

Sarawak

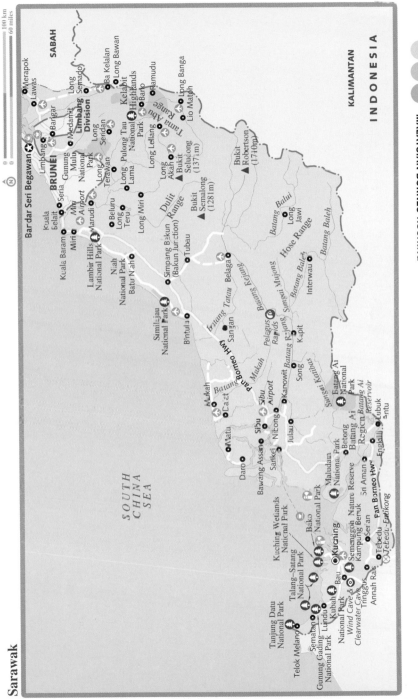

SABAH

BRUNEI

Bandar Seri Begawan

SOUTH CHINA SEA

KALIMANTAN

INDONESIA

100 km
60 miles

Merapok
Lawas
Bangar
Limbang
Medamit
Limbang Division
Long Semado
Ba Kelalan
Long Bawan
Kelabit Highlands
Pulong Tau National Park
Bario
Ramudu
Lipg Banga
Lio Matoh
Seria
Gunung Mulu National Park
Long Terawan
Long Lama
Long Seridan
Tama Abu Range
Long Lellang
Long Akah
Bukit Selucing (137 m)
Kuala Belait
Miri Airport
Marudi
Beluru
Long Teru
Long Miri
Dulit Range
Bukit Semalong (1281 m)
Bukit Robertson (1710 m)
Kuala Baram
Lambir Hills National Park
Niah National Park
Batu Niah
Tubau
Simpang Bakun (Bakun Junction)
Batang Balui
Long Jawi
Hose Range
Similajau National Park
Bintulu
Batang Rejang
Belaga
Batang Tatau
Sungai Mujong
Batang Baleh
Batang Baleh
Batang Balui
Interwau
Mukah
Batang Mukah
Pan Borneo Hwy
Sangan
Pelagus Rapids
Kapit
Daro
Matu
Sibu Airport
Sibu
Nitong
Mukah
Song
Kanowit
Batang Rejang
Sungai Katibas
Batang Ai National Park
Bawang Assan
Sarikei
Julau
Maludan
National Park
Betong
Batang Ai Region
Batang Ai Reservoir
Lubuk Antu
Kuching Wetlands National Park
Bako National Park
Kuching
Semenggoh Nature Reserve
Sri Aman
Engkilili
Kampung Benuk
Serian
Tebedu
Tebedu-Entikong
Pan Borneo Hwy
Talang-Satang National Park
Tanjung Datu National Park
Telok Melano
Sematan
Lundu
Gunung Gading National Park
Kubah National Park
Bau
Wind Cave & Clearwater Cave
Annah Rais
Tinggus

Kuching

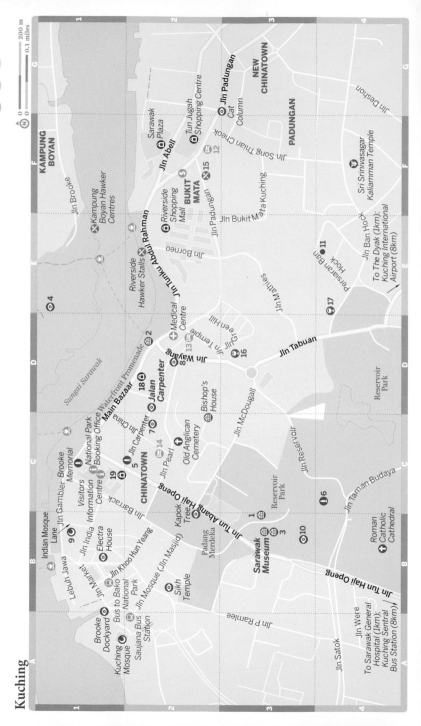

Kuching

MALAYSIAN BORNEO KUCHING

◉ Sights & Activities

Waterfront Promenade
The south bank of Sungai Sarawak, from the Indian Mosque east to the Hotel Grand Margherita Kuching, has been turned into a promenade, affording great views across the river to the white, crenellated towers and manicured gardens of the **Astana** (official residence of the governor of Sarawak); hilltop **Fort Margherita**, also white and crenellated; and, between the two, Sarawak's **State Assembly Building**, with its dramatic, golden pointy roof.

CHINESE HISTORY MUSEUM Museum
(Map p296; cnr Main Bazaar & Jln Wayang; ☺9am-4.45pm Mon-Fri, 10am-4pm Sat, Sun & holidays) Housed in the century-old Chinese Court building, the Chinese History Museum provides an excellent introduction to the nine Chinese communities – each with its own dialect, cuisine and temples – who began settling in Sarawak around 1830.

Old Chinatown
JALAN CARPENTER Street
(Map p296) Lined with evocative, colonial-era shophouses and home to several vibrantly coloured Chinese temples, Jln Carpenter – the heart of Kuching's Old Chinatown – stretches from ornamental **Harmony Arch**

(Map p296; cnr Jln Tun Abang Haji Openg & Jln Carpenter) eastward to **Hong San Si Temple** (Map p296; cnr Jln Wayang & Jln Carpenter; ☺6am-6pm), with its roofline of tiled dragons. It was established sometime before 1848 (and restored in 2004), and is also known by its Hokkien name, Say Ong Kong.

HIN HO BIO Temple
(Map p296; 36 Jln Carpenter; ☺6am-5pm) One of Kuching's hidden gems is tucked away on the roof of the Kuching Hainan Association. Mount the staircase to the top floor and you soon get to a vivid little Chinese shrine, Hin Ho Bio (Temple of the Queen of Heaven), with rooftop views of the area.

Jalan India Area
INDIAN MOSQUE Mosque
(Map p296; Indian Mosque Lane; ☺6am-8.30pm except during prayers) Turn off Jln India (between Nos 37 and 39A) or waterfront Jln Gambier (between Nos 24 and 25A) onto tiny **Indian Mosque Lane** (Lg Sempit) and you enter another world anchored by Kuching's oldest mosque. The mosque itself is a modest structure built in 1836 out of *belian* (ironwood) by Muslim traders from Tamil Nadu. Painted turquoise and notable for its simplicity, it's an island of peace and cooling shade in the middle of Kuching's commercial hullabaloo.

Detour:
Brunei Darussalam

Covering just 5765 sq km, Brunei is the last remnant of a naval empire that once ruled all of Borneo and much of the Philippines. The sultanate is known for the wealth that flows from some of the largest oil fields in Southeast Asia, but should be no less famous for having the foresight and wisdom to preserve its rainforests. Approximately 75% of Brunei retains its original forest cover.

The capital, Bandar Seri Begawan (BSB), overlooks the estuary of the mangrove-fringed Sungai Brunei (Brunei River), which opens onto Brunei Bay and the separate eastern part of the country, Temburong, a sparsely populated area where the highlight is the lush **Ulu Temburong National Park** (admission B$5). Given the country's riches, BSB is a surprisingly understated place – urban life pretty much revolves around malls, restaurants and, depending on your level of piety, illicit parties or Islam (and sometimes both).

If you have a few days spare, it's easily possible to squeeze a visit to Brunei from Malaysian Borneo. In BSB you can arrange a day trip to Ulu Temburong National Park, and explore the boardwalks of **Kampung Ayer** – the largest stilt village settlement in the world – and the gorgeous **Omar Ali Saifuddien Mosque** (Jln Stoney; ☉interior 8.30am-noon, 1.30-3pm & 4.30-5.30pm Sat-Wed, 4.30-5pm Fri, closed Thu, exterior compound 8am-8.30pm daily except prayer times). **Brunei Tourism** (www.bruneitourism.travel) can give you more ideas and plenty of useful information. When it comes to sleeping, the best-value option is the **Brunei Hotel** (📞224-4828; thebruneihotel.com; 95 Jln Pemancha; incl breakfast r B$91-220, ste B$242-440; ❄@🛜).

Brunei International Airport (📞233-1747, flight enquiries 233-6767; www.civil-aviation.gov.bn) has international connections; there are are also boat and bus links with Sabah and Sarawak. Note, if you're planning on travelling overland from Sarawak to Sabah via Burnei make sure you've got plenty of pages in your passport – the traverse will add 10 new chops (stamps).

North Bank of the River

FORT MARGHERITA   Historic Site
(Map p296; Kampung Boyan; ☉9am-4.30pm) Built by Charles Brooke in 1879 and named after his wife, Ranee Margaret, this hilltop fortress long protected Kuching against surprise attack by pirates. Inspired by an English Renaissance castle, the whitewashed fort manages to feel both medieval-European and tropical. A steep spiral staircase leads up three flights of stairs to the crenellated roof, a great place to take in panoramic views of the river and get a feel for the lie of the city.

SATOK WEEKEND MARKET   Market
(Pasar Minggu; Jln Satok; ☉about noon-10pm Sat, 6am-1pm or 2pm Sun) Kuching's biggest and liveliest market features rural folk selling fruits, vegies, fish and spices. At research time, the market was situated on Jln Satok about 1km west of the Sarawak Museum (from the centre, walk south on Jln Tun Abang Haji Openg and turn east at Jln Satok). But there were plans – bitterly opposed by vendors – to move (some would say exile) the market across the river to a complex about 2km further west.

 Tours

TELANG USAN TRAVEL & TOURS   Tour
(Map p296; 📞082-236945; www.telangusan.com; Telang Usan Hotel, Persiaran Ban Hock) A well-regarded, veteran agency based in the Telang Usan Hotel. Audry, currently

president of the Sarawak Tourism Federation, speaks English and French.

RAINFOREST KAYAKING Tour
(Borneo Trek & Kayak Adventure; ☏082-240571, 013-804 8338; www.rainforestkayaking.com) Specialises in river trips.

BORNEO À LA CARTE Tour
(☏082-236857; www.borneoalacarte.com) A Kuching-based agency offering innovative, tailor-made trips, mainly for a French-speaking clientele, to indigenous communities other agencies don't cover. Amélie, the owner, is known for having very reasonable prices and sharing receipts equitably with local communities.

 **Sleeping**

BATIK BOUTIQUE HOTEL Boutique Hotel $$
(Map p296; ☏082-422845; www.batikboutiquehotel.com; 38 Jln Padungan; d incl breakfast RM250; ❀ 🛜) A superb location, classy design and a super-friendly staff make this a top midrange choice. The 15 spacious rooms, six with balconies, are sleek and elegant, and even come with i-Pod docks.

THREEHOUSE B&B Guesthouse $
(Map p296; ☏082-423499; www.threehousebnb.com; 51 Upper China St; dm/d RM20/60; @ 🛜) A spotless, family-friendly guesthouse, in a great Old Chinatown location, with a warm and hugely welcoming vibe – everything a guesthouse should be! All nine rooms have shared bathrooms. Amenities include a common room with TV, DVDs and books, and a kitchen. Laundry costs RM8 per load, including drying.

SINGGAHSANA LODGE Guesthouse $
(Map p296; ☏082-429277; www.singgahsana.com; 1 Jln Temple; dm RM30, d with private/shared bathroom RM98/88; ❀ @ 🛜) Setting the Kuching standard for backpacker digs, this hugely popular guesthouse,

Traditional Arts & Crafts

If it's traditional Bornean arts and crafts you're after, then you've come to the right place – Kuching is the best shopping spot on the island for collectors and cultural enthusiasts. Don't expect many bargains, but don't be afraid to negotiate either – there's plenty to choose from, and the quality varies as much as the price. Dubiously aged items are common, so be sure to spend some time browsing to familiarise yourself with prices and range.

1 MAIN BAZAAR
(Map p296; Main Bazaar; ⊙some shops closed Sun) The row of old shophouses facing the Waterfront Promenade is chock full of handicrafts shops, some outfitted like art galleries, others with more of a 'garage sale' appeal, yet others (especially along the Main Bazaar's western section) stocking little more than kitschy-cute cat souvenirs.

2 SARAWAK CRAFT COUNCIL
(Map p296; cnr Jln Tun Abang Haji Openg & Jln India; ⊙9am-4.30pm Mon-Fri) Run by a nonprofit government agency, this two-storey shop has a pretty good selection of Malay, Bidayuh, Iban and Orang Ulu handicrafts – check out the cowboy hats made entirely of bark and the conical *terendak* (Melanau hats).

3 TANOTI
(56 Jln Tabuan; ⊙8am-6pm, closed public holidays) Using the supplementary weft technique (in which designs are woven into the fabric as it's made), a dozen women hand-weave silk shawls (RM400 to RM2000), wedding veils and the like. Designs at this not-for-profit studio are both traditional and modern.

decked out with stylish Dayak crafts, has an unbeatable location and a great chill-out lobby. Prices aren't low and the rooms, though colourful, are far from luxurious, but breakfast at the rooftop bar is included. The shared bathrooms are spotless. Laundry costs RM6.50 per kilo.

ANDREW WATSON/GETTY IMAGES ©

Don't Miss **Sarawak Museum Complex**

Established in 1891, the excellent Sarawak Museum complex has a first-rate collection of cultural artefacts gathered from around the state. A highlight of the complex is the **Ethnology Museum** (Map p296), which spotlights Borneo's incredibly rich indigenous cultures.

The landscaped **Museum Garden** (Map p296) stretches south from the Ethnology Museum, leading past flowers and fountains to a white-and-gold column called the **Heroes' Monument** (Map p296).

The **Art Museum** (Map p296) features sculpture and paintings inspired by Dayak motifs and traditions and by Borneo's flora, fauna and landscapes. It may be closed at lunchtime.

NEED TO KNOW

Map p296; www.museum.sarawak.gov.my; Jln Tun Abang Haji Openg; ⏰9am-4.45pm Mon-Fri, 10am-4pm Sat, Sun & holidays

 Eating

Kuching is the best place in Malaysian Borneo to work your way through the entire range of Sarawak-style cooking. At hawker centres you can pick and choose from a variety of Chinese and Malay stalls, each specialising in a particular culinary tradition or dish. Jln Padungan, home to some of the city's best noodle houses, is

undergoing something of a restaurant, cafe and bar boom.

DYAK   Dayak $$$
(☎082-234 068; Jln Mendu & Jln Simpang Tiga; mains RM18-30; ⏰noon -11pm, last order 9.30pm; ✈) Kuching's most important culinary event of the last few years was the opening of this elegant restaurant, the first to treat Dayak home cooking as true cuisine. The chef, classically trained

300

the Western tradition, takes traditional recipes, many of them Iban (a few are Kelabit, Kayan or Bidayuh), and fresh, organic jungle vegies to create mouthwatering dishes unlike anything else you've ever tasted. Vegetarian dishes, made without lard, are available upon request. Staff are happy to explain the origin of each dish. It's a good idea to reserve ahead on Thursday, Friday and Saturday nights. Dyak is situated 2km southeast of Old Chinatown. A taxi from the city centre – worth every cent – costs RM12.

TOP SPOT FOOD COURT Seafood **$$**
(Map p296; Jln Padungan; fish per kg RM35-70, vegetable dishes RM8-12; ◷noon-11pm) A perennial favourite among local foodies, this neon-lit courtyard and its half-a-dozen humming seafooderies sits, rather improbably, on the roof of a concrete parking garage – look for the giant backlit lobster sign. Grilled white pomfret is a particular delicacy. Ling Loong Seafood and the Bukit Mata Seafood Centre are particularly good.

JAMBU Mediterranean **$$$**
(☎082-235 292; www.jamburestaurant.com; 32 Jln Crookshank; mains RM28-55; ◷6-10.30pm, closed Mon) Once the venue for elegant colonial parties (check out the photos on the way to the bar), this 1920s mansion – with teak floors and soaring ceilings – is the best place in town for a romantic meal. Some of the tastiest dishes are Mediterranean inflected. Has a stylish lounge-bar that serves tapas. Named for the *jambu air* (water apple) tree in the yard. Situated 1.5km south of the centre.

🍷 Drinking

JUNK Bar
(Map p296; 80 Jln Wayang; ◷4pm-1.30am, closed Tue) Kuching's chicest hang-out is more than a restaurant – it also has two bars: Junk Bar, tucked away on the side, and the Backstage Bar, lit by red Chinese lanterns and chock full of old radios and musical instruments.

RUAI Bar
(Map p296; 7F Jln An Hock; ◷5pm-1am or 2am) This Iban-owned bar has a laid-back cool and welcoming spirit all its own. Decorated with old photos and Orang Ulu art (and, inexplicably, several Mexican sombreros), it serves as an urban *ruai* (the covered verandah of an Iban longhouse) for local and expat aficionados of vigorous outdoor activities such as caving, trekking and Hash House Harriers social runs. A great place to meet people. Starts to pick up after about 9pm.

MALAYSIAN BORNEO KUCHING

Satok Weekend Market (p298)
PETER PTSCHELINZEW/GETTY IMAGES ©

❶ Information

Tourist Information

National Park Booking Office (☎082-248088; www.sarawakforestry.com; Sarawak Tourism Complex, Jln Tun Abang Haji Openg; ⏰8am-5pm Mon-Fri) Bookings for accommodation at Bako and other national parks can be made in person, by phone or via http://ebooking.com.my.

Visitors Information Centre (☎082-410942, 082-410944; www.sarawaktourism.com; Jln Tun Abang Haji Openg, Sarawak Tourism Complex; ⏰8am-5pm Mon-Fri) Located in the atmospheric old courthouse complex, this office has helpful and well-informed staff, lots of brochures (including the useful *Kuching Visitors Guide*) and oodles of practical information (eg bus schedules), much of it on bulletin boards.

❶ Getting There & Away

Air

Kuching International Airport, 12km south of the city centre, has direct air links with Singapore, Johor Bahru, Kuala Lumpur (KL), Penang, Kota Kinabalu (KK) and Bandar Seri Begawan (BSB) in Brunei.

MASwings (Rural Air Service; www.maswings.com.my), a subsidiary of Malaysia Airlines, is basically Malaysian Borneo's very own domestic airline. Flights link its hubs in Miri and Kuching with 14 destinations around Sarawak.

Boat

Ekspress Bahagia (☎in Kuching 016-889 3013, in Kuching 082-412 246, in Sibu 016-800 5891, in Sibu 084-319-228) runs a daily express ferry from Kuching's Express Wharf, 6km east of the centre, to Sibu. Departures are at 8.30am from Kuching and at 11.30am from Sibu (RM45, five hours). It's a good idea to book a day ahead. A taxi from town to the wharf costs RM25.

Left: Sungai Kinabatangan (p288); **Below:** Rhinoceros hornbill

(LEFT) JUAN CARLOS MUÂ±OZ/GETTY IMAGES ©; (BELOW) NEVADA WIER/GETTY IMAGES ©

Bus

The massive Kuching Sentral (cnr Jln Penrissen & Jln Airport) bus station and shopping mall, handles almost all of Kuching's medium- and all long-haul routes. Situated about 10km south of the centre, it's also known as Six-and-a-Half-Mile Bus Station. Various buses run by City Public Link (eg K9) and STC (eg 3A, 4B, 6 and 2) link central Kuching's Saujana Bus Station with here. A taxi from the centre costs RM28 to RM30.

Taxi

For some destinations, the only transport option – other than taking a tour – is chartering a taxi through your hotel or guesthouse or via a company like Kuching City Radio Taxi (p304). Hiring a red-and-yellow cab for an eight-hour day should cost about RM250, with the price depending in part on distance; unofficial taxis may charge less. If you'd like your driver to wait at your destination and then take you back to town, count on paying about RM20 per hour of wait time.

ℹ️ Getting Around

Almost all of Kuching's attractions are within easy walking distance of each other so taxis or buses are only really needed to reach the airport, Kuching Sentral (the long-haul bus terminal) and the Express Wharf for the ferry to Sibu.

To/From the Airport

The price of a red-and-yellow taxi into Kuching is fixed at RM26, including luggage.

Boat

'Bow-steered wooden boats known as *tambang* shuttle passengers back and forth across Sungai Sarawak, linking jetties along the Waterfront Promenade with destinations such as Kampung Boyan (for Fort Margherita) and the Astana. The fare for Sarawak's cheapest cruise is 50 sen (more from 10pm to 6am); pay as you disembark.

Bus

Saujana Bus Station (Jln Masjid) handles local and short-haul routes.

Car

Not many tourists rent cars in Sarawak. The reasons: road signage is not great; even the best road maps are a useless 1:900,000 scale; and picking up a vehicle in one city and dropping it off in another incurs hefty fees. That said, having your own car can be unbelievably convenient. Half-a-dozen car-rental agencies have desks in the arrivals hall of Kuching airport.

Taxi

Kuching now has two kinds of taxis: the traditional red-and-yellow kind; and the larger, more comfortable – and pricier – executive taxis (*teksi eksekutiv*), which are painted blue.

Taxis can be hailed on the street, found at taxi ranks (of which the city centre has quite a few, eg at larger hotels) or ordered by phone 24 hours a day from:

ABC Radio Call Service (☎016-861 1611, 082-611 611)

Kuching City Radio Taxi (☎082-348 898, 082-480 000)

T&T Radio Call Taxi (☎016-888 2255, 082-343 343)

All Kuching taxis – except those on the flat-fare run to/from the airport (RM26) – are required to use meters; overcharging is not common. Flag fall is RM10; after the first 3km (or, in traffic, nine minutes of stop-and-go) the price is RM1.20 per km or for each three minutes. There's a RM2 charge to summon a cab by phone. Fares go up by 50% from midnight to 6am.

Bako National Park

Occupying a jagged peninsula jutting into the South China Sea, Sarawak's oldest **national park** (☎at Bako Bazaar 082-431336, at park HQ 082-478011; www.sarawakforestry. com; adult RM20; ⊙park office 8am-5pm) is just 37km northeast of downtown Kuching but feels like worlds and eons away. It's one of the best places in Sarawak to see rainforest animals in their native habitats.

The coast of the 27-sq-km peninsula consists of lovely pocket beaches tucked into secret bays interspersed with wind-sculpted cliffs, forested bluffs and stretches of brilliant mangrove swamp. The interior of the park is home to streams, waterfalls and a range of

Proboscis monkeys

Around Kuching

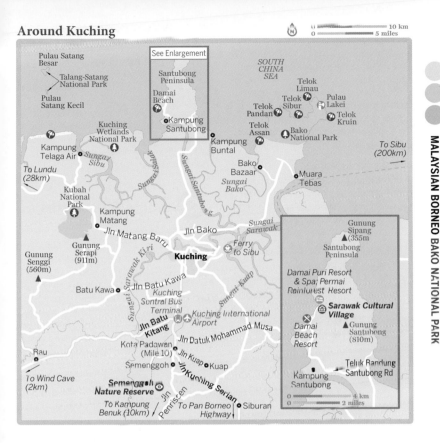

MALAYSIAN BORNEO BAKO NATIONAL PARK

distinct ecosystems, including classic lowland rainforest (mixed dipterocarp forest) and *kerangas* (heath forest). Hiking trails cross the sandstone plateau that forms the peninsula's backbone and connect with some of the main beaches, all of which can be reached by boat from park HQ.

Bako is notable for its incredible biodiversity, which includes almost every vegetation type in Borneo and encompasses everything from terrestrial orchids and pitcher plants to long-tailed macaques and bearded pigs. The stars of the show are the proboscis monkeys – this is one of the best places in Borneo to observe these endemics up close.

Bako's 17 trails are suitable for all levels of fitness and motivation, with routes ranging from short strolls to strenuous all-day treks to the far (ie eastern) end of

the peninsula. It's easy to find your way around because trails are colour-coded and clearly marked with stripes of paint. Plan your route before starting out and aim to be back at Telok Assam before dark, ie by about 6pm at the latest. It's possible to hire a boat to one of the far beaches and then hike back, or to hike to one of the beaches and arrange for a boat to meet you there.

🛏 Sleeping & Eating

In-park accommodation, which was being upgraded on our most recent visit, often fills up, especially from June to October. If you plan to stay over it's best to book ahead.

FOREST HOSTEL   Hostel **$**
(dm RM15.90, 4-bed r RM42) The new hostel,
made of concrete, will by the time you're
reading this have a private bathroom in
each simply furnished, three-bed room.
Bring your own towel and a top sheet
(bottom sheets are provided). Cooking is
not allowed in park accommodation but
there is an onsite **canteen (3-dish buffet
meal approx RM8.50; ⊙7.30am-10pm).**

FOREST LODGE TYPE 5   Chalet **$$**
(3-bed r RM106, 2-room chalet RM159) Each
two-room (six-bed) chalet, two of which
are being upgraded, has one bathroom
and one fridge. Fan-equipped.

ℹ Getting There & Away

Take one of the hourly buses from Kuching to
Bako Bazaar, then hop on a motorboat (RM94
return, 20 minutes) to Telok Assam jetty, about
400m along a wooden boardwalk from the park
HQ. Kuching travel agencies charge about RM230
per person for a tour, including the boat ride. A
cab from Kuching to Bako Bazaar (45 minutes)
costs RM40.

Santubong Peninsula

The Santubong Peninsula (also known
as Damai) is a 10km-long finger of land
jutting out into the South China Sea. The
main drawcards are the longhouses of the
Sarawak Cultural Village, some beaches,
jungle walks, a golf course and a great
seafood restaurant in the fishing village of
Kampung Buntal. Santubong is the best
place in Sarawak for a lazy, pampered
beach holiday.

◉ Sights & Activities

**SARAWAK CULTURAL
VILLAGE**   Eco-Museum
**(SCV; ☎082-846411; www.scv.com.my; adult/
child 6-12yr RM60/30, ⊙9am-5.15pm, last entry
4pm, 45-min cultural show 11.30am & 4pm)** This
living museum is centred on seven tradi-
tional dwellings: three Dayak longhouses
(including a Bidayuh headhouse with
skulls and the only Melanau tallhouse left
in Sarawak), a Penan hut, a Malay town-
house (the only place you have to remove
your shoes) and a Chinese farmhouse. It

Orang Ulu warrior re-enacting battle, Sarawak Cultural Village

may sound contrived and even hokey but the SCV is held in high esteem by locals for its role in keeping their cultures and traditions alive.

Twice a day, the **cultural show** showcases traditional music and dance. The lively Melanau entry involves whirling women and clacking bamboo poles, while the Orang Ulu dance (spoiler alert!) includes four women, several balloons and a blowpipe hunter.

Hotels and tour agencies in Kuching offer packages (per person RM125), but it's easy enough to get out here by shuttle bus. The SCV is a short walk from both the Damai Beach Resort and the Permai Rainforest Resort.

 **Sleeping**

PERMAI RAINFOREST RESORT Bungalow $$
(☎082-846490, 082-846487; www.permairainforest.com; Damai Beach; 6-bed longhouse RM260, 6-bed cabin RM305, 2-bed tree house RM300, camping per person RM15; @ 🛜) This lushly forested bungalow complex, on a beach-adjacent hillside, hosts macaques and silver-leaf monkeys in addition to paying guests. Accommodation ranges from rustic, simply furnished cabins to air-con wooden bungalows towering 6m off the ground. Prices drop from Sunday to Thursday.

DAMAI BEACH RESORT Resort $$$
(☎082-846999; www.damaibeachresort.com; Teluk Bandung, Santubong; d incl breakfast from RM440; ❄ @ 🛜 🏊) A great getaway for families, this 252-room beach resort has enough activities and amenities to make you feel like you're on a cruise ship (in a good way), including boat excursions, sea kayaking (RM15 to RM20 per hour) and even an 18-hole **golf course** (www.damai-golf.com) designed by Arnold Palmer.

ⓘ **Getting There & Away**
Kuching is linked to the Santubong Peninsula by the K15 bus (RM4, 45 minutes) from Saujana Bus Station and faster minibuses operated by Setia

Kawan (☎019-825 1619; adult/child under 12yr RM10/5) and the Damai Beach Resort. A cab from Kuching to the SCV or the resorts costs RM50 to RM60 (RM70 from the airport).

Semenggoh Nature Reserve

The **Semenggoh Wildlife Centre** (☎082-618325; www.sarawakforestry.com; ⏰8am-5pm), situated within the 6.8-sq-km Semenggoh Nature Reserve, is home to 25 orang-utans. It's one of the best places in the world to see semi-wild orang-utans in their natural jungle habitat, swinging from trees and scurrying up vines. Hour-long feedings, in the rainforest a few hundred metres from park HQ, run from 9am to 10am and from 3pm to 4pm. Note, orang-utans often turn up at park HQ, so don't rush off straightaway if everything seems quiet.

Semenggoh Nature Reserve has two beautiful trails that pass through primary rainforest: the **Masing Trail** (Main Trail; red trail markings; 30 minutes), which links the HQ with the highway; and the **Brooke's Pool Trail** (yellow and red trail markings), a 2km loop from HQ. At research time both were closed because of attacks on staff and visitors by two particularly aggressive orang-utans, Ritchie and Delima ('Hot Mama'), whom rangers guess were mistreated in captivity. When the trails reopen, it should be possible to hire a guide at the Information Centre for RM30 per hour (for up to 10 people). Tickets are valid for the whole day so it's possible to come for the morning feeding, visit a longhouse, and then see the afternoon feeding as well. Note: there's nowhere in the park to buy food.

ⓘ **Getting There & Away**
Two bus companies provide reliable public transport from Kuching's Saujana Bus Station to the park gate, which is 1.3km down the hill from park HQ (RM3, 45 minutes). A taxi from Kuching costs RM45 one way or RM90 to RM100 return, including one hour of wait time. Tours are organised by Kuching guesthouses and tour agencies.

TOM COCKREM/GETTY IMAGES ©

Don't Miss **Batang Rejang**

A trip up the tan, churning waters of 640km-long Batang Rejang (Rejang River) – the 'Amazon of Borneo' – is one of Southeast Asia's great river journeys. Express ferries barrel through the currents, eddies and whirlpools, the pilots expertly dodging angular black boulders half-hidden in the roiling waters. Though the area is no longer the jungle-lined wilderness it was in the days before Malaysian independence, it retains a frontier, *ulu-ulu* (upriver, ie back-of-the-beyond) vibe, especially in towns and longhouses accessible only by boat.

Annah Rais Longhouse

Although this Bidayuh longhouse has been on the tourist circuit for decades, it's still an excellent place to get a sense of what a longhouse is and what longhouse life is like.

The 500 residents of **Annah Rais (adult/ student RM8/4)** are as keen as the rest of us to enjoy the comforts of modern life – they do love their mobile phones and 3G internet access – but they've made a conscious decision to preserve their traditional architecture and the social interaction it engenders. They've also decided that welcoming modern tourists is a good way to earn a living without

moving to the city, something most young people end up doing.

Once you pay your entry fee (in an eight-sided wooden pavilion next to the parking lot), you're free to explore Annah Rais' three longhouses (Kupo Saba, Kupo Terekan and, across the river, Kupo Sijo) with a guide or on your own.

 **Sleeping**

EMILY & JOHN AHWANG   Homestay $$
(☎ Emily 010-977 8114, John 016-855 2195; http://22.com.my/homestay) Emily and John, both of whom speak fluent English, love to welcome guests to their spotless,

modern, two-storey home, built right into the longhouse.

AKAM GANJA Homestay **$$**
(📞010-984 3821; winniejagig@gmail.com) It's a pleasure to be hosted by Akam, a retired forestry official, and his wife Winnie, an English teacher, at their comfortable detached house on the riverbank.

ℹ️ Getting There & Away

Annah Rais is about 40km south of Kuching. A taxi from Kuching costs RM80 one-way.

A variety of Kuching guesthouses and tour agencies offer four-hour tours to Annah Rais (per person RM115, including Semenggoh Nature Reserve RM140).

Sibu

Gateway to the Batang Rejang, and situated 60km upriver from the open sea, Sibu has grown rich from trade with Sarawak's interior since the time of James Brooke. These days, although the 'swan city' does not rival Kuching in terms of charm, it's not a bad place to spend a day or two before or after a boat trip to the wild interior.

Sibu is Sarawak's most Chinese city. Of the two-thirds of locals who trace their roots to China, many are descendents of migrants who came from Foochow (Fujian or Fuzhou) province in the early years of the 20th century. The city was twice destroyed by fire, in 1889 and 1928. Much of Sibu's modern-day wealth can be traced to the timber trade.

👁️ Sights

Strolling around the city centre is a good way to get a feel for Sibu's fast-beating commercial pulse. Drop by the tourist office for a brochure covering the new **Sibu Heritage Trail**. Features of architectural interest include the old **shophouses** around the Visitors Information Centre, eg along Jln Tukang Besi, and the old art deco **Rex Cinema** (Jln Ramin).

TUA PEK KONG TEMPLE Temple
(Jln Temple; 🕐6.30am-8pm) Established sometime before 1871 and damaged by Allied bombs in 1945, this colourful river-front temple incorporates both a Taoist hall, on the ground floor, and a Chinese

Tua Pek Kong Temple

ANDERS BLOMQVIST/GETTY IMAGES ©

DBIMAGES/ALAMY ©

Buddhist sanctuary, on the 1st floor. For a brilliant view over the town and up and down the muddy Batang Rejang, climb the seven-storey **Kuan Yin Pagoda**; ask for a key at the ground-floor desk.

SIBU HERITAGE CENTRE   Museum
(Jln Central; ⊙9am-5pm, closed Mon & public holidays) This excellent museum explores the captivating history of Sarawak and Sibu. Panels, rich in evocative photographs, take a look at the various Chinese dialect groups, Sarawak's communist insurgency (1965-90), Sibu's Christian (including Methodist) traditions, and even local opposition to Sarawak's incorporation into Malaysia in 1963.

 Tours

Two well-regarded Sibu-based travel agencies – **Greatown Travel** (☎084-211243, 084-219243; www.greatowntravel.com; No 6, 1st fl, Lg Chew Siik Hiong 1A) and **Great Holiday Travel** (☎084-348196; www.ghtborneo.com; No 23, 1st fl, Pusat Pedada, Jln Pedada) – offer tours of the city and visits to sights both upriver and down.

 Sleeping

LI HUA HOTEL   Hotel **$$**
(☎084-324000; www.lihua.com.my; cnr Jln Maju & Lg Lanang 2; s/d/ste from RM50/65/150; ❀@◉) Sibu's best-value hotel has 68 spotless, tile-floor rooms spread out over nine stories and highly professional and friendly staff. The hotel is lift-equipped, and is especially convenient if you're arriving or leaving by boat. Book by phone or fax.

TANAHMAS HOTEL   Hotel **$$$**
(☎084-333188; www.tanahmas.com.my; Jln Kampung Nyabor; s/d RM250/270; ❀@◉≋) As comfortable as it is central, with 114 spacious rooms. Amenities include a small fitness centre and an open-air pool, both on the 3rd floor.

Eating

Sibu is famous for Foochow-style Chinese dishes such as *kam pua mee* (thin noodle strands soaked in pork fat and served with a side of roast pork), the city's signature dish, and *kompia* (sesame-flecked mini-bagels filled with pork).

SIBU CENTRAL MARKET   Market $

(Pasar Sentral Sibu, PSS; Jln Channel; dishes RM2.50-5; ⏰food stalls 3am-midnight) Malaysia's largest fruit and vegie market combines Sibu's former wet market and the Lembangan Market, used by upriver villagers and longhouse-dwellers. Upstairs, Chinese-, Malay- and a few Iban-owned food stalls serve up local specialities, including porridge, *kam pua mee* (some of the best is on offer at evening-only Stall 102) and *kompia* (try Stall 17 and Stall FL12; both are open from 7am to 5pm).

ISLAMIC NYONYA KAFÉ   Peranakan $$

(141 Jln Kampung Nyabor; mains RM8-18; ⏰10am-11pm; 📶📵) This Peranakan (Baba-Nonya, or Straits Chinese) cafe serves the deliciously spicy dishes of the Straits Chinese, including *ayam halia* (ginger chicken) and *kari kambing* (mutton curry). 'Islamic' means it's halal. The cafe has great lunch deals (RM5.90 to RM9.90) from 11am to 2pm.

ℹ Information

Visitors Information Centre (📞084-340980; www.sarawaktourism.com; 32 Jln Tukang Besi; ⏰8am-5pm Mon-Fri, closed public holidays) Has a friendly and informative staff, plenty of maps, bus and ferry schedules, and brochures on travel around Sarawak.

ℹ Getting There & Away

Air

MASwings (www.maswings.com.my) has services to Kuching, Bintulu, Miri and KK, **Malaysia Airlines** (www.malaysiaairlines.com) flies to KL, and **AirAsia** (www.airasia.com) flies to Kuching (40 minutes), KL and Johor Bahru.

Boat

At the entrance to the **Express Ferry Terminal** (Jln Kho Peng Long, Terminal Penumpang Sibu; 📶), ferry company booths indicate departure times using large clocks. Make sure you're on board 15 minutes before departure time – boats have been known to set sail early.

Unless you fly, the quickest way to get from Sibu to Kuching is by boat. **Ekspress Bahagia**

(📞in Kuching 016-889 3013, in Kuching 082-412246, in Sibu 016-800 5891, in sibu 084-319228) runs a daily express ferry to/from Kuching's Express Wharf (RM45, five hours). It's a good idea to book a day ahead.

'Flying coffin' express boats head up the Batang Rejang to Kapit (RM20 to RM30, 140km, 2½ to three hours) once or twice an hour from 5.45am to 2.30pm.

Bus

Sibu's **long-distance bus station** (Jln Pahlawan) is about 3.5km northeast of the centre along Jln Pedada. A variety of companies send buses to Kuching (RM50 to RM60, seven to eight hours, regular departures between 6.15am and 4am), Miri (RM50, 6½ hours, roughly hourly from 6am to 3.30am) and Bintulu (RM25, 3¼ hours, roughly hourly from 6am to 3.30am).

ℹ Getting Around

To/From the Airport

Sibu airport is 23km east of the centre; a taxi costs RM35.

Longhouse Tours

Longhouses, many of them quite modern and some accessible by road (river travel is both slower and pricier than going by minibus), can be found along the Batang Baleh, which conflows with the Batang Rejang 9km upstream from Kapit, and the Sungai Sut, a tributary of the Batang Baleh. Longhouses along these rivers tend to be more traditional (ie still have hunted heads on display) than their counterparts along the mainline Batang Rejang.

The problem is finding a good guide. Tours run by **Alice Chua** (📞019-859 3126; atta_kpt@yahoo.com), Kapit's only licensed guide, are pricey and, frankly, do not get rave reviews. You could also ask at your hotel for recommendations. A few lucky travellers get invitations from locals!

MALAYSIAN BORNEO KAPIT

Bus

To get from the local bus station (in front of the Express Ferry Terminal) to the long-distance bus station, take Lanang Bus 20 or 21 (RM1.20, 15 minutes, once or twice an hour 6.30am to 5.15pm).

Taxi

Taxis can be ordered 24 hours a day on 084-320773 or 084-311286. Taking a taxi from the city centre to the long-distance bus station costs RM13.

Kapit

The main upriver settlement on the Batang Rejang, Kapit is a bustling trading and transport centre dating back to the days of the White Rajas. A number of nearby longhouses can be visited by road or river but the pickings are thin when it comes to finding a good local guide.

◉ Sights & Activities

FORT SYLVIA Museum
(Jln Kubu; ◷10am-noon & 2-5pm, closed Mon & public holidays) A worthwhile stop before you head to a longhouse. Built by Charles Brooke in 1880 to take control of the Upper Rejang and to keep the peace, this wooden fort – built of *belian* – was renamed in 1925 to honour Ranee Sylvia, wife of Charles Vyner Brooke. Exhibits offer a pretty good intro to the traditional lifestyles of the Batang Rejang Dayaks and include evocative photos of the colonial era.

🛏 Sleeping & Eating

NEW REJANG INN Hotel $
(☏084-796600; 104 Jln Teo Chow Beng; d RM68; ❄🛜) A welcoming and well-run hotel whose 15 spotless, good-sized rooms

come with comfortable mattresses, hot water, TV, phone and mini-fridge. The best-value accommodation in town.

NIGHT MARKET Food Stalls $

(Taman Selera Empurau; mains RM2.50-5; ⏱5pm-11pm or midnight) An excellent place for satay or BBQ chicken. Situated a block up the slope from Kapit Town Sq.

ⓘ Getting There & Away

Boat

Express boats to Sibu (RM20 to RM30, 2½ to three hours, once or twice an hour) depart between 6.40am and 3.15pm from the Kapit Passenger Terminal (Jln Panglima Balang; ☎).

Van

A small road network around Kapit, unconnected to the outside world, links the town to a number of longhouses. Vans that ply these byways congregate at Kapit Town Sq.

Miri

The dynamic oil town of Miri is busy and modern – not much about it is Borneo – but there's plenty of money sloshing around so the eating is good, the broad avenues are brightly lit and there's plenty to do when it's raining. The city's friendly guesthouses are a good place to meet other travellers. The population is about 40% Dayak (mainly Iban), 30% Chinese and 18% Malay.

Miri serves as a major transport hub, so if you're travelling to/from Brunei, Sabah, the Kelabit Highlands or Gunung Mulu National Park chances are you'll pass this way.

Sights

Miri is not big on historical sites – it was pretty much destroyed during WWII – but it's not an unattractive city. A walk around the centre is a good way to get a feel for the local vibe – streets worth a wander include (from north to south) Jln North Yu Seng, Jln South Yu Seng, Jln Maju and Jln High Street.

SABERKAS WEEKEND MARKET Market (⏱3pm Fri-evening Saturday, daily during Ramadan) One of the most colourful and friendly markets in Sarawak. Vendors are more than happy to answer questions about their colourful products, which include tropical fruits and vegies, BBQ chicken, satay, grilled stingray and handicrafts. Situated about 3km northeast of the centre near the Boulevard Commercial Centre, Miri's newest shopping mall.

 Sleeping

DILLENIA GUESTHOUSE Guesthouse $$ (☎085-434204; https://sites.google.com/site/dilleniaguesthouse; 1st fl, 846 Jln Sida; dm/s/d/q incl breakfast RM30/50/80/110; ❄@🛜) This super-welcoming hostel, with 11 rooms and lots of nice little touches (plants in the bathrooms, for example), lives up

to its motto, 'a home away from home'. Incredibly helpful Mrs Lee is an artesian well of useful travel information and tips – and leech socks. All rooms have shared bathrooms. The guesthouse is served by local bus 42.

Eating

MENG CHAI SEAFOOD Seafood $$ (11a Jln Merbau; fish per kg RM25-80; ⏱4.30pm-midnight) Discerning locals crowd this first-rate eatery, which is housed in two very unassuming adjacent buildings. Specialities include barbequed garlic fish, *kampung*-raised chicken and *midin* fern. Seawater tanks hold live clams and prawns. The restaurant doesn't serve pork.

SUMMIT CAFE Dayak $ (Centre Point Commercial Centre, Jln Melayu; mains from RM3; ⏱6am-early afternoon Mon-Sat) If you've never tried Kelabit cuisine, this place will open up whole new worlds for your tastebuds. Try the colourful array of 'jungle food' – *canko manis* (forest ferns), *dure'* (fried jungle leaf), minced tapioca leaves, and (sometimes) wild boar. The best selection is available before 11.30am – once the food runs out they close! Gets rave reviews.

ⓘ Information

Visitors Information Centre (☎085-434 181; www.sarawaktourism.com; 452 Jln Melayu; ⏱8am-5pm Mon-Fri, 9am-3pm Sat, Sun & public holidays) The helpful staff can provide city maps, information on accommodation and a list of licensed guides. The National Park booking office is also here.

Mulu Canopy Skywalk (p317)
ANDERS BLOMQVIST/GETTY IMAGES ©

ℹ Getting There & Away

Air

AirAsia (www.airasia.com) can get you to Kuching, KK, KL, Johor Bahru (across the causeway from Singapore) and Singapore, while **Malaysia Airlines** (www.malaysiaairlines.com) flies to KL.

Miri is the main hub of the Malaysia Airlines subsidiary **MASwings** (www.maswings.com.my) for connections around Borneo.

Bus & Van

Long-distance buses use the Pujut Bus Terminal, about 4km northeast of the centre.

Once or twice an hour, buses head to Kuching (RM80, 12 to 14 hours, departures from 6am to 10pm) via the inland (old) Miri–Bintulu highway. Stops include Sibu (RM40 to RM50, seven to eight hours). This route is highly competitive so it pays to shop around. Companies include **Bintang Jaya** (☏085-432178, 085-438301), **Bus Asia** (Biaramas; ☏085-414999, hotline 082-411111; http://mybus.com.my) and **Miri Transport Company** (MTC; ☏085-438161; www.mtcmiri.com). Bintang Jaya and **Borneo Bus** (☏010-967 6648) travel northeast to KK (RM90, 10 hours).

ℹ Getting Around

To/From the Airport

A red-and-yellow **taxi** (☏013-838 1000; ⊘24hr) from the airport to the city centre (15 minutes, in traffic 25 minutes) costs RM22 (RM33 from 11.45pm to 6am). If you're heading from town to the airport, the fare is RM20. Spacious blue 'executive taxis' charge RM30.

Bus 28 links the local bus station with the airport (RM2.60) every 1½ hours or so; last departures are at 5.20pm (from the airport) and 6.30pm (from the local bus station).

Bus

The **local bus station** (Jln Padang), next to the Visitors Information Centre, has schedules posted. Fares start at RM1; most lines run from 7am to about 6pm.

Car

Most of Miri's guesthouses are happy to organise private transport. A half-dozen car rental companies have desks at Miri airport.

Taxi

Taxi stations are sprinkled around the city centre. A short cab ride around downtown is RM10, while a ride from the centre to the Pujut Bus Terminal costs RM15.

Gunung Mulu National Park

Also known as the **Gunung Mulu World Heritage Area** (☏085-792300; www.mulupark.com; adult/child 5-day pass RM30/10; ⊘HQ office 8am-5pm), this World Heritage Site is one of the most majestic and thrilling nature destinations anywhere in Southeast Asia.

Few national parks anywhere in the world pack so many natural marvels into such a small area. Home to **caves** (www.mulucaves.org) of mind-boggling proportions, other worldly geological phenomena, such as the Pinnacles and brilliant old-growth tropical rainforest, this is truly one of the world's wonders.

◉ Sights & Activities

When you register, park staff will give you a placemat-sized schematic map of the park on which you can plan out your daily activities. HQ staff are generally very helpful in planning itineraries and are happy to (try to) accommodate special needs and interests (eg for family-friendly activities). You can take a number of **jungle walks** unaccompanied so long as you inform the park office. For instance, you can walk to the **Bat Observatory** near the entrance to the Deer Cave and to **Paku Waterfall** (3km one way), where it's possible to swim.

MULU DISCOVERY CENTRE   Museum
(⊘7.30am-9pm) Offers a fine introduction to the park as a 'biodiversity hotspot' and to its extraordinary geology. Situated in the new HQ building, between the park office and Café Mulu.

NIGHTWALK   Walking
(Night Shift; per person RM10; ⊘7pm except if raining) The ideal first-night introduction

TRISTAN SAVATIER/GETTY IMAGES ©

Don't Miss **Gunung Mulu's Show Caves**

Mulu's show caves (the park's name for caves that can be visited without specialised training or equipment) are its most popular attraction and for good reason: they are, quite simply, awesome. All are accessible on guided walks from park HQ. Bring a powerful torch.

Deer Cave & Lang's Cave A lovely 3km walk (40 minutes to 60 minutes) through the rainforest along a plankwalk takes you to these adjacent caverns. Deer Cave – over 2km in length and 174m high – is the world's largest cave passage open to the public. It is home to two million to three million bats – more than in any other single cave in the world. Every evening around dusk (unless it's raining) they emerge in spiralling, twirling clouds that look a bit like swarms of cartoon bees. It's an awe-inspiring sight. Count on getting back to park HQ at around 7pm.

Wind Cave & Clearwater Cave The Wind Cave, named for the deliciously cool breezes that flow through it, has several chambers – including the cathedral-like King's Chamber – filled with phantasmagorical forests of stalactites and stalagmites. Clearwater Cave is vast – over 170km of passages – and only a tiny segment is open to casual visitors. The tour takes about four hours and, as the name suggests, the highlight here is an underground river.

NEED TO KNOW

Deer Cave & Lang's Cave per person RM20; ⊙departures at 2pm & 2.30pm; Wind Cave & Clearwater Cave per person incl boat ride RM50; ⊙departures at 8.45am & 9.15am

to the park's nocturnal fauna, this 1½- to two-hour walk (the route varies) wends its way through alluvial forest. Creatures you're very likely to see – but only after the guide points them out – include tree frogs just 1cm long, enormous spiders, vine snakes that are a dead ringer for a vine wrapped around a branch, and stick insects (phasmids), extraordinary creatures up to 30cm long.

MULU CANOPY SKYWALK   Walking
(per person RM35; ⊙ departures every 1-2 hr 7am-2pm) Mulu's 480m-long skywalk, unforgettably anchored to a series of huge trees, has excellent signage and is one of the best in Southeast Asia. Often gets booked out early – for a specific time slot, reserve as soon as you've got your flight.

PINNACLES   Trekking
(per person RM325) The Pinnacles are an incredible formation of 45m-high stone spires protruding from the forested flanks of Gunung Api. Getting there involves a boat ride (you can stop off at Wind Cave and Clearwater Cave for a fee of RM20) and, between two overnights at Camp 5, an unrelentingly steep 2.4km ascent; the final section – much more gruelling than anything on Mt Kinabalu – involves some serious clambering and some rope and ladder work. Coming down is just as taxing so when you stagger into Camp 5,

a swim in the cool, clear river may look pretty enticing. The trail passes through some gorgeous jungle.

GUNUNG MULU SUMMIT   Trekking
(per person RM385, with a porter RM475) The climb to the summit of Gunung Mulu (2376m) is a classic Borneo adventure. If you're very fit and looking for real adventure, this 24km trek may be for you. However, you must be fully prepared for a grueling trip that takes four days and three nights.

Guides & Reservations

For almost all of the caves, walks and treks in the park, visitors must be accompanied by a guide licensed by Sarawak Forestry, generally supplied either by the park or by an adventure tour agency. For adventure caving, trekking to the Pinnacles or up to the summit of Gunung Mulu, advance reservations are a must. They're doubly important if you'll be coming in July, August or September, when some routes are booked out several months

Swimming hole outside Clearwater Cave

ANDERS BLOMQVIST/GETTY IMAGES ©

ahead, and are absolutely crucial if your travel dates are not flexible.

 Sleeping

Accommodation options range from longhouse-style luxury to extremely basic. Park HQ, a lovely spot set amid semi-wild jungle, has 24-hour electricity, tap water that's safe to drink and a total of 88 beds. All private rooms have attached bathroom.

GARDEN BUNGALOWS Bungalow **$$**
(s/d/tr incl breakfast RM200/230/250; ❄) Opened in 2011, these eight spacious units come with verandahs.

CHALETS Chalet **$$**
(s/d/tr/q incl breakfast RM170/180/215/250; ❄) Each of the two chalets has two rooms and a huge living room.

LONGHOUSE ROOMS Guesthouse **$$**
(s/d/tr/q incl breakfast RM170/180/215/250; ❄) There are eight of these, four in each of two wooden buildings.

Eating

Cooking is not allowed at any park accommodation except Camps 1, 3, 4 and 5.

CAFÉ MULU Asian, Western **$$**
(mains RM7.40-17; ⏱7.30am-9.30pm, last orders 9pm) The Berawan women who work here make excellent breakfasts (free if you're staying in the park, RM15.90 otherwise) and a few Western items, but the standouts are local dishes such as the spectacular *Mulu laksa*.

❶ Getting There & Away

Air

MASwings (www.maswings.com.my) flies 68-seat ATR 72-500 turboprops from/to Miri and Kuching.

❶ Getting Around

Park HQ is a walkable 1.5km from the airport. Vans run by Melinau Transportation (☎012-871 1372) and other companies meet incoming flights at the airport; transport to park HQ and the adjacent guesthouses costs RM5 per person. Oversized

Iban man with traditional tattoos

VICTOR PAUL BORG/ALAMY ©

Don't Miss **Trekking in the Kelabit Highlands**

The temperate highlands up along Sarawak's far eastern border with Indonesia offer some of the best jungle trekking in Borneo, taking in farming villages, rugged peaks and supremely remote settlements. Most trails traverse a variety of primary and secondary forest, as well as an increasing number of logged areas.

With very few exceptions, the only way to explore the Kelabit Highlands is to hire a local guide. Fortunately, this could hardly be easier. Any of the guesthouses in Bario can organise a wide variety of short walks and longer treks led by guides they know and rely on.

The going rate for guides is RM100 per day for either a Bario-based day trip or a longer trek. Some itineraries involve either river trips (highly recommended if the water is high enough) or travel by 4WD – naturally, these significantly increase the cost. The going rate for a porter is RM80 to RM100 a day.

If you are connecting the dots between rural longhouses, expect to pay RM70 for a night's sleep plus three meals (you can opt out of lunch and save RM10 or RM15).

tuk-tuks ferry guests between park HQ and Mulu Marriott Resort & Spa (RM6 per person one way).

It's possible to hire local longboats for excursions to destinations such as the government-built Penan longhouse village of Long Iman (RM60 per person return, minimum three people), 40 minutes away by river.

Kelabit Highlands

Nestled in Sarawak's northeastern corner, the upland rainforests of the Kelabit (keh-*lah*-bit) Highlands are sandwiched between Gunung Mulu National Park and the Indonesian state of East Kalimantan. The main activity here, other than enjoying the clean, cool air, is trekking from longhouse to longhouse on mountain trails. Unfortunately, logging roads – ostensibly for 'selective' logging – are encroaching and some of the Highlands' primary forests have already succumbed to the chainsaw.

The area is home to the Kelabits, an Orang Ulu (inland Dayak) group who number only about 6500 worldwide and who inspire awe throughout Sarawak for their unparalleled ability to wrangle government investments and subsidies.

Bario

The 'capital' of the highlands, Bario consists of about a dozen 'villages' – each with its own church – spread over a beautiful valley, much (though less and less) of it given over to growing the renowned local rice. Some of the appeal lies in the mountain climate (the valley is 1500m above sea level) and splendid isolation (the only access is by air and torturous 4WD track), but above all it's the unforced hospitality of the Kelabit people that will quickly win you over.

Sights & Activities

The Bario area offers plenty of opportunities for jungle exploration even if you're not a hardcore trekker. Guides can arrange activities such as **fishing**, **bird-watching** and **kayaking** (☏Stu 019-807 1640; per boat RM60).

BARIO ASAL LONGHOUSE Longhouse

This all-wood, 22-door longhouse has the traditional Kelabit layout. On the *dapur* (enclosed front verandah) each family has a hearth, while on the other side of the family units is the *tawa'*, a wide back verandah – essentially an enclosed hall over 100m long – used for weddings, funerals and celebrations and decorated with historic family photos.

🛏 Sleeping

Bario's various component villages are home to lots of guesthouses where you can meet English-speaking locals and dine on delicious Kelabit cuisine (accommodation prices almost always include board). Some of the most relaxing establishments are a bit out of town (up to 5km). Almost all rooms have shared bathroom facilities. If you're on a very tight budget, enquire about renting a bed without board.

No need to book ahead – available rooms outstrip the space available on flights, and guesthouse owners meet

Bario Asal Longhouse

VICTOR PAUL BORG/ALAMY ©

incoming flights at the airport. The places below are listed alphabetically.

BARIO AIRPORT
HOMESTAY Guesthouse **$**
(☎ 013-835 9009; barioairporthomestay@gmail.com; beds RM20, per person incl board RM80; 📶)
These five rooms across the road from the airport terminal are run by Joanna, the airport's personable dynamo of an operations manager.

BARIO ASAL
LEMBAA LONGHOUSE Homestay **$**
(☎ Jenette 014-590 7500, Peter 014-893 1139; jenetteulun@yahoo.com; beds RM20, per person incl 3 meals RM60; 📶) Run as a cooperative by the entire longhouse. Some local families let out rooms, while others do the cooking. A great way to experience longhouse living. Transport from the airport costs RM10 per person each way.

GEM'S LODGE Guesthouse **$**
(☎ 013-828 0507; gems_lodge@yahoo.com; per person incl meals RM70) Situated 5km southeast of town (bear right at the fork), five minutes from the longhouse village of Pa' Umor. Managed by Jaman, one of Bario's nicest and most experienced guides, this place is tranquillity incarnate.

JUNGLEBLUESDREAM Guesthouse **$**
(☎ 019-884 9892; http://junglebluesdream.weebly.com; per person incl board RM80; 📶) This super-welcoming lodge (and art gallery)

has four mural-decorated rooms, good-quality beds and quilts, and fantastic Kelabit food.

ℹ Information

There are no banks, ATMs or credit-card facilities anywhere in the Kelabit Highlands.

The best Malaysian cellphone company to have up here is Celcom (Maxis works at the airport and in parts of Bario; Digi is useless). The airport has wi-fi, as do several guesthouses.

ℹ Getting There & Around

AIR

Bario airport (☎ Joanna 013-835 9009, Norman Peter 013-824 8006) is linked with Miri twice a day by Twin Otters operated by MASwings (www.maswings.com.my). Weather (especially high winds) frequently causes delays and cancellations to this service. Checked baggage is limited to 10kg, carry-ons to 5kg and passengers themselves are weighed on a giant scale when they check in.

CAR

The overland trip between Bario and Miri, possible only by 4WD (per person RM150), takes 12 hours at the very least and sometimes a lot more, depending on the weather and road conditions.

In Bario, 4WD vehicles can be hired for RM250 or RM300 a day including a driver and petrol; guesthouses can make arrangements.

Malaysia & Singapore

In Focus

Johor storekeeper
EIGHTFISH/GETTY IMAGES ©

Malaysia & Singapore Today

Boat Quay and the Singapore skyline

> *Rallies brought tens of thousands onto the streets of central Kuala Lumpur*

if Malaysia were 100 people

50 would be Malay
24 would be Chinese
11 would be Orang Asli
7 would be Indian
8 would be other

if Singapore were 100 people

14 would be Malay
76 would be Chinese
8 would be Indian
2 would be other

population per sq km

♦ ≈ 86 people

Malaysia   Singapore

Malaysia's 2013 Election

Malaysia's Prime Minister Najib Razak has until April 2013 to call the country's next general election – all the indications at the time of research suggested that he would leave it until the last minute to do so. Ever since the previous elections in 2008 – in which Barisan Nasional (BN) saw their parliamentary dominance slashed to less than the customary two-thirds majority – the ruling coalition has been looking nervously at the increasing popularity of Pakatan Rakyat (PR), the opposition People's Alliance, led by Anwar Ibrahim. PR already is in control of three of Malaysia's 13 state governments.

In July 2011 and April 2012 rallies by Bersih (www.bersih.org), a civil rights organisation seeking fairer elections, brought tens of thousands onto the streets of central Kuala Lumpur. Both rallies were broken up by police using tear gas and water cannons. Charges against Anwar were thrown out in January 2012 because of unreliable evidence; the trial had dragged on for two years by that point.

PHOTO BY WILLIAM CHO/GETTY IMAGES ©

Information Minister Rais Yatim said that the verdict showed that judges were free to rule as they saw fit. For more on Anwar's trial and political career see p332.

Winning Policies?

Malaysia saw strong economic growth in 2012, partly linked to the government's $444 billion Economic Transformation Program (ETP), which aims to lift the country to high-income status by 2020. To tackle public concerns about widespread graft, Najib set up the independent Malaysian Anti-Corruption Commission (MACC), which in 2011 resulted in 900 individuals being arrested on corruption charges.

The hope is that such policies will persuade voters to stick with the ruling coalition rather than take a chance with PR; however, other government actions have played into the opposition's hands. The replacing of the draconian Internal Security Act (ISA) has been criticised by many, including Human Rights Watch who believe the new legislation doesn't go far enough to protect the fundamental rights and freedoms of Malaysians.

Uneven Society in Singapore

With a per capita GDP of S$63,000 in 2011, Singaporeans enjoy one of the world's highest standards of living. However, modern Singapore is grappling with several social and lifestyle issues, particularly the soaring cost of living and the growing gap between the haves and have nots. A 2009 study by the United Nations Development Programme found that Singapore has the second most uneven distribution of wealth in the developed world, after Hong Kong.

There are also worries about ethnic tension created by an ever-increasing foreign population versus a declining citizen base. Singapore's birthrate is among the lowest in the world (7.7 births per 1000 people), yet its population doubled from 1980 to 2010 because of the influx of foreign workers, who now make up around 27% of the population. To diffuse tensions, the government has put the brakes on the intake of migrants and offers many incentives to Singaporean couples who procreate.

Social media is now a viable voice alongside the mainstream media, which is often accused of being mouthpieces of the government. Prime Minister Lee Hsien Loong participated in an online chat for the 2011 election. However, on his Facebook page in October 2012 Lee posted, 'Let us be mindful of what we say, online and in person,' following community anger sparked when a Singaporean resident's racially abusive Facebook rant went viral.

Portraits in Kuala Lumpur of Malaysia's former prime ministers

AFP/GETTY IMAGES

Malaysia and Singapore have been around since 1963 and 1965 respectively, though British colonial rule on the peninsula ended in 1957. The region's early history is hazy because of the lack of written records. Events are well recorded from the Melaka Sultanate in the 16th century onward, however, both locally and by the nations that came to trade with and later rule over the region, including the Portuguese and the Dutch.

Early Trade & Empire

Traders from India and China stopped by the region from around the 1st century AD. By the 2nd century Malaya was known as far away as Europe. From the 7th century to the 13th century, the area fell under the sway of the Buddhist Srivijaya empire, based in southern Sumatra. Under the protection of the Srivijayans, a significant Malay trading state grew up in the Bujang Valley area in the far northwest of the Thai-Malay peninsula. The growing

200

Langkasuka, one of the first Hindu-Malay kingdoms, is established on the peninsula around the area now known as Kedah.

power of the southern Thai kingdom of Ligor, and the Hindu Majapahit empire of Java finally led to the demise of the Srivijayans in the 14th century.

The Melaka Empire

Parameswara, a renegade Hindu pirate prince from a little kingdom in southern Sumatra, washed up around 1401 in the tiny fishing village that would become Melaka. He immediately lobbied the Ming emperor of China for protection from the Thais in exchange for generous trade deals, and thus the Chinese came to Peninsular Malaysia.

Equidistant between India and China, Melaka developed into a major trading port. The Melaka sultans soon ruled over the greatest empire in Malaysia's history, which lasted a century until the Portuguese turned up in 1509.

The Portuguese & the Dutch

In 1511 the Portuguese drove the sultan and his forces out of Melaka to Johor. While their rule lasted 130 years, unlike with Indian-Muslim traders the Portuguese contributed little to Malay culture. Attempts to introduce Christianity and the Portuguese language were never a big success, though a dialect of Portuguese, Cristang, is still spoken in Melaka.

In 1641 the Dutch formed an allegiance with the sultans of Johor, and ousted the Portuguese from Melaka, which fell under Dutch control for the next 150 years. Johor was made exempt from most of the tariffs and trade restrictions imposed on other vassal states of the Dutch.

Enter the East India Company

British interest in the region began with the East India Company (EIC) establishing a base on the island of Penang in 1786. Napoleon overran the Netherlands in 1795, prompting the British to take over Dutch Java and Melaka to protect their interests. When Napoleon was defeated in 1818, the British handed the Dutch colonies back.

The British lieutenant-governor of Java, Stamford Raffles, soon persuaded the EIC that a settlement south of the Malay peninsula was crucial to the India–China maritime route. In 1819 he landed in Singapore and negotiated a trade deal with Johor that saw the island ceded to Britain in perpetuity, in exchange for a significant cash tribute.

In 1824 Britain and the Netherlands signed the Anglo–Dutch Treaty, dividing the region into two distinct spheres of influence. The Dutch controlled what is now

1402
Hindu prince and pirate Parameswara founds the great trading port and sultanate of Melaka.

1511
The Portuguese conquer Melaka; the sultan and his court flee to Perak and Johor.

1641
The Dutch, with the help of the Johor sultanate, wrest Melaka from the Portuguese.

Indonesia, and the British controlled Penang, Melaka, Dinding and Singapore, which were soon combined to create the 'Straits Settlements'.

Borneo Developments

Britain did not include Borneo in the Anglo–Dutch Treaty, preferring that the EIC concentrate its efforts on consolidating their power on the peninsula. Into the breach jumped opportunistic British adventurer James Brooke. In 1841, having helped the local viceroy quell a rebellion, Brooke was installed as raja of Sarawak, with the fishing village of Kuching as his capital.

Through brutal naval force and skilful negotiation, Brooke extracted further territory from the Brunei sultan and eventually brought peace to a land where piracy, headhunting and violent tribal rivalry had been the norm. The 'white raja' dynasty of the Brookes was to rule Sarawak until 1941 and the arrival of the Japanese.

British Malaya

In Peninsular Malaya, Britain's policy of 'trade, not territory' was challenged when trade was disrupted by civil wars within the Malay sultanates of Negeri Sembilan, Selangor, Pahang and Perak. In 1874 the British started to take political control by appointing the first colonial governor of Perak and, in 1896, Perak, Selangor, Negeri

The Rise of Singapore

'It is impossible to conceive a place combining more advantages...it is the Navel of the Malay countries,' wrote a delighted Raffles soon after landing in Singapore in 1819. The statement proves his foresight because at the time the island was an inhospitable swamp. Raffles returned to his post in Bencoolen, Sumatra, but left instructions on Singapore's development as a free port with the new British Resident, Colonel William Farquhar.

In 1822 Raffles returned to Singapore and governed it for one more year. He initiated a town plan that included erecting government buildings around Forbidden Hill (now Fort Canning Hill), building shipyards, churches and streets of shophouses with covered walkways, and planting a botanical garden. Raffles' blueprint also separated the population according to discrete racial categories, with the Europeans, Indians, Chinese and Malays living and working in their own delineated quarters.

1786
Francis Light cuts a deal with the sultan of Kedah to establish a settlement on the island of Penang.

1819
Stamford Raffles gains sole rights to build a trading base on the island of Singapore. Statue of Stamford Raffles, Singapore

DAJ/GETTY IMAGES ©

Sembilan and Pahang were united under the banner of the Federated Malay States, each governed by a British Resident.

Kelantan, Terengganu, Perlis and Kedah were then purchased from the Thais, in exchange for the construction of the southern Thai railway, much to the dismay of local sultans. The 'Unfederated Malay States' eventually accepted British 'advisers', though the sultan of Terengganu held out till 1919. By the eve of WWII Malays were pushing for independence.

WWII Period

A few hours before the bombing of Pearl Harbor in December 1941, Japanese forces landed on the northeast coast of Malaya. Within a few months they had taken over the entire peninsula and Singapore. The poorly defended Bornean states fell even more rapidly.

In Singapore, Europeans were slung into the infamous Changi Prison, and Chinese communists and intellectuals were targeted for Japanese brutality. Thousands were executed in a single week. In Borneo, early resistance by the Chinese was also brutally put down. The Malayan People's Anti-Japanese Army (MPAJA), comprising remnants

Portuguese ship at the Maritime Museum & Naval Museum (p199), Melaka

1826
The British East India Company combines Melaka with Penang and Singapore to create the Straits Settlements.

1874
British take control of Peninsular Malaysia after signing the Pankor Treaty with the sultan of Perak.

1941
The Japanese land on Malaya's northeast coast. Within two months they are at Singapore's doorstep.

of the British army and Chinese from the fledgling Malayan Communist Party, waged a weak, jungle-based guerrilla struggle throughout the war.

The Japanese surrendered to the British in Singapore in 1945. However, the easy loss of Malaya and Singapore to the Japanese had humiliated the empire and its days of controlling the region were now numbered.

Federation of Malaya

In 1946 the British persuaded the sultans to agree to the Malayan Union, which amalgamated all the Malayan peninsula states into a central authority with citizenship to all residents regardless of race. The sultans were reduced to the level of paid advisers and the system of special privileges for Malays was abandoned. Rowdy protest meetings were held throughout the country, leading to the formation of the first Malay political party, the United Malays National Organisation (UMNO). In 1948 the Federation of Malaya was created, which reinstated the sovereignty of the sultans and the special privileges of the Malays.

Merdeka & Malaysia

UMNO formed a strategic alliance with the Malayan Chinese Association (MCA) and the Malayan Indian Congress (MIC). The new Alliance Party led by Tunku Abdul

The Emergency

While the creation of the Federation of Malaya appeased Malays, the Chinese felt betrayed, particularly after their massive contribution to the war effort. Many joined the Malayan Communist Party (MCP), and in 1948 many of their members took to the jungles and embarked on a protracted guerrilla war against the British. Even though the insurrection was on par with the Malay civil wars of the 19th century, it was classified as an 'Emergency' for insurance purposes.

The effects of the Emergency were felt most strongly in the countryside, where villages and plantation owners were repeatedly targeted by rebels. Almost 500,000 rural Chinese were forceably resettled into protected *kampung baru* ('new villages') and the jungle-dwelling Orang Asli were bought into the fight to help the police track down the insurgents. In 1960 the Emergency was declared over, although sporadic fighting continued and the formal surrender was signed only in 1989.

1946
The United Malays National Organisation (UMNO) is formed to campaign for political independence from Britain.

1957
On 31 August Merdeka (independence) is declared in Malaya; Tunku Abdul Rahman becomes first prime minister.

1963
The British Borneo territories of Sabah and Sarawak are combined with Singapore and Malaya to form Malaysia.

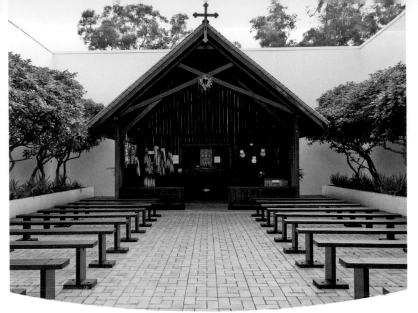

Rahman won a landslide victory in the 1955 election and, on 31 August 1957, Merdeka (Independence) was declared. Sarawak, Sabah (then North Borneo) and Brunei remained under British rule.

In 1961 Tunku Abdul Rahman proposed a merger of Singapore, Malaya, Sabah, Sarawak and Brunei, which the British agreed to the following year. At the 11th hour Brunei pulled out of the deal.

When modern Malaysia was born, on July 1963, it immediately faced a diplomatic crisis. The Philippines broke off relations, claiming that Sabah was part of its territory (a claim upheld to this day), while Indonesia laid claim to the whole of Borneo, invading parts of Sabah and Sarawak before eventually giving up its claim in 1966.

Ethnic Chinese outnumbered Malays in both Malaysia and Singapore, and the new ruler of the island-state, Lee Kuan Yew, refused to extend constitutional privileges to the Malays in Singapore. Riots broke out in Singapore in 1964 and in August 1965 Tunku Abdul Rahman was forced to boot Singapore out of the federation.

Chapel at the site of Changi Prison, Singapore
KC HUNTER/ALAMY ©

1965

Singapore is booted out of Malaysia. Lee Kuan Yew becomes Singapore's first prime minister.

1969

Race riots erupt in Kuala Lumpur, killing 198. The government responds with the New Economic Policy of positive discrimination.

1981

Dr Mahathir Mohamad becomes Malaysia's prime minister. He urges the country to emulate Japan, South Korea and Taiwan.

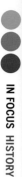

The Best... Historical Sights

1 St Paul's Church, Melaka

2 Merdeka Sq, Kuala Lumpur

3 National Museum of Singapore

4 Fort Margherita, Kuching

Ethnic Tensions

In the 1969 general elections the Alliance Party lost its two-thirds majority in parliament. A celebration march by the opposition Democratic Action Party (DAP) and Gerakan (The People's Movement) in Kuala Lumpur led to a full-scale riot, which Malay gangs used as a pretext to loot Chinese businesses, killing hundreds of Chinese in the process.

Stunned by the savageness of the riots the government decided that the Malay community needed to achieve economic parity for there to be harmony between the races. To this end the New Economic Policy (NEP), a socioeconomic affirmative action plan, was introduced. The Alliance Party invited opposition parties to join them and work from within, with the expanded coalition renamed the Barisan Nasional (BN; National Front).

The Era of Mahathir

In the 1980s, under Prime Minister Mahathir Mohamad, Malaysia's economy went into overdrive. Multinationals were successfully wooed to set up in Malaysia, and manufactured exports began to dominate the trade figures rather than traditional commodities like rubber.

At the same time the main media outlets became little more than government mouthpieces. The sultans lost their right to give final assent on legislation, and the independent judiciary appeared to become subservient to government wishes. The draconian Internal Security Act (ISA), a hangover from the Emergency, was used to silence opposition leaders and social activists.

Economic & Political Crisis

In 1997 Malaysia was hit by the regional currency crisis. Mahathir and his deputy prime minister and heir apparent Anwar Ibrahim disagreed on the best course action. Their falling out was so severe that in September 1998 Anwar was sacked and soon after charged with corruption and sodomy.

Many Malaysians, feeling that Anwar had been falsely arrested, took to the streets chanting Anwar's call for 'reformasi'. The demonstrations were harshly quelled and, in trials that were widely criticised as unfair, Anwar was sentenced to a total of 15 years' imprisonment. The international community rallied around Anwar with Amnesty International proclaiming him a prisoner of conscience.

1990
Lee Kuan Yew steps down as prime minister of Singapore, handing over to Goh Chok Tong'.

1998
Anwar Ibrahim is sacked, arrested, sent for trial and jailed following disagreements with PM Mahathir.

2003
Dr Mahathir steps down as prime minister in favour of Abdullah Badawi.

In the following year's general elections BN suffered huge losses, particularly in the rural Malay areas. The gainers were the fundamentalist Islamic party, PAS (standing for Parti Islam se-Malaysia), which had vociferously supported Anwar, and a new political party, Keadilan (People's Justice Party), headed by Anwar's wife Wan Azizah.

BN on the Ropes

Prime Minister Mahathir's successor, Abdullah Badawi, was sworn into office in 2003 and went on to lead BN to a landslide victory in the following year's election. In stark contrast to his feisty predecessor, the pious Abdullah impressed voters by taking a nonconfrontational, consensus-seeking approach and calling time on several of the massively expensive mega projects that had been the hallmark of the Mahathir era.

Released from jail in 2004, Anwar returned to national politics in August 2008 on winning the bi election for the seat vacated by his wife. However, sodomy charges were again laid against the politician in June and he was arrested in July.

In the March 2008 election, UMNO and its coalition partners in Barisan Nasional (BN) saw their parliamentary dominance slashed to less than the customary two-thirds majority. Pakatan Rakyat (PR), the opposition People's Alliance, led by Anwar Ibrahim bagged 82 of parliament's 222 seats and took control of four out of Malaysia's 13 states including the key economic bases of Selangor and Penang. PR subsequently lost Perak following a complex powerplay between various defecting MPs.

Abdullah Badawi resigned in favour of his urbane deputy Mohammad Najib bin Tun Abdul Razak (typically known as Najib Razak) in April 2008.

2008

BN retains power in general election but suffers heavy defeats to opposition coalition Pakatan Rakyat.

2011

Tens of thousands rally in Kuala Lumpur in support of fairer elections.
Demonstrations in Kuala Lumpur

HOWARD HARRISON/ALAMY ©

Family Travel

LONELY PLANET/GETTY IMAGES ©
MATTHEW NGUI, THE BUILDING REMEMBERS, 2006 © NATIONAL MUSEUM OF SINGAPORE

Malaysia and Singapore are among the easiest countries in Asia to travel in. Both are great places for a family to watch temple ceremonies, take trishaw rides, spot wildlife in national parks or a world-class zoo and taste some of the best food on the continent – all with access to clean accommodation, modern malls with all the necessities you'll find at home, and brilliant beaches.

Sights & Activities

Malaysia and Singapore's multiplicity of gorgeous beach-fringed islands and dense jungles, with soaring trees peopled by cheeky monkeys, are straight out of exotic storyland. The cities have verdant parks often with top-grade play areas.

Those with older children might enjoy some of the jungle parks including Taman Negara, Penang National Park and, over in Sarawak, the Bako and Gunung Mulu national parks. As long as your kids are not afraid of heights the canopy walkways strung through the treetops are usually a huge hit.

For guaranteed animal and bird encounters also consider the KL Bird Park; the Sepilok Orang-Utan Rehabilitation Centre in Sabah; and Singapore's excellent Zoo, Night Safari and River Safari. Snorkelling off some of the safer island beaches will give you a peek at sea life;

there are also good aquariums in KL, Langkawi and Singapore.

Singapore's museums are super kid-friendly with creative audio-visual displays. Malaysia's museums are not quite in the same grade but still worth visiting for cultural and educational background.

Dining Out

Food is a highlight here and there's a lot on offer that kids will love. Contrary to Western impulse, a busy street food stall is usually the safest place to eat – you can see the food being prepared, the ingredients are often very fresh and there's little chance of harmful bacteria existing in a scalding hot wok. Grownups can also try more adventurous dishes while the kids get something more familiar.

Many restaurants attached to hotels and guesthouses will serve familiar Western food, while international fast food is everywhere.

Breastfeeding in public should be discreet if at all (Malaysia is a Muslim country so avoid showing any skin). Local women publicly breastfeed very rarely, using their headscarves for extra coverage.

Local drinks tend to be very sweet and even fresh juices may have sugar added. It's not a bad idea to ask for drinks without sugar or to order bottled water.

The Best... Kid-Friendly Beaches

1 Pantai Cenang, Pulau Langkawi

2 Tekek, Pulau Tioman

3 Teluk Dalam, Pulau Perhentian Besar

4 Siloso Beach, Sentosa

Need to Know

Cots By special request at midrange and top-end hotels.

Health Drink a lot of water; wash hands regularly; warn children against playing with animals.

Highchairs Sometimes available in Kuala Lumpur and Singapore restaurants as well as resort areas.

Nappies Available in supermarkets and convenience stores.

Strollers Bring a compact umbrella stroller.

Toilets Western-style toilets are common but always carry some toilet paper with you – most will not have any.

Changing facilities Available in large malls and some top-end hotels.

Kids' menus Common in big cities but usually in Western-style establishments.

Transport Discounted fares are available.

Multicultural Malaysia & Singapore

Dayak longhouse, Sarawak

DAVID KIRKLAND/GETTY IMAGES ©

Malaysians and Singaporeans hold a strong sense of shared experience and national identity. However, there are distinct cultural differences between the region's three main ethnic groups – Malays, Chinese and Indians – as well as the Peranakan (Straits Chinese) and other mixed blood communities. Older aboriginal groups, the Orang Asli and Dayaks, belong to scores of different tribal groups and speak well over 100 languages and dialects.

The Malays

All Malays, Muslims by birth, are supposed to follow Islam, but many also adhere to older spiritual beliefs and adat. Adat, a Hindu tradition, emphasises collective responsibility and maintaining harmony within the community.

The enduring appeal of the *kampung* (village) spirit cannot be underestimated. Many urban Malays hanker after it, despite their affluent lifestyles. In principle villagers are of equal status, though a headman is appointed on the basis of his wealth, greater experience or spiritual knowledge. Traditionally a village's founder was appointed leader (*penghulu* or ketua kampung), and the title passed on to their family members. A *penghulu* is usually a haji, one who has made the pilgrimage to Mecca.

The Muslim religious leader, the imam, holds a position of great importance in the community as the keeper of Islamic knowledge and the leader of prayer, but even educated urban Malaysians periodically turn to *pawang* (shamans who possess a supernatural knowledge of harvests and nature) or *bomoh* (spiritual healers with knowledge of curative plants and the ability to harness the power of the spirit world) for advice before making any life-changing decisions.

The Chinese

Religious customs govern much of the Chinese community's home life, from the moment of birth, which is carefully recorded for astrological consultations later in life, to funerals, which also have many rites and rituals. The Chinese, who started arriving in the region in the early 15th century, came mostly from the southern Chinese province of Fujian and eventually formed one half of the group known as Peranakans. They developed their own distinct hybrid culture whereas later settlers, from the Guangdong and Hainan provinces, stuck more closely to the culture of their homelands, including keeping their dialects.

If there's one cultural aspect that all Chinese in the region agree on it's the importance of education. It has been a very sensitive subject among the Malaysian Chinese community since the 1960s, when there was an attempt to phase out Chinese-language secondary schools, followed by government policies in the 1970s that favoured Malays. The constraining of educational opportunities within Malaysia for the ethnic Chinese has resulted in many families working doubly hard to afford the tuition fees needed to send their offspring to private schools within the country and to overseas institutions.

The Peranakans

Peranakans – meaning 'half-caste' in Malay – are the descendants of Chinese immigrants who from the 16th century onwards settled principally in Singapore, Melaka and Penang and married Malay women.

The culture and language of the Peranakans is a fascinating melange of Chinese and Malay traditions. The Peranakans took the name and religion of their Chinese fathers, but the customs, language and dress of their Malay mothers. They also used the terms Straits-born or Straits Chinese to distinguish themselves from later arrivals from China. They are also known as Baba-Nonyas, after the Peranakan words for men *(baba)* and women *(nonya)*.

The Peranakans were often wealthy traders who could afford to indulge their passion for sumptuous furnishings, jewellery and brocades. Their terrace houses were brightly painted, with patterned tiles embedded in the walls for extra decoration. When it came to the interior, Peranakans favoured heavily carved and inlaid furniture.

Traditional Peranakan dress was similarly ornate. Women wore fabulously embroidered *kasot manek* (beaded slippers) and *kebaya* (blouses worn over a sarong), tied with beautiful *kerasong* (brooches), usually of fine filigree gold or silver. Men – who assumed Western dress in the 19th century, reflecting their wealth and contacts with the British – saved their finery for important occasions such as the wedding ceremony, a highly stylised and intricate ritual dictated by adat.

The Indians

Like the Chinese settlers, Indians in this region hail from many parts of the subcontinent and have different cultures depending on their religions – mainly Hinduism, Islam, Sikhism and Christianity. Most are Tamils, originally coming from the area now known as Tamil Nadu in southern India, where Hindu traditions are strong. Later Muslim Indians

Dayaks & the People of Borneo

Not all of Borneo's indigenous tribes refer to themselves as Dayaks but the term usefully groups together peoples who have a great deal in common.

In Sarawak Dayaks make up about 48% of the population. About 29% of Sarawakians are Iban, a group that migrated from West Kalimantan's Kapuas River starting five to eight centuries ago. Also known as Sea Dyaks for their exploits as pirates, the Iban are traditionally rice growers and longhouse dwellers. The Bidayuh (8% of the population), many of whom also trace their roots to what is now West Kalimantan, are concentrated in the hills south and southwest of Kuching. Adjacent villages sometimes speak different dialects. Few Bidayuh still live in longhouses.

Upland groups such as the Kelabit, Kayan and Kenyah (ie everyone except the Bidayuh, Iban and coastal dwelling Melenau) are often grouped under the term Orang Ulu ('upriver people'). There are also the Penan, originally a nomadic hunter-gatherer group living in northern Sarawak.

None of Sabah's 30-odd indigenous ethnicities are particularly keen on the term 'Dayak'. The state's largest ethnic group, known as the Kadazan-Dusun, make up 18% of the population. Mainly Roman Catholic, the Kadazan and the Dusun share a common language and have similar customs.

from northern India followed along with Sikhs. These religious affiliations dictate many of the home life customs and practices of Malaysian Indians although one celebration that all Hindus and much of the rest of the region takes part in is Deepavali.

A small, English-educated Indian elite has always played a prominent role in Malaysian and Singaporean society, and a significant merchant class exists. However, a large percentage of Indians – imported as indentured labourers by the British – remain a poor working class in both countries.

The Orang Asli

The indigenous people of Malaysia, known collectively as Orang Asli, are generally classified into three groups: the Negrito; the Senoi; and the Proto-Malays, who are further subdivided into 18 tribes. There are dozens of different tribal languages and most Orang Asli follow animist beliefs, though there are vigorous attempts to convert them to Islam.

Data from the Department of Orang Asli Affairs (JHEOA) puts the total Orang Asli population of Peninsular Malaysia at around 150,000, of whom 80% live below the poverty line, compared with an 8.5% national average. Although the JHEOA was set up to represent Orang Asli concerns to the government (ie land rights), the department has evolved into a conduit for government decisions. Asli land rights are not recognised, and when logging, agricultural or infrastructure projects require their land, their claims are generally regarded as illegal.

In 2010 the government put forward plans to corporatise JHEOA so it could take charge of Orang Asli lands (currently the Orang Asli manage their own small holdings). The Centre for Orang Asli Concerns (www.coac.org.my) has criticised the plan saying it will further impoverish an already poor group of people.

Religion

Sultan Mosque, Singapore (p239)

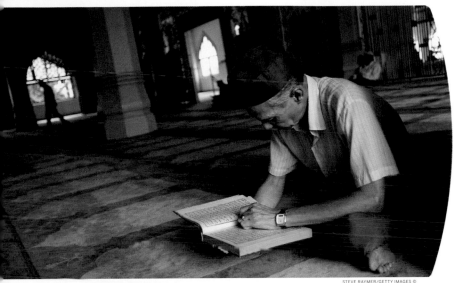

STEVE RAYMER/GETTY IMAGES ©

Freedom of religion is guaranteed throughout this mainly Islamic region. Hinduism's roots in the region long predate Islam, and the various Chinese religions are also strongly entrenched. Christianity has a presence, more so in Singapore than peninsula Malaysia where it has never been strong. In Malaysian Borneo many indigenous people have converted to Christianity, although others still follow their animist traditions.

Islam

Most likely Islam came to the region in the 14th century with the South Indian traders and was not of the more-orthodox Islamic tradition of Arabia. It was adopted peacefully by the locals, absorbing rather than conquering existing beliefs. Islamic sultanates replaced Hindu kingdoms, though the Hindu concept of kings remained.

Malay ceremonies and beliefs still exhibit pre-Islamic traditions, but most Malays are ardent Muslims and to suggest otherwise to a Malay would cause great offence. With the rise of Islamic fundamentalism, the calls to introduce Islamic law and purify the practices of Islam have increased, but while the federal government of Malaysia is keen to espouse Muslim ideals, it is wary of religious extremism. *Syariah* (Islamic law) is the preserve of state governments, as is the establishment of Muslim courts of law, which since 1988 cannot be overruled by secular courts.

Chinese Religions

The Chinese in the region usually follow a mix of Buddhism, Confucianism and Taoism. Buddhism takes care of the afterlife, Confucianism looks after the political and moral aspects of life, and Taoism contributes animistic beliefs to teach people to maintain harmony with the universe. But to say that the Chinese have three religions is too simple a view of their traditional religious life. At the first level Chinese religion is animistic, with a belief in the innate vital energy in rocks, trees, rivers and springs. At the second level people from the distant past, both real and mythological, are worshipped as gods. Overlaid on this are popular Taoist, Mahayana Buddhist and Confucian beliefs.

Chinese religion incorporates elements of what Westerners might call 'superstition' – if you want your fortune told, for instance, you go to a temple. The other thing to remember is that Chinese religion is polytheistic. Apart from the Buddha, Lao Zi and Confucius there are many divinities, such as house gods, and gods and goddesses for particular professions.

Hinduism

Hinduism in the region dates back at least 1500 years and there are Hindu influences in cultural traditions, such as *wayang kulit* and the wedding ceremony. However, it is only in the last 100 years or so, following the influx of Indian contract labourers and settlers, that it has again become widely practised.

Hinduism has three basic practices: puja (worship), the cremation of the dead, and the rules and regulations of the caste system. Although still very strong in India, the caste system was never significant in Malaysia, mainly because the labourers brought here from India were mostly from the lower classes.

Major Religious Festivals

○ The highpoint of the Islamic calendar is **Ramadan**, when Muslims fast from sunrise to sunset. Ramadan always occurs in the ninth month of the Muslim calendar and lasts between 29 and 30 days based on sightings of the moon. The start of Ramadan moves forward 11 days every year in line with the Muslim lunar calendar.

○ **Hari Raya Puasa** (also known as Hari Raya Aidilfitri) marks the end of the month-long fast, with two days of joyful celebration and feasting. During this major holiday it can be difficult to find accommodation, particularly on the coast.

○ The Hindu festival of **Thaipusam**, famously involving body piercing, falls between mid-January and mid-February. Enormous crowds converge at the Batu Caves north of Kuala Lumpur and Nattukotai Chettiar Temple in Penang and in Singapore for the celebrations.

○ From mid- to late August, the Chinese communities of Malaysia and Singapore mark the **Festival of the Hungry Ghosts** with street performances of traditional Chinese opera.

Hinduism has a vast pantheon of deities although the one omnipresent god usually has three physical representations: Brahma, the creator; Vishnu, the preserver; and Shiva, the destroyer or reproducer. All three gods are usually shown with four arms, but Brahma has the added advantage of four heads to represent his all-seeing presence.

Animism

The animist religions of Malaysia's indigenous peoples are as diverse as the peoples themselves. While animism does not have a rigid system of tenets or codified beliefs, it can be said of animist peoples that they perceive natural phenomena to be animated by various spirits or deities, and a complex system of practices is used to propitiate these spirits.

Ancestor worship is also a common feature of animist societies and departed souls are considered to be intermediaries between this world and the next. Examples of elaborate burial rituals can still be found in some parts of Sarawak, where the remains of monolithic burial markers and funerary objects still dot the jungle around longhouses in the Kelabit Highlands. However, most of these are no longer maintained and they're being rapidly swallowed up by the fast-growing jungle.

The Best... Mosques

1 Masjid Negara, Kuala Lumpur

2 Masjid Jamek, Kuala Lumpur

3 Masjid Zahir, Alor Setar

4 Sultan Mosque, Singapore

Arts & Architecture

Kite-maker in Kota Bharu

GAVIN HELLIER/GETTY IMAGES ©

Traditional Malay art forms such as wayang kulit *(shadow puppetry) and* mak yong *(dance and music performances) continue and stand alongside contemporary art, drama, dance and music. There's a distinctive look to vernacular architecture – particulary the vividly painted and handsomely proportioned, traditional wooden Malay houses – as well as a daring and originality in contemporary constructions in Kuala Lumpur and Singapore.*

Literature

The classic colonial expat experience is recounted by Anthony Burgess in *The Malayan Trilogy* written in the 1950s. In the late 1960s Paul Theroux lived in Singapore which, together with Malaysia, forms the backdrop to his novel *Saint Jack* and his short-story collection *The Consul's Wife.*

Leading lights of the contemporary Malaysian literary scene include Tash Aw (www.tash-aw.com/index2.html), whose debut novel, *The Harmony Silk Factory,* won the 2005 Whitbread First Novel Award; and the Man Booker Prize–nominated author Tan Twan Eng (www.tantwaneng. com), whose novels mix a fascination with Malaysia's past and the impact of Japanese culture.

Foreign Bodies and *Mammon Inc* by Hwee Hwee Tan (www.geocities.com/hweehwee_

tan) are among the best of contemporary Singaporean fiction. Other celebrated novels by Singaporean writers include *Tigers in Paradise* by Philip Jeyaretnam, *Juniper Loa* by Lin Yutang, *Tangerine* by Colin Cheong and *Playing Madame Mao* by Lau Siew Mai.

Traditional Architecture

Vividly painted and handsomely proportioned, traditional wooden Malay houses are built on stilts, with high, peaked roofs, to take advantage of even the slightest cooling breeze. Further ventilation is achieved by full-length windows, no internal partitions, and latticelike grilles in the walls.

Although their numbers are dwindling, this type of house has not disappeared altogether. The best places to see examples are in the *kampung* (villages) of Peninsular Malaysia, particularly along the east coast in the states of Kelantan and Terengganu. Here you'll see that roofs are often tiled, showing a Thai and Cambodian influence.

In Melaka, the Malay house has a distinctive tiled front stairway leading up to the front verandah – examples can be seen around Kampung Morten. The Minangkabau-style houses found in Negeri Sembilan are the most distinctive of the *kampung* houses, with curved roofs resembling buffalo horns – the design is imported from Sumatra.

Few Malay-style houses have survived Singapore's rapid modernisation – the main place they remain is on Pulau Ubin. Instead, the island state has some truly magnificent examples of Chinese shophouse architecture, particularly in Chinatown, Emerald Hill (off Orchard Rd) and around Katong. There are also the distinctive 'black and white' bungalows built during colonial times; find survivors lurking in the residential areas off Orchard Rd.

Drama & Dance

Traditional Malay dances include *menora,* a dance-drama of Thai origin performed by an all-male cast dressed in grotesque masks; and the similar *mak yong,* where the

Traditional Crafts

Batik While it's made across Malaysia, Kelantan and Terengganu are batik's true homes. It's created by printing fabric with wax and then dyeing the material.

Basketry & weaving Materials include rattan, bamboo, swamp nipah grass and pandanus palms. While each ethnic group has certain distinctive motifs, centuries of interaction has led to an intermingling of patterns.

Kain songket This hand-woven fabric with gold and silver threads through the material is a speciality of Kelantan and Terengganu.

Kites & puppets The *wau bulan* (moon kite) of Kelantan is a traditional paper and bamboo crescent-shaped kite that can be as large as 3m in length and breadth, while kite makers in Terengganu specialise in the *wau kucing* (cat kite). *Wayang kulit* (shadow puppets) are made from buffalo hide and reenact Hindu legends.

Metalwork Kelantan is famed for its silversmiths, who work in a variety of ways and specialise in filigree and repoussé work. In Selangor you'll find the Royal Selangor Pewter Factory as well as other pewter manufacturers.

fun – steamed rice flour sheets – are sliced into strips and topped with sweet brown and red chilli sauces. Round yellow noodles are served in soup and stir-fried with curry leaves, bean sprouts and chilli sauce for the Muslim-Indian speciality *mee mamak*.

Meat

Chicken *(ayam)* is tremendously popular. The meat regularly turns up in curries (rarely prohibitively spicy), on skewers, grilled and served with peanut sauce for satay. Another oft-enjoyed fowl is *itik* (duck), roasted and served over rice, simmered in star anise-scented broth and eaten with yellow *mee*, or stewed with aromatics for an Indian-Muslim curry.

Tough local beef *(daging)* is best cooked long and slowly, for dishes like coconut milk–based rendang. Chinese-style beef noodles feature tender chunks of beef and springy meatballs in a rich, mildly spiced broth lightened with pickled mustard. Indian Muslims do amazing things with mutton; it's worth searching out *sup kambing*, stewed mutton riblets (and other parts, if you wish) in a thick soup, flavoured with loads of aromatics and chillies that's eaten with sliced white bread.

Pork *(babi)* is the king of meats for Chinese. Whether roasted till crispy-skinned *(char yoke)* or marinated and barbecued till sweetly charred *(char siew)*, the meat is eaten with rice, added to noodles, and stuffed into steamed and baked buns.

Fish & Seafood

Lengthy coastlines and abundant rivers and estuaries mean that seafood forms much of the diet for many of the region's residents. Fresh fish *(ikan)* is left whole, slathered and stuffed with *rempah* (a pounded paste of chillies, dried spices and aromatics such as garlic, lemongrass and turmeric). It may be cooked on the grill (often wrapped in banana leaves) or rubbed with turmeric and deep-fried to accompany Indian rice meals. Cut into chunks or steaks, it's cooked in hot and sour stews or aromatic coconut curries.

The head and shoulders of large fish are prized; a Chinese cook might steam and serve it smothered in a garlic and *taucu* (salted bean paste) sauce, while an Indian would cook it in spicy and sour curry; Malaysians chop fish heads, deep-fry them, and serve

Tips on Tipples

○ Half the fun of taking breakfast in one of Singapore's or Malaysia's Little Indias is watching the tea wallah toss-pour an order of *teh tarik* ('pulled' tea) from one cup to the other.

○ *Kopi* (coffee) is also extremely popular; the inky, thick brew owes its distinctive colour and flavour to the fact that its beans are roasted with sugar.

○ Caffeine-free alternatives include freshly squeezed or blended vegetable and fruit juices, sticky-sweet fresh sugar-cane juice and *kelapa muda*, or young coconut water, drunk straight from the fruit with a straw.

○ Other, more unusual drinks are *ee bee chui* (barley boiled with water, pandan leaf and rock sugar), *air mata kucing* (made with dried longan), and *cincau* or herbal grass jelly. Chinese salted plums add an oddly refreshing dimension to sweetened lime juice, in *asam boi*.

○ Alcohol is pricey; for a cheap, boozy night out stick to locally brewed beers such as Tiger and Carlsberg.

them with noodles in a fish and tomato broth redolent of ginger and rice wine, enriched with evaporated milk.

Sotong (squid) is deep-fried, stirred into curries or griddle-grilled on a banana leaf with sambal. Shellfish is much adored; Singaporeans stir-fry crab with chillies or black pepper; and Malaysians insist that if it doesn't have fresh cockles it's not a real *char kway teow*.

Vegetables & Fruit

Every rice-based Malay meal includes *ulam,* a selection vegetables and fresh herbs to eat on their own or dip into sambal. Indians cook cauliflower and leafy vegetables like cabbage, spinach and roselle (sturdy leaves with an appealing sourness) with coconut milk and turmeric. *Tahu* (soy beans) are consumed in many forms including soy milk, *dou fu* (soft fresh bean curd) and *fucuk* (the chewy skin that forms on the surface of boiling soy milk). Malays often cook with tempeh, a fermented soy bean cake with a nutty flavour, stir-frying it with lemongrass and chillies, and stewing it with vegetables in mild coconut gravy.

Pineapples, watermelon, papaya and guava are abundant in this region. In December, January, June and July, follow your nose to sample notoriously odiferous love-it-or-hate it durian. Should the king of fruits prove too repellent, consider the slightly smelly but wonderfully sweet yellow flesh of the young *nangka* (jackfruit).

Regional Cuisines

Penang is known for its Nonya cooking, born of intermarriage between Chinese immigrants and local women. This is also the home of *nasi kandar,* rice eaten with a variety of curries, a *mamak* (Indian Muslim) speciality named after the *kandar* (shoulder pole) from which ambulant vendors once suspended their pots of rice and curry

Culinary fusion is also a theme in Melaka, the former Portuguese outpost where you'll find Cristang (a blend of Portuguese and local cooking styles) dishes such as *debal,* a fiery Eurasian stew that marries European-originated red wine vinegar, Indian black-mustard seeds, Chinese soy sauce and Malay candlenuts.

The peninsular east coast is the heartland of traditional Malay cooking. The states of Kelantan and Terengganu were isolated from the rest of the country, receiving few Chinese and Indian immigrants. Consequently, regional specialities have remained staunchly Malay. Local cooks excel at making all manner of *kuih* (sweet rice cakes) and even savoury dishes have a noticeably sweet edge.

If you're looking to diverge from the local cuisine altogether, look no further than Singapore; its high-end dining scene is second to none in Southeast Asia.

The Best... Culinary Treats

1 **Cendol** Shaved ice, fresh coconut milk, pandan 'pasta' and sweet, smoky palm sugar beat the heat deliciously.

2 **Roti canai** Flaky, crispy griddled bread dipped in curry and dhal and accompanied by a mug of frothy *teh tarik* ('pulled' tea) is one of the world's best ways to wake up.

3 **Char kway teow** Silky rice noodles, plump prawns, briny cockles, chewy Chinese sausage, crispy sprouts, fluffy egg, a hint of chilli – all kissed by the smoke of a red-hot wok. Need we say more?

4 **Hainanese chicken-rice** Tender poached chicken accompanied by rice scented with stock and garlic and a trio of dipping sauces plain and spicy.

5 **Popiah** Fresh spring rolls stuffed with shredded turnip and other vegetables and dressed with sweet-spicy bean sauce.

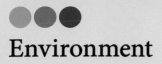

Environment

Mulu Canopy Skywalk (p317)

FELIX HUG/GETTY IMAGES ©

Malaysia and Singapore's lush natural habitats teem with thousands of mammals, birds, amphibians, reptiles and insects, many of them found nowhere else on earth. Although vast areas of old-growth forest have been cleared, a few magnificent stands remain, mostly protected within reserves and parks. Tropical flora and fauna are so abundant that this region is considered to be one of the world's 'mega-diversity' hotspots.

Peninsular Malaysia

Large parts of Peninsular Malaysia are covered by dense jungle, particularly its mountainous centre and thinly populated northern half. However, the predominant vegetation constitutes palm oil and rubber plantations.

On the western side of the peninsula there is a long, fertile plain running down to the sea; this is where you'll find the country's major urban centres, Kuala Lumpur and the Klang Valley, Penang and Melaka. On the more sparsely populated eastern side the mountains descend more steeply and the coast is fringed with sandy beaches.

East Malaysia

East Malaysia, also known as Malaysian Borneo, occupies the northern part of the island of Borneo (the larger, southern part is the Indonesian state of Kalimantan). It is divided into the states of Sarawak and Sabah, with the tiny Sultanate of Brunei a small enclave between them.

Eons ago Borneo was joined to the peninsula, but since the last ice age it has been separated by the South China Sea. Jungle features heavily here along with many large river systems, particularly in Sarawak.

Singapore

Consisting of the main, low-lying Singapore island and 63 much smaller islands within its territorial waters, Singapore is a mere 137km north of the equator. In the centre of Singapore island, Bukit Timah (162m) is the nation's highest point. This central area is an igneous outcrop, containing most of Singapore's remaining forest and open areas. The western part of the island is a sedimentary area of low-lying hills and valleys, while the southeast is mostly flat and sandy. The undeveloped northern coast and the offshore islands are home to some mangrove forest.

National Parks & Protected Areas

Fancy seeing what life was possibly like 100 million years ago? Trekking into the deepest parts of Malaysia's jungles will give you a clue as they were largely unaffected by the far-reaching climatic changes brought on elsewhere by the ice age. Significant chunks of these rainforests have been made into national parks, in which all commercial activities apart from tourism are banned.

The British established the region's first national park in 1938 and it is now included in Taman Negara, the crowning glory of Malaysia's network of national parks, which crosses the state borders of Terengganu, Kelantan and Pahang. In addition to this and the 27 other national and state parks across the country (23 of them located in Malaysian Borneo), there are various government-protected reserves and sanctuaries for forests, birds, mammals and marine life.

Even in the heart of KL it's possible to stretch your legs in the Lake Gardens Park or the Bukit Nanas Forest Reserve. Singapore also offers up trekking possibilities: the country's National Parks Board manages 10% of the island's total land area,

Environmental Triva

o Over half Malaysia's total of 329,758 sq km is covered by East Malaysia which takes up 198,847 sq km of Borneo.

o Malaysia includes 877 islands. Popular ones with visitors include Penang, Langkawi and Pulau Pangkor off the west coast of the peninsula; and Pulau Tioman, Pulau Redang and Pulau Perhentian off the peninsula's east coast.

o Mt Kinabalu (4095m) in Sabah is Malaysia's highest mountain.

o There's a disparity between government figures and those of environmental groups, but it's probable that 60% of Peninsula Malaysia's rainforests have been logged with similar figures applying to Malaysian Borneo.

o Singapore island is 42km long and 23km wide; with the other islands, the republic has a total landmass of 704 sq km (and this is growing through land reclamation).

The Best... National Parks

1 Taman Negara National Park

2 Gunung Mulu National Park

3 Kinabalu National Park

4 Endau-Rompin National Park

5 Bako National Park

which comprises over 50 major parks and four nature reserves, including the excellent Bukit Timah Nature Reserve.

Mega-Diversity Area

The wet, tropical climate of this region produces an amazing range of flora, some unique to the area, such as certain species of orchid and pitcher plants. A single hectare of rainforest (or dipterocarp forest) can support many species of tree, plus a vast diversity of other plants, including many thousands of species of orchid, fungi, fern and moss – some of them epiphytes (plants that grow on other plants).

Other important vegetation types include mangroves, which fringe coasts and estuaries and provide nurseries for fish and crustaceans; the stunted rhododendron forests of Borneo's high peaks, which also support epiphytic communities of orchids and hanging lichens (beard moss); and the *kerangas* of Sarawak, which grows on dry, sandy soil and can support many types of pitcher plant.

Survival Guide

Morning traffic in Kuala Lumpur
ROB WHITWORTH/GETTY IMAGES ©

Directory

●●●
Accommodation

Malaysia and Singapore's accommodation options range from rock-bottom flophouses to luxurious five-star resorts. In Malaysia, inquire about homestays with Tourism Malaysia (www.tourismmalaysia.gov.my) or each of the state tourism bodies. In Sarawak it's also possible to stay in longhouses, the age-old dwellings of many (but not all) of the region's indigenous people.

Outside the peak holiday seasons (around major festivals like Chinese New Year in January/February) big discounts are frequently available.

Budget listings (denoted with a '$') offer a double room with attached bathroom or dorm bed for under RM100/S$100; midrange properties ($$) have double rooms for

RM100 to RM400/S$100 to S$250; top-end places ($$$) charge over RM400/over $250.

Credit cards are widely accepted at midrange and top-end hotels; cash payment is expected at cheaper places.

HOTELS

Standard rooms at top-end hotels are often called 'superior' in the local parlance. Most hotels have slightly more expensive 'deluxe' or 'club' rooms, which tend to be larger, have a better view and include extras like breakfast or free internet access. Many also have suites.

Where a room rate is expressed as '++' (plus, plus) it means service of 10% and tax of 6% is added in Malaysia; in Singapore it's 10% service plus 7% tax.

At the lower end of the price scale are the traditional Chinese-run hotels usually offering little more than simple rooms with a bed, a table and chair, and a sink. The showers and toilets (which will sometimes be Asian squat-style) may be down the corridor.

●●●
Business Hours

Reviews won't list operating hours unless they deviate from the following:

Book Your Stay Online

For more accommodation reviews by Lonely Planet authors, check out http://hotels.lonelyplanet.com. You'll find independent reviews, as well as recommendations on the best places to stay. Best of all, you can book online.

Banks 10am to 3pm Monday to Friday, 9.30am to 11.30am Sat

Restaurants noon to 2.30pm and 6pm to 10.30pm

Shops 9.30am to 7pm, malls 10am to 10pm

●●●
Climate

Malaysia and Singapore are hot and steamy year-round, with temperatures rarely dropping below 20°C, even at night.

Although Malaysia is monsoonal, only the east coast of the peninsula has a real rainy season – elsewhere there is just a little more rain than usual. Rain tends to arrive in brief torrential downpours, providing a welcome relief from the heat. During the monsoon it may rain every day, but it rarely rains all day. Humidity tends to hover around the 90% mark; escape the clammy heat by retreating to the cooler hills.

For current weather forecasts check the website of the Malaysian Meteorological Department (www.kjc.gov.my/english/weather/weather.html).

●●●
Customs Regulations

MALAYSIA

The following can be brought into Malaysia duty free:

- 1L of alcohol

- 225g of tobacco (200 cigarettes or 50 cigars)

Climate

Kuala Lumpur

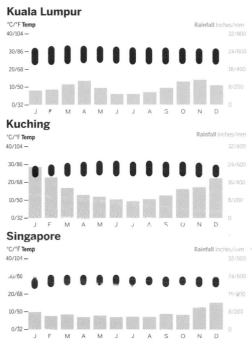

Kuching

Singapore

and pirated recordings and publications are prohibited.

Penalties for importation or exportation of illegal drugs ranges from jail and strokes of the rotan (a rattan cane) to death. If you bring in prescription drugs, you should have a doctor's letter or a prescription.

There is no restriction on the importation of currency.

Electricity

Connect to the reliable electricity supply (220V to 240V, 50 cycles) with a UK-type three-square-pin plug.

250V/50Hz

Food

Our listed price ranges (p354) refer to a two course meal including a soft drink. Unless otherwise stated, tax is included in the price. For more on food specialties and dining see p345.

○ souvenirs and gifts not exceeding RM200 (RM500 when coming from Bandar Labuan or Pulau Langkawi).

Cameras, portable radios, perfume, cosmetics and watches do not incur duty. Prohibited items include weapons (including imitations), fireworks and 'obscene and prejudicial articles' (pornography, for example, and items that may be considered inflammatory, or religiously offensive).

Drug smuggling carries the death penalty in Malaysia.

Visitors can carry only RM1000 in and out of Malaysia; there's no limit on foreign currency.

SINGAPORE

Visitors to Singapore are allowed to bring in 1L of wine, beer or spirits duty-free. Electronic goods, cosmetics, watches, cameras, jewellery, footwear, toys, arts and crafts are not dutiable.

It is forbidden to bring any tobacco products, though they'll turn a blind eye to the odd pack of smokes.

Duty-free concessions are not available if you are arriving in Singapore from Malaysia or if you leave Singapore for less than 48 hours.

Fire crackers, toy currency and coins, obscene or seditious material, gun-shaped cigarette lighters, endangered species or their by-products,

Gay & Lesbian Travellers

Sex between males is illegal in both Malaysia and Singapore. However, prosecution is rare and in both Kuala Lumpur and Singapore there are fairly active gay scenes.

Malaysians and Singaporeans are conservative about displays of public affection. Although same-sex hand-holding is quite common for men and women, this is rarely an indication of sexuality; an overtly gay couple doing the same would attract attention, though there is little risk of vocal or aggressive homophobia.

The websites Utopia (www.utopia-asia.com) and Fridae (www.fridae.com) provide excellent coverage of gay venues and events across Asia.

Health

BEFORE YOU GO

- Take out health insurance.

- Pack medications in their original, clearly labelled containers.

- Carry a signed and dated letter from your physician describing your medical conditions and medications, including their generic names.

- If you have a heart condition bring a copy of your ECG taken just prior to travelling

- Bring a double supply of any regular medication in case of loss or theft.

RECOMMENDED VACCINATIONS

Proof of yellow fever vaccination will be required if you have visited a country in the yellow-fever zone (ie Africa or South America) within the six days prior to entering Malaysia. Otherwise the World Health Organization (WHO) recommends the following vaccinations for travellers to Malaysia:

Adult diphtheria and tetanus Single booster recommended if none in the previous 10 years.

Hepatitis A Provides almost 100% protection for up to a year. A booster after 12 months provides at least another 20 years' protection.

Hepatitis B Now considered routine for most travellers. Given as three shots over six months. A rapid schedule is also available, as is a combined vaccination with Hepatitis A.

Measles, mumps and rubella (MMR) Two doses of MMR are required unless you have had the diseases. Many young adults require a booster.

Polio There have been no reported cases of polio in Malaysia in recent years. Only one booster is required as an adult for lifetime protection.

Typhoid Recommended unless your trip is less than a week and only to developed cities. The vaccine offers around 70% protection, lasts for two to three years and comes as a single shot. Tablets are also available. However, the injection is usually recommended as it has fewer side effects.

Varicella If you haven't had chickenpox, discuss this vaccination with your doctor.

IN MALAYSIA & SINGAPORE

AVAILABILITY & COST OF HEALTH CARE

In Malaysia the standard of medical care in the major centres is good, and most problems can be adequately dealt with in Kuala Lumpur.

Singapore has excellent medical facilities. You cannot buy medication over the counter without a doctor's prescription.

INFECTIOUS DISEASES

The following are the most common for travellers:

Dengue Fever Becoming increasingly common in cities. The mosquito that carries dengue bites day and night, so use insect avoidance measures at all times. Symptoms can include high fever, severe

Eating Price Ranges

	MALAYSIA	SINGAPORE
$	less than RM10	less than S$10
$$	RM10–50	S$10–30
$$$	more than RM50	more than S$30

headache, body ache, a rash and diarrhoea. There is no specific treatment, just rest and paracetamol - do not take aspirin as it increases the likelihood of hemorrhaging.

Hepatitis A This food- and water-borne virus infects the liver, causing jaundice (yellow skin and eyes), nausea and lethargy. All travellers to Malaysia should be vaccinated against it.

Hepatitis B The only sexually transmitted disease (STD) that can be prevented by vaccination, hepatitis B is spread by body fluids, including sexual contact.

Hepatitis E Transmitted through contaminated food and water and has similar symptoms to hepatitis A, but is far less common. It is a severe problem in pregnant women and can result in the death of both mother and baby. There is currently no vaccine, and prevention is by following safe eating and drinking guidelines.

HIV Unprotected heterosexual sex is the main method of transmission.

Malaria Uncommon in the region and antimalarial drugs are rarely recommended for travellers. However, there may be a small risk in rural areas. Remember that malaria can be fatal. Before you travel, seek medical advice on the right medication and dosage for you.

Rabies A potential risk, and invariably fatal if untreated, rabies is spread by the bite or lick of an infected animal, most commonly a dog or monkey. Pretravel vaccination means the postbite treatment is greatly simplified. If an animal bites you, gently wash the wound with soap and water, and apply iodine-based antiseptic. If you are not prevaccinated you will need to receive rabies immunoglobulin as soon as possible.

Typhoid This serious bacterial infection is spread via food and water. Symptoms include high and slowly progressive fever, headache, a dry cough and stomach pain. Vaccination, recommended for all travellers spending more than a week in Malaysia, is not 100% effective so you must still be careful with what you eat and drink.

Traveller's Diarrhoea
Diarrhoea, commonly caused by bacteria, is by far the most common problem affecting travellers. The treatment consists of staying well-hydrated; replenish lost fluids with plenty of water and a solution like Gastrolyte. Antibiotics such as Norfloxacin, Ciprofloxacin or Azithromycin will kill the bacteria quickly.

Loperamide is just a 'stopper', but it can be helpful in certain situations, like if you have to go on a long bus ride. Seek medical attention quickly if you do not respond to an appropriate antibiotic.

Giardiasis is also relatively common. Symptoms include nausea, bloating, excess gas, fatigue and intermittent diarrhoea. The treatment of choice is Tinidazole; Metroniadzole is a second option.

ENVIRONMENTAL HAZARDS

Air Pollution If you have severe respiratory problems, speak with your doctor before travelling to any heavily polluted urban centres. If troubled by the pollution, leave the city for a few days to get some fresh air.

Diving & Surfing If planning on diving or surfing, seek specialised advice before you travel to ensure your medical kit contains treatment for coral cuts and tropical ear infections, as well as the standard problems. Have a dive medical before you leave your home country – there are certain medical conditions that are incompatible with diving, and economic

Further Resources

Lonely Planet's *Asia & India: Healthy Travel* contains useful information. Other recommended references include *Traveller's Health* by Dr Richard Dawood and *Travelling Well* by Dr Deborah Mills. Online resources include the following:

Centres for Disease Control and Prevention (CDC; www.cdc.gov)

MD Travel Health (www.mdtravelhealth.com)

World Health Organization (www.who.int/ith)

Drinking Water

o Never drink tap water unless you've verified that it's safe (many parts of Malaysia and Singapore have modern treatment plants).

o Bottled water is generally safe – check the seal is intact at purchase.

o Avoid ice in places that look dubious.

o Avoid fruit juices if they have not been freshly squeezed or you suspect they may have been watered down.

o Boiling water is the most efficient method of purifying it.

o The best chemical purifier is iodine. It should not be used by pregnant women or those with thyroid problems.

o Water filters should also filter out viruses. Ensure your filter has a chemical barrier such as iodine and a small pore size, ie less than 4 microns.

Snakes Assume all snakes are poisonous and never try to catch one. Always wear boots and long pants if walking in an area that may have snakes. First aid in the event of a snake bite involves pressure immobilisation via an elastic bandage firmly wrapped around the affected limb, starting at the bite site and working up towards the chest. The bandage should not be so tight that the circulation is cut off; the fingers or toes should be kept free so the circulation can be checked. Immobilise the limb with a splint and carry the victim to medical attention. Don't use tourniquets or try to suck out the venom. Antivenin is available for most species.

considerations may override health considerations at some dive operations in Asia.

Heat It can take up to two weeks to adapt to the region's hot climate. Swelling of the feet and ankles is common, as are muscle cramps caused by excessive sweating. Prevent these by avoiding excessive activity in the heat.

Prickly heat – an itchy rash of tiny lumps – is caused by sweat being trapped under the skin. Treat by moving out of the heat and into an air-conditioned area for a few hours and by having cool showers. Avoid creams and ointments as they clog the pores.

Skin Problems There are two common fungal rashes that affect travellers in the tropics. The first occurs in moist areas that get less air, such as the groin, armpits and between

the toes. It starts as a red patch that slowly spreads and is usually itchy. Treatment involves keeping the skin dry, avoiding chafing and using an anti-fungal cream such as Clotrimazole or Lamisil. Tinea versicolour is also common – this fungus causes small, light-coloured patches, most commonly on the back, chest and shoulders. Consult a doctor.

Cuts and scratches become easily infected in humid climates. Take meticulous care of any cuts and scratches to prevent complications such as abscesses. Immediately wash all wounds in clean water and apply antiseptic. If you develop signs of infection (increasing pain and redness), see a doctor. Divers and surfers should be particularly careful with coral cuts as they become easily infected.

Sunburn Even on a cloudy day, sunburn can occur rapidly. Always use a strong sunscreen (at least SPF 30), making sure to reapply after a swim, and always wear a wide-brimmed hat and sunglasses outdoors. Avoid lying in the sun during the hottest part of the day (10am to 2pm). If you're sunburnt stay out of the sun until you've recovered, apply cool compresses and take painkillers for the discomfort. Applied twice daily, 1% hydrocortisone cream is also helpful in treating sunburn.

TRAVELLING WITH CHILDREN

There are specific issues you should consider before travelling with your child.

All routine vaccinations should be up to date, as many of the common childhood diseases that have been eliminated in the West are still present in parts of Southeast Asia. A travel-health clinic can advise on specific vaccines, but think seriously about rabies vaccination if you're visiting rural areas or travelling for more than a month, as children are more vulnerable to severe animal bites.

Children are more prone to getting serious forms of mosquito-borne diseases such as malaria, Japanese B encephalitis and dengue fever. In particular, malaria is very serious in children and can rapidly lead to death – think seriously before taking your child into a malaria-risk area. Permethrin-impregnated clothing is safe to use, and insect repellents should contain between 10% and 20% DEET.

Diarrhoea can cause rapid dehydration and you should pay particular attention to keeping your child well hydrated. The best antibiotic for children with diarrhoea is Azithromycin.

Children can get very sick very quickly so locate good medical facilities at your destination and make contact if you are worried – it's always better to get a medical opinion than to try to treat your own children.

WOMEN'S HEALTH

Pregnant women should receive specialised advice before travelling. The ideal time to travel is in the second trimester (between 16 and 28 weeks), when the risk of pregnancy-related problems is at its lowest and pregnant women generally feel at their best. During the first trimester there's a risk of miscarriage and in the third trimester complications such as premature labour and high blood pressure are possible. At any stage, it's wise to travel with a companion. Always carry a list of quality medical facilities available at your destination and ensure you continue your standard antenatal care at these facilities. Avoid travel in rural areas with poor transport and medical facilities and, most of all, ensure travel insurance covers all pregnancy-related possibilities, including premature labour.

Malaria is a high-risk disease in pregnancy. The World Health Organization recommends that pregnant women do not travel to areas with malaria resistant to chloroquine, but none of the more effective antimalarial drugs are completely safe in pregnancy.

Traveller's diarrhoea can quickly lead to dehydration and result in inadequate blood flow to the placenta. Many of the drugs used to treat various diarrhoea bugs are not recommended in pregnancy, although Azithromycin is considered safe.

In urban areas, supplies of sanitary products are readily available. Birth-control options may be limited so bring adequate supplies of your own form

Insect Bites & Stings

Bedbugs Live in the cracks of furniture and walls and migrate to the bed at night to feed on you; they are a particular problem in cheaper hotels in the region. Treat the itch with antihistamine.

Lice Most commonly inhabit your head and pubic area. Transmission is via close contact with an infected person. Treat with numerous applications of an antilice shampoo such as Permethrin.

Ticks Contracted after walking in rural areas. If you are bitten and experience symptoms such as a rash at the site of the bite or elsewhere, fever, or muscle aches, see a doctor. Doxycycline prevents tick-borne diseases.

Leeches Found in humid rainforest areas. Don't transmit any disease but their bites can be itchy for weeks afterwards and can easily become infected. Apply an iodine-based antiseptic to any leech bite to help prevent infection.

Bees or wasps If allergic to their stings, carry an injection of adrenaline (eg an Epipen) for emergency treatment.

Jellyfish Most are not dangerous. If stung, pour vinegar onto the affected area to neutralise the poison. Take painkillers, and seek medical advice if your condition worsens.

Practicalities

- Read the English-language newspapers the *New Straits Times,* the *Star* and the *Malay Mail*. In Malaysian Borneo you'll also find the *Borneo Post,* the *New Sarawak Tribune* and the *New Sabah Times*. In Singapore there's the *Straits Times*, *Business Times* and *New Paper*.

- Listen to Traxx FM (www.traxxfm.net; 90.3FM), HITZ FM (www.hitz.fm; 92.9FM) and MIX FM (www.mix.fm; 94.5FM) for pop music and BFM (www.bfm.my; 89.9FM) or Fly FM (www.flyfm.com.my; 95.8FM) for news. All frequencies are for the KL area. In Sabah, listen to Traxx FM (90.7FM) or Muzik FM (88.9FM); in Sarawak tune in to Traxx FM (89.9FM), or Wai FM (101.3FM) for tribal music.

- Watch Malaysia's two government TV channels (TV1 and TV2), four commercial stations (TV3, NTV7, 8TV and TV9) and a host of satellite channels.

- Use the metric system for weights and measures.

of contraception. Heat, humidity and antibiotics can all contribute to thrush. Treatment is with anti-fungal creams and pessaries such as Clotrimazole, a single tablet of Fluconazole (Diflucan) is a practical alternative. Urinary-tract infections can be precipitated by dehydration or long bus journeys without toilet stops, so if you're prone to these you may want to bring suitable antibiotics.

Insurance

It's always a good idea to take out travel insurance. Check the small print to see if the policy covers potentially dangerous sporting activities like caving, diving or trekking, and make sure that it adequately covers your valuables. Health-wise, you may prefer a policy that pays doctors or hospitals directly rather than

your having to pay on the spot and claim later. If you have to claim later, make sure that you keep all documentation. Check that the policy covers ambulances, an emergency flight home and, if you plan on trekking in remote areas, a helicopter evacuation.

A few credit cards offer limited, although sometimes full, travel insurance to the holder.

Internet Access

Urban centres in Malaysia and Singapore have ubiquitous hot spots for wi-fi connections (often free) and internet cafes typically charging RM3/S$3 to S$5 per hour for broadband access. You can also use a smartphone to access the internet via wi-fi. Don't expect fast internet in the remote reaches of the peninsula and Malaysian Borneo.

Legal Matters

In any dealings with the local police it pays to be deferential. You're most likely to come into contact with them either through reporting a crime (some of the big cities in Malaysia have tourist police stations for this purpose) or while driving. Minor misdemeanours may be overlooked, but don't count on it.

Drug trafficking carries a mandatory death penalty in both countries and a number of foreigners have been executed over the years. Even possession of tiny amounts can incur a lengthy jail sentence and a beating with the rotan (cane). Just don't do it.

Money
ATMS & CREDIT CARDS

MasterCard and Visa are the most widely accepted brands. You can make ATM withdrawals with your PIN, and Maybank (Malaysia's biggest bank), HSBC and Standard Chartered will accept credit cards for over-the-counter cash advances. Many banks are also linked to international banking networks such as Cirrus (the most common), Maestro and Plus, allowing withdrawals from overseas savings or checking accounts.

Contact details for credit card companies in Malaysia and Singapore:

American Express
Malaysia (🔊 2050 0000;
www.americanexpress.com/
malaysia) Singapore (🔊 6396
6000, local calls only 1800-299
1997; www.americanexpress.
com/sg)

MasterCard Malaysia
(🔊 1800-804 594; www.
mastercard.com/sea) Singapore
MasterCard (🔊 800-1100
113; www.mastercard.com)

Visa Malaysia (🔊 1800-802
997; www.visa-asia.com)
Singapore **Visa** (🔊 800-4481
250; www.visa.com.sg)

CURRENCY
MALAYSIA
The ringgit (RM) is made up
of 100 sen. Coins in use are
1 sen, 5 sen, 10 sen, 20 sen
and 50 sen; notes come in
RM1, RM2 (rare), RM5, RM10,
RM20, RM50 and RM100.

Malaysians sometimes
refer to ringgit as 'dollars',
the old name used for the
country's currency – if in
doubt ask if people mean US
dollars or 'Malaysian dollars'
(le ringgit).

Carry small bills with you
when venturing outside cities.

SINGAPORE
The Singapore dollar, locally
referred to as the 'singdol-
lar', is made up of 100 cents.
Singapore uses 5¢, 10¢, 20¢,
50¢ and $1 coins, while notes
come in denominations of $2,
$5, $10, $50, $100, $500 and
$1000.

TAXES & REFUNDS
MALAYSIA
There is no general sales tax
but there is a government tax
of 6% at some midrange and
all top-end hotels and many
larger restaurants (in addition
to an establishment's 10%
service fee).

SINGAPORE
As a visitor you are entitled
to claim a refund of the 7%
Goods and Services Tax on
your purchases, provided you
meet certain conditions.

TRAVELLERS CHEQUES & CASH
Banks in the region are efficient and there are plenty
of moneychangers. Banks
usually charge a commission
(around RM10/S$5 per trans-
action, with a possible small
fee per cheque) to change
cash and travellers cheques,
whereas moneychangers
have no charges but their
rates vary more. Compared
with a bank, you'll generally
get a better rate for cash at a
moneychanger – it's usually
quicker too. Away from the
tourist centres, moneychangers' rates are often poorer and
they may not change travellers cheques.

All major brands of
travellers cheques are
accepted across the region.
Cash in major currencies
is also readily exchanged,
though – like everywhere else
in the world – the US dollar
has a slight edge.

Public Holidays
In addition to fixed secular
holidays, both countries have
various religious festivals
(which change dates annually)
that are national holidays, too.
These include Chinese New
Year (in January/February),
the Hindu festival of Deepavali
(in October/November), the
Buddhist festival of Wesak
(April/May) and the Muslim
festivals of Hari Raya Haji,
Hari Raya Puasa, Mawlid
al-Nabi and Awal Muharram
(Muslim New Year).

MALAYSIA
Schools break for holidays
five times a year. The actual
dates vary from state to state
but are generally in January
(one week), March (two
weeks), May (three weeks),
August (one week) and October (four weeks).

New Year's Day 1 January

Federal Territory Day 1
February (in Kuala Lumpur
and Putrajaya only)

Good Friday March or April
(in Malaysian Borneo only)

Labour Day 1 May

**Yang di-Pertuan Agong's
(King's) Birthday** 1st
Saturday in June

**Governor of Penang's
Birthday** 2nd Saturday in July
(in Penang only)

National Day (Hari
Kebangsaan) 31 August

Malaysia Day 16 September

Christmas Day 25 December

SINGAPORE
There are two long school
breaks; the first is a four-week
break in June and the second

is usually the entire month of December.

New Year's Day 1 January

Labour Day 1 May

National Day 9 August

Christmas Day 25 December

● ● ●
Safe Travel
ANIMAL HAZARDS

Rabies occurs in Malaysia, so any bite from an animal should be treated very seriously (see p354). In the jungles and mangrove forests, living hazards include leeches (annoying but harmless), snakes (some kinds are highly venomous; see p355), macaques (prone to bag-snatching in some locales), orang-utans (occasionally aggressive) and saltwater crocodiles (found in muddy estuaries, and deadly if they drag you under).

THEFT & VIOLENCE

Theft and violence are not particularly common in either country and compared with Indonesia or Thailand both are extremely safe. Nevertheless, it pays to keep a close eye on your belongings, especially your travel documents (passport, travellers cheques etc), which should be kept with you at all times.

Muggings do happen, particularly in KL and Penang, and physical attacks have been known to occur, particularly after hours and in the poorer, run-down areas of cities. We've been told that thieves on motorbikes particularly target women for

grab raids on their handbags. Also keep a watch out for sleazy local 'beach boys' in Langkawi and the Perhentians.

Credit-card fraud is a growing problem in Malaysia. Use your cards only at established businesses and guard your credit-card numbers closely.

A small, sturdy padlock is well worth carrying, especially if you are going to be staying at any of the cheap chalets found on Malaysia's beaches, where flimsy padlocks are the norm.

● ● ●
Telephone

Operators mentioned here have been personally checked by the authors and should be reliable. However, you should always check terms and conditions carefully.

MALAYSIA
FAX

Fax facilities are available at Telekom Malaysia (TM; www.tm.com.my) offices in larger cities and at some main post offices. If you can't find one of these try a travel agency or large hotel.

INTERNATIONAL CALLS

The easiest and cheapest way to make international calls is to buy a local SIM card for your cellular phone. Only certain payphones permit international calls. You can make operator-assisted international calls from local TM offices. To save money on landline calls, buy a prepaid international calling card (available from convenience stores).

LOCAL CALLS

Landline services are provided by the national monopoly Telekom Malaysia.

Local calls cost 10 sen for three minutes. Payphones take coins or prepaid cards, which are available from TM offices and convenience stores. Some also take international credit cards. You'll also find a range of discount calling cards at convenience stores and mobile-phone counters.

MOBILE PHONES

If you have arranged global-roaming with your home provider, your GSM digital phone will automatically tune into one of the region's digital networks. If not, cheap prepaid SIM cards (RM8.50; passport required) are available almost everywhere from mobile phone shops and kiosks (including at airports). If you bring along your own phone, make sure it can handle 900/1800MHz and is not locked. In Borneo, the cheapest cell phones start at about US$40.

Local calls cost RM0.12 to RM0.15 per minute; international direct dialling costs just RM0.18 per minute to North America and to land-line numbers in Australia and the UK (mobile lines cost RM0.88 a minute). SMSs (text messages; RM0.06 or less each) are hugely popular and are a great way to communicate with locals and expats.

There are three cell phone companies, all with similar call rates and prepaid packages:

Celcom (www.celcom.com.
my; numbers beginning with
013 or 019) This is the best
company to use if you'll be
spending time in remote
regions of Malaysian Borneo.

DiGi (www.digi.com.my;
numbers beginning with 016)

Maxis (www.maxis.com.my;
numbers beginning with 012
or 017).

SINGAPORE
LOCAL CALLS
You can make local and
international calls from public
phone booths. Most phone
booths take phonecards.
Singapore also has credit-card
phones that can be used by
running your card through the
slot. At SingTel centres, there
are also Home Country Direct
phones – press a country
button to contact the operator
and reverse the charges, or
have the call charged to an
international telephone card
acceptable in your country.

There are no area codes
within Singapore; telephone
numbers are eight digits
unless you're calling toll-free
(☎1800). If you're calling
from outside the country,
numbers are preceded by the
country code ☎65. Calls to
Malaysia (from Singapore)
are considered to be STD
(trunk or long-distance) calls.
Dial the access code ☎020,
followed by the area code
(minus the leading zero) and
then your party's number.
Thus, for a call to ☎346
7890 in Kuala Lumpur (area
code ☎03) you would dial
☎02-3-346 7890. Call ☎109
for assistance with Malaysian
area codes.

MOBILE PHONES
Mobile phone numbers start
with ☎9. As long as you have
arranged to have 'global roaming' facilities with your home
provider, your GSM digital
phone will automatically connect with one of Singapore's
networks. Singapore uses
GSM900 and GSM1800 and
there is complete coverage
over the whole island. Check
roaming rates with your operator, as they can be very high.
Alternatively, you can buy a
local SIM card for around $28
(including credit) from post
offices and 7-Eleven stores
– by law you must show your
passport to get one.

●●●
Time

Malaysia and Singapore are
eight hours ahead of GMT/
UTC (London). Noon in the
region is

- 8pm in Los Angeles
- 11pm in New York
- 4am in London
- 2pm in Sydney and
  Melbourne

●●●
Toilets

Although there are still some
places with Asian squat-style
toilets, you'll most often find
Western-style ones these days.
At public facilities toilet paper
is not usually provided. Instead,
you will find a hose which you
are supposed to use as a bidet
or, in cheaper places, a bucket
of water and a tap. If you're not
comfortable with this, remember to take packets of tissues or
toilet paper wherever you go.

●●●
Tourist Information

MALAYSIA
Tourism Malaysia (www.
tourismmalaysia.gov.my) has an
efficient network of overseas
offices, which are useful for
predeparture planning. Unfortunately, its domestic offices
are less helpful and are often
unable to give specific information about destinations
and transport. Nonetheless,
they do stock some decent
brochures as well as the excellent *Map of Malaysia*.

Within Malaysia there are
also a number of state tourist-
promotion organisations,
which often have more
detailed information about
specific areas. These include
the following:

Johor Tourism (www.
johortourism.com.my)

Pahang Tourism (www.
pahangtourism.com.my)

Perak Tourism (www.
peraktourism.com)

Sabah Tourism (www.
sabahtourism.com)

Sarawak Tourism (www.
sarawaktourism.com)

Tourism Melaka (http://
melakatourism.gov.my)

Tourism Penang (www.
tourismpenang.gov.my)

Tourism Selangor (www.
tourismselangor.org)

Tourism Terengganu
(http://tourism.terengganu.
gov.my)

SINGAPORE

A good place to check for information is the website of the Singapore Tourism Board (www.visitsingapore.com).

Several tourism centres offer a wide range of services, including tour bookings and event ticketing, plus a couple of electronic information kiosks.

Liang Court Tourist Service Centre (☎ 6336 7184; Level 1, Liang Court Shopping Centre, 177 River Valley Rd; ☉ 10am-10pm; M Clarke Quay)

Singapore Visitors Centre@ Little India (☎ 6296 4280; InnCrowd Backpackers Hostel, 73 Dunlop St; ☉ 10am-10pm; M Little India)

Singapore Visitors@Orchard Information Centre (☎ 1800 736 2000; cnr Orchard & Cairnhill Rds; ☉ 8am-10.30pm; M Somerset)

Suntec City Visitors Centre (☎ 1800-332 5066; 01-35/37/39/41 Suntec City Mall, 3 Temasek Blvd; ☉ 10am-6pm; M City Hall)

Travellers with Disabilities

Before setting off get in touch with your national support organisation (preferably with the travel officer, if there is one). Also try the following:

Accessible Journeys (☎ 800-846 4537; www.disabilitytravel.com) In the US

Mobility International USA (☎ 541-343 1284; www.miusa.org) In the US

Nican (☎ 02-6241 1220; www.nican.com.au) In Australia

Tourism For All (☎ 0845 124 9971; www.tourismforall.org.uk) In the UK

MALAYSIA

For the mobility impaired, Malaysia can be a nightmare. In most cities and towns there are often no footpaths, kerbs are very high, construction sites are everywhere, and crossings are few and far between. On the upside, taxis are cheap and both Malaysia Airlines and KTM (the national rail service) offer 50% discounts on travel for travellers with disabilities.

SINGAPORE

In recent years a large government campaign to assist those in wheelchairs has seen ramps, lifts and other facilities progressively installed around the island. The pavements in the city are nearly all immaculate, MRT stations all have lifts and there are even some buses equipped with wheelchair-friendly equipment.

Access Singapore is a useful guidebook by the Disabled Persons Association of Singapore; it has a complete rundown on services and other information, and can be found online at www.dpa.org.sg. The booklet is also available from STB offices or from the **National Council of Social Services** (☎ 6210 2500; www.ncss.org.sg).

Visas
MALAYSIA

Visitors must have a passport valid for at least six months beyond the date of entry into Malaysia. The following gives a brief overview of other requirements – full details of visa regulations are available on the website www.kln.gov.my.

Nationals of most countries are given a 30- or 60-day visa on arrival, depending on the expected length of stay. As a general rule, if you arrive by air you will be given 60 days automatically, though coming overland you may be given 30 days unless you specifically ask for a 60-day permit. It's possible to get an extension at an immigration office in Malaysia for a total stay of up to three months. This is a straightforward procedure that is easily done in major Malaysian cities.

Only under special circumstances can Israeli citizens enter Malaysia.

Both Sabah and Sarawak retain a certain degree of state-level control of their borders. Tourists must go through passport control and have their passports stamped whenever they:

◉ arrive in Sabah or Sarawak from Peninsular Malaysia or the federal district of Pulau Labuan

◉ exit Sabah or Sarawak on their way to Peninsular Malaysia or Pulau Labuan

◉ travel between Sabah and Sarawak.

When entering Sabah or Sarawak from another part of Malaysia, your new visa stamp will be valid only for the remainder of the period left on your original Malaysian visa. In Sarawak, an easy way to extend your visa is to make a 'visa run' to Brunei or Indonesia (through the Tebedu-Entikong land crossing).

SINGAPORE

Citizens of most countries are granted 30-day visas on arrival by air or overland (though the latter may get 14-day visas). The exceptions are the Commonwealth of Independent States, India, Myanmar, China and most Middle Eastern countries. Extensions can be applied for at the **Immigration Department** (☎ 6391 6100; 10 Kallang Rd; Ⓜ Lavender).

Women Travellers

The key to travelling with minimum hassle in Malaysia and Singapore is to blend in with the locals, which means dressing modestly and being respectful, especially in areas of stronger Muslim religious sensibilities such as the northeastern states of Peninsula Malaysia. Regardless of what local non-Muslim women wear, it's better to be safe than sorry – we've had reports of attacks on women ranging from minor verbal aggravation to physical assault. Hard as it is to say, the truth is that women are much more likely to have problems in Malay-dominated areas, where attitudes are more conservative.

In Malay-dominated areas, you can halve your hassles just by tying a bandanna over your hair (a minimal concession to the headscarf worn by most Muslim women). When visiting mosques, cover your head and limbs with a headscarf and sarong (many mosques lend these out at the entrance). At the beach, most Malaysian women swim fully clothed in T-shirts and shorts, so don't even think about going topless.

Be proactive about your own safety. Treat overly friendly strangers, both male and female, with a good deal of caution. In cheap hotels check for small peepholes in the walls and doors; when you have a choice, stay in a Chinese-operated hotel. On island resorts, stick to crowded beaches, and choose a chalet close to reception and other travellers. Take taxis after dark and avoid walking alone at night in quiet or seedy parts of town.

Transport

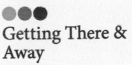

Getting There & Away

Flights and tours can be booked online at www.lonelyplanet.com/travel_services.

ENTERING MALAYSIA & SINGAPORE

The main requirements are a passport that's valid for travel for at least six months, proof of an onward ticket and adequate funds for your stay, although you will rarely be asked to prove this.

The Causeway linking Johor Bahru (JB) with Singapore handles most traffic between the countries. Trains and buses run from all over Malaysia straight through to Singapore terminating at Woodlands, or you can take a bus to JB and get a taxi or one of the frequent buses from JB to Singapore.

A good website with details of express buses between Singapore, Malaysia and Thailand is the Express Bus Travel Guide (www.myexpressbus.com).

There is also a causeway linking Tuas, in western Singapore, with Geylang Patah in JB. This is known as the Second Link, and some bus services to Melaka and up the west coast head this way. If you have a car, tolls on the Second Link are much higher than those on the main Causeway.

✈ AIR

AIRPORTS

Kuala Lumpur International Airport (KLIA; ☎ 8777 8888; www.klia.com.my), 75km south of Kuala Lumpur (KL), is Malaysia's main gateway. Near KLIA, the Low Cost Carrier Terminal (LCCT), from which **AirAsia** (☎ 600 85 8888; www.airasia.com) currently operates, will be replaced in 2013 by a new terminal KLIA2. These terminals handle the bulk of international flights, with the exception of a few flights from Asia and Australia, which come via Penang, Kuching, Kota Kinabalu and a few other cities.

Singapore's main airport is **Changi** (☎ 6595 6868, flight information 1800 542 4422; www.changiairport.com).

●●●
Getting Around

✈ AIR

The two main Malaysian domestic operators are **Malaysia Airlines** (MAS; ☎ 1300-883 000, outside Malaysia 03-2161 0555; www.malaysia-airlines.com.my) and AirAsia (www.airasia.com). AirAsia also operates out of Singapore along with **Jetstar** (☎ 800-852 9507; www.jetstar.com) and **Tiger Airways** (☎ 6808 4437; www.tigerairways.com).

The MAS subsidiary **Firefly** (☎ 03-7845 4543; www.fireflyz.com.my) has flights from KL (SkyPark Subang Terminal) to Penang, Kota Bharu, Kuala Terengganu, Kerteh, Langkawi, Johor Bahru, Alor Setar and Kuantan, and from Penang to KL, Johor Bahru and Langkawi.

Berjaya Air (☎ 03-7847 8228; www.berjaya-air.com) flies between KL (SkyPark Subang Terminal), Pulau Tioman, Pulau Pangkor and Pulau Redang in Peninsular Malaysia, as well as Singapore and Koh Samui in Thailand.

In Malaysian Borneo, Malaysia Airlines' subsidiary MASwings (www.maswings.com.my) offers local flights within and between Sarawak and Sabah; it's main hub

is Miri. These services, especially those handled by 18-seat Twin Otters, are very much reliant on the vagaries of the weather. In the wet season (October to March in Sarawak and on Sabah's northeast coast; May to November on Sabah's west coast), places like Bario in Sarawak can be isolated for days at a time, so don't venture into this area if you have a very tight schedule.

🚌 BUS

Bus travel in Malaysia is economical and generally comfortable, and seats can be reserved. It's also fast – sometimes too fast. In a bid to pack in as many trips as possible, some bus drivers speed recklessly, resulting in frequent, often fatal, accidents. Konsortium Transnasional Berhad (www.ktb.com.my) is Malaysia's largest bus operator running services under the **Transnasional** (☎ 1300-888 582; www.transnasional.com.my), **Nice** (☎ 2272 1586; www.nice-coaches.com.my), Plusliner (www.plusliner.com) and Cityliner (www.cityliner.com.my) brands. Its services tend to be slower than rivals, but its buses have also been involved in several major accidents. They have competition from a variety of privately operated buses on the longer domestic routes including Aeroline (www.aeroline.com.my) and Supernice (www.supernice.com.my). There are so many buses on major runs that you can often turn up and get a seat on the next bus.

On main routes most private buses have air-con (often turned to frigid so bring

a sweater!) and cost only a few ringgit more than regular buses.

In larger towns there may be a number of bus stations; local/regional buses often operate from one station and long-distance buses from another; in other cases, KL for example, bus stations are differentiated by the destinations they serve.

CAR & MOTORCYCLE

It's technically possible to bring your vehicle into Malaysia and Singapore, but there are reams of red tape and the costs are prohibitively expensive – a hire car is a much better proposition. You drive on the left-hand side of the road and it is compulsory to wear seat belts in the front and back of the car.

MALAYSIA

Driving in the cities, particularly KL, can be a nightmare, due to traffic and confusing one-way systems. Malaysian drivers aren't always the safest when it comes to obeying road rules – they mightn't be as reckless as those you might see elsewhere in Southeast Asia, but they still take risks. For example, hardly any of the drivers keep to the official 110km/h speed limit on the main highways and tailgating is a common problem.

The Lebuhraya (North–South Hwy) is a six-lane expressway that runs for 966km along the length of the peninsula from the Thai border in the north to JB in the south. There are quite steep toll charges for using the expressway and these vary according to the distance travelled. As a result the normal highways remain crowded while traffic on the expressway is light. Many other highways are in excellent condition and many are under construction.

Driving Licence A valid overseas licence is needed to rent a car. An International Driving Permit (a translation of your state or national driver's license and its vehicle categories) is usually not required by local car-hire companies, but it is recommended that you bring one. Most rental copanies also require that drivers are at least 23 years old (and less than 65) with at least one year of driving experience.

Hire Major rent-a-car operations include Avis (www.avis.com.my), Hertz (www.simedarbycarrental. com), Mayflower (www. mayflowercarrental.com) and Orix (www.orixcarrentals. com.my); there are many others, though, including local operators only found in one city. Unlimited distance rates for a 1.3L Proton Saga, one of the cheapest and most popular cars in Malaysia, are posted at around RM190/1320 per day/week, including insurance and collision-damage waiver. The Proton is basically a Mitsubishi assembled under licence in Malaysia.

You can often get better deals, either through smaller local companies or when the major companies offer special deals. Rates drop substantially for longer rentals, and if you shop around by phone, you can get wheels for as little as RM2500 per month, including unlimited kilometres and insurance. The advantage of dealing with a large company is that it has offices all over the country, giving better backup if something goes wrong and allowing you to pick up in one city and drop off in another (typically for a RM50 surcharge). Mayflower is one local company with offices all over and some competitive rates.

The best place to look for car hire is KL, though Penang is also good. In Sabah and Sarawak there is less competition and rates are higher, partly because of road conditions; there's also likely to be a surcharge if you drop your car off in a different city from the one you rented it in.

Insurance Rental companies will provide insurance when you hire a car, but always check what the extent of your coverage will be, particularly if you're involved in an accident You might want to take out your own insurance or pay the rental company an extra premium for an insurance excess reduction.

SINGAPORE

Singapore once boasted fairly clear roads, but in recent years congestion has significantly worsened. The roads themselves are immaculate, but don't let that lull you into a false sense of security – nowhere is the infamous *kiasu* (Hokkien for 'afraid to lose') Singaporean character more evident than on the roads. Aggressive driving is common, speeding and tailgating endemic, use of signals rare, and wild lane-changing universal. Given Singapore's reputation for strict punishment, penalties for serious offences – even killing pedestrians while drunk – are breathtakingly lenient.

In short, we don't recommend driving in Singapore, but if you do, practise extreme defensive driving, and have your road rage under control!

As for motorcycles, they are held in very low esteem (we speak from experience here). At best, drivers display almost no regard for bike safety. At worst, they appear to violently object to the right of a lowly motorcycle to be in front of them and try to hunt you down.

Hire If you want a car for local driving only, it's worth checking smaller operators, whose rates are often cheaper than the big global rental firms. If you're going into Malaysia, you're better off renting in Johor Bahru, where the rates are significantly lower (besides, Malaysian police are renowned for targeting Singapore licence plates).

Rates start from around S$60 a day. Special deals may be available, especially for longer-term rental. There are hire booths at Singapore Changi Airport as well as in the city. These are some of the major companies:

Avis (6737 1668; www.avis. com.sg; 01-07 Waterfront Plaza, 390A Havelock Rd)

Express Car (6748 9963; www.expresscar.com.sg; 1 Sims Lane)

Hawk (☎ 6469 4468; www.
hawkrentacar.com.sg; 32A
Hillview Terrace)

Hertz Rent-a-Car (☎ 6734
4646; www.hertz.com;
Singapore Changi Airport
Terminal 2 & 3)

Premier (www-singapore.
com/premier; 03-05 Balmoral
Plaza, 271 Bukit Timah Rd)

Restricted Zone Parking From
7.30am to 7pm weekdays,
and from 10.15am to 2pm
Saturday, the CBD, Chinatown
and Orchard Rd is considered
a restricted zone, and cars
incur a toll. Vehicles must
be fitted with an in-vehicle
unit, into which drivers must
insert a cashcard (available at
petrol stations and 7-Elevens).
The toll is extracted from the
card. The same system is
also in operation on certain
expressways. Rental cars are
subject to the same rules.

Parking in the city centre is
expensive, but relatively easy
to find – almost every major
mall has a car park. Outdoor
car parks and street parking
spaces are usually operated
by the government – you
can buy booklets of parking
coupons, which must be
displayed in the window, from
post offices and 7-Elevens.

LOCAL TRANSPORT

MALAYSIA

Local transport varies widely
from place to place. Taxis are
found in all large cities, and
most have meters. Fares in
KL and other cities on the peninsula are as follows: flagfall
(first 2km) is RM3, with an additional 20 sen for each 200m
or 45 seconds thereafter; 20
sen for each additional passenger over two passengers;
RM1 for each piece of luggage
in the boot (trunk); plus 50%
on each of these charges
between midnight and 6am.
Drivers are legally required to
use meters if they exist – you
can try insisting that they do
so, but sometimes you'll just
have to negotiate the fare
before you get in.

Bicycle rickshaws (trishaws)
supplement the taxi service in
George Town and Melaka and
are definitely handy ways of
getting around the older parts
of town, which have convoluted
and narrow streets.

In major cities there are also
buses, which are extremely
cheap and convenient,
provided you can figure out
which one is going your way.
KL also has commuter trains,
a Light Rail Transit (LRT) and
monorail system.

In the bigger cities across
Malaysian Borneo, such as
Kuching and Kota Kinabalu,
you will find taxis, buses and
minibuses. Once you're out of
the big cities, though, you're
basically on your own and must
either walk or hitch. If you're
really in the bush, of course,
riverboats and aeroplanes are
the only alternatives to lengthy
jungle treks.

Long Distance Taxi In almost
every Malaysian town there
will be a *teksi* stand where
the cars are lined up and
ready to go to their various
destinations. Taxis are ideal
for groups of four, and are also
available on a share basis. As
soon as a full complement of
four passengers turns up then
you're ready to go.

If you're travelling between
major towns, you have a
reasonable chance of finding
other passengers to share
without having to wait too long,
but otherwise you will have to
charter a whole taxi, which is
four times the single-fare rate.

As Malaysia becomes
increasingly wealthy, and
people can afford to hire a
whole taxi, the share system
is becoming less reliable.
Early morning is generally
the best time to find people
to share a taxi, but you can
inquire at the taxi stand the
day before as to the best time.

Taxi rates to specific
destinations are fixed by the
government and are posted
at the taxi stands. Air-con
taxis cost a few more ringgit
than non-air-con, and fares
are generally about twice the
comparable bus fares. If you
want to charter a taxi to an
obscure destination, or by the
hour, you'll probably have to
do some negotiating. On the
peninsula you're likely to pay
around 50 sen per kilometre.
In Sarawak, the taxi metre
price (for kilometres beyond
the first 3km which is RM10) is
RM1.20 per km.

Taxi drivers often drive at
frighteningly high speeds. They
don't have as many head-on
collisions as you might expect,
but closing your eyes at times
of high stress certainly helps!
You also have the option of
demanding that the driver slow
down, but this can be met with
varying degrees of hostility.
Another tactic is to look for
ageing taxis and taxi drivers –
they must be doing something
right to have made it this far!

SINGAPORE

With a typical mixture of far-
sighted social planning and
authoritarianism, the government has built, and continues

to extend, its Mass Rapid Transit (MRT) rail system and its road network.

If you're going to be using public transport heavily, buy the TransitLink Guide ($2.50 from MRT ticket offices), which lists all bus and MRT routes. Maps show the surrounding areas for all MRT stations, including bus stops.

For online bus information, including a searchable bus guide and the useful IRIS service (which tells you in real time when your next bus will arrive), see www.sbstransit. com.sg. For train information, see www.smrt.com.sg.

Taxi Poor Singapore has endless problems with its taxi system. Finding a taxi in the city at certain times (during peak hours, at night, or when it's raining) remains a major headache. The fare system is also hugely complicated, but thankfully it's metered, so there's no haggling over fares. The basic flagfall is $2.80, then $0.20 for every 385m.

These are the taxi companies:

Comfort Taxi and CityCab (🕿 6552 1111)

Premier Taxis (🕿 6363 6888)

SMRT Taxis (🕿 6555 8888)

Ordering a taxi by phone from any of these companies during nonpeak hours is usually quick, but during peak hours you'll often be waiting a long time. An automated message gives you the estimated time of arrival.

You can flag down a taxi any time, but in the city centre taxis are not allowed to stop anywhere except at designated taxi stands.

🚆 TRAIN
Malaysia's privatised national railway company is **Keretapi Tanah Melayu (KTM;** 🕿 1300-885 862; www.ktmb.com.my). It runs a modern, comfortable and economical railway service, although there are basically only two lines and for the most part services are slow.

One line runs up the west coast from Singapore, through KL, Butterworth and on into Thailand. The other branches off from this line at Gemas and runs through Kuala Lipis up to the northeastern corner of the country near Kota Bharu in Kelantan. Often referred to as the 'jungle train', this line is properly known as the 'east-coast line'.

In Sabah the North Borneo Railway (www. suteraharbour.com), a small narrow-gauge line running through the Sungai Padas gorge from Tenom to Beaufort, offers tourist trips lasting four hours on Wednesday and Saturday.

SERVICES & CLASSES
There are two main types of rail services: express and local trains. Express trains are air-conditioned and have 'premier' (1st class), 'superior' (2nd class) and sometimes 'economy' (3rd class) seats. Similarly on overnight trains you'll find 'premier night deluxe' cabins (upper/lower berth RM50/70 extra), 'premier night standard' cabins (upper/lower berth RM18/26), and 'standard night' cabins (upper/lower berth RM12/17). Local trains are usually economy class only, but some have superior seats.

Express trains stop only at main stations, while local services, which operate mostly on the east-coast line, stop anywhere, even in remote jungle, to let passengers off. Consequently local services take more than twice as long as the express trains and run to erratic schedules, but if you're in no hurry they provide a colourful experience and are good for short journeys.

Train schedules are reviewed biannually, so check the KTM website (www.ktmb. com.my) where you can make bookings and buy tickets.

Climate Change & Travel
Every form of transport that relies on carbon-based fuel generates CO_2, the main cause of human-induced climate change. Modern travel is dependent on aeroplanes, which might use less fuel per kilometres per person than most cars but travel much greater distances. The altitude at which aircraft emit gases (including CO_2) and particles also contributes to their climate change impact. Many websites offer 'carbon calculators' that allow people to estimate the carbon emissions generated by their journey and, for those who wish to do so, to offset the impact of the greenhouse gases emitted with contributions to portfolios of climate-friendly initiatives throughout the world. Lonely Planet offsets the carbon footprint of all staff and author travel.

Language

In Malay most letters are pronounced the same as their English counterparts, except for *c* which is always pronounced as the 'ch' in 'chair'. The second-last syllable is lightly stressed, except for the unstressed *e* – eg in *besar* (big) – which sounds like the 'a' in 'ago'.

To enhance your trip with a phrasebook, visit **lonelyplanet.com**. Lonely Planet iPhone phrasebooks are available through the Apple App store.

BASICS

Hello.	*Helo.*
Goodbye.	*Selamat tinggal/jalan.* (by person leaving/staying)
Yes./No.	*Ya./Tidak.*
Excuse me.	*Maaf.*
Sorry.	*Maaf.*
Please.	*Silakan.*
Thank you.	*Terima kasih.*
You're welcome.	*Sama-sama.*
How are you?	*Apa kabar?*
I'm fine.	*Kabar baik.*
What's your name?	*Siapa nama kamu*
My name is ...	*Nama saya ...*
Do you speak English?	*Adakah anda berbahasa Inggeris?*
I don't understand.	*Saya tidak faham.*

ACCOMMODATION

Do you have any rooms available?	*Ada bilik kosong?*
How much is it per day/person?	*Berapa harga satu malam/orang?*
Is breakfast included?	*Makan pagi termasukkah?*

EATING & DRINKING

A table for (two), please.	*Meja untuk (dua) orang.*
I'd like (the menu).	*Saya minta (daftar makanan).*
What's in that dish?	*Ada apa dalam masakan itu?*
The bill, please.	*Tolong bawa bil.*
I don't eat ...	*Saya tak suka makan ...*
fish	*ikan*
(red) meat	*daging (merah)*
nuts	*kacang*

SHOPPING

I'd like to buy ...	*Saya nak beli ...*
Can I look at it?	*Boleh saya tengok barang itu?*
How much is it?	*Berapa harganya?*
It's too expensive.	*Mahalnya.*

EMERGENCIES

Help!	*Tolong!*
Go away!	*Pergi!*
Call the police!	*Panggil polis!*
Call a doctor!	*Panggil doktor!*
I'm ill.	*Saya sakit.*
I'm lost.	*Saya sesat.*

TRANSPORT & DIRECTIONS

When's the (next bus)?	*Jam berapa (bis yang berikutnya)?*
I want to go to ...	*Saya nak ke ...*
I'd like a ... ticket.	*Saya nak tiket ...*
one-way	*sehala*
return	*pergi balik*
Where is ...?	*Di mana ...?*
Can you show me (on the map)?	*Tolong tunjukkan (di peta)?*
hotel	*hotel*
internet cafe	*cyber cafe*
market	*pasar*
post office	*pejabat pos*
public phone	*telpon awam*
restaurant	*restoran*
station	*stasiun*
toilets	*tandas*
tourist office	*pejabat pelancong*

Behind the Scenes

Author Thanks
Simon Richmond

Terima kasih to the great team of coauthors and to Errol, Diana and Sasha for support from LP HQ. In Malaysia, many thanks to Alex Yong, Honey Ahmad, Andrew Sebastian, David Hogan Jr, Narelle McMurtrie, Bee Yin Low, Howard Tan, Yu-mei Balasingamchow, Leslie Tay and Quek I-Gek.

Acknowledgments

Climate map data adapted from Peel MC, Finlayson BL & McMahon TA (2007) 'Updated World Map of the Köppen-Geiger Climate Classification', Hydrology and Earth System Sciences, 11, 163344.

Integrated Transit Network of Kuala Lumpur Map © 2012 Tourism Malaysia
Cover photographs
Front: Malaysian Borneo, Reinhard Dirscherl/Alamy©
Back: Vegetable market, Kuala Lumpur, Bruno Morandi/SIME/4Corners

This Book

This 1st edition of Lonely Planet's *Discover Malaysia & Singapore* guidebook was coordinated and written by Simon Richmond, and researched on the ground by Simon, Cristian Bonetto, Celeste Brash, Joshua Samuel Brown, Austin Bush, Adam Karlin and Daniel Robinson. This guidebook was commissioned in Lonely Planet's Melbourne office, and produced by the following:

Commissioning Editors Errol Hunt, Ilaria Walker
Coordinating Editor Mardi O'Connor
Coordinating Cartographer Alex Leung
Coordinating Layout Designer Nicholas Colicchia
Managing Editors Sasha Baskett, Barbara Delissen
Managing Cartographers Adrian Persoglia, Diana Von Holdt
Managing Layout Designers Chris Girdler, Jane Hart
Assisting Editor Andrea Dobbin
Assisting Cartographer Mick Garrett
Assisting Layout Designer Katherine Marsh
Cover Research Naomi Parker
Internal Image Research Aude Vauconsant
Language Content Branislava Vladisavljevic
Thanks to David Carroll, Daniel Corbett, Bruce Evans, Ryan Evans, Larissa Frost, Genesys India, Jouve India, Asha Ioculari, Shawn Low, Maryanne Netto, Trent Paton, Martine Power, Raphael Richards, Gerard Walker

SEND US YOUR FEEDBACK

Index

Map pages 000

NOTES

NOTES